Version Control Git and GitHub

Discover the most popular source control solutions used by developers worldwide

Alex Magana

Joseph Muli

Packt>

Version Control with Git and GitHub

Copyright © 2018 Packt Publishing

All rights reserved. No part of this book may be reproduced, stored in a retrieval system, or transmitted in any form or by any means, without the prior written permission of the publisher, except in the case of brief quotations embedded in critical articles or reviews.

Every effort has been made in the preparation of this book to ensure the accuracy of the information presented. However, the information contained in this book is sold without warranty, either express or implied. Neither the authors, nor Packt Publishing, and its dealers and distributors will be held liable for any damages caused or alleged to be caused directly or indirectly by this book.

Packt Publishing has endeavored to provide trademark information about all of the companies and products mentioned in this book by the appropriate use of capitals. However, Packt Publishing cannot guarantee the accuracy of this information.

Authors: Alex Magana and Joseph Muli

Managing Editor: Darren Patel

Acquisitions Editor: Koushik Sen

Production Editor: Samita Warang

Editorial Board: David Barnes, Ewan Buckingham, Simon Cox, Manasa Kumar, Alex Mazonowicz, Douglas Paterson, Dominic Pereira, Shiny Poojary, Saman Siddiqui, Erol Staveley, Ankita Thakur, and Mohita Vyas

First Published: November 2018

Production Reference: 1271118

ISBN: 978-1-78980-897-1

Table of Contents

Preface	i
Introducing Version Control	1
Introduction	2
Defining Version Control	2
Applications of Version Control	4
Common Terminologies	4
Feature branch workflow	6
Forking Workflow	6
Navigating GitHub	7
Exercise 1: Setting Up a GitHub Account	7
Exercise 2: Utilizing Two-Factor Authentication	12
Organizations	15
Exercise 3: Setting Up an Organization	16
Exercise 4: Setting Up a Team	18
Marketplace	20
Exercise 5: Setting Up Codacy for Accounts	20
Runtime Config	23
Exercise 6: Setting User Credentials	24
Removing Configuration	25
SSH Configuration	26
Exercise 7: Setting Up SSH	26
Creating a Repository	30
Exercise 8: Creating a Repository in a Local Environment	30
Exercise 9: Creating a Repository on GitHub	35

| Navigating a Repository 38

| Collaborators 38

| Exercise 10: Adding and Deleting Contributors 38

| Navigating Branches, Commits, and Insights
| (Contributors, Pulse, Forks) 41

| GitHub Etiquette 42

| Repository Names, Tags, and Descriptions 43

| Exercise 11: Adding Licenses 48

| Wikis and Issues 48

| Activity 1: Creating a Repository 52

| Summary 54

Versioning Commits   57

| Introduction 58

| Introduction to Versioning Commits 58

| Exercise 12: Viewing and Establishing the Status of a File 59

| Comparing the Working Tree to the Index 63

| Comparing the Working Tree to an Arbitrary Commit or Branch 64

| Comparing the Index to an Arbitrary Commit 64

| Comparing Commits and Branches 65

| Exercise 13: Examining Differences Between Files 66

| Exercise 14: Adding Files to the Index 73

| Exercise 15: Removing Files from the Working Tree and the Index 80

| Exercise 16: Moving and Renaming Files 82

| History and Logs 84

| Amending Commits 96

| Amending a Single Most Recent Commit 96

| Exercise 17: Editing the Most Recent Commit 97

| Amending Multiple Commits 98

Exercise 18: Editing Commits Using the reword Command 99

Exercise 19: Editing Commits Using the edit Command 101

Activity 2: Tracking Files 104

Summary 106

Fetching and Delivering Code   109

Introduction 110

Fetching the Code 110

Exercise 20: Configuring the Remote Repository 111

Default and Protected Branches 114

Exercise 21: Configuring the Base Branch and Branch Protection 115

Fetching, Pushing, and Pulling Changes 118

Exercise 22: Retrieving Changes 120

Dealing with Non-Fast-Forward Commits 124

Reversing Commits 126

Exercise 23: Reversing Changes 126

Other Possible Uses 130

Activity 3: Handling Changes and Enforcing Branch Restrictions 135

Summary 137

Branches   139

Introduction 140

Utilizing Workflows 140

Creating a Centralized Workflow 141

Feature Branch Workflow 141

Forking Workflow 141

Feature-Branch Workflow 141

Exercise 24: Feature-Branch Workflow-Driven Delivery 143

Creating, Renaming, Deleting, and Listing Branches 153

Creating:	154
Merging	158
Cherry-Pick	160
Pull Request (PR)	162
Exercise 25: Examining Branch Differences	162
Pull Request Templates	165
Exercise 26: Standardizing Procedures through Ordered Templates	165
Identifying and Fixing Merge Issues	171
Exercise 27: Merge Conflict Resolution	173
Exercise 28: Resolving Conflicts	177
Merging and Reverting Pull Requests	180
Exercise 29: Pull Request Reversal	183
Activity 4: Managing Branches and Experimentation with Selective Changes	186
Summary	188

Collaborative Git — 191

Introduction	192
Forking the Workflow	192
Exercise 30: Forking a Repository	192
Why Do We Fork Repositories?	194
Embedding Upstream Changes	195
Exercise 31: Modifying the Upstream Repository Remote Address	197
Rebasing	204
Exercise 32: Rebasing in GitHub	206
Fixup and Squash Commits	210
Exercise 33: Utilizing the Autosquash Feature	211
Drop Commits	214
Exercise 34: Dropping Commits	216

Submodules 218

　　Exercise 35: Utilizing Gitmodules 219

　　Activity 5: Rebasing 223

Debugging and Maintenance 224

　　Exercise 36: Identifying Revisions Using Git Blame 225

　　Exercise 37: Finding Commits using Git Bisect 228

Housekeeping 233

　　Exercise 38: Removing Untracked Files using Git Clean 233

　　Removing Merged Local and Remote Branches 236

　　Exercise 39: Deleting Branches 237

　　Activity 6: Utilizing Pre-Commit Hooks for Housekeeping 238

Summary 239

Automated Testing and Release Management   241

Introduction 242

Test Automation 242

　　Webhooks and GitHub Applications 242

　　Exercise 40: Setting up a Webhook 243

　　GitHub Applications 246

　　Exercise 41: Setting Up CircleCi CI 246

Automated Pull Requests 253

　　Exercise 42: Utilizing Automated Pull Requests 254

　　Activity 7: Integrating a Build Pipeline on CircleCi 256

Release Management 257

　　Tagging 258

　　Exercise 43: Creating Tags 259

　　Exercise 44: Publishing GitHub Releases 264

Git Archive 267

Exercise 45: Packaging through GitHub Archive 267

Activity 8: Tagging and Releasing with Git 268

Summary 269

Appendix   271

Index   323

Preface

About

This section briefly introduces the author, the coverage of this book, the technical skills you'll need to get started, and the hardware and software required to complete all of the included activities and exercises.

About the Book

Version control refers to the tracking and traceability of changes. It is, in a way, akin to the use of a bookmark in a book, to mark the point the reader should return to when they resume reading. In version control, this metaphorical bookmark marks a reference to a snapshot of the code base. Git is a version control tool. Using Git, you can make, track, retrieve, and share changes on a repository. GitHub is a hosting service where a repository resides.

This book begins by providing you with a thorough understanding of what version control is, why it's necessary, and how it lends itself to application development and version management. With thorough explanations and interesting activities, you will learn all about using Git and GitHub optimally. By the end of the book, you will have the skills to safeguard your application and ensure its speedy development.

About the Authors

Alex Magana is a software engineer keen on developing solutions that matter. He is interested in HCI, machine learning, agritech, information storage and retrieval, and effective backup and recovery. Alex has helped to deliver projects for clients on context-aware and location-based services, point-of-sale software, data analytics for mobile-based banking, and AMP-based performant news pages across a myriad of locales. To let his hair down, Alex enjoys music, dance, adventure, reading, and exploring architecture. He is an avid gastronome at heart.

Joseph Muli loves programming, writing, teaching, gaming, and travelling. Currently, he is working as a software engineer at Andela and Fathom, specializing in DevOps and site reliability. Previously, he worked as a software engineer and technical mentor at Moringa School.

Objectives

- Understand and implement best practices in version control
- Explain the GitHub User Interface
- Understand what the Feature-Branch Workflow is and implement its features.
- Use forking features, such as submodules and rebasing
- Master commands for debugging and maintaining a repository
- Implement continuous integration with CircleCI
- Gain insight into release management and how GitHub enables software releases

Audience

This book is meant for developers, who want to migrate from other version control tools, or want to learn more about Git. Prior experience in coding or familiarity with using the bash command-line interface will enable you to easily grasp the concepts introduced.

Approach

This book thoroughly explains the technology in an easy-to-understand language, while perfectly balancing theory and exercises. Each chapter is designed to build on the learnings of the previous chapter. The book also contains multiple activities that use real-life business scenarios for you to practice and apply your new skills in a highly relevant context.

Minimum Hardware Requirements

For the optimal student experience, we recommend the following hardware configuration:

- Processor: Intel Core i3 or equivalent
- Memory: 4 GB RAM
- Storage: 35 GB available space
- 5400 RPM hard disk drive
- DirectX 9-compatible video card (1024 x 768 or higher resolution)
- An internet connection

Software Requirements

You'll also need the following software installed in advance:

- Operating System: Linux, Ubuntu, or macOS
- Google Chrome (https://www.google.com/chrome/)
- Atom IDE (https://atom.io/)
- Git (https://git-scm.com/download/linux)

Installing the Code Bundle

Copy the code bundle for the class to the `C:/Code` folder.

Additional Resources

The code bundle for this book is also hosted on GitHub at: https://github.com/TrainingByPackt/Version-Control-with-Git-and-GitHub.

We also have other code bundles from our rich catalog of books and videos available at: https://github.com/PacktPublishing/. Check them out!

Conventions

Code words in text, database table names, folder names, filenames, file extensions, pathnames, dummy URLs, user input, and Twitter handles are shown as follows: "On macOS, edit `~/.ssh/config` to enable the `ssh-agent` to automatically load keys and store passphrases in the keychain."

A block of code is set as follows:

```
Host *
    AddKeysToAgent yes
    UseKeychain yes
    IdentityFile [location_of_the_generated_private_key]
```

New terms and important words are shown in **bold**. Words that you see on the screen, for example, in menus or dialog boxes, appear in the text like this: "A **license** governs the utilization of an application by its users..."

Installing Atom IDE

1. To install Atom IDE, go to https://atom.io/ in your browser.
2. Click on **Download Windows Installer** for Windows, to download the setup file called **AtomSetup-x64.exe**.
3. Run the executable file.
4. Add the atom and apm commands to you path.
5. Create shortcuts on the desktop and start menu.

Installing Git

1. To install Git via the package installer, go to https://git-scm.com/download/linux.
2. Run the following command: `# apt-get install git` on the terminal window.
3. Enter your password if prompted.

Introducing Version Control

Learning Objectives

By the end of this chapter, you will be able to:

- Define version control and various types of workflows
- Explain the GitHub User Interface
- Set up various GitHub functions such as teams and SSH
- Create a repository using the GitHub etiquette

This chapter describes the working of version control, workflows and setting up a local and GitHub repository.

Introduction

This chapter will cover the basic concepts of version control, using illustrative examples. This book draws attention to the facets that make up version control, thus encompassing tracking of code base changes, how to host a code base to support remote access, managing contributors and contributions, and best practices to adhere to. By implementing version control, the creation and enforcement of team-driven checks and controls for introduction, scrutiny, approval, merging, and the reversal of changes, when the occasion necessitates, can be realized.

Version control alludes to the tracking and traceability of changes. It is, in a way, akin to the use of a bookmark, to mark the point to return to when the reader wants to continue reading. In version control, this metaphorical bookmark marks a reference to a snapshot of the code base. This snapshot indicates the state of the product or the code base at a given point.

To appreciate version control and—more so—Git, we need to consider what nature software development takes when it's void of version control and, by extension, distributed version control that's provided by Git.

In the case of development without employing version control, the handling of code and making changes to the same code translates to a chaotic environment where changes to a code base are uncoordinated. No information exists to track changes to a file, apart from the metadata that is offered by the operating system that you are working from, and an archiving approach where file naming is used to refer to different snapshots of a code base.

The result of this is derailed and delayed changes. This is due to the overhead of requiring the development team to constantly physically investigate files to integrate changes successfully, as well as the resources spent in rectifying incorrect integrations that result in unintended and unforeseen bugs in the production environment.

Defining Version Control

Version control is aimed at supporting the tracking of changes to a file, that is, the reversal of changes made to a file and the annotation of changes introduced to a code base. Prior to the inception of version control software, version control itself took an approach that was contrived and agreed upon by a team of developers working on a code base.

To introduce and roll out a change to a product, a developer would, for instance, retrieve an archived version corresponding to the version in the production environment. They would proceed to make and test the change. To deploy the new version, a version number would be assigned to the release, and notes detailing a change would be annotated alongside the release. To revert changes, you would be required to do the following:

- Match the release notes to specific files.
- Establish the actual changes introduced in the respective files.
- Revert the changes and deploy the rectified version.

Software developers' building products need to coordinate concurrent pieces of work to achieve an effective product development flexibility.

Consider a team working on a bus ticket sale platform for the city of Tunis needs to roll out a mobile app for ticket sales. In this project, the developers may split the work into the following categories:

- User authentication
- Ticket purchase

This work can be assigned to different members of the development team. Each member can focus their efforts on a task and share the work through a central repository on GitHub. Each feature can be rolled out incrementally in bits, before being tested and merged to the production environment for use by the residents of Tunis.

Documentation maintainers use version control for collaboration on shared documents. A documentation maintainer allows for the review of proposed changes from concerned stakeholders, after which the final version of a document can be released for use by an organization.

Software documentation may be maintained by the personnel responsible for managing information resources of an organization using version control. For example, a repository may be used to archive documents that are no longer in use.

This process would be more challenging in the event that documentation material such as release notes were lacking from a project. As you may have established by now, this is a process marred with frustrations, stress, and inefficacies.

The advent of version control software was instigated by a need to address the issues that plagued the incorporation of the change and release of software. Version control software has seen an evolution of three generations.

In the **first generation**, version control software utilized a **locking mechanism** on files to allow a change to occur on the file. A file could only be worked on by one individual at a given point in time. The lock put in place on a file would be lifted once an individual who was working on the said file had persisted their changes by way of commits. **Change management** was conducted by managing a history on each file. During this period, **SCCS (Source Code Control System)** and **RCS (Revision Control System)** were the common version control software in use.

The **second generation** was characterized by the use of a **merge-before-commit mechanism** to support concurrent editing of a file by multiple users. To incorporate changes into a file, you would be are required to merge changes made by others to the same file. Once done, you would then proceed to commit your change to the file of interest. This generation of software introduced the use of **centralized repositories**. Developers were able to access the code base remotely and collaborate with other developers from a shared repository. Additionally, the unit of change was tracked as the change on a set of files in lieu of a single file.

The **third generation** is **decentralized** in nature. Each developer obtains a copy of the repository. Changes to the remote repository are introduced by way of a merge. To allow multiple individuals to work on the same file, a **commit-before-merge mechanism** is used. Here, you make changes to the local repository. To incorporate changes made to the remote repository, you commit the local changes, after which you are able to merge changes made by other individuals. This will be demonstrated in later sections. Git is a third-generation version control tool.

Version control provides an integral part of work, that is, **change management**. Git and GitHub, as you'll see in this book, provide tools that allow both teams and individuals to effect change in the book of work in a fast and effective manner. This is achieved through the facilities of division of work and integration of change provided by Git and GitHub.

Applications of Version Control

Version control is applicable to both technical and non-technical pieces of work. It lends itself to software development projects just as well as it does to projects that require teams to collaborate on the formulation and usage of documents. A good example to consider is when a building's construction plans may be shared and collaboratively contrived by a team of architects. Such a project could be managed using Git and GitHub to share documents and plans.

Common Terminologies

Let's take a look at some of the common terms that you will come across in this book:

Repository

A unit of storage and change tracking that represents a directory whose contents are tracked by Git.

Branch

A version of a repository that represents the current state of the set of files that constitute a repository.

In a repository, there exists a default or main branch that represents the single source of truth.

Master

The default or main branch. A version of the repository that is considered the single source of truth.

To use the analogy of a river, the master is the main stream of a river. Other branches depart from the main stream, just like a distributary would, but instead of not returning to the main stream, the branches rejoin the main stream, just like a tributary would. This process of joining the main stream is referred to as **merging**.

Reference

A Git ref or reference is a name corresponding to a commit hash. The references are stored in a files in the `.git/refs` directory, of a repository.

HEAD

A reference to the most recent commit on a branch. The most recent commit is commonly referred to as the **tip** of the branch.

Working Tree

This refers to the section in which we view and make changes to the files in a branch. The files that are changed are then moved to a staging area once they are ready for a commit.

Index

This is an area where Git holds files that have been changed, added, or removed in readiness for a commit. It's a staging area from where you commit changes.

Commit

This is an entry into Git's history that represents a change made to a set of files at a given point in time. A commit references the files that have been added to the index and updates the `HEAD` to point to the new state of the branch.

Merge

Using the analogy of a river, a merge refers to the process through which a tributary joins the main river.

In Git, a merge is the process of incorporating changes from one branch to another. Here, the branch bringing in changes is the tributary, whereas the branch receiving the changes is the main stream of a river.

Workflows

Workflows refer to the approach a team takes to introduce changes to a code base. A workflow is characterized by a distinct approach in the usage of branches (or lack thereof) to introduce changes into a repository.

Gitflow workflow

This uses two branches: **master** and **develop**. The master branch is used to track release history, while the develop branch is used to track feature integration into the product.

Centralized workflow

This approach uses the master branch as the default development branch. The changes are committed to the master branch. It's a suitable workflow for small size teams and teams transitioning from Apache Subversion. In Apache Subversion, the trunk is the equivalent of the master branch.

Feature branch workflow

In this workflow, feature development is carried out in a dedicated branch. The branch is then merged to the master once the intended changes are approved.

Forking Workflow

In this approach, the individual seeking to make a change to a repository, makes a copy of the desired repository in their respective GitHub account. The changes are made in the copy of the source repository and then it's merged to the source repository through a pull request.

Navigating GitHub

Version control with Git takes on a distributed nature. The code resides on each local computer where the code base is being worked on, as well as on a central remote point where every individual who wishes to work on the code base can obtain it. GitHub is one such central remote point. GitHub hosts repositories and enables users to obtain, alter, and integrate changes to a code base through Git:

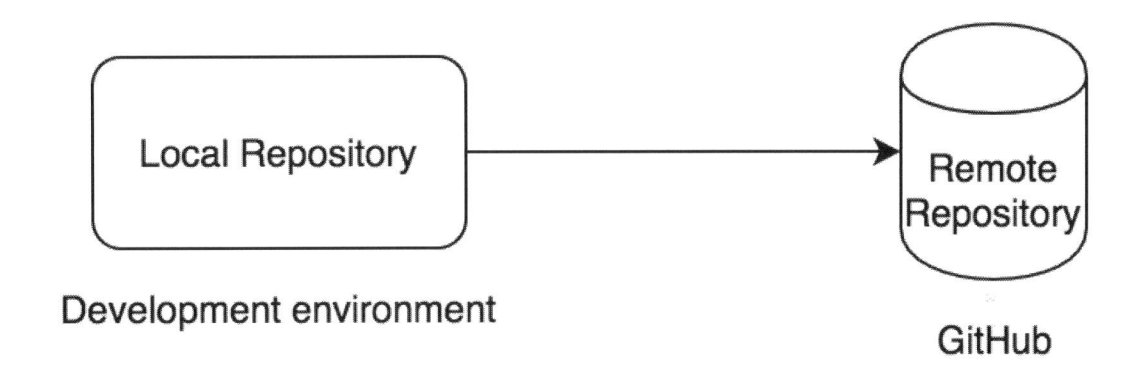

Figure 1.1: Relationship between the Development environment and GitHub

Exercise 1: Setting Up a GitHub Account

To capture how GitHub serves as a hosting utility, we shall now proceed to explore the features that are offered by exploring the user interface:

1. Enter your user details, as shown in the following screenshot, and press the **Sign up for GitHub** button:

   > **Note**
   >
   > You'll be requested by GitHub to verify the email address that you used when signing up. Please check your email for instructions.

8 | Introducing Version Control

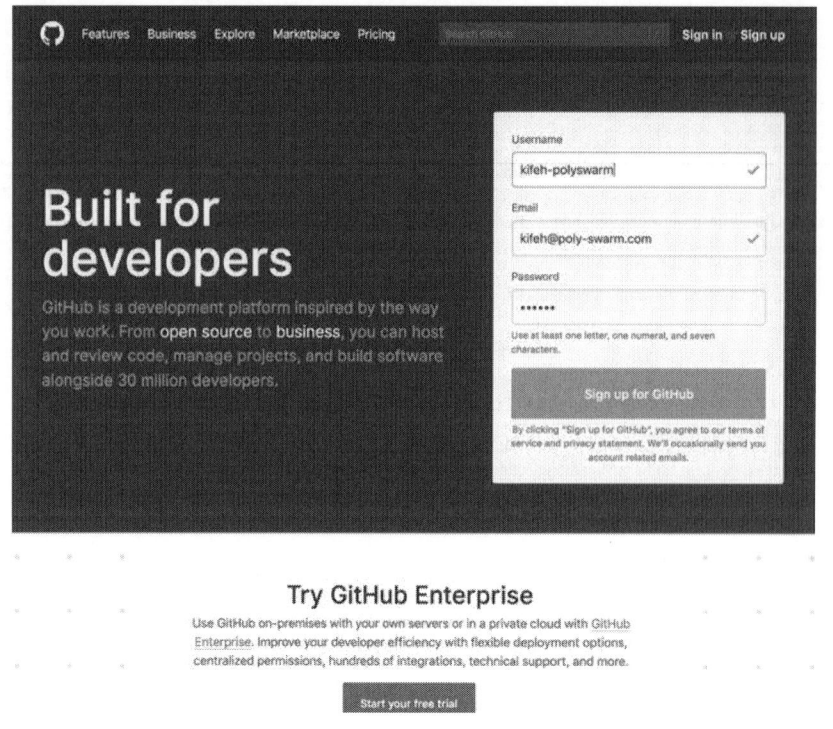

Figure 1.2: The GitHub home page

2. Choose a plan and set the preferences that best indicate your utilization of GitHub as seen in the following screenshot:

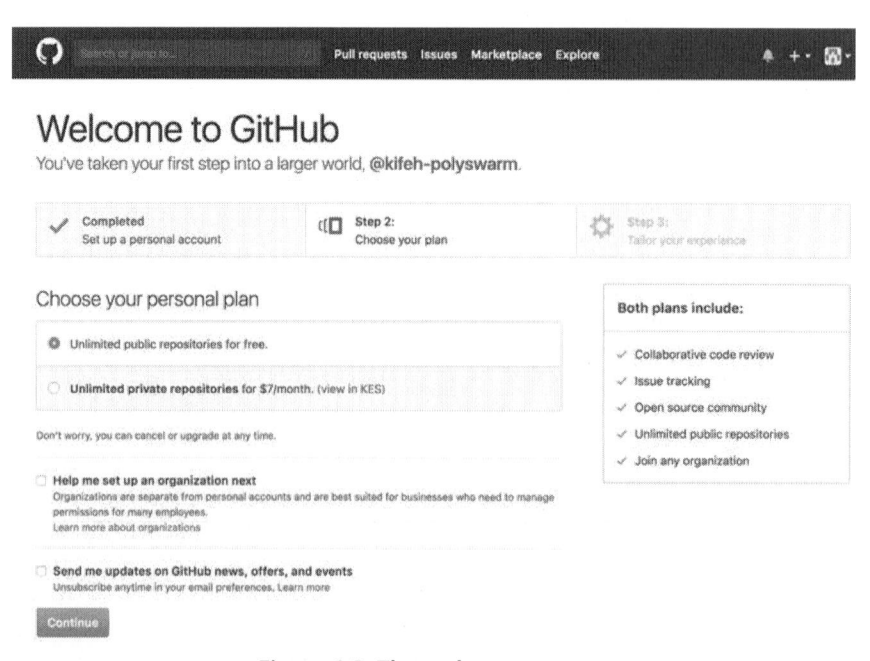

Figure 1.3: The welcome screen

Figure 1.4: Registration details

3. With account registration completed, you should see the page pictured as follows:

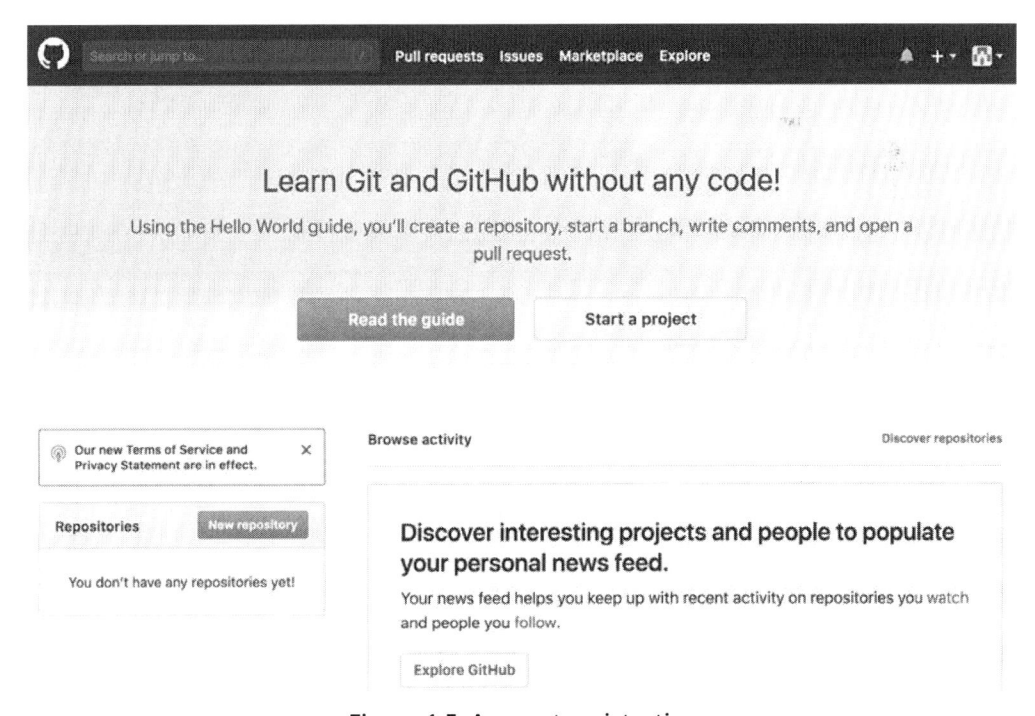

Figure 1.5: Account registration

10 | Introducing Version Control

4. To further configure your account, please select the right-most drop-down button and select the **Settings** option. The account settings should be listed, as pictured in the following screenshots:

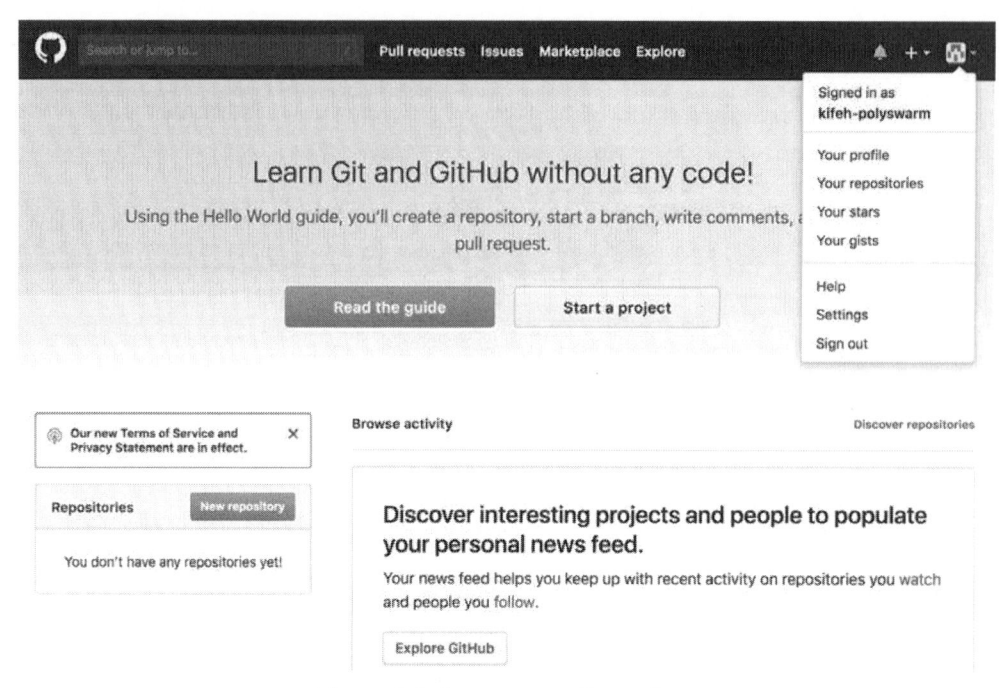

Figure 1.6: Account configuration

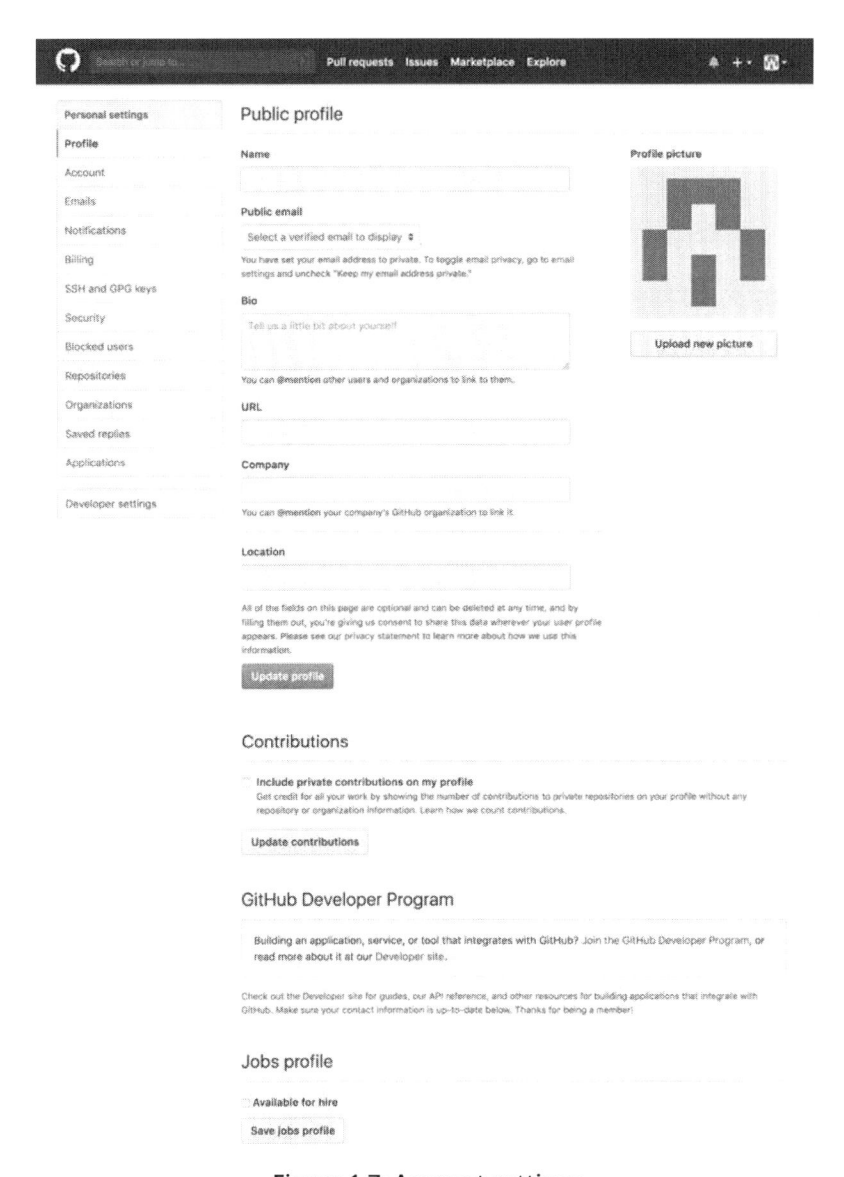

Figure 1.7: Account settings

Outcome

You have successfully set up a GitHub account as a hosting utility.

We shall now look at using the **Settings** menu to enable two-factor authentication and create an organization.

Exercise 2: Utilizing Two-Factor Authentication

You'll need to have **Google Authenticator** installed on your phone. The app is available on Android and iOS.

To enable two-factor authentication on the account so that you have enhanced security, follow these steps:

1. Go to **Settings** and select **Security**.

2. Click the **Enable two-factor authentication** button and enter your password on the next prompt:

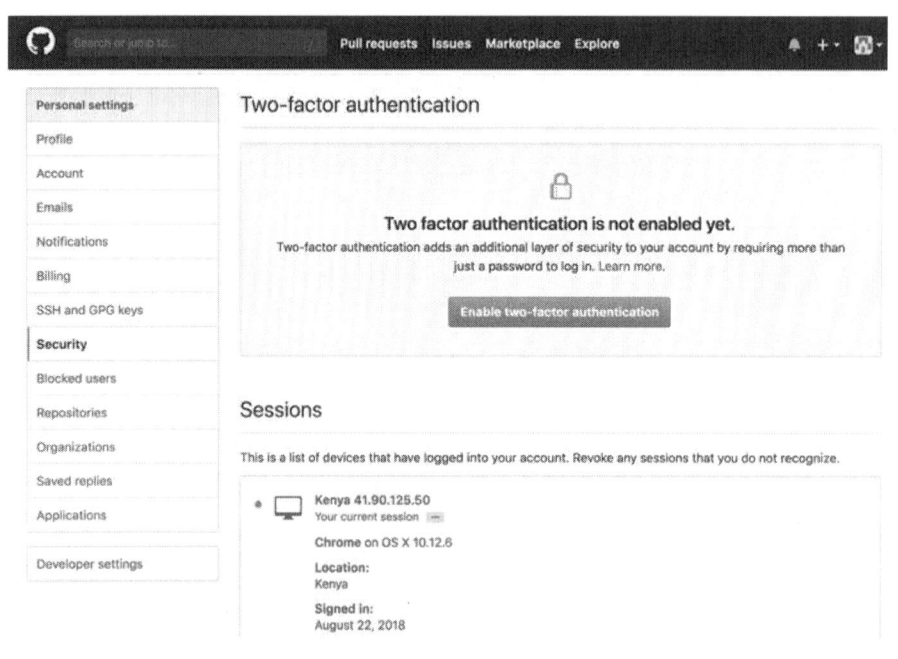

Figure 1.8: Two-factor authentication

3. Select the method you wish to use to set up two-factor authentication.

> **Note**
>
> We shall use an app for this demonstration. The SMS option may not be supported for all regions.

4. Click **Set up using an app**:

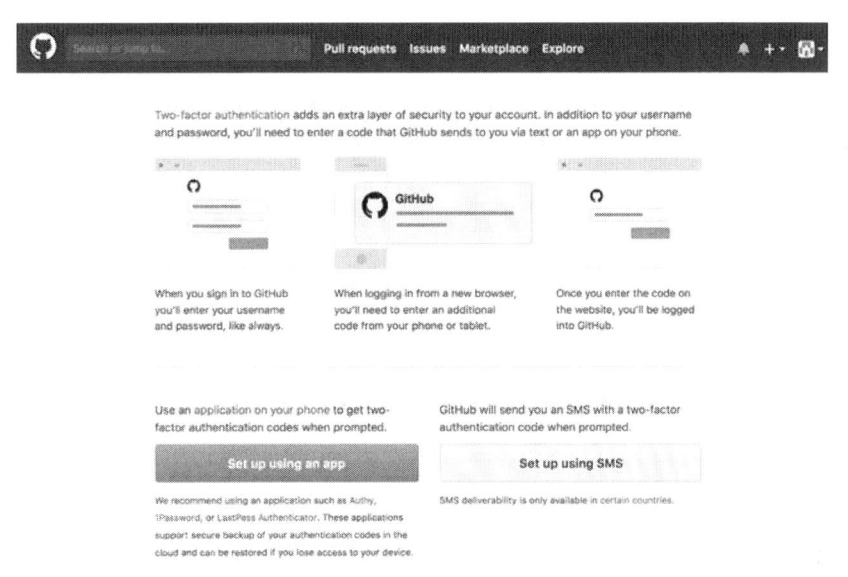

Figure 1.9: Setting up using an app

5. Download the recovery codes and store them in your preferred location.
6. Press **Next** to proceed to the next step.
7. On your phone, select **Set up an account**.
8. Select **Scan a barcode** to scan the QR code presented on your browser, as shown in the following screenshot:

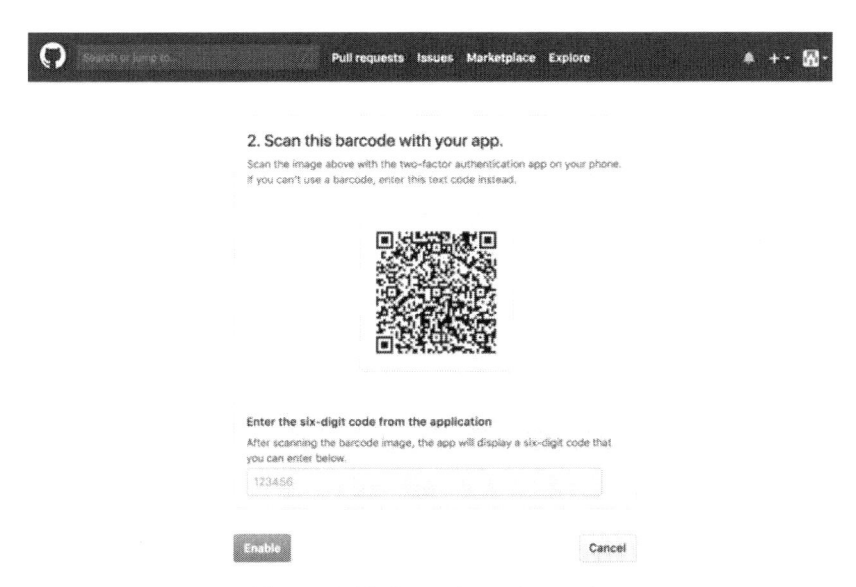

Figure 1.10: Scanning a barcode

14 | Introducing Version Control

9. Insert the six-digit code shown on the app into the text field below the label that reads **Enter the six-digit code from the application** and press **Next**:

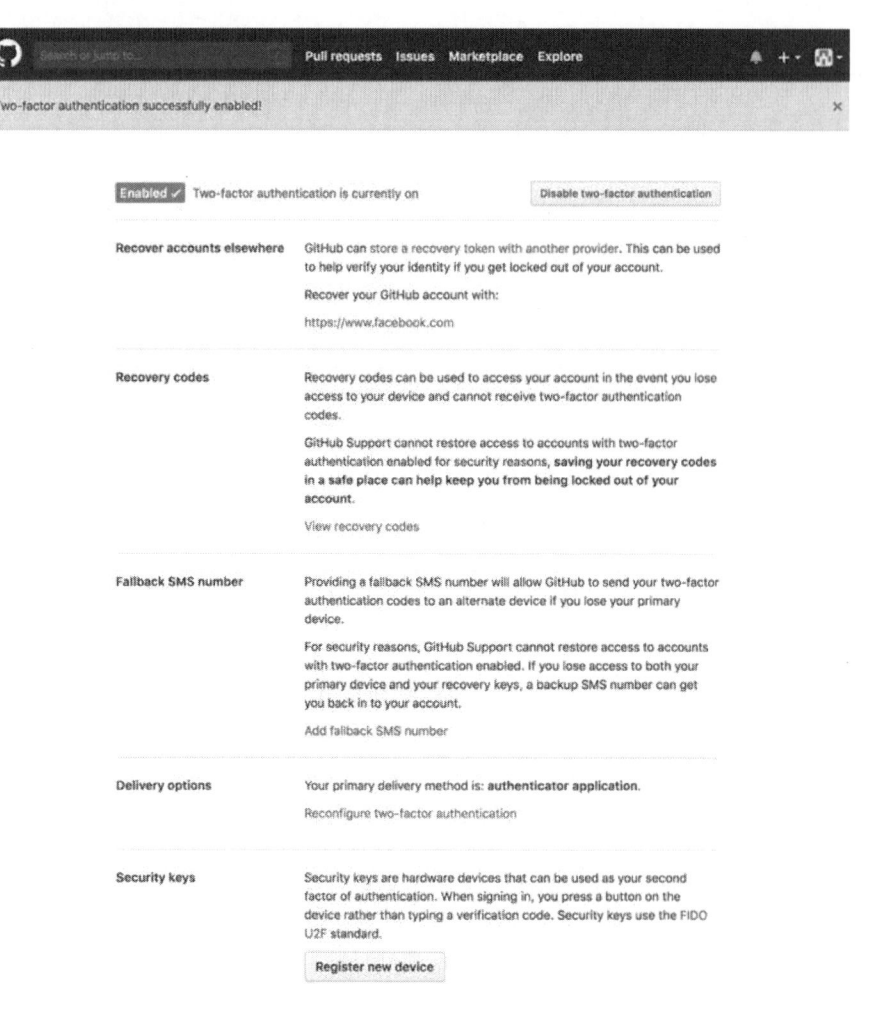

Figure 1.11: Completed two-factor authentication setup

> **Note**
>
> With two-factor authentication configured for your account, you should be able log in using your password and the code provided by the app. You can configure your account to use a registered SIM card by using the **callback SMS number** option. Additionally, you can change your account to use SMS as the default login method for receiving the authentication code instead of the app. This can be achieved using the **Delivery options**.

Outcome

You have successfully configured two-factor authentication for your account.

Organizations

GitHub offers the ability to manage multiple projects and, by extension, repositories using a shared account that's referred to as an organization. Using an organization, you can arrange contributors in a project to reflect your organization's structure. This structure corresponds to the teams that work on the respective projects as well as the access rights assigned to the individual contributors on each team.

Organizations spur seamless coordination of work through the following features availed by GitHub:

1. **Role-based membership**. Three roles exist in role-based membership, that is, **owner**, **billing manager**, and **member**. Each personal account that is added to an organization can belong to one of the aforementioned roles. The owner role is the most superior and is used to conduct administrative procedures.

2. **Repository level permissions**. Teams or their respective members can be assigned read, write, or admin-level permissions to a repository. Each level dictates activities that the assigned members undertake, with a varying degree of limitations. The following diagram shows the three levels of permission, in order of increasing capabilities, that are available in the respective levels:

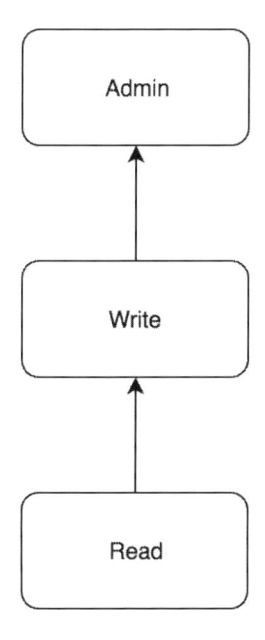

Figure 1.12: Block diagram

16 | Introducing Version Control

3. **Teams:** These are members of an organization that can be grouped into teams, with the option of nesting the teams to match an organization's structure.

4. **Multi-factor authentication:** Organizations support the enforcement of two-factor authentication as well as business-specific single sign-on approaches such as Security Assertion Markup Language (SAML) and System for Cross-domain Identity Management (SCIM).

Exercise 3: Setting Up an Organization

To create an organization, you may convert your personal account to an organization or create an organization which you can then associate with your personal account.

1. On GitHub, go to **Settings** and select **Organizations**. Then, click **New organization**:

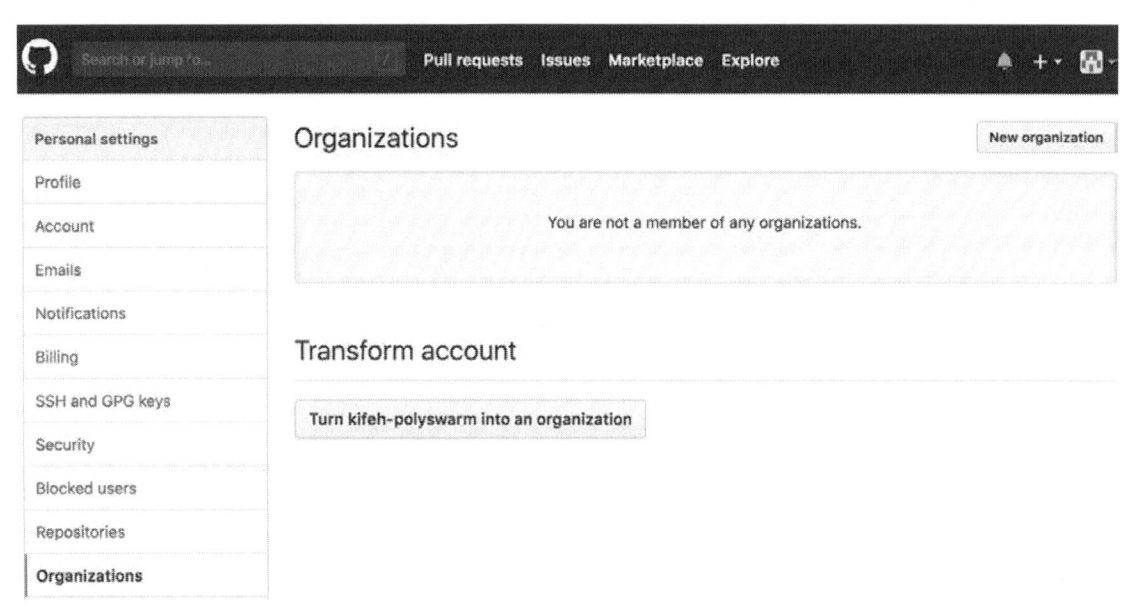

Figure 1.13: Setting up the organization

2. Enter the organization's details, choose a plan, and click **Create organization**:

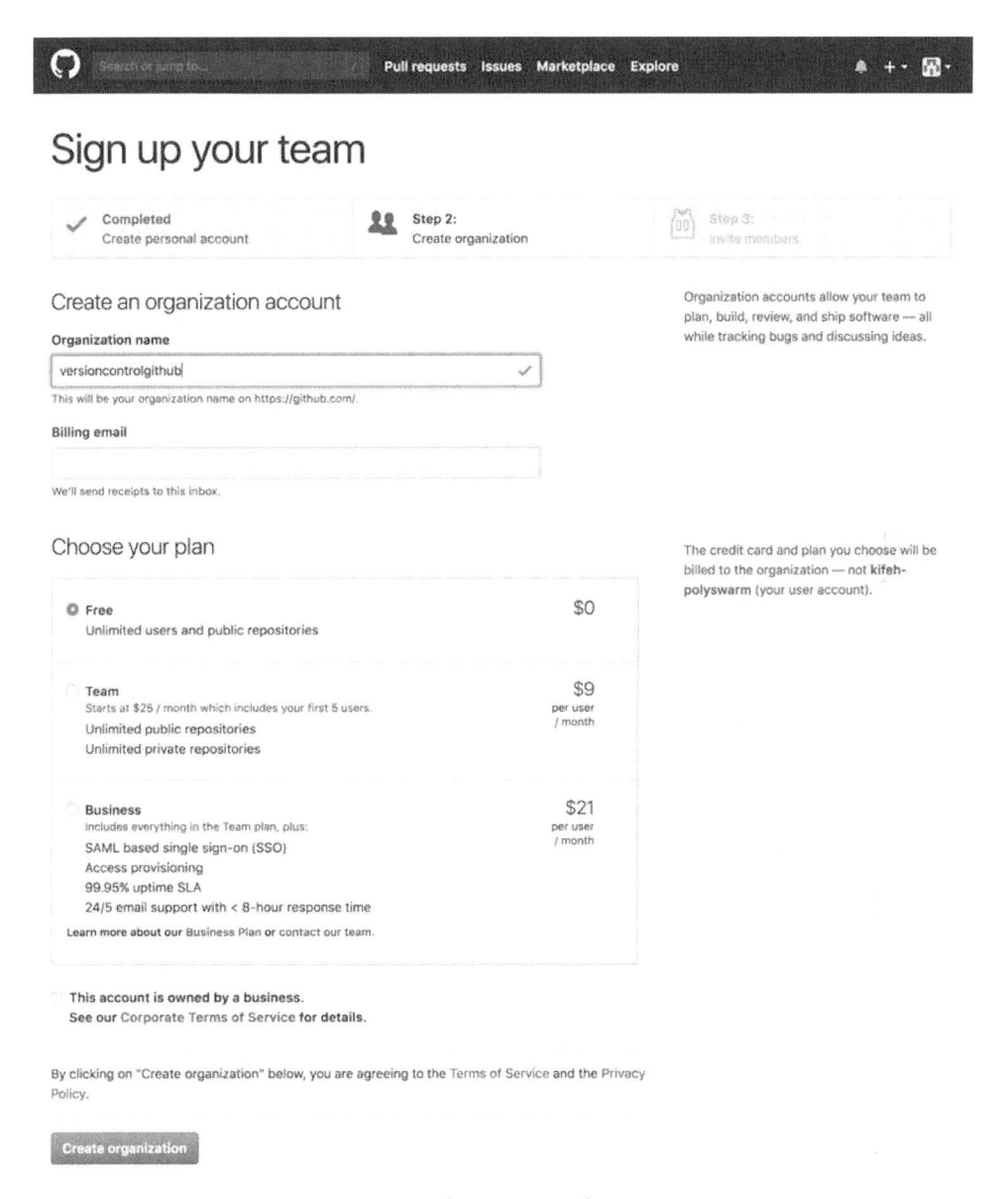

Figure 1.14: Creating an organization account

3. Search and add users, or click **Finish** to conclude the process on the next prompt.

Outcome

You have successfully set up an organization for your account.

18 | Introducing Version Control

Exercise 4: Setting Up a Team

With GitHub organizations, you can, as stated previously, organize contributors in teams and manage permissions and restrictions at a team level and repository level.

To create a team under the **versioncontrolgithub** organization, follow these steps:

1. Go to https://github.com/.

2. On your left, you should find a drop-down menu with your username. Click on the dropdown to reveal the organizations that you belong to:

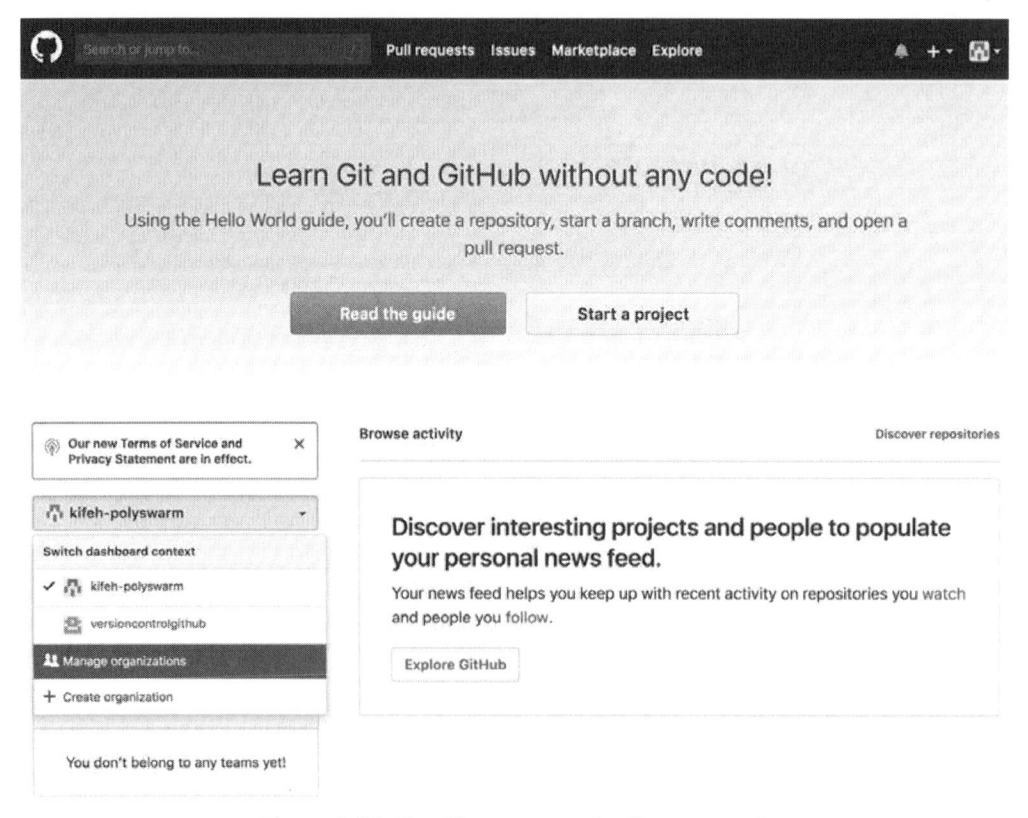

Figure 1.15: Creating an organization account

3. Click **Manage organizations** and then click the **versioncontrolgithub** organization on the next prompt.
4. Click on the **Teams** tab on the organization's dashboard:

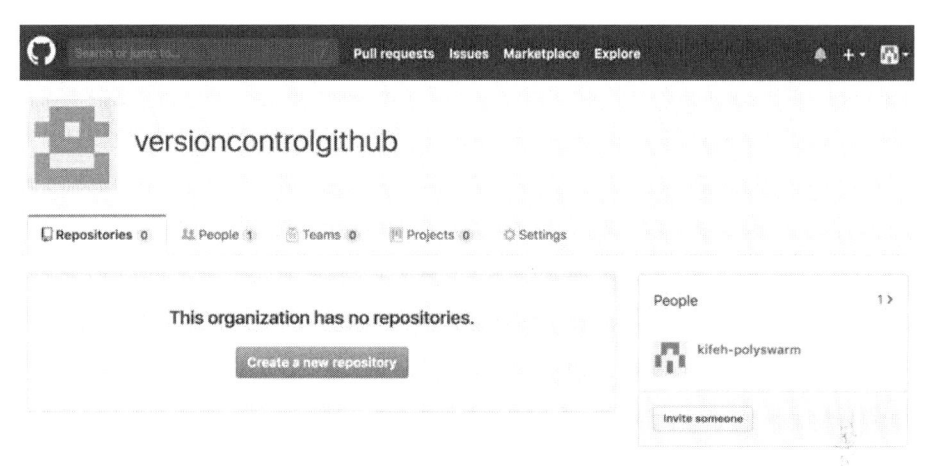

Figure 1.16: versioncontrolgithub

5. Click on the **New team** button on the next prompt.
6. Set the team details and click **Create team**:

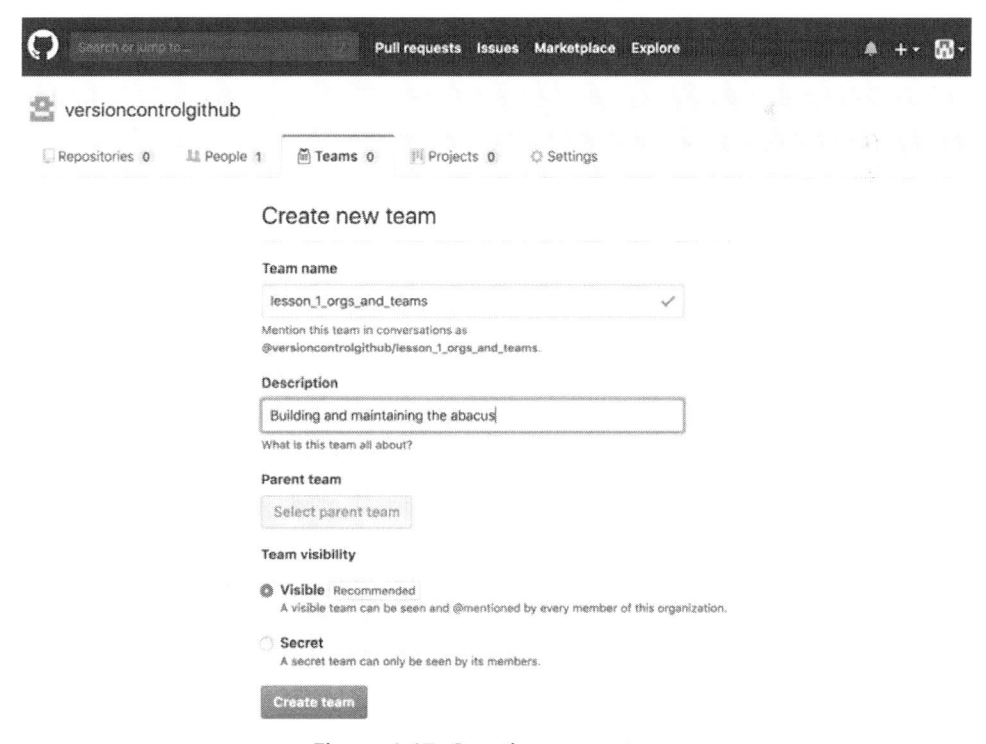

Figure 1.17: Creating a new team

20 | Introducing Version Control

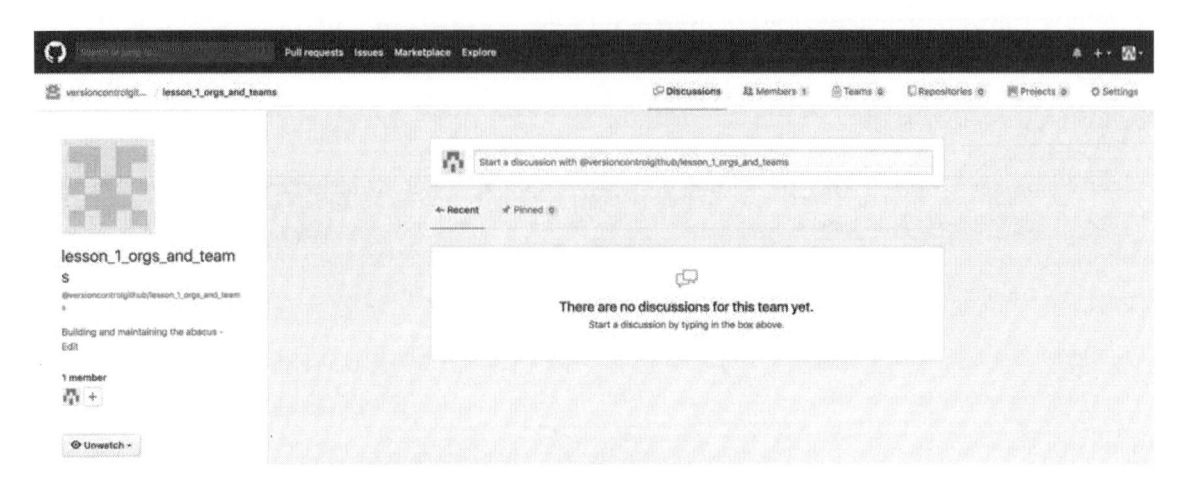

Figure 1.18: Team home page

Outcome

You have successfully created a team under the **versioncontrolgithub** organization.

As seen from the preceding steps, a team can:

- Be utilized to manage pieces of work organized under repositories.
- Have members assigned to it to collaborate on specific repositories.
- Be assigned task-tracking boards under **Projects**.
- Have nested or child teams created under it. This can be achieved from the **Team** tab, which is shown in the preceding screenshot.

Marketplace

GitHub offers the ability to integrate applications with your account. These applications serve a range of roles such as continuous integration, code quality analysis, and dependency management analysis. Next, we shall set up **Codacy** for our accounts. **Codacy** is used to analyze code that's introduced into a project to identify areas of improvements where action can be taken before changes are merged.

Exercise 5: Setting Up Codacy for Accounts

Consider using the following text as the description text for the exercise.

To set-up Codacy follow the steps below.

1. Go to https://github.com/.
2. Click **Marketplace** on the top navigation bar.

3. Click **Code quality** from the categories list.
4. Click **Codacy**, which is listed on the right:

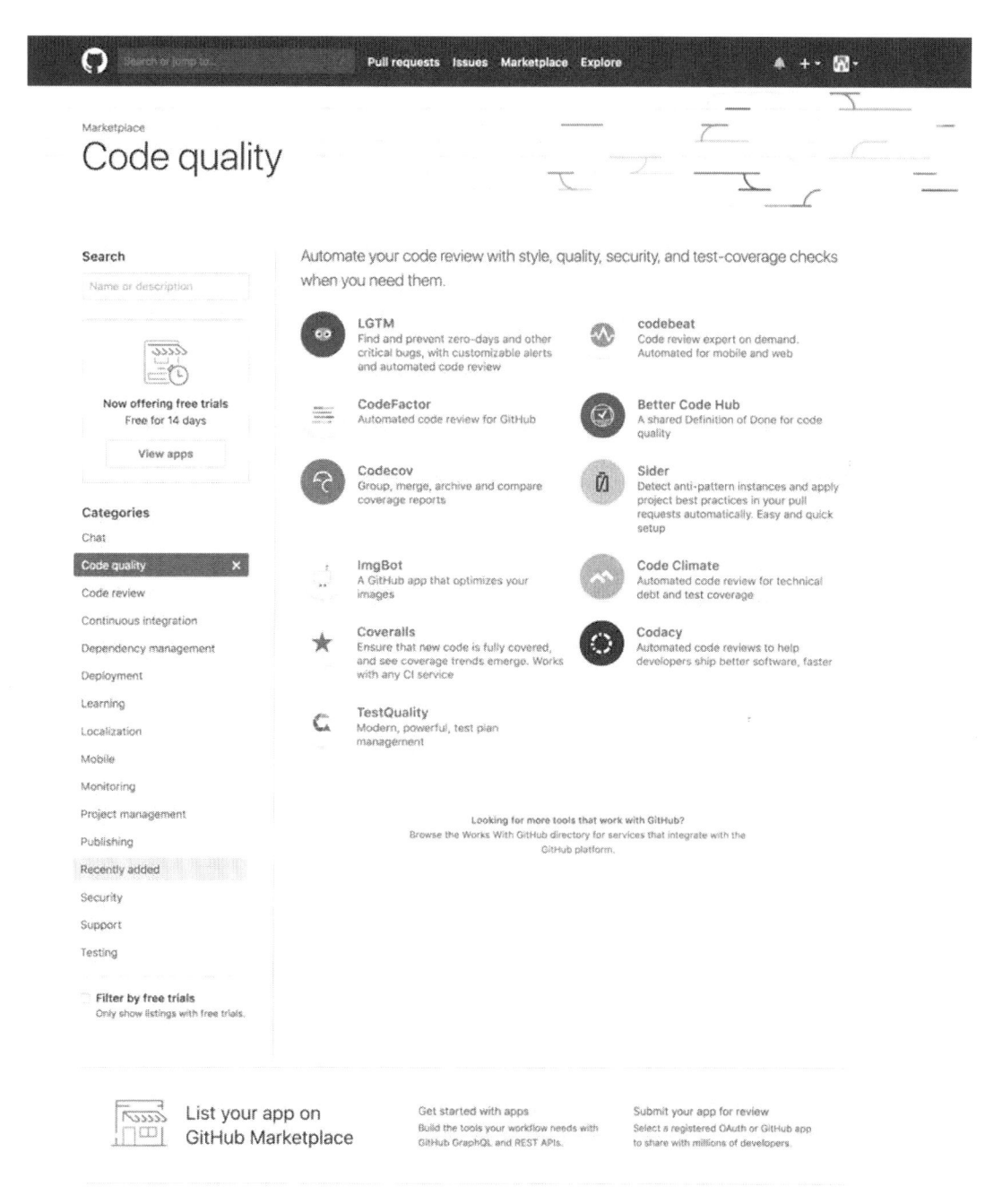

Figure 1.19: Code quality

22 | Introducing Version Control

5. From there, click **Set up a plan** and **Install it for free**:

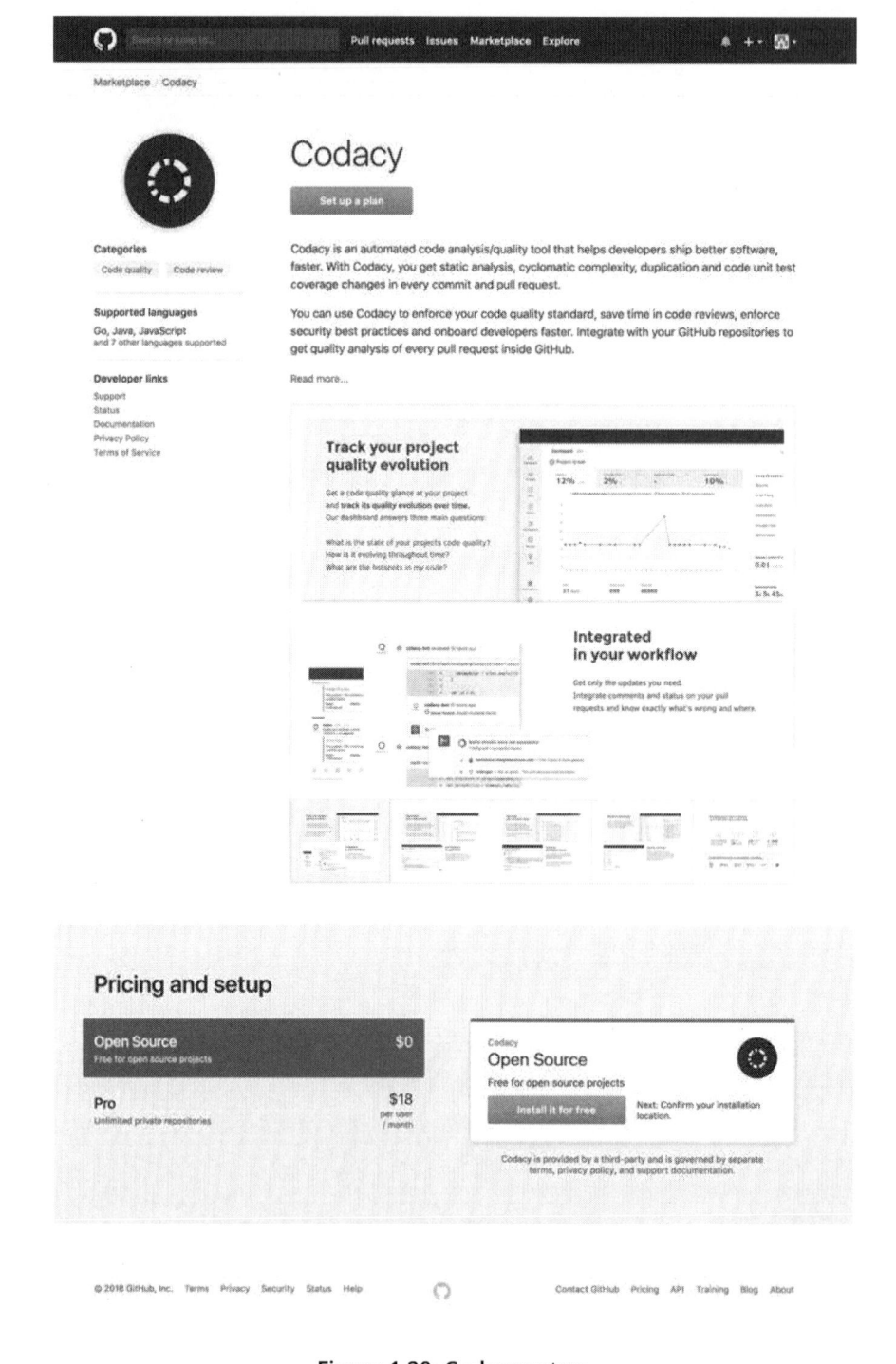

Figure 1.20: Codacy setup

6. Click **Complete order and begin installation**.

7. Authorize the application by clicking the **Authorize qamine** button:

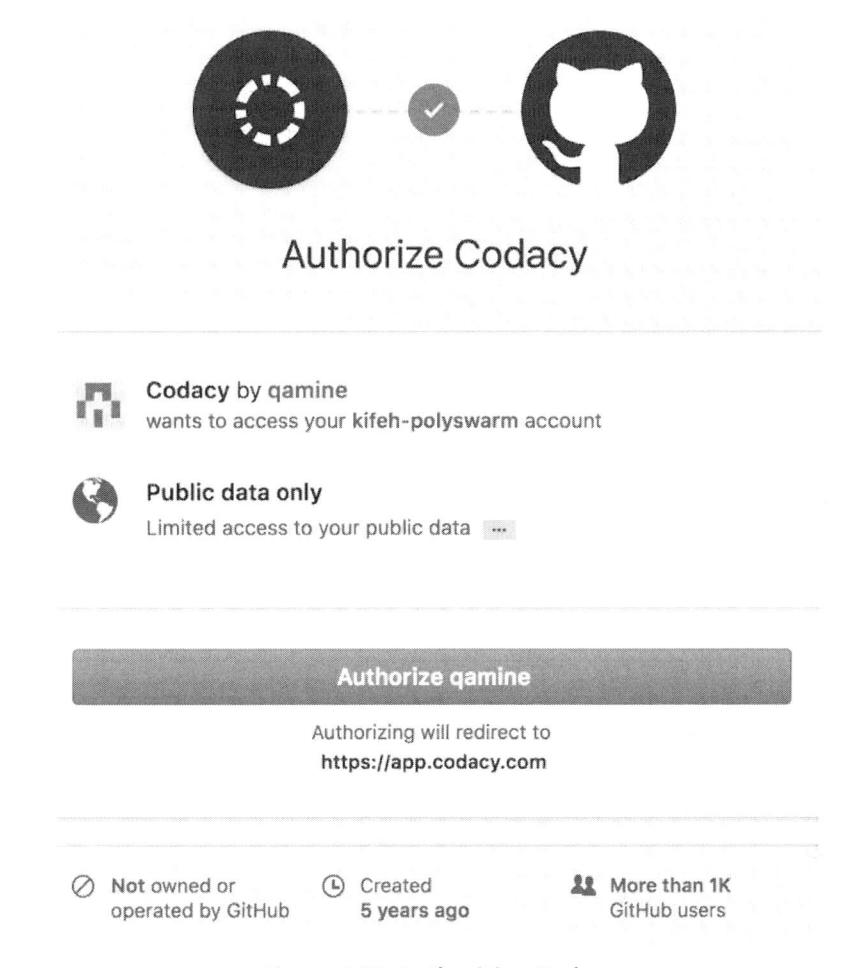

Figure 1.21: Authorizing Codacy

8. Enter your password and click **Confirm password** to complete the setup process.

Outcome

You have integrated Codacy into your account for use in quality control of code.

Runtime Config

Git supports the configuration of runtime options. These options and/or values are used by other Git commands to dictate behavior. Runtime configurations are set using the `git config` command.

The `git config` command allows for the setting, retrieving, removal, and replacement of configurations. Git configurations are set in three levels, namely:

System wide configuration

These options are set in the **/etc/gitconfig** file. The presets specified in this category are used for all of the users on a computer.

To access these settings, you use the `git config --system` flag specifies that system wide configuration should be used.

User-specific configuration

These options are set in the **~/.gitconfig** file. The presets provided here are used for the user account that is in use on a computer.

The user-specific settings are accessed via the `git config --global` flag specifies that user specific configuration should be used.

Repository-specific configuration

Repository-specific settings are set in the **path_to_repository/.git/config** file. The options set here are used at the repository level. An example of configuration here is the GitHub URL of a repository, which is set at this level.

These settings are accessed via the `git config --local` flag specifies that repository specific configuration should be used.

You may specify a specific config file using the `-f` or `--file` option.

Exercise 6: Setting User Credentials

To set up the user credentials for an account, follow these steps:

1. Launch the Terminal or command prompt.
2. Set the username by using the following command: `git config --global user.name kifeh-polyswarm`:

```
alexmagana@ALEXs-MacBook-Pro    git config --global user.name kifeh-polyswarm
alexmagana@ALEXs-MacBook-Pro
```

Figure 1.22: Setting up a username

3. Set up the email by using the following command: `git config --global user.email kifeh@poly-swarm.com`:

Figure 1.23: Setting up an email

4. List the configuration using one of the following commands:

`git config --global --list`

Or, `git config --list`, to fetch all the available presets

Figure 1.24: Setting up the user credentials

Outcome

You have successfully set up the user credentials for an account.

Removing Configuration

Using `git config`, we can remove configuration in the event that a change is required. The `git config` utility supports this by using the `--unset` option.

The syntax of the command is indicated as follows:

`git config --global --unset [section_name].[section_variable]`

Example

`git config --global --unset user.name`

The preceding command will remove the value set for the user's username.

SSH Configuration

To interact with a repository and/or conduct tasks on GitHub from your local environment, you need to assert you are who you say you are. Git supports this by using a combination of a username and password, or using an SSH key to authenticate a connection or requests made to GitHub from your local environment.

The use of SSH keys ensures enhanced security and averts the need to provide a username and password for each request.

Exercise 7: Setting Up SSH

To set up the SSH key for the account, follow these steps:

1. Launch the Terminal or command prompt.
2. Generate a SSH key using the following command:

`ssh-keygen -t rsa -b 4096 -C "[email_address]"`

Example: `ssh-keygen -t rsa -b 4096 -C "kifeh@poly-swarm.com"`

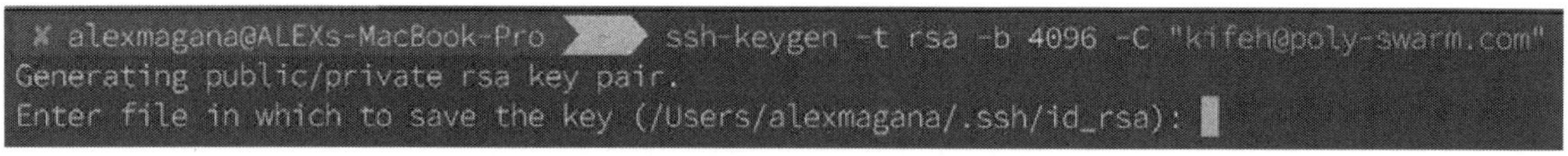

Figure 1.25: Generating an SSH key

3. Specify the location where the generated key is to be stored. You may press **Enter** to instruct the key generator to use the default location:

Figure 1.26: Specifying the storage location

4. Type a passphrase to secure the generated key as seen in the following screenshots:

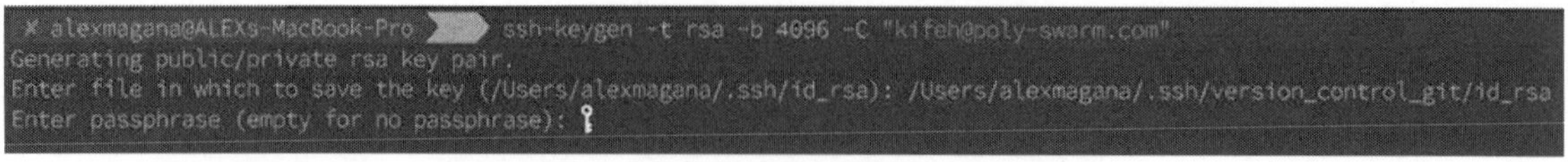

Figure 1.27: Using a passphrase for security

Figure 1.28: Using a passphrase for security part 2

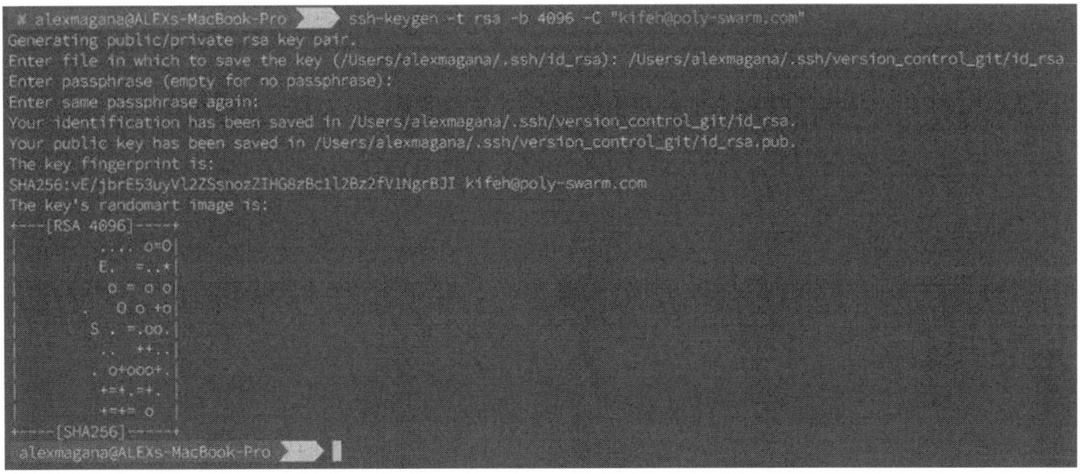

Figure 1.29: Generating the SSH key

The key is stored in the specified location, as pictured in the preceding screenshots:

1. Start the SSH agent using the following command: `eval "$(ssh-agent -s)"`.

2. On macOS, edit `~/.ssh/config` to enable the ssh-agent to automatically load keys and store passphrases in the keychain:

Host *

AddKeysToAgent yes

UseKeychain yes

IdentityFile [location_of_the_generated_private_key]

Example: Host *:

AddKeysToAgent yes

UseKeychain yes

IdentityFile ~/.ssh/version_control_git/id_rsa

28 | Introducing Version Control

3. Add the SSH private key to the ssh-agent.

> **Note**
>
> -K adds the passphrase to the keychain when a private key is added to the ssh-agent.

```
ssh-add -K [location_of_the_generated_private_key]
```

Example: `ssh-add -K ~/.ssh/version_control_git/id_rsa`

4. Add the public SSH key to your GitHub account. Go to https://github.com/, and then go to **Settings** as shown in the following screenshot::

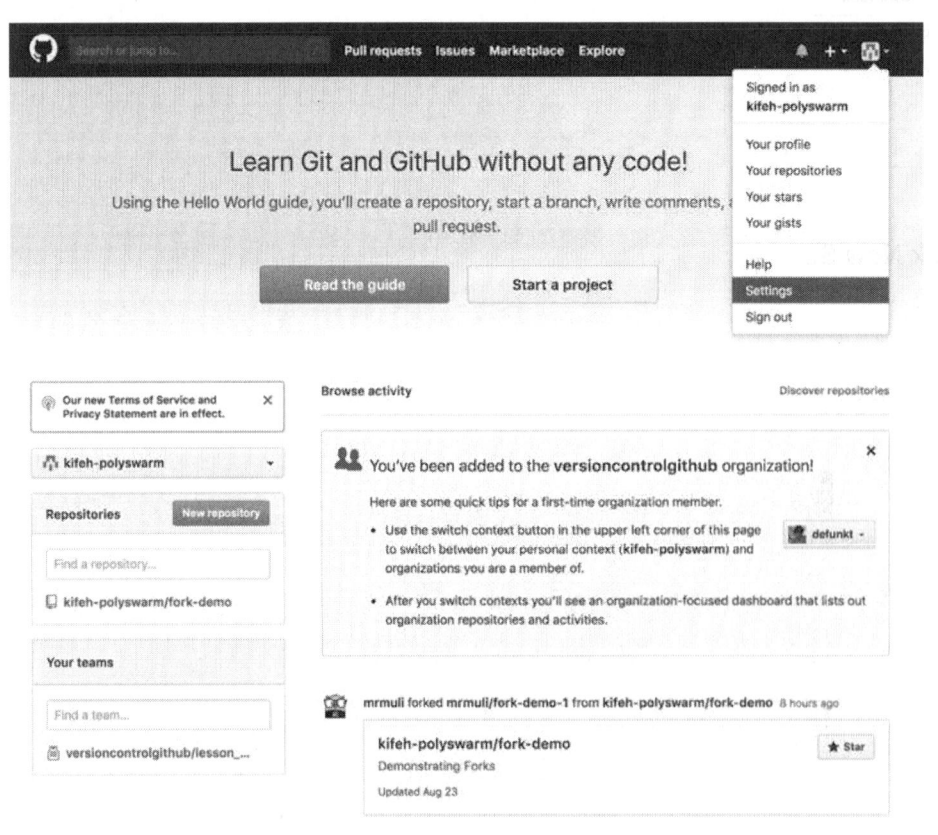

Figure 1.30: GitHub Settings

5. Click **SSH and GPG keys** as shown in the following screenshot::

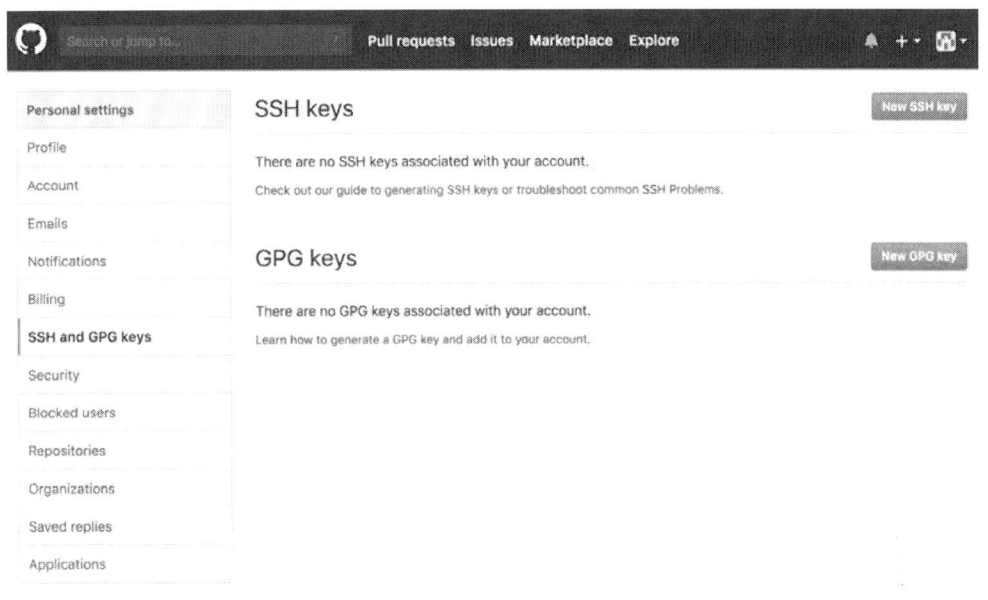

Figure 1.31: SSH and GPG keys

6. Click **New SSH key** and set a title for your public SSH key.

7. Launch the Terminal and copy the contents of the public SSH key to the clipboard using the following command: `pbcopy < ~/.ssh/version_control_git/id_rsa.pub`.

8. Paste the contents of the public key into the field under the label **Key**:

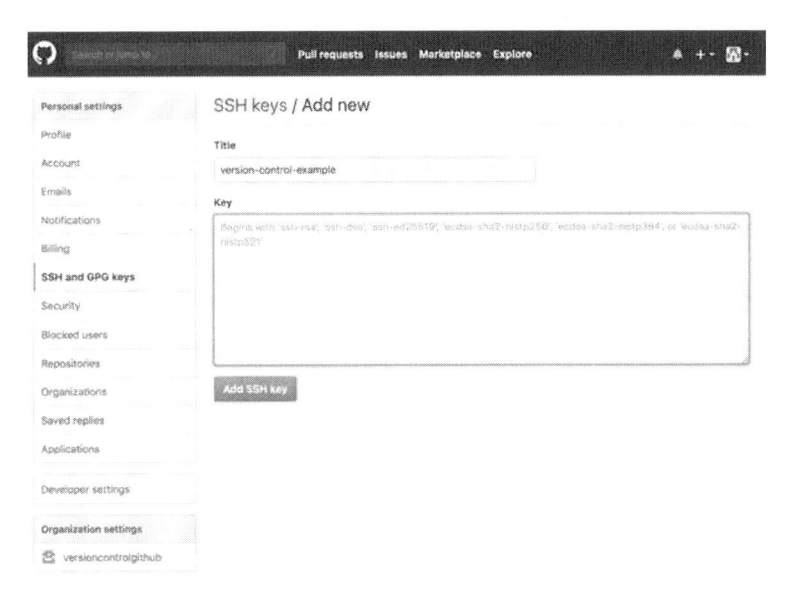

Figure 1.32: SSH keys/Add new

30 | Introducing Version Control

9. Click **Add SSH key** to add the public key to your GitHub account.

10. Test that the **SSH key** has been set up properly by making a request to GitHub using the following command:

    ```
    ssh -T git@github.com
    ```

Figure 1.33: Testing the SSH key's setup

You have successfully set up the SSH key for the account.

Creating a Repository

Version control requires that the files and associated changes that need to be tracked are organized in a repository which is the unit that Git identifies as the candidate for source control. To commence a piece of work, we need to create a repository.

In this section, we shall explore two approaches that you may use to initialize a repository.

Exercise 8: Creating a Repository in a Local Environment

Initializing a repository locally entails using `git init` and mapping the local repository to its corresponding remote repository:

1. Launch the Terminal.

    a. On a Linux computer: Press *Ctrl* + *Alt* + *T*.

    b. On a macOS computer: Press ⌘ + *spacebar,* Type **Terminal** or **iTerm**, and then click the application logo to launch the Terminal:

Figure 1.34: Launching a Terminal on macOS

c. On a Microsoft Windows computer: Press *Win* + *R* on your keyboard to launch the **Run** window. Then, type **cmd.exe** and press *Enter* on your keyboard, or click **OK** on the **Run** window.

2. Create a directory for the application using the following command: `mkdir abacus`:

Figure 1.35: Creating a directory

3. Change the working directory to the project directory using the following command: `cd abacus`

4. Initialize the repository using the following command: `git init`.

5. Go to https://github.com/

6. Click **New repository** on the left-hand pane on the page:

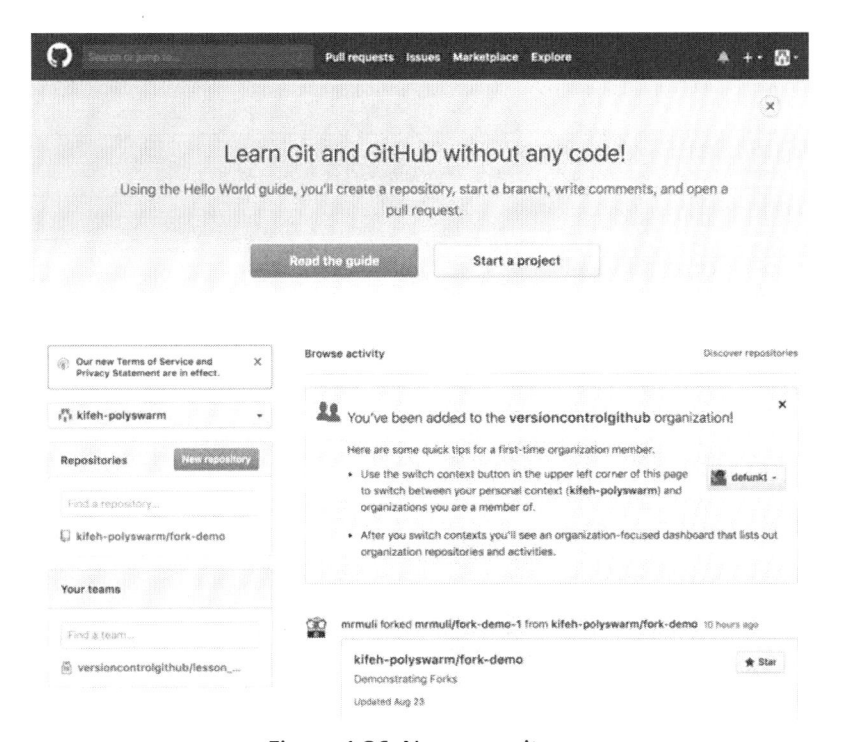

Figure 1.36: New repository

32 | Introducing Version Control

7. Specify the name of the repository as shown in the following screenshot:

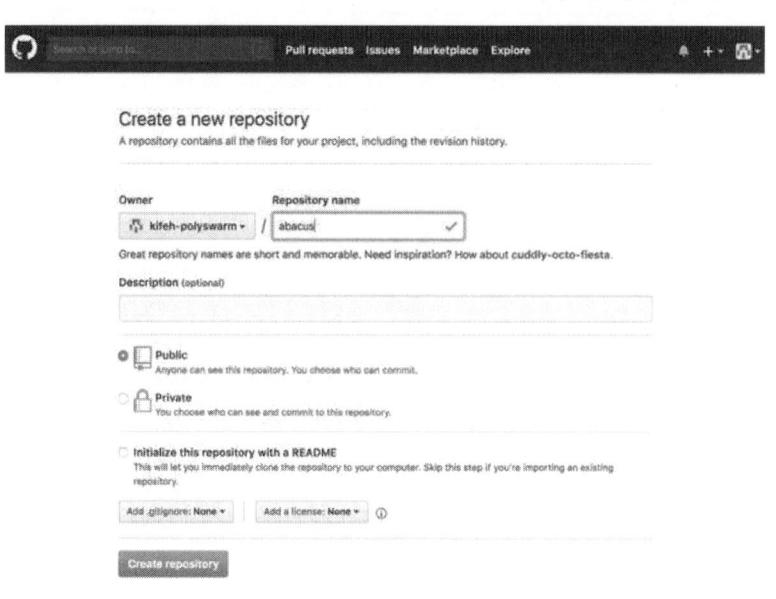

Figure 1.37: Creating a repository

8. Click **Create repository**.

9. Click on the **SSH** button to obtain the SSH URL. This button is below the text that reads **Quick setup - if you've done this kind of thing before**:

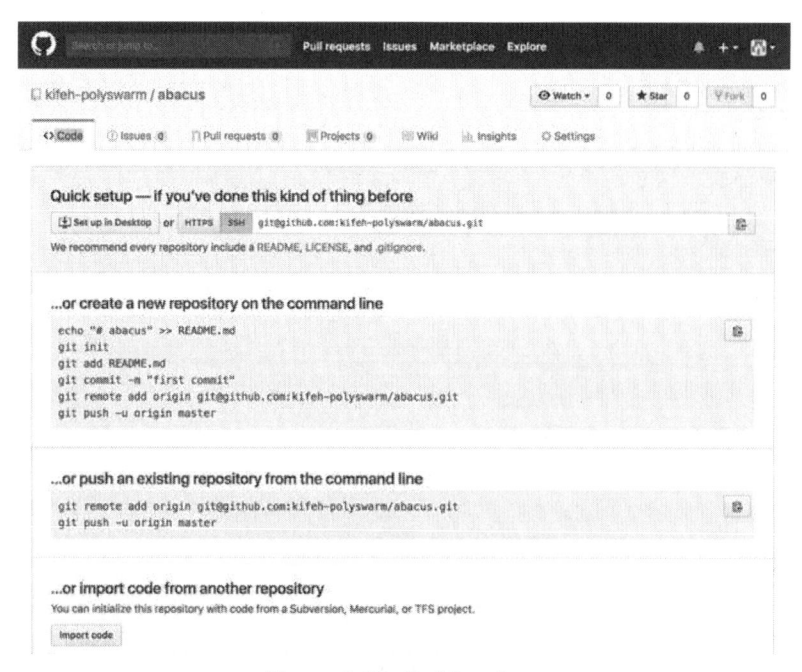

Figure 1.38: Quick setup

Navigating GitHub | 33

10. On the Terminal, specify the GitHub URL of the repository, that is, abacus:

    `git remote add origin [repository_url]`

Here is an example: `git remote add origin git@github.com:kifeh-polyswarm/abacus.git`

Figure 1.39: Specifying the GitHub URL

11. Add the file where we'll host the class that will host our code using the following code as seen in the following screenshots:

    `mkdir -p src/lib`

    `touch src/lib/compute.py`

Figure 1.40: Hosting the code

Figure 1.41: Hosting the code part

12. Prepare the files for the first commit using the following command: `git add src/lib/compute.py`

Figure 1.42: Preparing the files for commit

34 | Introducing Version Control

13. Commit the files using the following command: `git commit -m "Initial commit"`

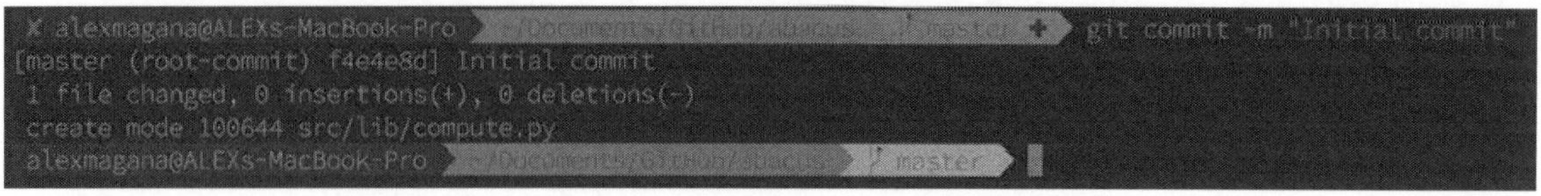

Figure 1.43: Preparing the files for commit part 2

> **Note**
>
> The `-m` option that's used with the `commit` command specifies the message we wish to use for a commit.

You can push the repository files to the repository on GitHub using the following command: `git push -u origin master`

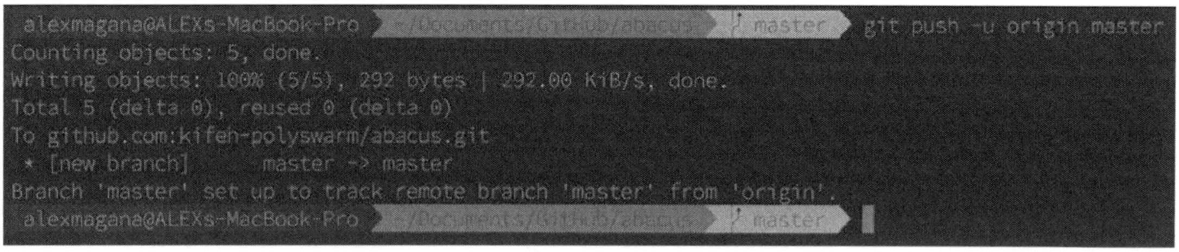

Figure 1.44: Pushing to the GitHub repository

Outcome

You have successfully initialized a repository locally by using `git init` and mapping the local repository to the remote repository.

> **Note**
>
> The `-u` option that's used with the `push` command sets the remote branch of the remote repository that the local repository is linked to. This option is used to create a tracking reference between a local and remote branch. It enables you to run `git push` or `git pull` without having to specify arguments such as the branch name as shown in the following screenshot:

Figure 1.45: Pulling from Git

Exercise 9: Creating a Repository on GitHub

To start a piece of work, you may, instead of initializing a repository locally, create the repository on GitHub, after which you can then clone it locally:

1. Go to https://github.com/.
2. Go to your account's repository listing by clicking **Your repositories** and then click the **New** button as shown in the following screenshots:

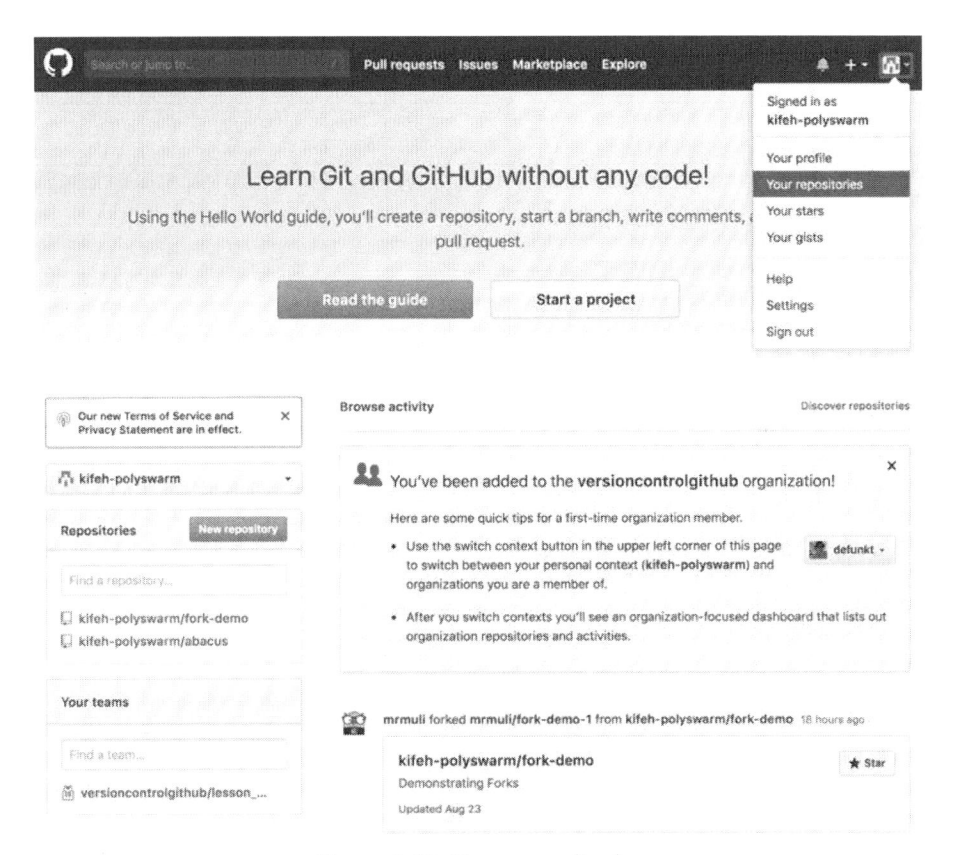

Figure 1.46: Your repositories

36 | Introducing Version Control

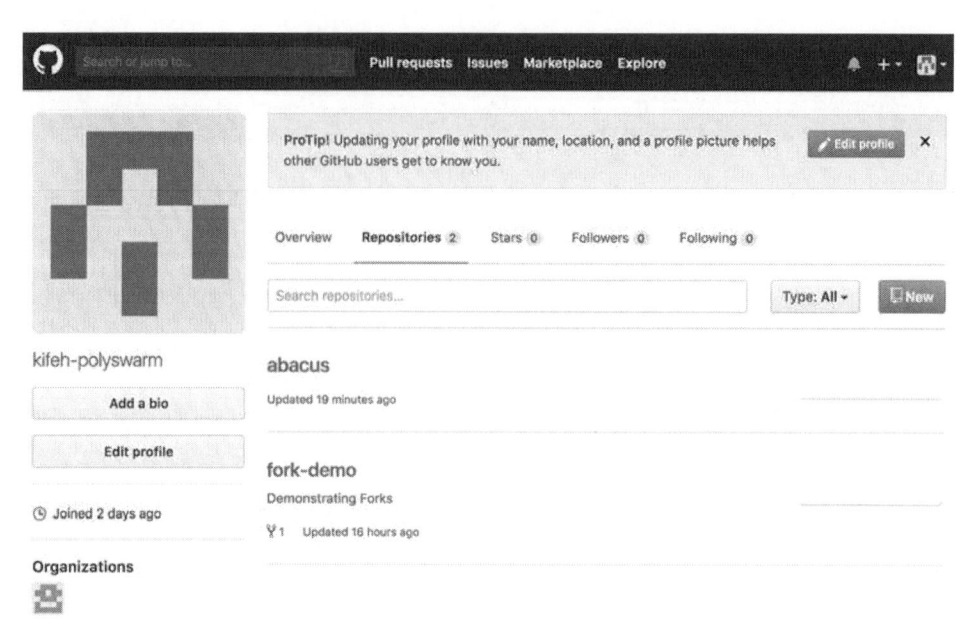

Figure 1.47: New repository button

3. Specify the repository name and description:

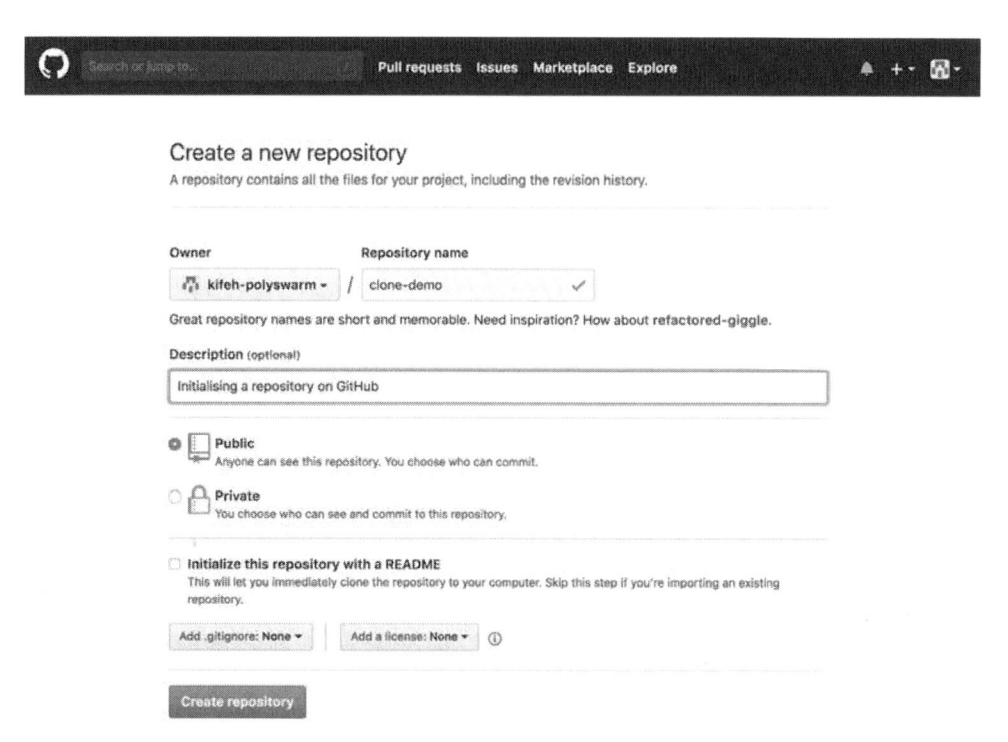

Figure 1.48: Creating a new repository

4. Click the **Create repository** button.

5. Retrieve the SSH URL:

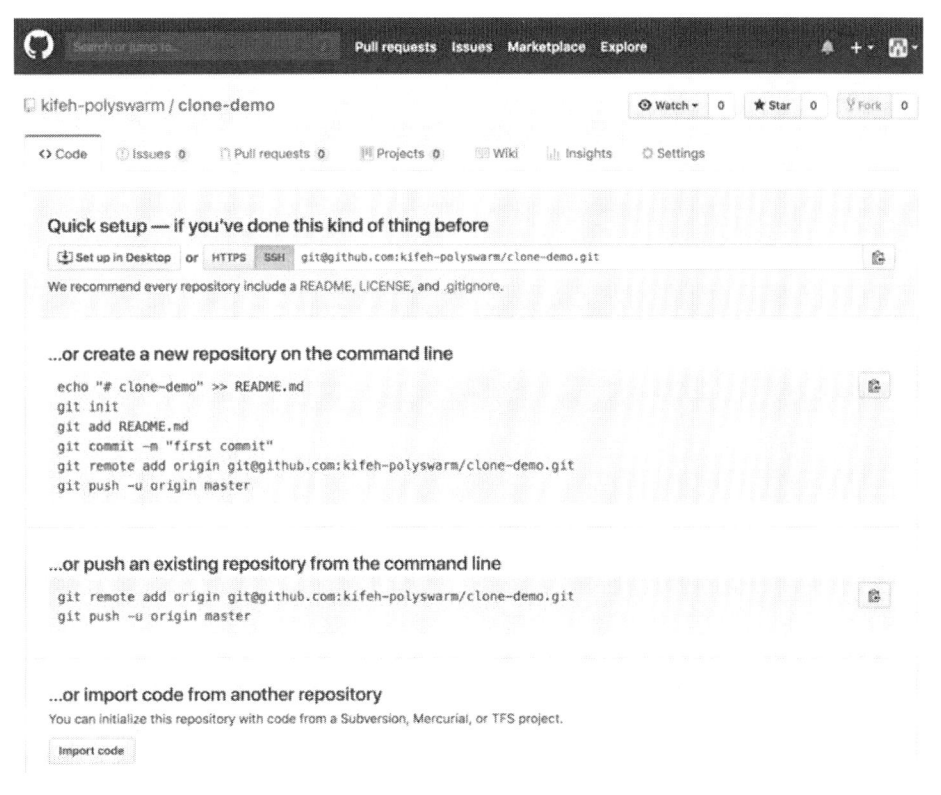

Figure 1.49: Quick setup

6. Clone the repository on your local environment using the following command as seen in the following screenshot:

`git clone [repository_url]`.

Example: `git clone git@github.com:kifeh-polyswarm/clone-demo.git`

Figure 1.50: Cloning a repository

Outcome

You have successfully created the repository on GitHub, which you can now clone locally.

Navigating a Repository

GitHub offers features on a repository level. These features provide an outlook of work and progress on a repository by offering insights related to velocity, adherence to community standards, and utilization of a repository by the community.

Collaborators

GitHub supports adding and removing contributors to/from a repository.

Exercise 10: Adding and Deleting Contributors

To add or remove contributors from a given repository, follow these steps:

1. Go to a repository on your account, for example, https://github.com/kifeh-polyswarm/abacus.

2. Click **Settings** and then click on **Collaborators**:

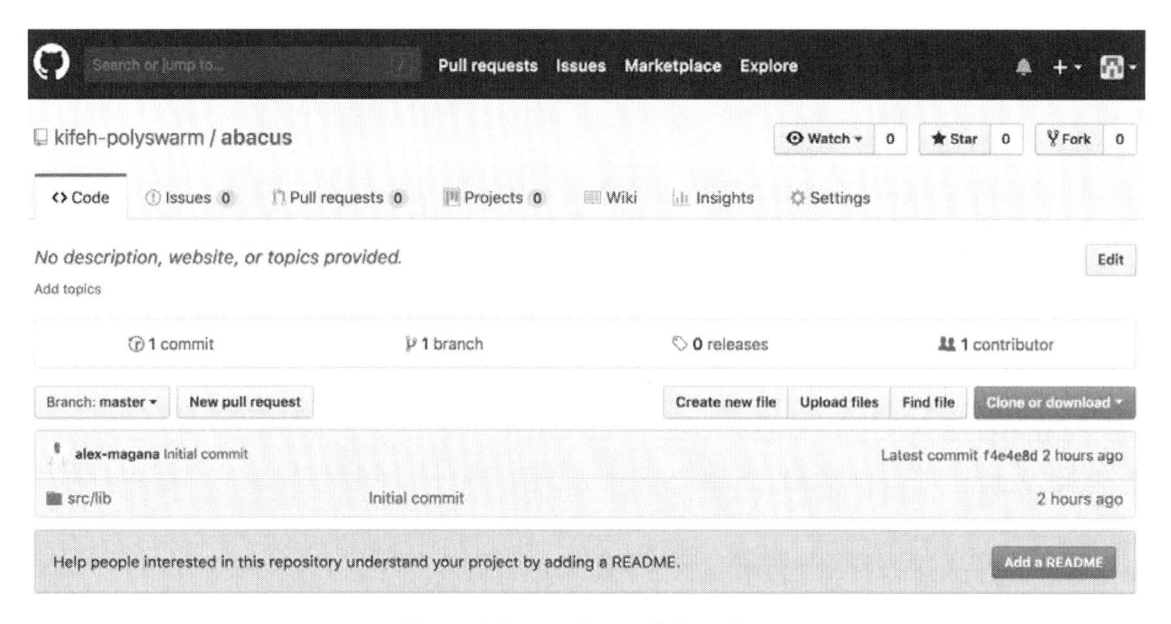

Figure 1.51: Settings tab location

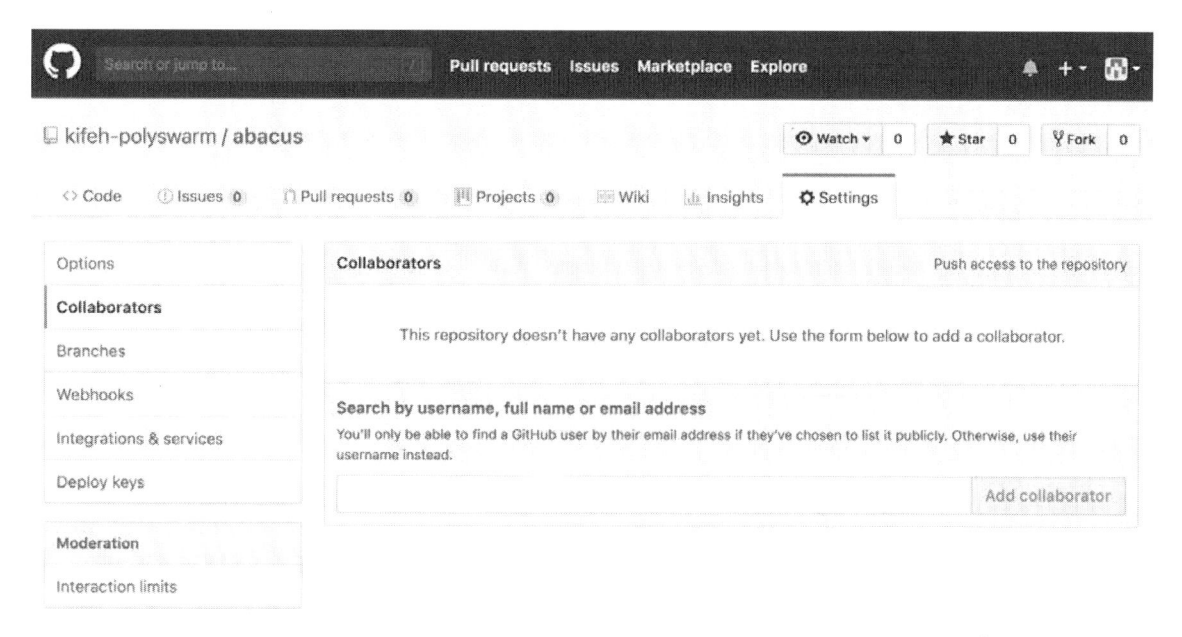

Figure 1.52: Settings part 2

3. Search for a user by their email address, username, or full name, for example, **alex-magana** as shown in the following screenshot:

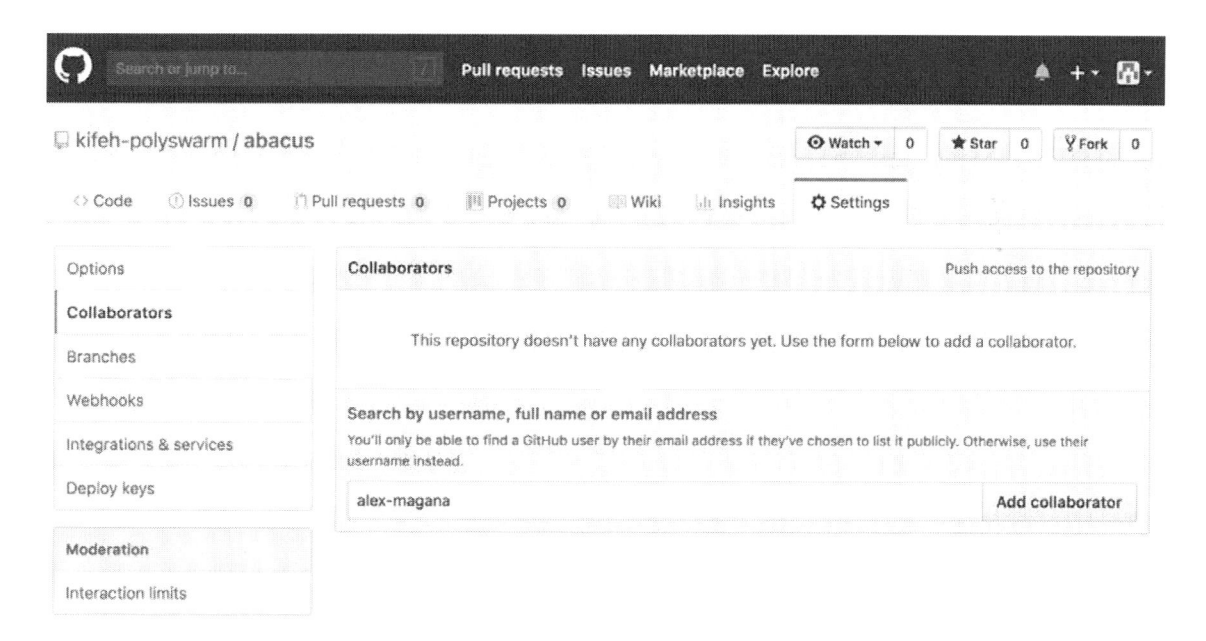

Figure 1.53: Adding collaborators

40 | Introducing Version Control

4. Select the resultant user and click **Add collaborator** as seen in the following screenshots:

> **Note**
>
> Once the user to whom you've sent an invite accepts the invite, they should be able to make contributions to the repository.

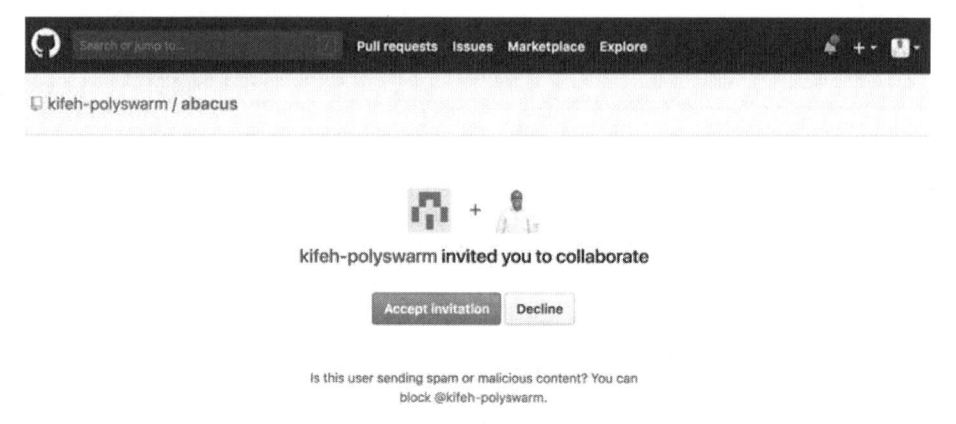

Figure 1.54: Accepting invitation

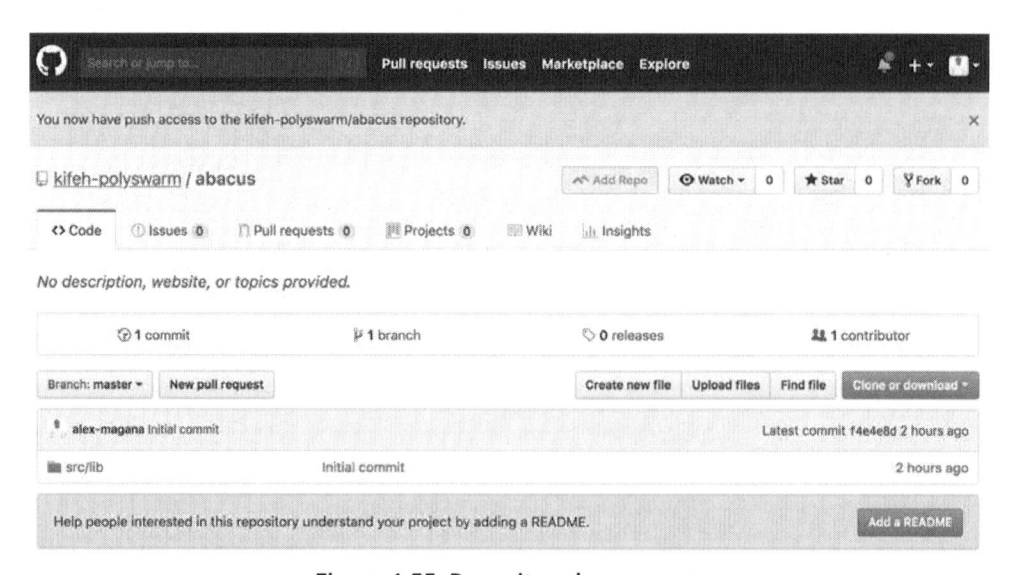

Figure 1.55: Repository home page

Outcome

You have successfully added contributors to a given repository.

Navigating Branches, Commits, and Insights (Contributors, Pulse, Forks)

Branches can be viewed and deleted in line with housekeeping processes. This can be done by going to the repository on your account, for example, https://github.com/kifeh-polyswarm/abacus. Next, you have to click the **Forked 1 Branch** button on the top bar to view a list of branches. Then, you should be directed to a page with an overview of the branches present on a repository:

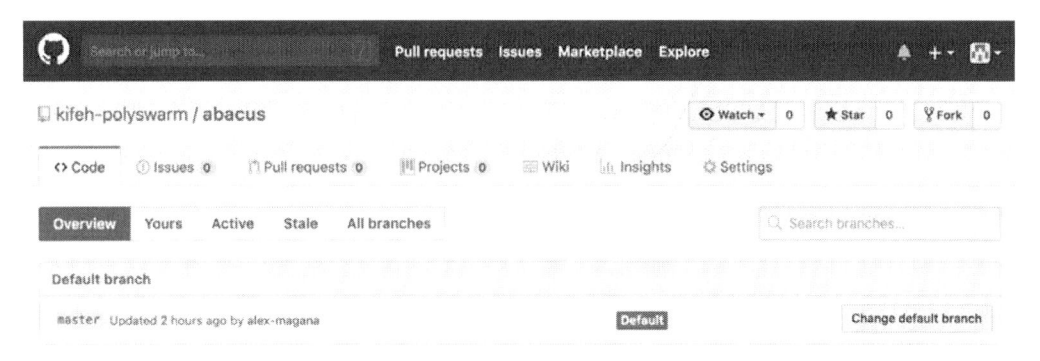

Figure 1.56: Repository overview

Commits present the state of a repository at the time of their creation. You can browse a repository at a commit's point in history and explore files that have been altered by a commit. Then, go to a repository on your account, for example, https://github.com/kifeh-polyswarm/abacus and click the **1 commit** icon to view the commits on a repository. In order to view file alterations on a commit, click the commit hash, for example, **f4e4e8d** as shown in the following screenshot:

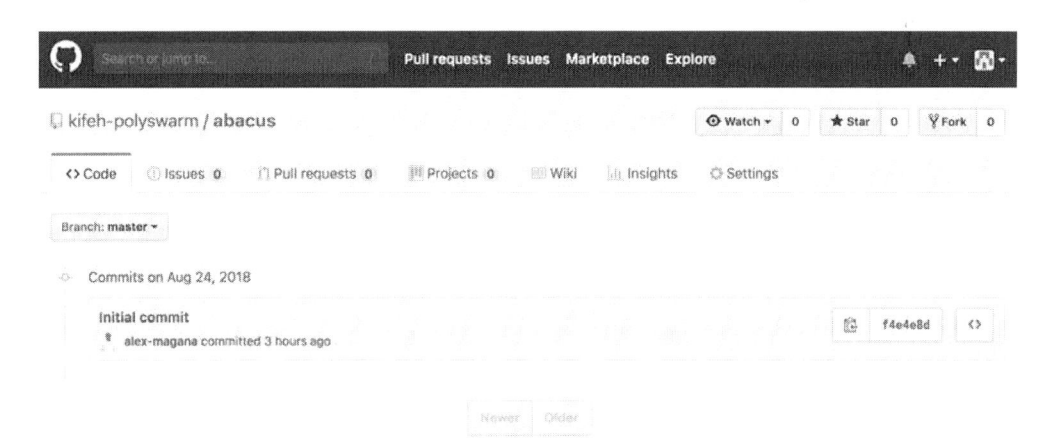

Figure 1.57: Repository part 2

Then, to browse the state of a repository at a given point in time, click the double arrow icon. This can be found on the far right of each commit that's listed. Lastly, you can observe commits that have been organized in order of the respective contributors.

This plays an imperative role of coordinating matters such as knowledge sharing across teams by leveraging the different strengths of the contributors. On a repository of your choice, click **Insights** and then click **Contributors** to view the contributors, along with details of the specific contributions that have been made as shown in the following screenshot:

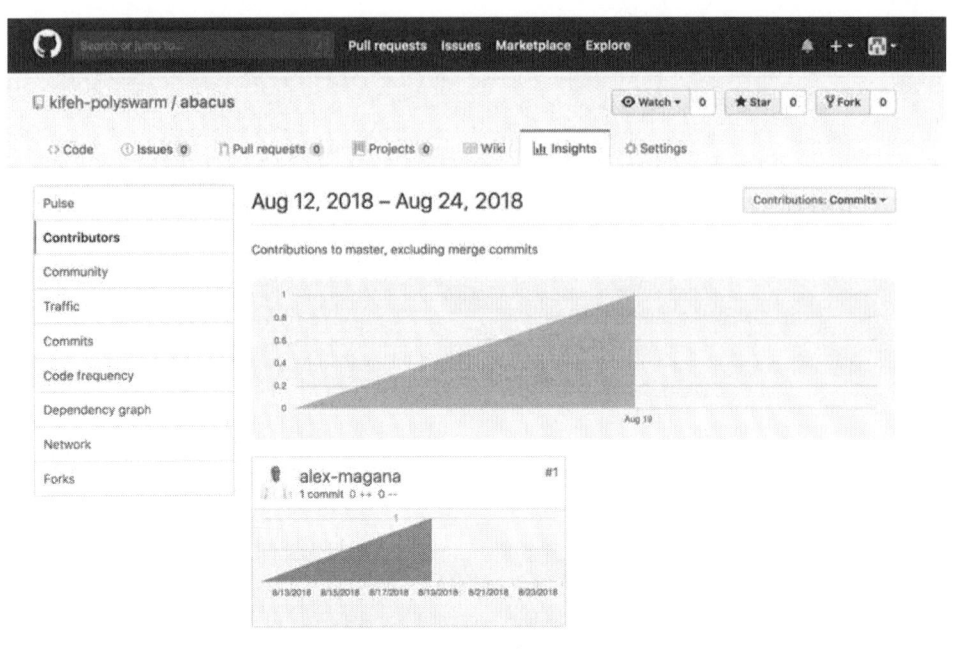

Figure 1.58: Repository part 3

GitHub Etiquette

A certain decorum is expected of repositories and users in using Version control and collaborating on GitHub. This propriety ensures that contributions are carried out in an orderly manner and promotes constructive working environments that focus on delivering value.

GitHub provides a checklist through a **Community profile** that can be accessed through the **Insights** tab of a repository navigation as shown in the following screenshot as follows:

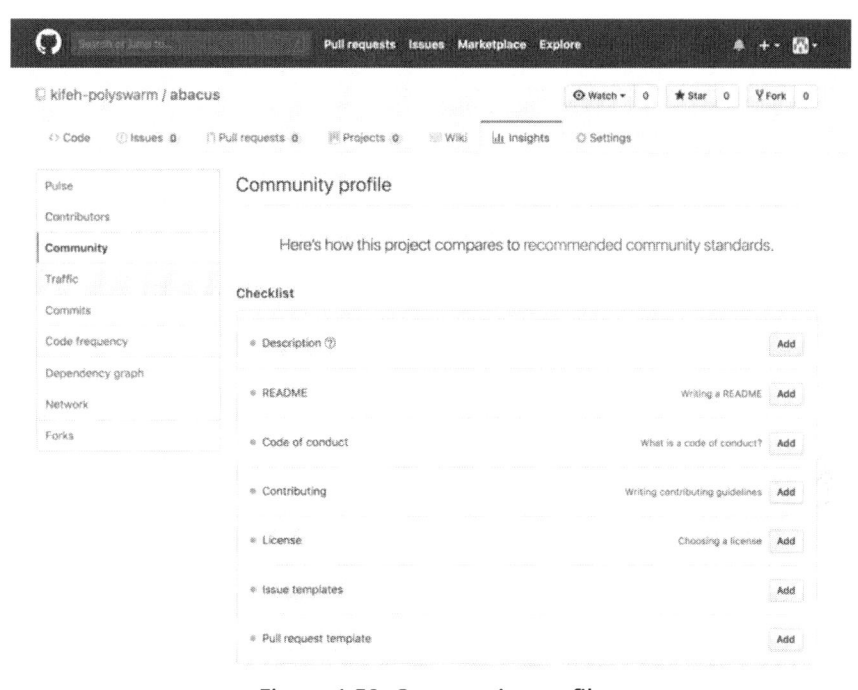

Figure 1.59: Community profile

Repository Names, Tags, and Descriptions

Take a look at the following definitions:

Names

A repository should bear a descriptive name that relates to the functionality an application seeks to deliver.

Tags

These are used for the purpose of identifying specific significant points on a repository's history, for example, software releases, Git supports the creation of markers, referred to as *tags*, to correspond to software versions.

Tags are of two types: *lightweight* and *annotated*.

44 | Introducing Version Control

Lightweight tags act as pointers to a specific commit. It only stores the reference to the commit:

```
git tag v2.5
```

Annotated tags act as pointers to a specific commit and additionally store information about the creator of the tag, the email, and date of creation:

```
git tag -a v2.6 -m "Support sdk version 3"
```

Tags shall be further covered in detail later in this book.

Descriptions

A repository description is required as a best practice. This serves as the first point of introduction and sets the basis on which a repository's functionality is understood.

Adding a Description

This is done by clicking the **Add** button to the right of **Description** on the **Community profile** and then adding the description and clicking **Save**:

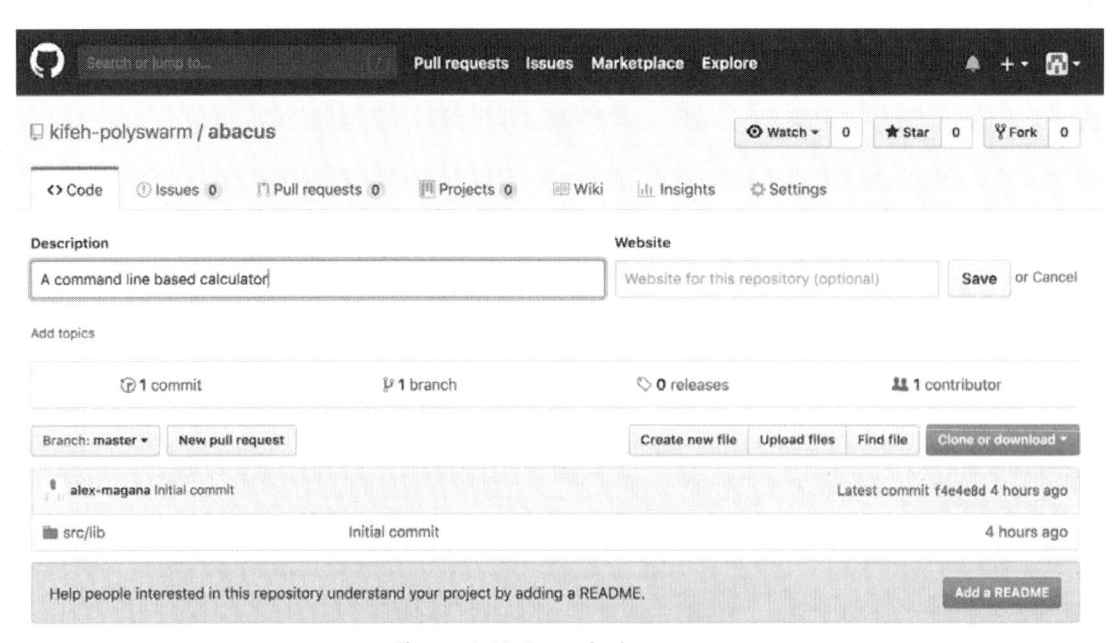

Figure 1.60: Description entry

README.md

This document provides a brief on the project handled by a repository. It encompasses a getting started guide, references to wikis, and conduct and contribution guidelines.

Adding a README.md, CODE_OF_CONDUCT.md and CONTRIBUTING.md

This is achieved by clicking the **Add** button to the right of **README** on the **Community profile**. From here, you should add the necessary details and commit the changes:

Figure 1.61: Committing a new file

This file will be altered as we add features to our application throughout the book.

46 | Introducing Version Control

Then, click the **Add** button to the right of **Code of conduct** on the **Community profile**. Next, select a preferred code of conduct guide as follows:

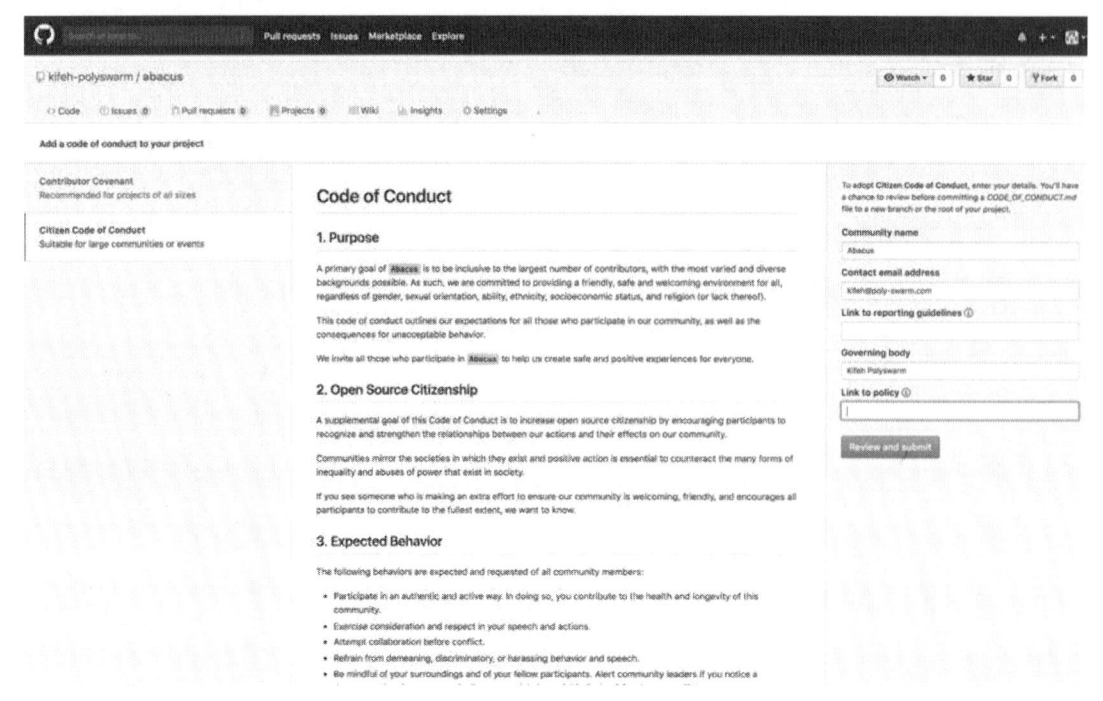

Figure 1.62: Code of Conduct

Then, commit the document to your repository:

Figure 1.63: Committing a new file

Next, click the **Add** button to the right of **Contributing** on the **Community profile**. Lastly, you may commit the document and alter it to fit your project.

LICENSE

A **license** governs the utilization of an application by its users by dictating the obligations and responsibilities of the creator and user of a software application.

Licenses are applicable, for example, in averting a creator from indemnifying a user when an application is used contrary to its terms of use.

Exercise 11: Adding Licenses

To add the appropriate license to the document, follow these steps:

1. Click the **Add** button to the right of **License** on the **Community profile**.
2. Choose a preferred license. In this case, we shall choose the **MIT License**.
3. Click **Review and submit** once you have finished reviewing the document:

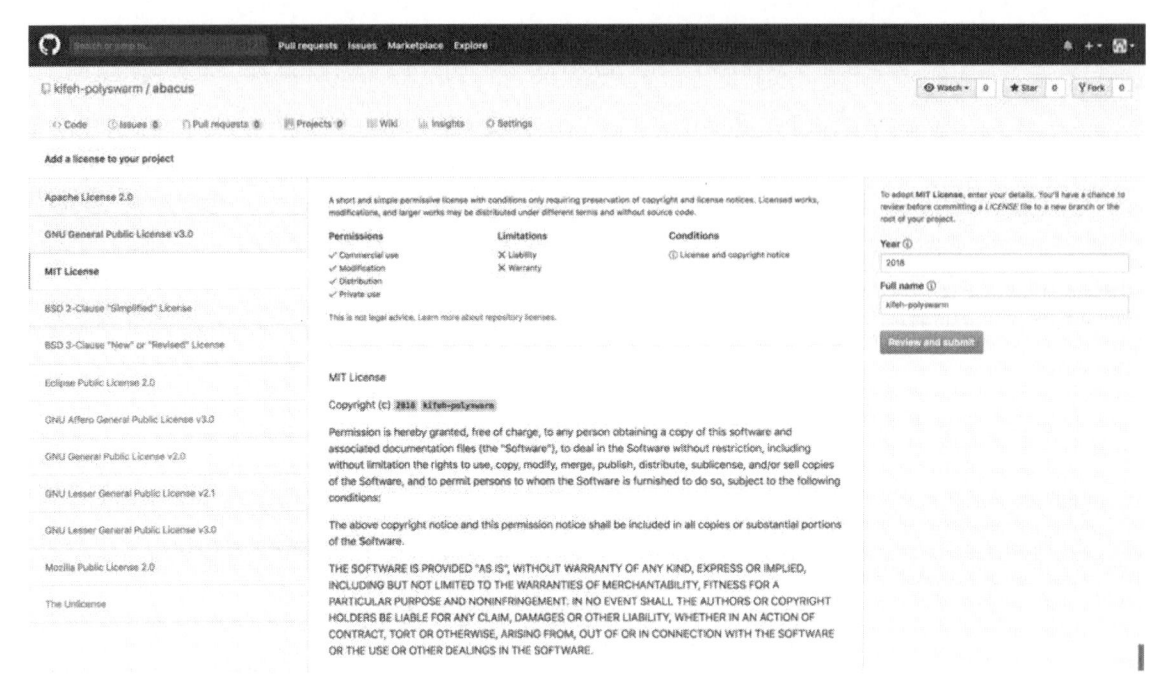

Figure 1.64: MIT License

4. Commit the document. You can alter this document to fit your project.

Outcome

You have successfully added the MIT license to a given repository.

Wikis and Issues

Take a look at the following definitions:

Wiki

Wikis provide an avenue for documenting processes and guides for the usage of a certain piece of software.

You can use wikis to document conventions that should be applied in creating branches, reporting issues, and making feature requests.

To access and/or create wikis, use the **Wiki** button on the top navigation bar:

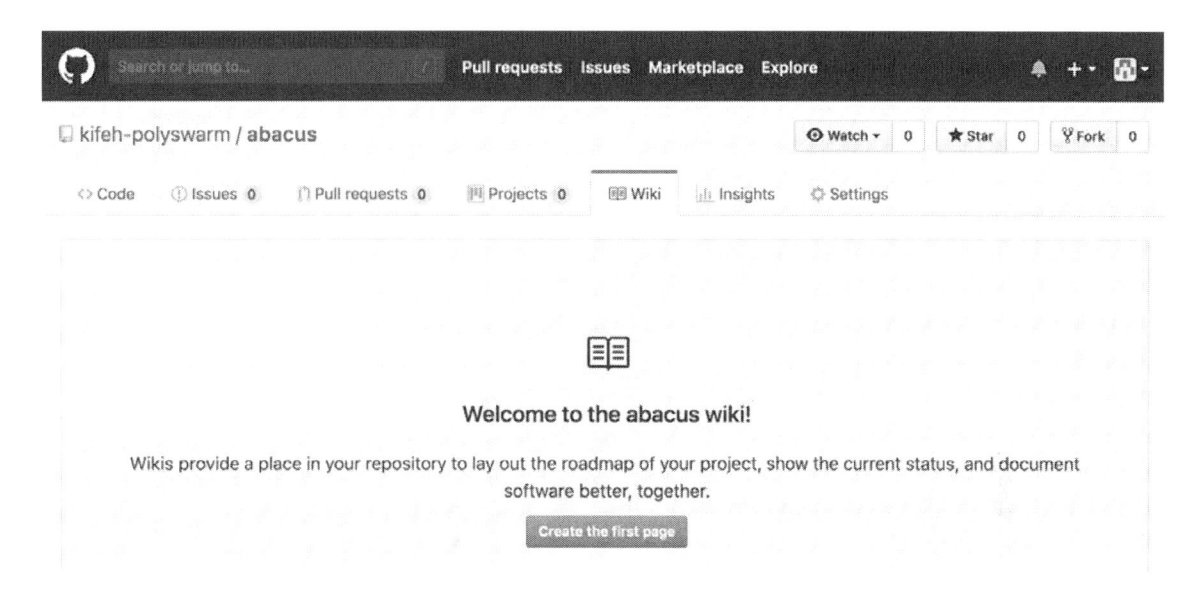

Figure 1.65: Abacus wiki

We shall use wikis to document best practices and conventions for the application we will be building in this book.

Issues

GitHub issues are suitable in reporting challenges or bugs that are encountered when using an application, as well as in making feature requests. Issues aid in tracking tasks that:

- Need to be undertaken as part of a products roadmap
- Respond to user requests and challenges reported, for example, bugs

50 | Introducing Version Control

To facilitate the filing of issues, we need to create templates that serves to ease the reporting process. You will need to click the **Add** button to the right of **Issues template** on the **Community profile**. Then, select the **Bug report** and **Feature request** templates. Lastly, preview and edit the templates if need be as seen in the following screenshots:

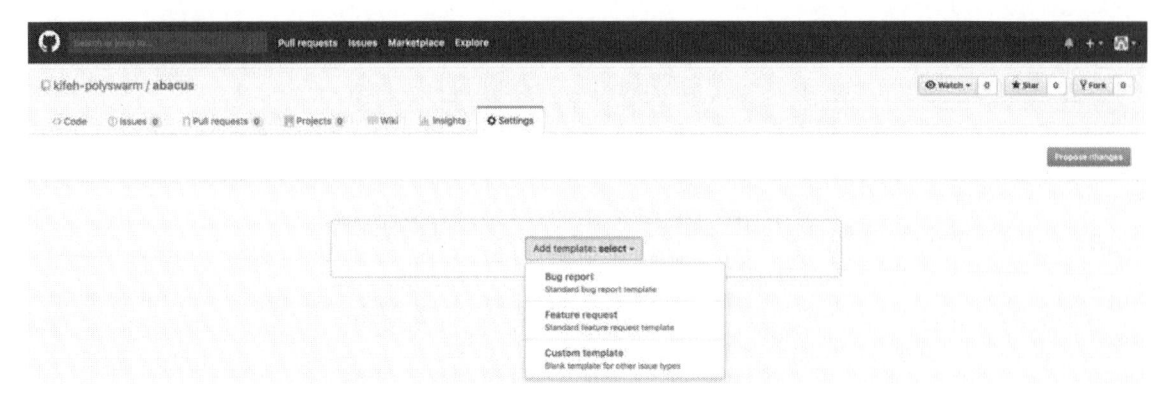

Figure 1.66: Abacus Bug report

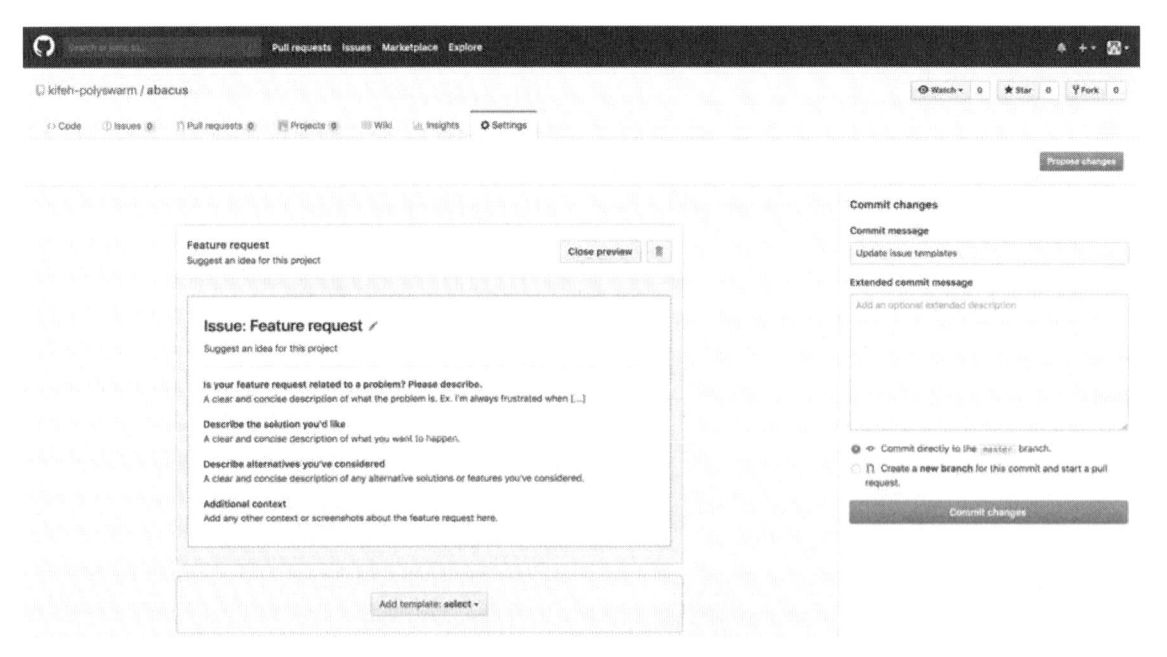

Figure 1.67: Issue: Feature request

By clicking the **Propose changes** button and **Commit changes** thereafter to add the template to your repository, you will be able to file the issues request.

Raising an Issue

This is easily achieved by selecting the **Issues** tab on the top repository navigation bar:

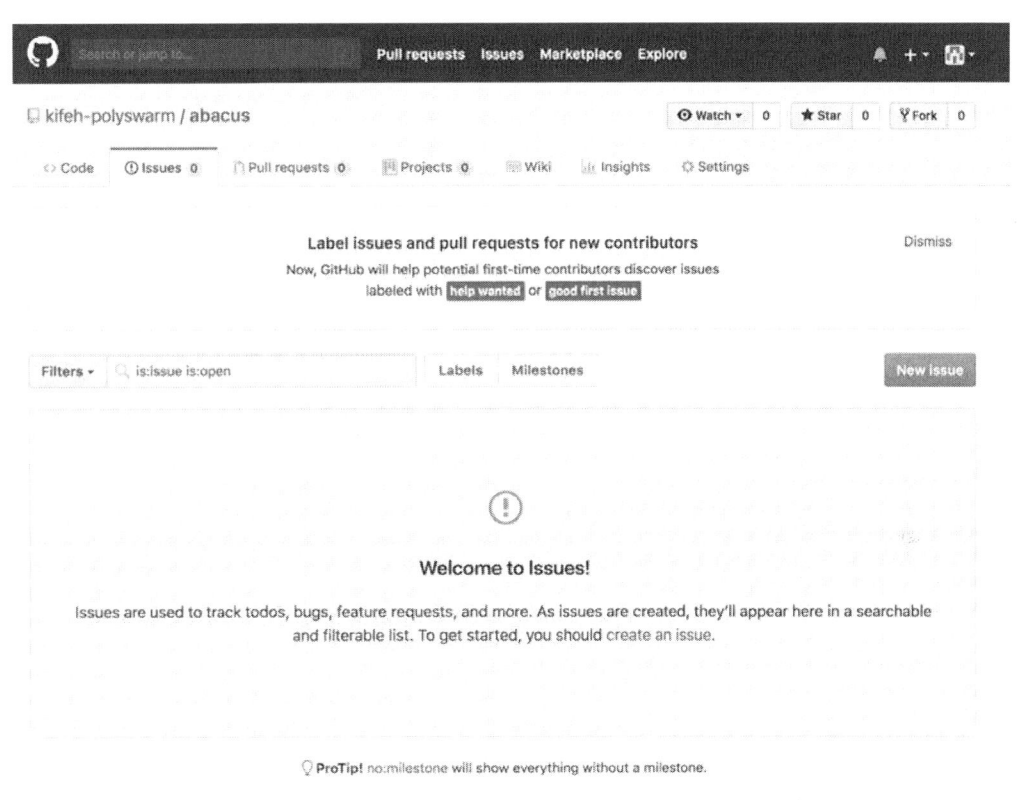

Figure 1.68: Labeling issues and pulling requests

Then, click **New issue** to file an issue. On the next prompt, select the appropriate issue type, for example, **Bug report**. Lastly, you can provide details of your issue and click **Submit new issue** to complete the process, as shown in the following screenshot:

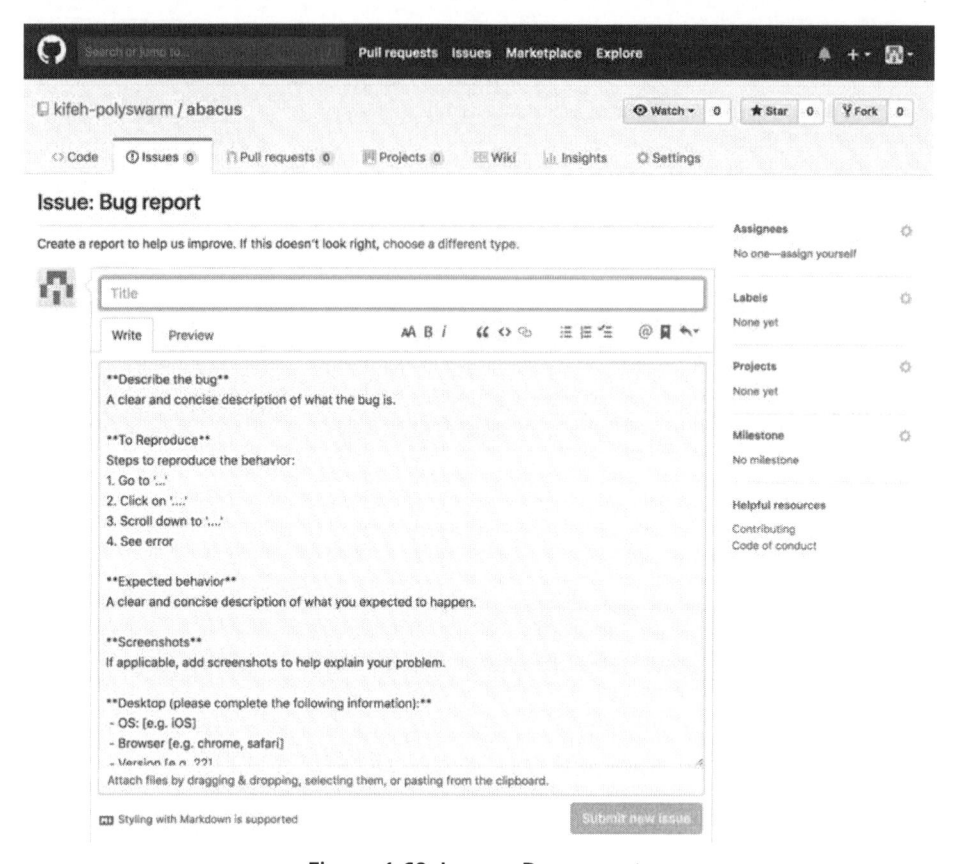

Figure 1.69: Issues: Bug report

Activity 1: Creating a Repository

You have been instructed to build an application that enables its user to order food from a restaurant and have it delivered. To commence this piece of work, you need to build the application while leveraging version control. You need to create a repository that will host the application. This repository will be used to track task completion and the deployment of the application.

To get started, you need to have the Git command-line tool installed on your computer. Additionally, you need to have an account on https://github.com/ and be logged into your account on GitHub:

1. Launch the Terminal.

2. Create a directory named [dine-in] for the application and navigate to the dine-in directory.

3. Initialize the repository.

4. Go to https://github.com/ to create a new repository with the name **dine-in**.

5. Obtain the HTTPS or SSH URL of the repository from GitHub.

6. Set the remote URL on the local repository:

Figure 1.70: Setting the remote URL

7. Create a README file and a .gitignore file, both of which are going to be added to the index.

8. Commit the files and then push them to the remote repository:

Figure 1.71: Setting the remote URL

Outcome

You have successfully created a repository on your GitHub account with README.md and .gitignore files

> **Note**
>
> For detailed steps of this activity, refer to the **Appendix** section on page 272.

Logistics

Conduct a recap of the concepts that have been covered in this topic.

Summary

In this chapter, we defined version control and the various types of workflows that are used. Then, we looked at what Git and GitHub are, and how they relate to each other. Last, but not least, we created a repository on GitHub, cloned it, and initialized a repository on a local environment before uploading (pushing) it to GitHub. Basic building blocks of version control and the application context were also introduced.

In the next chapter, you will finally see how to version commits and file stages to track file increments. You will also raise a pull request and merge it to the primary branch of a repository.

2

Versioning Commits

Learning Objectives

By the end of this chapter, you will be able to:

- Explain the need for versioning commits
- Compare commits, branches, indexes, and working trees
- Define the various Git commands and state their functions
- Amend commits

This chapter describes the comparison and editing of commits

Introduction

In the previous chapter, we covered the concept of version control and various types of workflows. We then analyzed the GitHub UI and GitHub functions, such as teams and SSH. Finally, we created a repository by using GitHub etiquette.

In this chapter, we will explain the logic behind the need for versioning commits. Additionally, we will compare commits, branches, indexes, and working trees. By the end of this chapter, you'll be able to demonstrate how to amend commits.

Introduction to Versioning Commits

We have already discussed version control, and we have established that it aids in tracking changes. In this topic, we will address the following question:

How can we make Git track and monitor the changes in a file?

Our aim is to examine and demonstrate the various stages that a file passes through to become a candidate for a **commit.**

In Git, files can have the following statuses:

1. **Untracked**: This a file that exists in the working tree whose changes are not being monitored by Git and aren't listed in the `gitignore` file.

2. **Unstaged**: This a file whose changes are being tracked by Git; the file has been changed since the last commit and has yet to be moved to the **index**.

3. **Staged**: This is a file whose changes are being tracked by Git; the file has been changed since the last commit and has been moved to the index. This file is a file that is ready for the Git commit. Staged files are the files in the index that are different from their corresponding files in the **HEAD**, that is, the version of the file in the most recent commit.

git status

git status is a utility that is used by Git. It's used to retrieve the details of files that are untracked, unstaged, or staged. `git status` lists files in order of their statuses.

The `git status` output is lengthy in nature. To view a brief list and status, use the `-s` or `--short` option with the `git status` command.

Exercise 12: Viewing and Establishing the Status of a File

To complete this exercise, you will need to create a class in the **abacus** application, so that you can host the functions that you'll be building for this application.

To establish the status of a file in a repository, follow these steps:

1. Create a branch to host this modification by using the following command:

`git branch ft-add-encapsulating-class`

> **Note**
>
> The changes made on this branch will later be incorporated into the branch **master**, that is, the primary branch. Take a look at the following screenshot:

Figure 2.1: Branch master

> **Note**
>
> The modification is done by using the command below. Take a look at the following screenshot:

`git checkout ft-add-encapsulating-class`

60 | Versioning Commits

Figure 2.2: Encapsulating a class

> **Note**
>
> You can create a branch by using `git checkout -b ft-add-encapsulating-class`. The prefix `ft` on the branch name is based on the best practices for enforcing a naming convention for different branch types.
>
> `ft`: Use this prefix for a feature branch.
>
> `bg`: This prefix should be used for bug branches.
>
> `fx`: The `fx` prefix is utilized to identify a branch for rolling out hotfixes.
>
> `ch`: This prefix is used for chore branches. Chores refer to tasks like styling code and rearranging files in a repository.

2. Create the `.gitignore` file by using the following command:

`echo '.DS_Store' > .gitignore`

Figure 2.3: Encapsulating a class

3. Run the `git status` command to view untracked files:

Figure 2.4: Creating the gitignore file

Introduction to Versioning Commits | 61

4. Open the **abacus** repository in a text editor of your choice.
5. Open `compute.py` in the text editor.
6. Add the following lines to `compute.py` and save the changes:

Live Link for exercise_1_step_6.py: https://bit.ly/2S34xaF

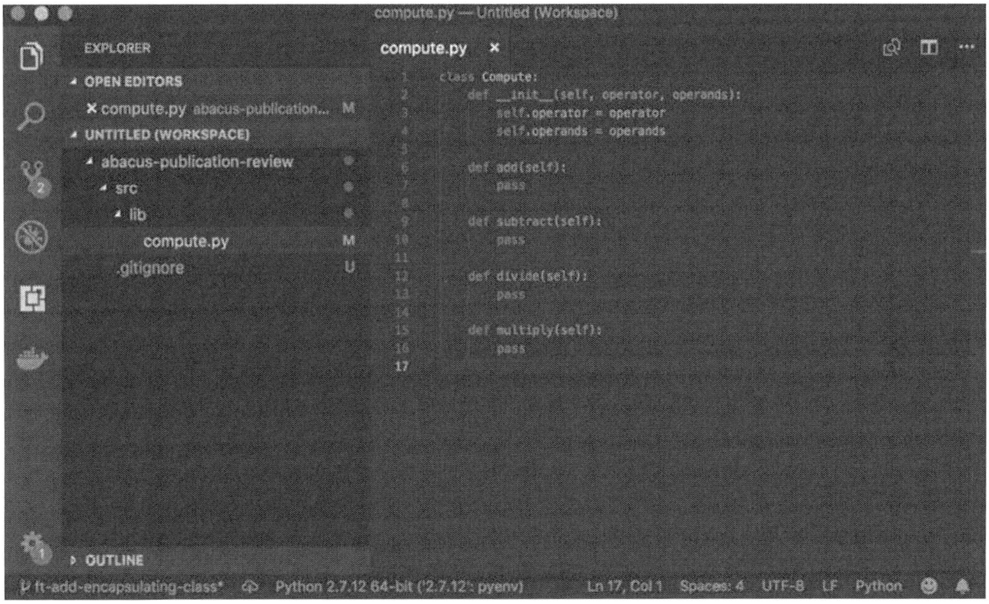

Figure 2.5: The compute.py file

7. Run `git status` to view any untracked and unstaged files:

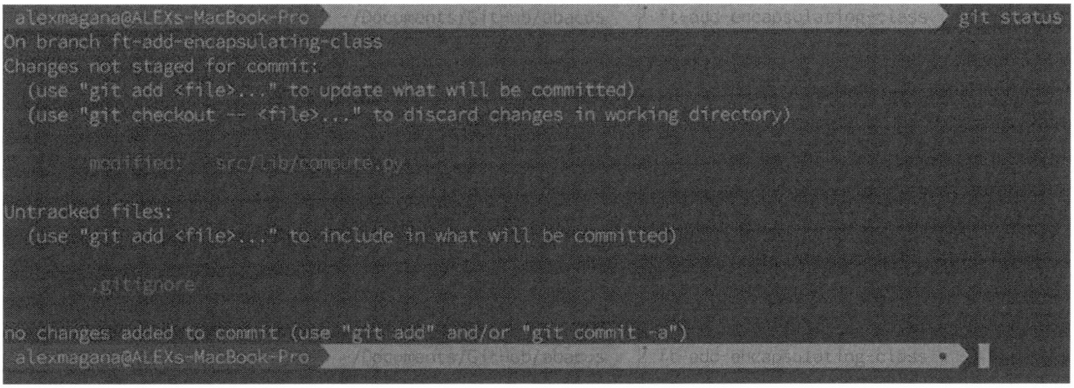

Figure 2.6: The modified compute.py file

62 | Versioning Commits

8. Run `git add src/lib/compute.py` to stage the changes made to the file.
9. Run `git status` to view untracked and staged files:

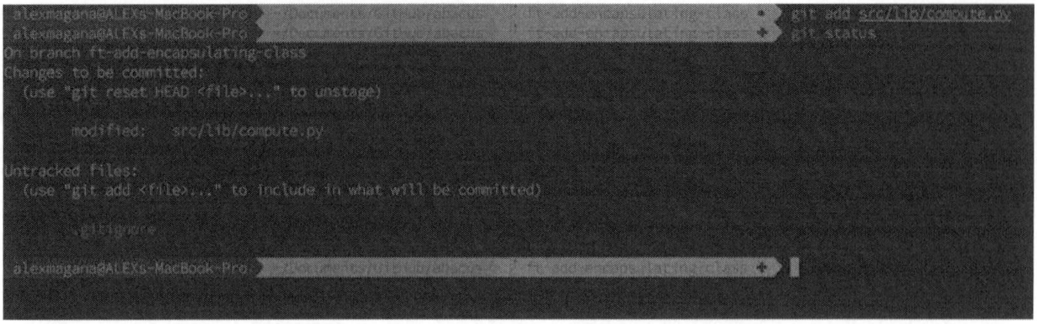

Figure 2.7: Running the git status command

10. Run `git add .gitignore` to start tracking the `.gitignore` file:

Figure 2.8: Tracking the .gitignore file

11. Commit the staged changes by using the following command:

`git commit -m "Add a class for math functions"`

Figure 2.9: Committing the changes

> **Note**
>
> To ensure flexibility, atomic commits are preferred and emphasized in version control. The term atomic commits refers to units of change that can be treated as a single unit. This normally implies a single file or a small set of files. This enables the addition and removal of changes without affecting a large set of files.

12. Push the changes made to a remote branch by using the following command:

```
git push origin ft-add-encapsulating-class
```

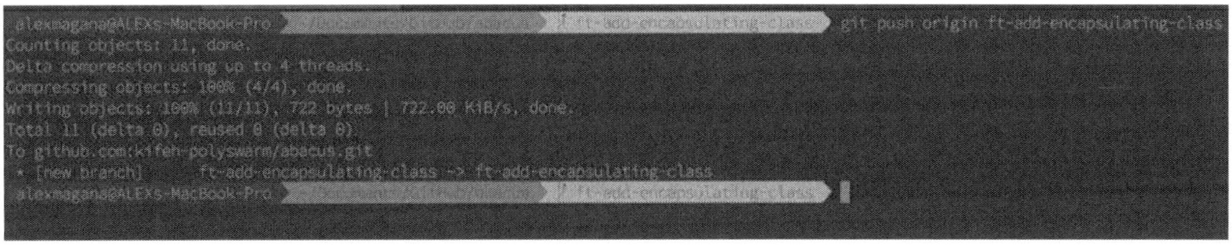

Figure 2.10: Pushing the changes to a branch

> **Note**
>
> Refer to the complete code at `abacus/.gitignore` and `abacus/src/lib/compute.py` for the files used in this exercise.
>
> Go to https://github.com/TrainingByPackt/Version-Control-with-Git-and-GitHub/tree/master/Lesson%202-Versioning%20Commits to access this code.

Outcome

By following the steps that we have outlined, you should be able to use `git status` to view untracked, unstaged, and staged files.

git diff

The `git diff` command is used to compare one snapshot of changes to another. As the name suggests, this utility supports evaluating the differences between two snapshots of a repository.

In this section, we will explore some use cases of the `git diff` command.

Comparing the Working Tree to the Index

To compare the entire working tree to the index, run the `git diff` command without specifying a path:

```
git diff
```

64 | Versioning Commits

This command supports examining the differences of a specific file or directory by accepting a path:

```
git diff -- [path_to_a_file_or_directory]
```

1. `git diff -- src/lib/`
2. `git diff -- src/lib/compute.py`

(1) and (2) compare the version in the working directory of the specified paths to the version that's present in the index.

Comparing the Working Tree to an Arbitrary Commit or Branch

A comparison can be made between the working tree and a specific commit on the same branch, or even the tip of a given branch. To compare the working tree to a given commit, use the following syntax:

```
git diff [commit_hash] -- [path_to_a_file_or_directory]
```

1. `git diff HEAD -- src/`
2. `git diff f4e4e8d5b292dc94468b6f88223cac4f55c03743 -- src/lib/`
3. `git diff master`

(1) Compares the version in the working directory of the `src` directory, to the version of the most recent commit on the current branch.

(2) Compares the version in the working directory of the `src` directory to the version in the snapshot represented by the hash `f4e4e8d5b292dc94468b6f88223cac4f55c03743`.

(3) Compares the version in the working directory of the `src` directory to the version at the tip of the branch `master`.

Comparing the Index to an Arbitrary Commit

To compare the files in the index to a specific commit, (for example, the most recent commit, also referred to as the tip of the branch), you can use the `--staged` or `--cached` option with the `git diff` command. A commit hash is required for this scenario. The `git diff` command defaults to HEAD in the absence of a specific commit hash:

```
git diff --cached [commit_hash] or
git diff --cached [commit_hash] -- [path_to_a_file_or_directory]
```

4. `git diff --cached HEAD -- /src/lib/compute.py`

(1) compares the version in the index of the `compute.py` file to the version at the tip of the current branch.

Comparing Commits and Branches

`git diff` provides a variant of the command's usage that supports comparing commits and branches.

To compare two commits or the tips of two branches, use the following syntax:

    git diff [commit_hash or branch_name] [commit_hash or branch_name] or
    git diff [commit_hash or branch_name] [commit_hash or branch_name] -- [path_to_a_file_or_directory] or
    git diff [commit_hash or branch_name]..[commit_hash or branch_name]

1. `git diff ft-add-encapsulating-class master`
2. `git diff ft-add-encapsulating-class..master`
3. `git diff da39a3ee5e6b4b0d3255bfef9560.890afd80709 86f7e437faa5a7fce15d1ddcb9eaeaea37766768`

(1) and (2) compare the differences between the tips of the specified branches.

(3) compares the differences between the files at the point referenced by the specified hashes.

Using the ... notation, `git diff` is capable of comparing the changes that have been made on branch A to branch B. This occurs from the point where the two branches share an ancestor to the most recent commit of branch B.

To achieve this, use the following syntax:

    git diff [branch_A]...[branch_B] -- [path_to_a_file_or_directory]

1. `git diff ft-add-encapsulating-class...master`

(1) lists the changes that have occurred in the branch master, since the ft-add-encapsulating-class branch was created from the branch master.

> **Note**
>
> When .. or ... are used with the `git diff` command, it implies the comparison of two points in history, and not a range.
>
> `git diff` defaults to HEAD when a commit hash or branch name is not specified.

Exercise 13: Examining Differences Between Files

To determine the differences in a branch or file, follow these steps:

1. Launch the Terminal.
2. Create a branch that comes off the ft-add-encapsulating-class branch by using the following command:

`git checkout -b ft-support-multiplication-arithmetic`

> **Note**
>
> This branch will be used to add a new feature to our application.

Figure 2.11: Creating a branch

3. Open the abacus repository in a text editor of your choice.
4. Open compute.py in the text editor.

5. Add the following lines to **compute.py** and save the changes:

Live Link for file exercise_2_step_5.py: https://bit.ly/2QvS04B

```
def multiply(self):
    sum = 1
    for item in self.operands:
        sum *= item
    print(sum)
```

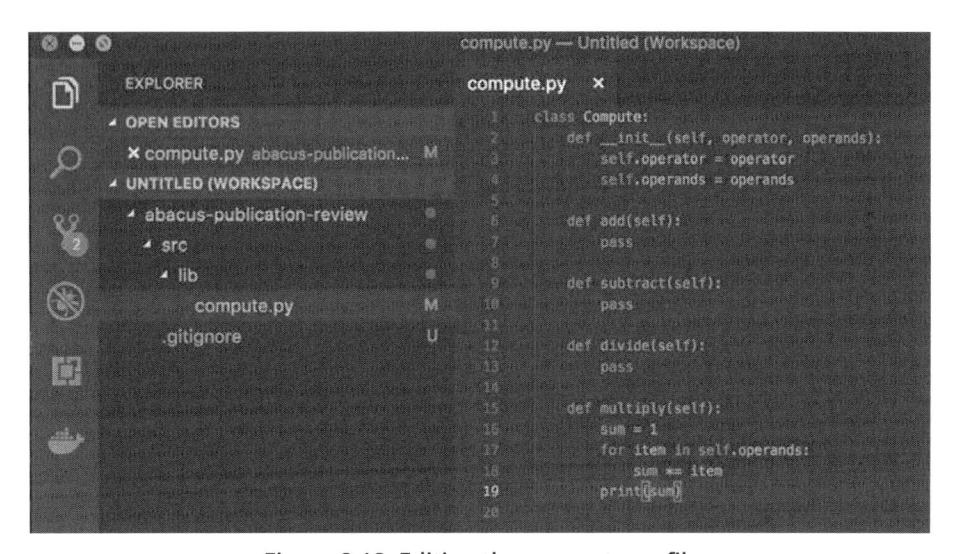

Figure 2.12: Editing the compute.py file

68 | Versioning Commits

6. Compare the working tree to the index by using the `git diff` command:

```
diff --git a/src/lib/compute.py b/src/lib/compute.py
index 5607ea4..555980a 100644
--- a/src/lib/compute.py
+++ b/src/lib/compute.py
@@ -13,4 +13,7 @@ class Compute:
         pass

     def multiply(self):
-        pass
+        sum = 1
+        for item in self.operands:
+            sum *= item
+        print(sum)
(END)
```

Figure 2.13: Comparing the working tree by using the diff command

7. Compare the working tree to the `master` branch by using the `git diff master` command:

```
less                  ⌘ 1
diff --git a/.gitignore b/.gitignore
new file mode 100644
index 0000000..e43b0f9
--- /dev/null
+++ b/.gitignore
@@ -0,0 +1 @@
+.DS_Store
diff --git a/src/lib/compute.py b/src/lib/compute.py
index e69de29..555980a 100644
--- a/src/lib/compute.py
+++ b/src/lib/compute.py
@@ -0,0 +1,19 @@
+class Compute:
+    def __init__(self, operator, operands):
+        self.operator = operator
+        self.operands = operands
+
+    def add(self):
+        pass
+
+    def subtract(self):
+        pass
+
+    def divide(self):
+        pass
+
+    def multiply(self):
+        sum = 1
+        for item in self.operands:
+            sum *= item
+        print(sum)
(END)
```

Figure 2.14: Comparing the working tree to the master branch

8. Compare the index to an arbitrary commit by using the following commands:

```
git add src/lib/compute.py
```

Figure 2.15: Comparing the index

```
git diff --cached
```

```
diff --git a/src/lib/compute.py b/src/lib/compute.py
index 5607ea4..555980a 100644
--- a/src/lib/compute.py
+++ b/src/lib/compute.py
@@ -13,4 +13,7 @@ class Compute:
         pass

     def multiply(self):
-        pass
+        sum = 1
+        for item in self.operands:
+            sum *= item
+        print(sum)
(END)
```

Figure 2.16: Comparing the index to an arbitrary commit

```
git diff --cached f4e4e8d5b292dc9446866f88223cac4f55c03743
```

```
diff --git a/.gitignore b/.gitignore
new file mode 100644
index 0000000..e43b0f9
--- /dev/null
+++ b/.gitignore
@@ -0,0 +1 @@
+.DS_Store
diff --git a/src/lib/compute.py b/src/lib/compute.py
index e69de29..555980a 100644
--- a/src/lib/compute.py
+++ b/src/lib/compute.py
@@ -0,0 +1,19 @@
+class Compute:
+    def __init__(self, operator, operands):
+        self.operator = operator
+        self.operands = operands
+
+    def add(self):
+        pass
+
+    def subtract(self):
+        pass
+
+    def divide(self):
+        pass
+
+    def multiply(self):
+        sum = 1
+        for item in self.operands:
+            sum *= item
+        print(sum)
(END)
```

Figure 2.17: Comparing the index to an arbitrary commit

> **Note**
>
> To retrieve a commit hash, run the git log command

9. You can compare different branches by using the following commands:

```
git commit -m "Add support for multiplication"
```

Figure 2.18: Comparing branches

```
git diff ft-support-multiplication-arithmetic..ft-add-encapsulating-class
```

```
diff --git a/src/lib/compute.py b/src/lib/compute.py
index 555980a..5607ea4 100644
--- a/src/lib/compute.py
+++ b/src/lib/compute.py
@@ -13,7 +13,4 @@ class Compute:
         pass

     def multiply(self):
-        sum = 1
-        for item in self.operands:
-            sum *= item
-        print(sum)
+        pass
(END)
```

Figure 2.19: Comparing branches

10. Push the changes to a remote branch by using the following command:

```
git push origin ft-support-multiplication-arithmetic
```

Outcome

By completing this exercise, you should be able to list and examine the differences between varying snapshots of a branch.

> **Note**
>
> Refer to the complete code at `abacus/.gitignore` and `exercise_2_step_5.py` for the files that were used in this exercise. Go to https://github.com/TrainingByPackt/Version-Control-with-Git-and-GitHub/blob/master/Lesson%202-Versioning%20Commits/exercise_2_step_5.py to access this code.

git add

So far, we've established that a file exists in three forms, that is, untracked, unstaged, and staged. We've also explored how to determine the status of a file and examine the changes on a tracked file, whether it be unstaged or staged.

We will now explore how to add files to the index from the working tree. This is achieved by using the `git add` command.

The `git add` command uses the following syntax:

```
git add [options] [path_to_files]
```

The `[options]` used with `git add` include the following:

```
-n or --dry-run
```

This option simulates the behavior of `git add` for the specified file:

> `-f` or `--force`

This option adds ignored files to the index:

> `-i` or `--interactive`

This option creates an interactive prompt that can be used to add files from the working tree to the index:

> `-p` or `--patch`

The `--patch` option caters to adding portions of a file to the index.

Once this option is chosen, it presents the differences in parts, referred to as **hunks**. You will then need to use the following options to instruct the `git add` utility on how to treat a hunk. Take a look at the patch interactive interface options that are given in the following table:

Option	Meaning
?	Print help.
y	Stage this hunk
n	Do not stage this hunk
q	Exit or quit. Do not stage this hunk or any of the remaining hunks
a	Stage this hunk and all later hunks in the specified files
d	Do not stage this hunk or any of the remaining hunks in the file
g	Select a hunk to go to
/	Search for the hunk that matches the specified regex pattern
j	Leave this hunk undecided; see the next undecided hunk
J	Leave this hunk undecided; see the next hunk
k	Leave this hunk undecided; see the previous undecided hunk
K	Leave this hunk undecided; see the previous hunk
s	Split the current hunk into more granular hunks
e	Manually edit the current hunk

Exercise 14: Adding Files to the Index

To determine the stage of a file in order to ensure that it is ready for the commit process, follow these steps:

1. Launch the Terminal.
2. Create a branch that comes off the ft-support-multiplication-arithmetic branch by using the git checkout -b ft-support-subtraction-arithmetic command:

> **Note**
> This branch will be used to add a new feature to our application.

Figure 2.20: Creating a branch off the branch

3. Open the abacus repository in a text editor of your choice.
4. Open compute.py in the text editor.
5. Make the following changes to compute.py and save the changes:

Live Link for file exercise_3_step_5.py: https://bit.ly/2zo4PM5

```python
def subtract(self):
    difference = 0
    for item in self.operands:
        difference -= item
    print(difference)

def multiply(self):
    if self.operands is None:
        return
    product = 1
    for item in self.operands:
        product *= item
    print(product)
```

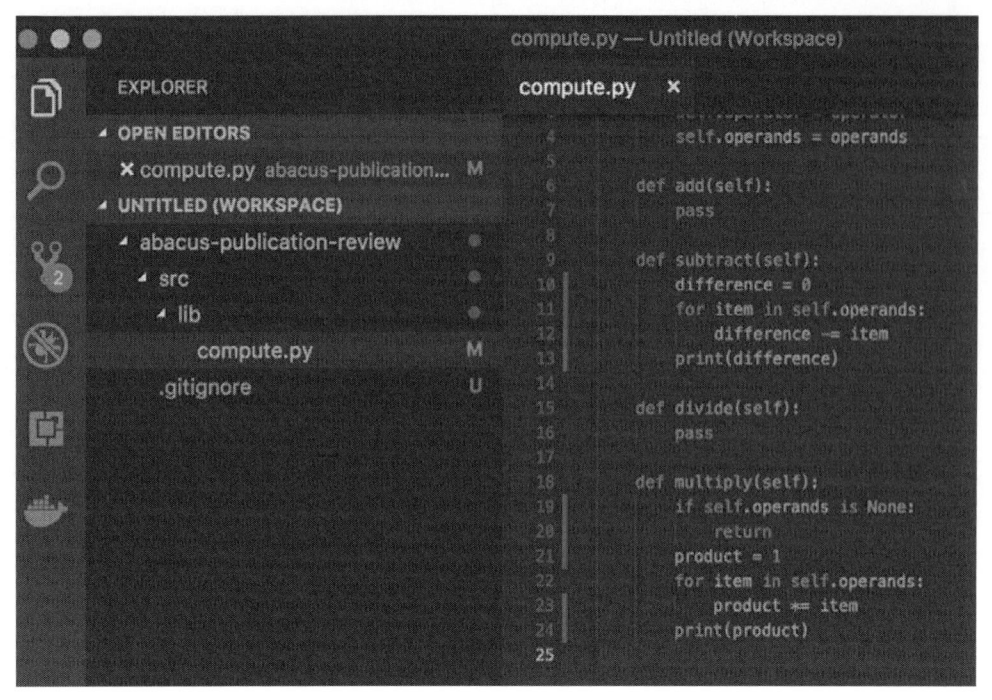

Figure 2.21: Editing the compute.py file

6. Add files to the index in parts as seen in the screenshots below by using the following command:

```
git add --patch src/lib/compute.py
```

Figure 2.22: Adding files to the index

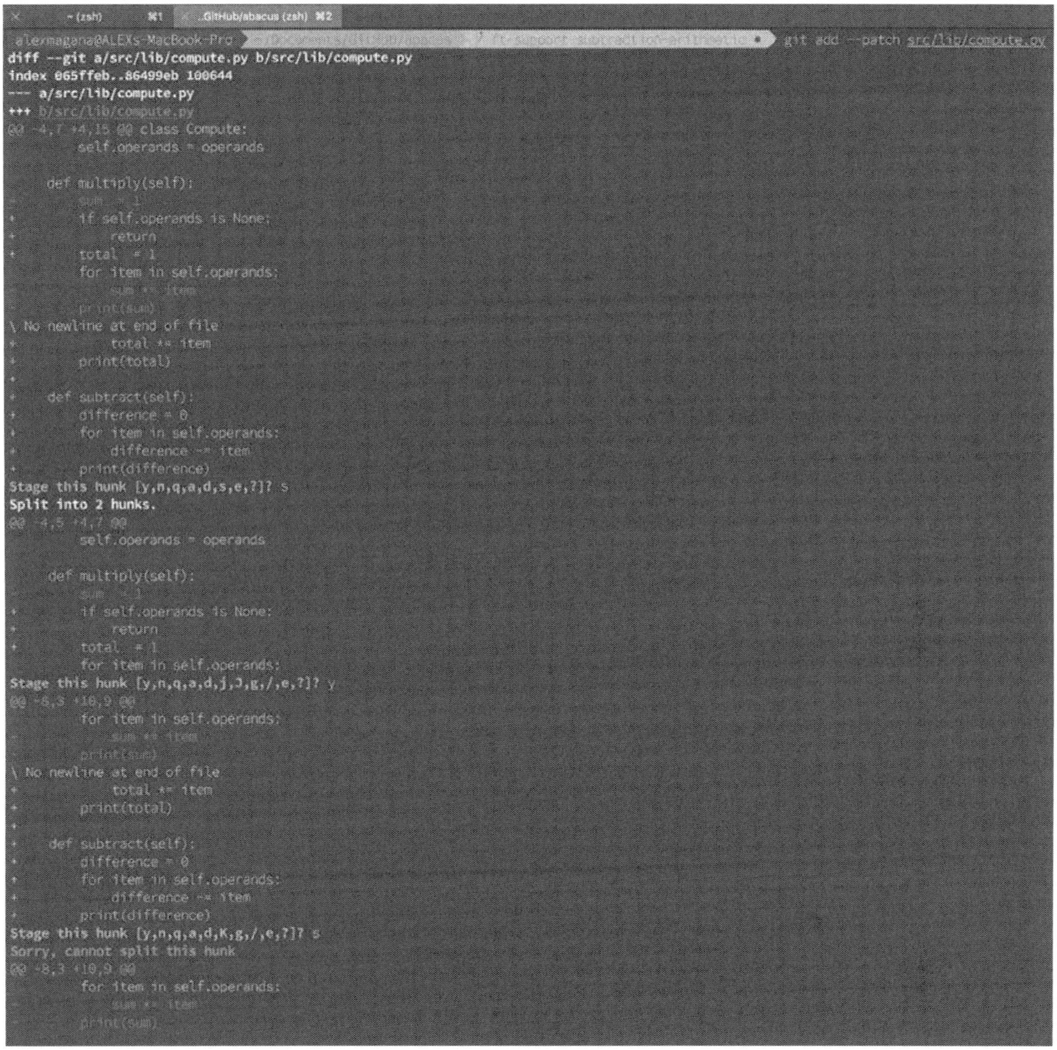

Figure 2.23: Adding files to the index

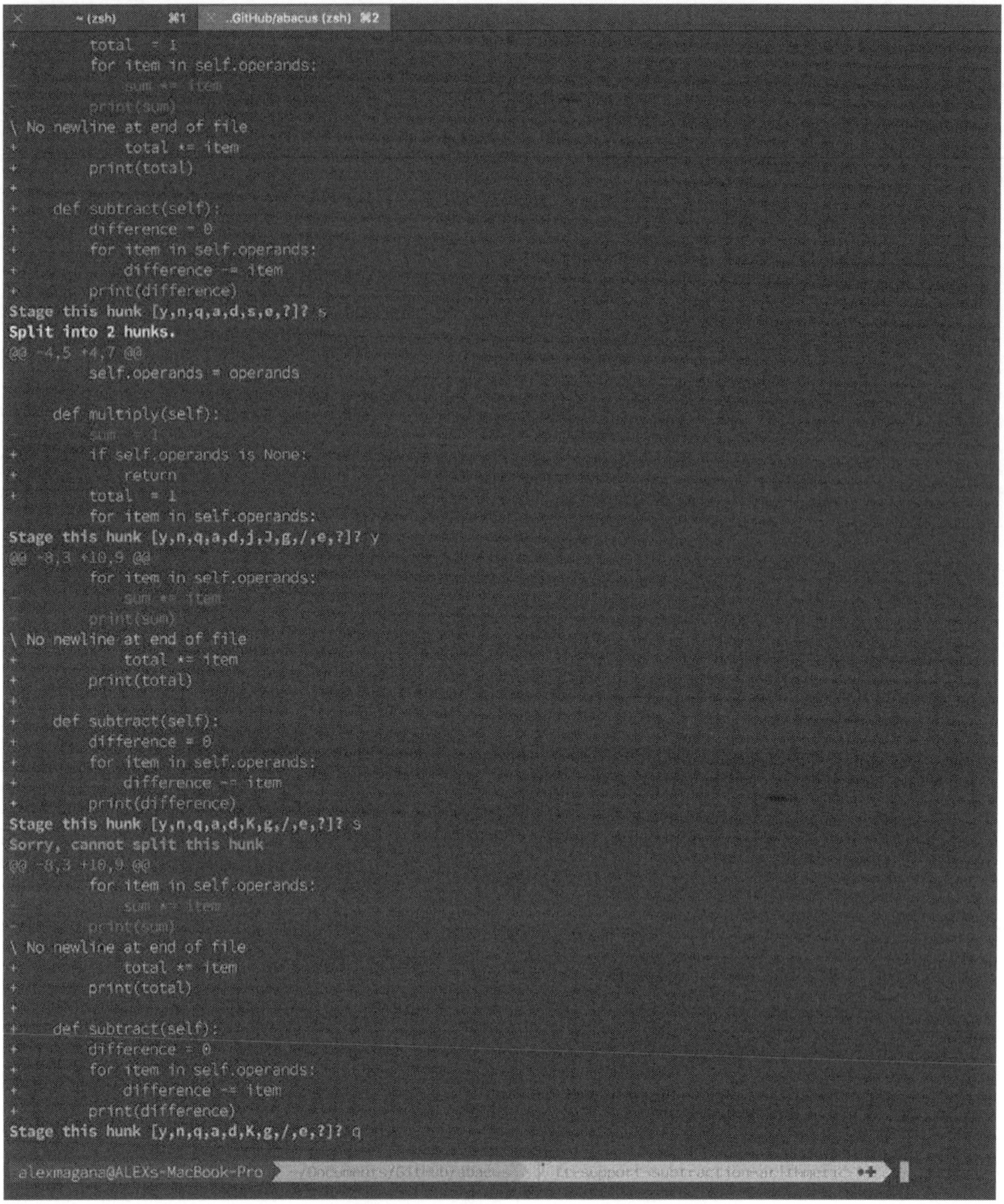

Figure 2.24: Adding files to the index

7. Check the staged changes by using the git status command

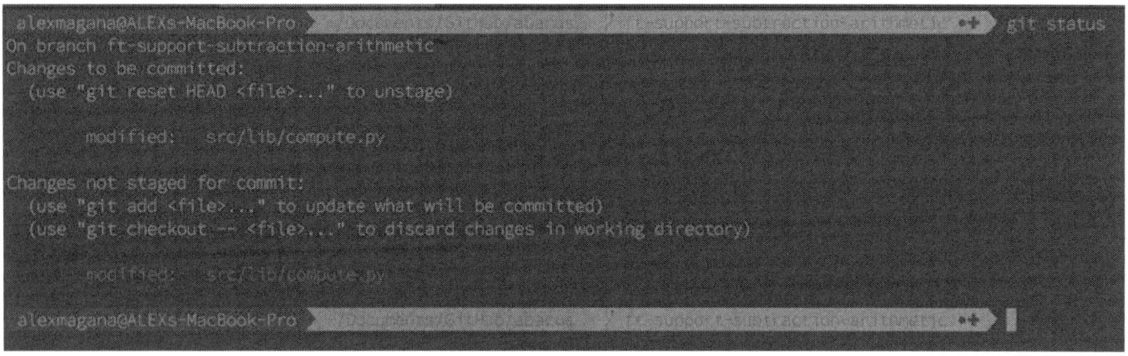

Figure 2.25: Checking the staged changes

8. Commit the changes by using the following command:

git commit -m "Remove usage of a reserved word"

9. Stage the remainder of the alterations by using the following command:

git add src/lib/compute.py

Figure 2.26: Staging the remainder of the alterations

10. Commit the staged changes using the following command:

git commit -m "Add subtraction support"

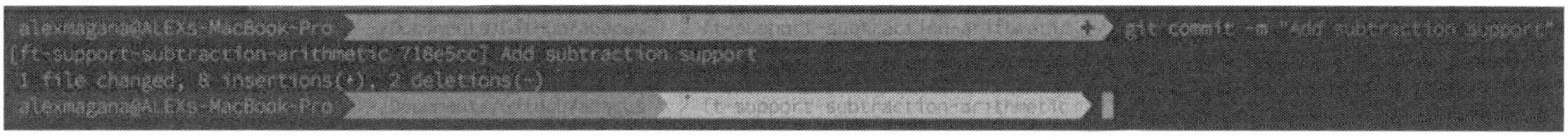

Figure 2.27: Committing the staged changes

11. Push the changes to a remote repository by using the following command:

git push origin ft-support-subtraction-arithmetic

Outcome

Having followed these steps, you should be able to add files to the index, commit the files, and push the files to a remote repository.

> **Note**
>
> `git add` will ignore files specified in the `.gitignore` file. Refer to the complete code at `abacus/.gitignore` and `version-Control-with-Git-and-Gitnub/Lesson 2-versioning Commits/exercise_3_step_5.py` for the files used in this exercise.
>
> Go to https://github.com/TrainingByPackt/Version-Control-with-Git-and-GitHub/blob/master/Lesson%202-Versioning%20Commits/exercise_3_step_5.py to access this code.

git commit

The `git commit` command saves the files in the index. This commit operation stores a message along with the commit. The message describes the additions or alterations associated with the created snapshot.

The syntax of this command is as follows: `git commit [options]`.

> **Note**
>
> The `git commit` command requires that a message be provided for each commit operation.

The options supported by this command include `-m [text]` or `--message [text]`.

This message is used to associate the index file with the commit action:

`-a` or `-all`

This option instructs the `git commit` utility to stage tracked files that are unstaged, that is, the tracked files have been added to the index if the files are yet to be staged. Untracked files are not added to the index.

`-p` or `--patch`

This launches the interactive patch tool. The options are akin to those that are available through the `git add` command. See the preceding table for more information on this.

`-C [commit hash]` or `--reuse-message=[commit hash]`

Introduction to Versioning Commits | 79

This instructs `git commit` to reuse a commit message and the author information of the specified commit hash.

`-F [file]` or `--file=[file]`

This command specifies a file from which a commit message should be obtained.

`-t [file]` or `--template [file]`

This command specifies the commit message template file.

`-e` or `--edit`

This command edits the provided commit message. This refers to the message provided by the `-F`, `-t`, and `-m` options.

`--no-edit`

This command uses the specified message as is. Do not launch an editor to edit the message.

`--author=[author]`

This command overrides the details of a commit author, and takes the following form:

`git commit --author="Kifeh Polyswarm <kifeh@poly-swarm.com>"`

`--date=[date]`

As you can see, this overrides the date details used in a commit.

`-q` or `--quiet`

This command suppresses the summary message that's returned after running the `git commit` command.

git rm

The `git rm` command performs two roles. These roles are used to remove files from the working directory and the index.

Removing Files From the Index

What doesn't `git rm` do?

`git rm` cannot remove a file from the working tree and retain the same file in the index.

`git rm` follows the following syntax:

`git rm [options] [path_file_or_directory]`

The options available for the `git rm` command are `-n` or `--dry-run`.

80 | Versioning Commits

This option simulates the behavior of `git rm` for the specified files. `-n` and `--dry-run` do not do the actual removal.

`-r`

This option is applicable when using the `git rm` command in a directory. It removes the directory's contents recursively. This means that the directory and its contents are removed.

`--cached`

This option removes the specified files from the index only.

`-f` or `--force`

`git rm` checks the files marked for removal for matches, with the files in HEAD, at the tip of the current branch. This check is conducted before the file(s) are removed. The `-f` option overrides this check.

Exercise 15: Removing Files from the Working Tree and the Index

To remove files from the index or the working tree.

1. Launch the Terminal and navigate to the location of the abacus repository.
2. Create the `scientific.py` file in `src/lib` by using the following command:

```
echo '# Scientific arithmetic module' > src/lib/scientific.py
```

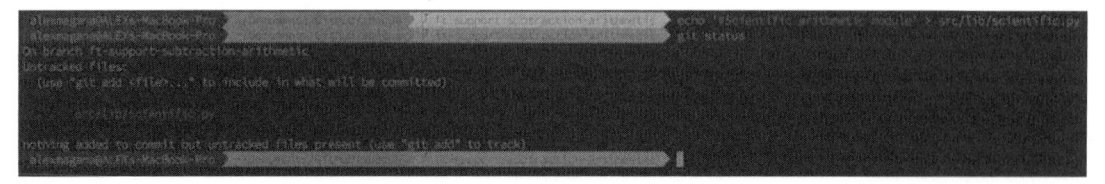

Figure 2.28: Creating the scientific.py file

3. Track the added file by using the `git add src/lib/scientific.py` command:

Figure 2.29: Tracking the added file

Introduction to Versioning Commits | 81

4. Remove the file from the index by using the `git rm --cached src/lib/scientific.py` command:

Figure 2.30: Removing the file from the index

5. Remove the file from the index and the working tree by using the following code:

```
git add src/lib/scientific.py
git commit -m "Add scientific module"
git rm src/lib/scientific.py
git status
git commit -m "Remove scientific module"
ls src/lib
```

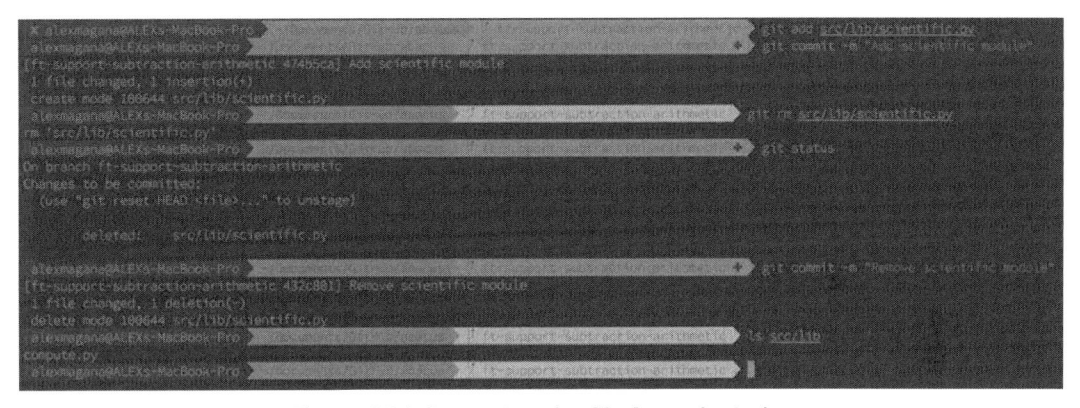

Figure 2.31: Removing the file from the index

Outcome

By completing this exercise, you should be able to remove an undesired file from the index and the working tree.

> **Note**
>
> The `rm` command removes the specified file from the working tree only. The `git rm` command, on the other hand, removes the file from the index and the working tree. This provides a shorter process for deleting files, since with `rm`, you need to run `git add` to impact the deletion process in the index.

git mv

In the event that you need to update the index for both, old and new paths automatically, the `git mv` command serves that purpose.

This command has two forms of implementation:

1. `git mv [options] [source] [destination]`
2. `git mv [options] [source] … [destination]`

(1) is used to rename a file.

(2) is used to move a file.

Exercise 16: Moving and Renaming Files

To learn how to handle files and directories using Git, follow these steps:

1. Launch the Terminal and navigate to the location of the `abacus` repository.
2. Create the `scientific.py` file in `src/lib` by using the following command:

`echo '# Scientific arithmetic module' > src/lib/scientific.py`

Figure 2.32: Creating the scientific.py file

3. Add the file to the index and commit it by using the following command:

`git add src/lib/scientific.py && git commit -C 474b5caaf480f7a367c4c456a53868c7fe32b9df --no-edit`

Figure 2.33: Adding the file to the index

Introduction to Versioning Commits | 83

4. Rename the file by using the `git mv src/lib/scientific.py src/lib/advanced_compute.py` command:

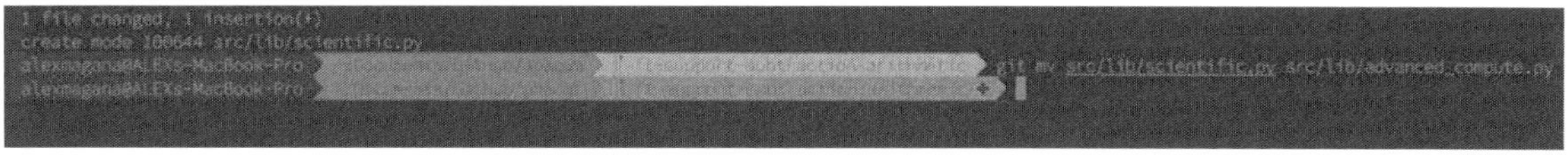

Figure 2.34: Renaming the file

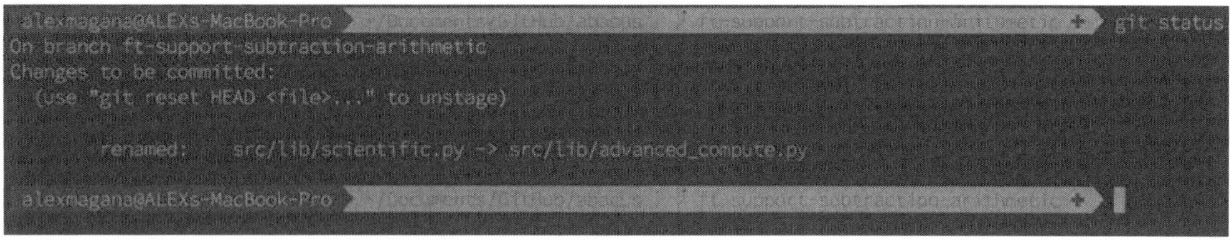

Figure 2.35: Renaming the file

5. Commit the file by using the `git commit -m "Rename scientific module"` command:

Figure 2.36: Committing the file

6. Move the file by using the following commands:

`mkdir -p src/lib/advanced/`

`git mv src/lib/advanced_compute.py src/lib/advanced/`

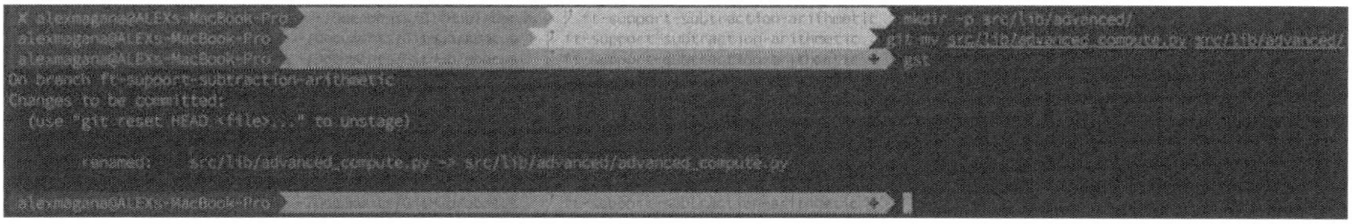

Figure 2.37: Moving the file

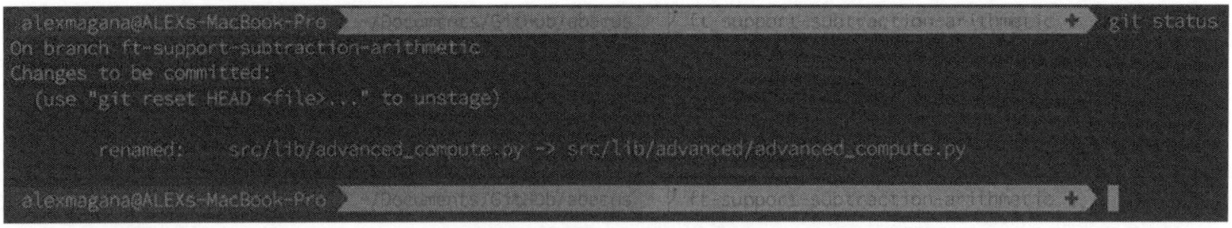

84 | Versioning Commits

Figure 2.38: Moving the file

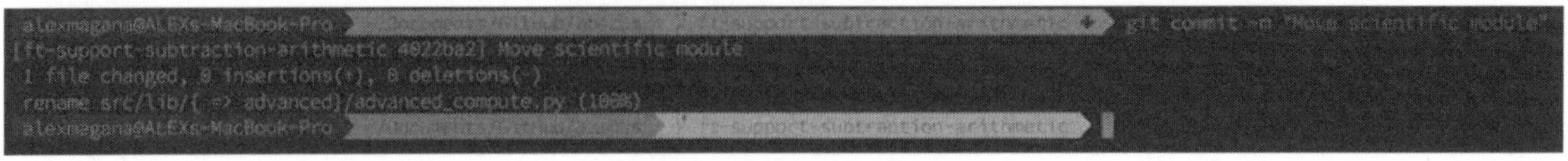

Figure 2.39: Moving the file

Outcome

By completing this exercise, you should be able to rename and move files and directories using `git mv`.

History and Logs

Take a look at the following command to access the history: `git log`

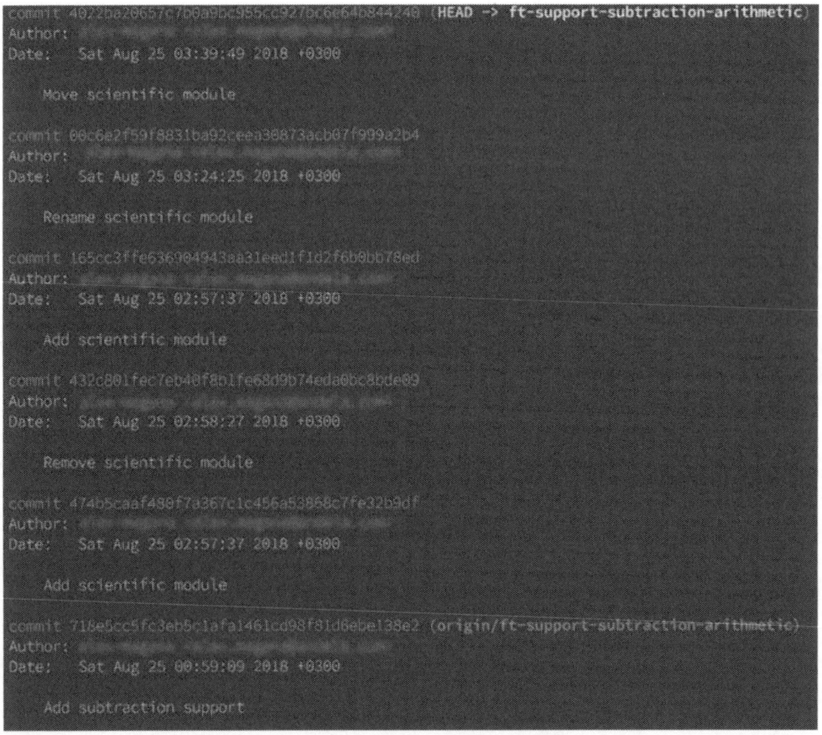

Figure 2.40: A git log file

Introduction to Versioning Commits | 85

The `git log` command lists the history of a branch and the repository, by extension. It uses options and a range to define the duration for which the logs should be retrieved:

```
git log [options] [version range] [path_to_file_or_directory] [version range]
```

The `git log` command can display the history of a branch when given a range of version hashes:

```
git log [hash_1]..[hash_2]
```

```
git log
```

718e5cc5fc3eb5c1afa146cd98f81d6ebe138e2..

4022ba20657c7b0a9bc955cc927bc6e64b844240

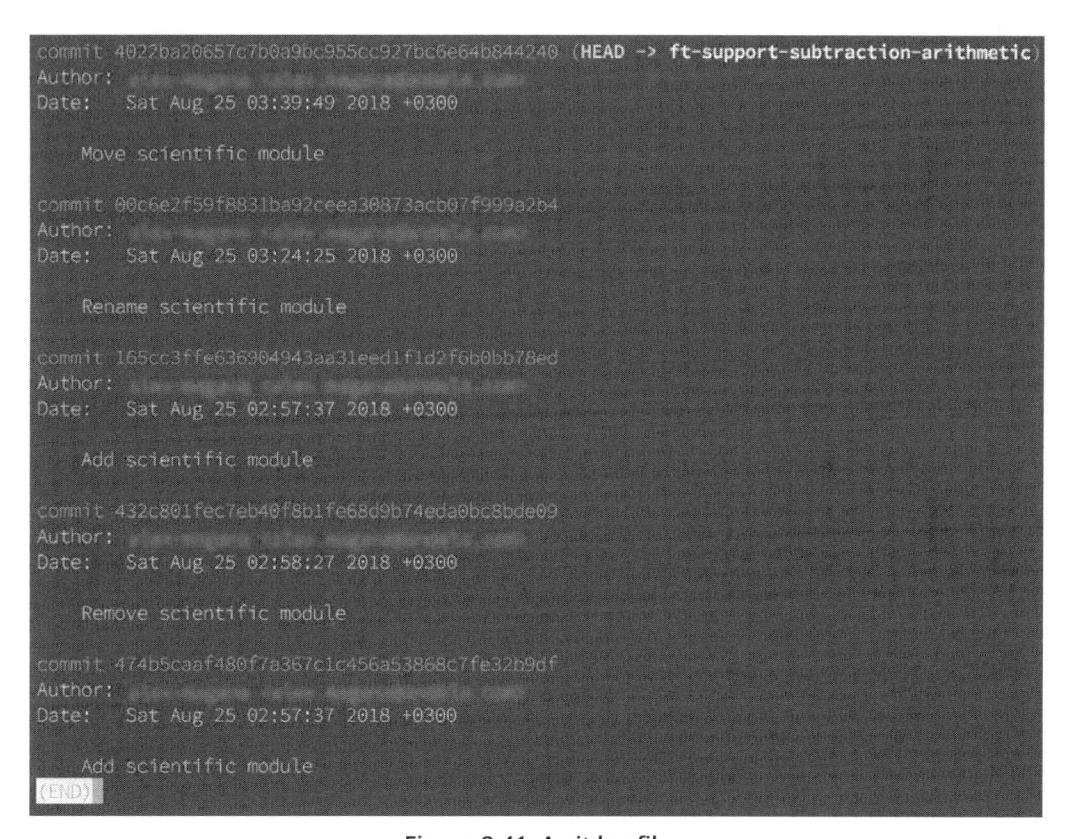

Figure 2.41: A git log file

Options

The `--follow` command retrieves and displays the history of a file, beyond rename events:

```
git log --follow ./src/lib/advanced/advanced_compute.py
```

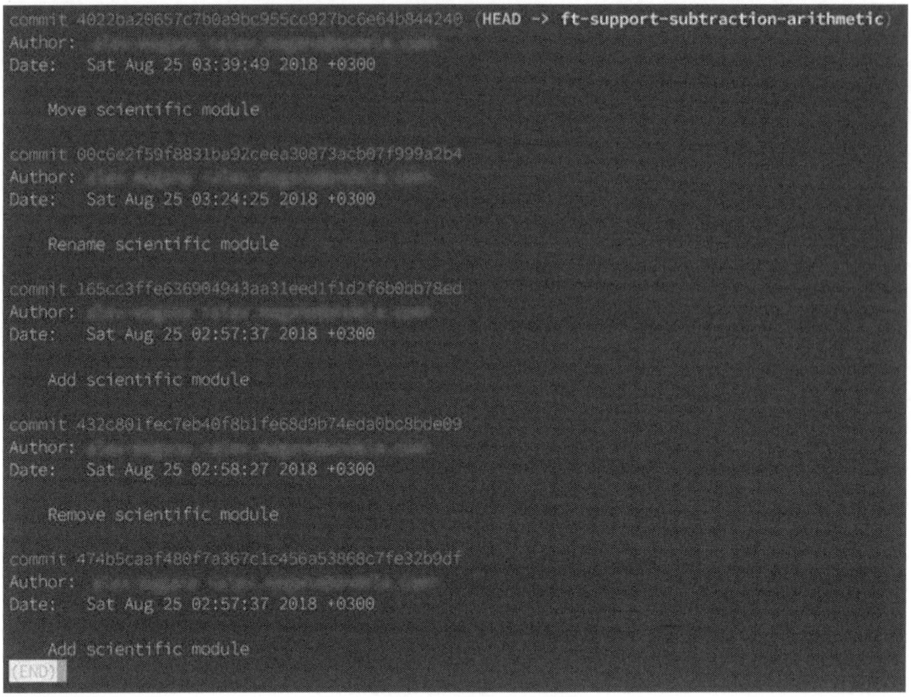

Figure 2.42: A git log file

Introduction to Versioning Commits | 87

The `--decorate[=short or full or no]` command displays the `ref` name of the listed commits as seen in the following screenshots:

```
git log --decorate=short
```

> **Note**
>
> The short option omits the `ref/heads/`, `ref/remotes/`, and `ref/tags/` prefixes from the `ref` name that is displayed.

Figure 2.43: A git log file

```
git log --decorate=full
```

> **Note**
>
> The full option displays the full ref name. It includes the `ref/heads/`, `ref/remotes/`, and `ref/tags/` prefixes in the ref name that is displayed.

Versioning Commits

Figure 2.44: A git log file

```
git log --decorate=no
```

> **Note**
>
> The **no** option omits the entire ref name from the commits.

Introduction to Versioning Commits | 89

```
commit 4022ba20657c7b0a9bc955cc927bc6e64b844240
Author:
Date:    Sat Aug 25 03:39:49 2018 +0300

    Move scientific module

commit 00c6e2f59f8831ba92ceea30873acb07f999a2b4
Author:
Date:    Sat Aug 25 03:24:25 2018 +0300

    Rename scientific module

commit 165cc3ffe636904943aa31eed1f1d2f6b0bb78ed
Author:
Date:    Sat Aug 25 02:57:37 2018 +0300

    Add scientific module

commit 432c801fec7eb40f8b1fe68d9b74eda0bc8bde09
Author:
Date:    Sat Aug 25 02:58:27 2018 +0300

    Remove scientific module

commit 474b5caaf480f7a367c1c456a53868c7fe32b9df
Author:
Date:    Sat Aug 25 02:57:37 2018 +0300

    Add scientific module
```

Figure 2.45: A git log file

> **Note**
>
> As shown in the preceding screenshot, the commit with the message Move `scientific module` does not include a ref name.

90 | Versioning Commits

The `-L [start]:[end]:[path_to_file]` command views the changes that have been made to a section of a file, from line number X to line number Y:

```
git log -L 6:12:./src/lib/compute.py
```

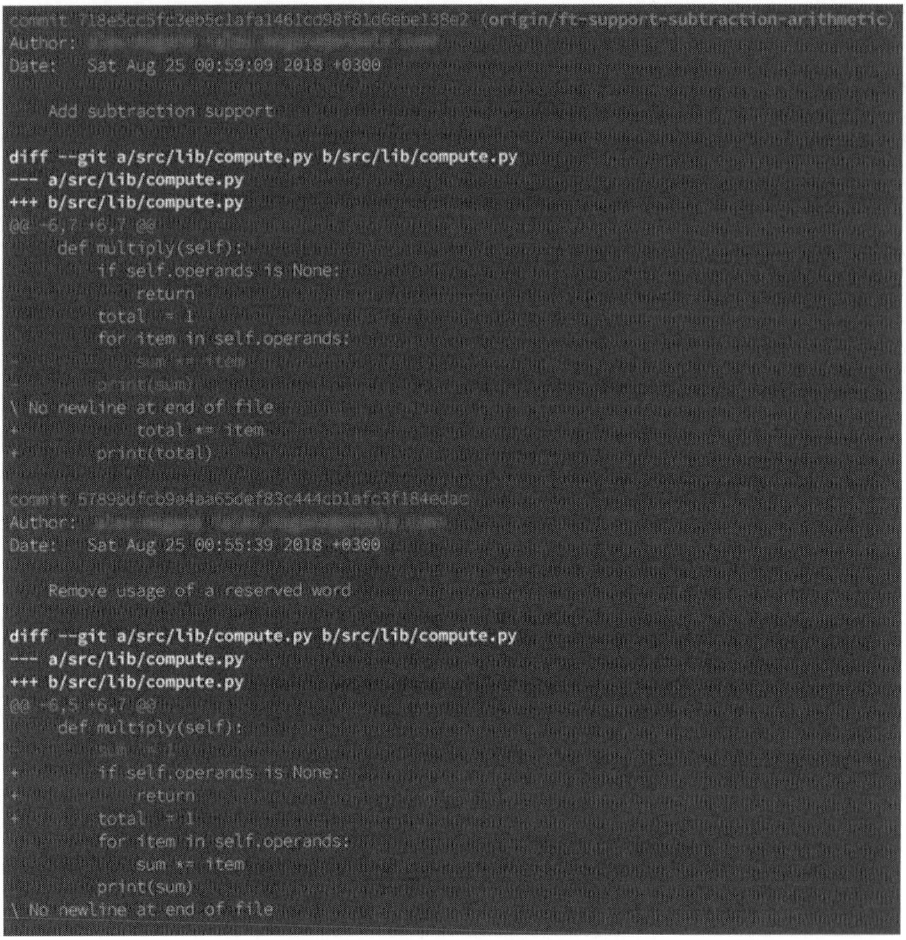

Figure 2.46: Viewing the changes to a section of a file

> **Note**
>
> The preceding screenshot demonstrates the changes made to the source code in `/src/lib/compute.py`, for the content in line 6 to line 12, with each commit indicating the alterations it represents.

Introduction to Versioning Commits | 91

The `--[number]`, `-n [number]`, and `--max-count=[number]` the specified number of commits only:

    `git log -3 or git log -n 3`

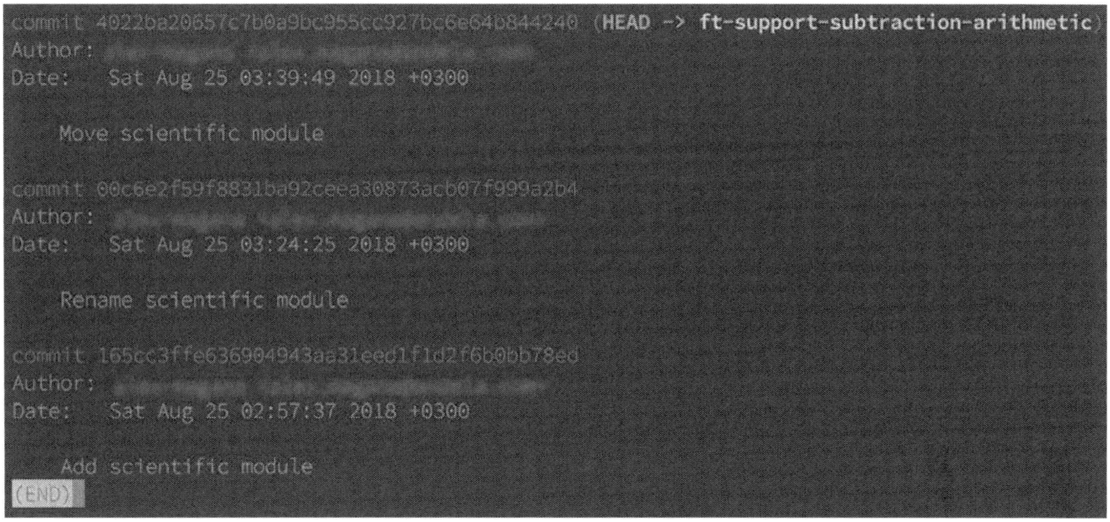

Figure 2.47: Adding the scientific module

The `--skip=[number]` command skips the specified commits and displays the rest:

    `git log --skip=4`

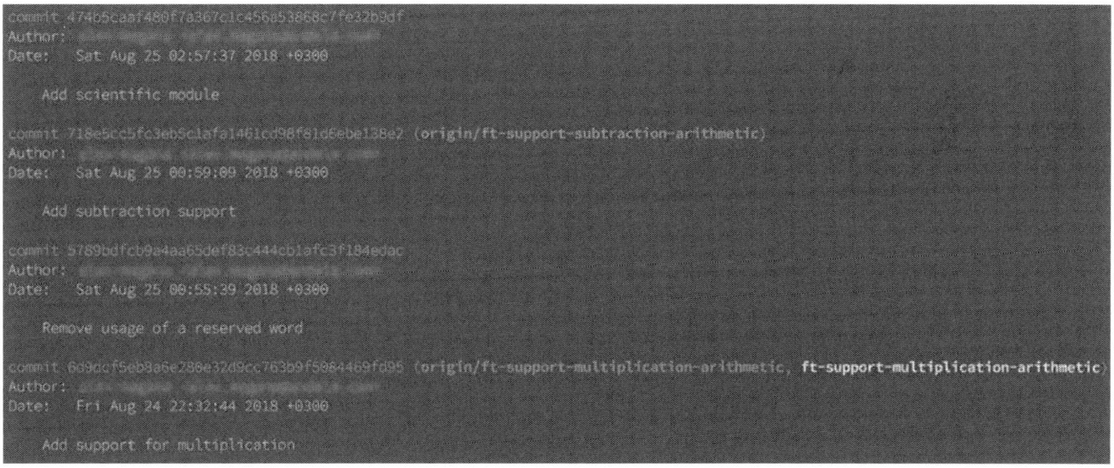

Figure 2.48: Adding scientific support

The `--since=[date]` or `--after=[date]` commits that have been created after a given date:

```
git log --after=25/08/2018
```

The `--until=[date]` or `--before=[date]` commits that precede a given date:

```
git log --before=24/08/2018
```

The `--pretty=[format]` command displays the history of a branch using a prescribed format:

```
git log --pretty=oneline
```

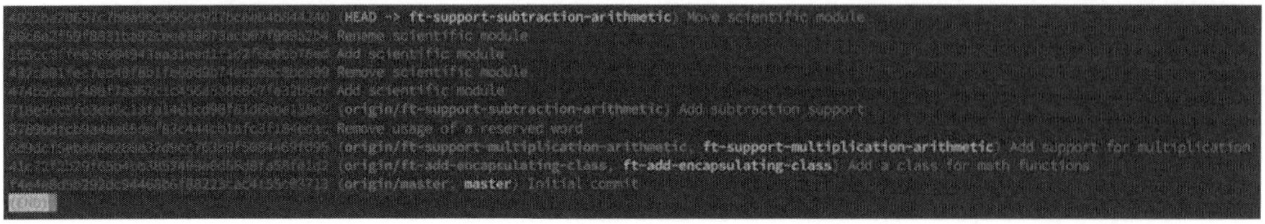

Figure 2.49: Modifying the scientific module

The following code displays the commit history details in a reverse chronological order:

```
[commit_hash] [commit title]
git log --pretty=short
```

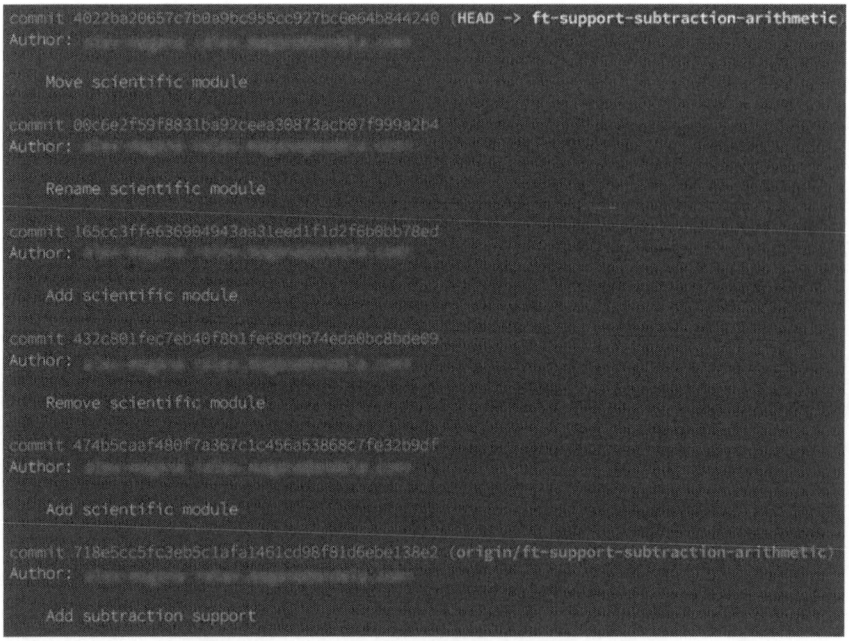

Figure 2.50: Modifying the scientific module

Introduction to Versioning Commits | 93

The following code displays the commit history details in a reverse chronological order:

[commit commit_hash]

[Author: author_details]

[commit title]

> **Note**
>
> In the preceding screenshot, the commits are listed in the following format:
>
> ```
> commit 4022ba20657c7b0a9bc955cc927bc6e64b844240
>
> Author: alex-magana <alex.magana@andela.com>
>
> Move scientific module
>
> git log --pretty=medium
> ```

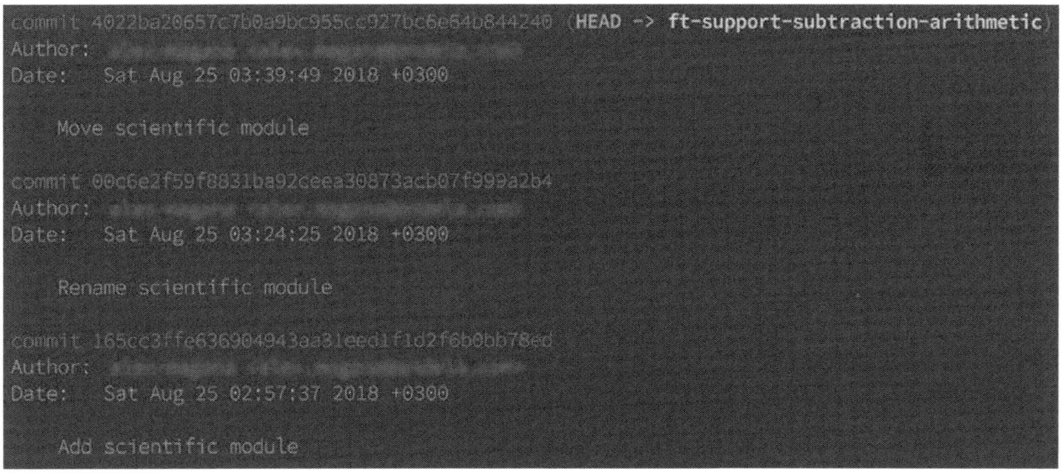

Figure 2.51: Modifying the scientific module

This command displays the commit history details in the following order:

[commit commit_hash]

[Author: author_details]

[Date: date_details]

[commit title]

> **Note**
>
> In the preceding screenshot, the commits are listed in the following format:
>
> commit 4022ba20657c7b0a9bc955cc927bc6e64b844240
>
> Author: alex-magana <alex.magana@andela.com>
>
> Date: Sat Aug 25 03:39:49 2018 +0300
>
> move scientific module

```
git log --pretty=format:[format string]
```

The format is a string that's in the form of `%placeholder₁ %placeholder2 %placeholderN`.

The supported placeholders include the following and are shown in the following screenshots:

- **%H**: The commit hash
- **%h**: The abbreviated commit hash
- **%T**: A tree hash
- **%t**: An abbreviated tree hash
- **%P**: The parent hash
- **%p**: The abbreviated parent hash
- **%an**: Author name
- **%ae**: Author email

- %a^d: Author date
- %a^r: A relative author date
- %at: The Unix timestamp version of the author date
- %s: The subject of the commit
- %b: The body of the commit
- %n: A newline

```
git log --pretty=format:"%n %an"
```

```
4022ba20657c7b0a9bc955cc927bc6e64b844240 alex-magana
00c6e2f59f8831ba92ceea30873acb07f999a2b4 alex-magana
165cc3ffe636904943aa31eed1f1d2f6b0bb78ed alex-magana
432c801fec7eb40f8b1fe68d9b74eda0bc8bde09 alex-magana
474b5caaf480f7a367c1c456a53868c7fe32b9df alex-magana
718e5cc5fc3eb5c1afa1461cd98f81d6ebe138e2 alex-magana
5789bdfcb9a4aa65def83c444cb1afc3f184edac alex-magana
6d9dcf5eb8a6e280e32d9cc763b9f5084469fd95 alex-magana
41c72f2b29f65b4bb3852499e0d58d8fa58fe1d2 alex-magana
f4e4e8d5b292dc94468b6f88223cac4f55c03713 alex-magana
(END)
```

Figure 2.52: String format

```
git log --pretty=format:"%n %an %ae"
```

```
4022ba20657c7b0a9bc955cc927bc6e64b844240
00c6e2f59f8831ba92ceea30873acb07f999a2b4
165cc3ffe636904943aa31eed1f1d2f6b0bb78ed
432c801fec7eb40f8b1fe68d9b74eda0bc8bde09
474b5caaf480f7a367c1c456a53868c7fe32b9df
718e5cc5fc3eb5c1afa1461cd98f81d6ebe138e2
5789bdfcb9a4aa65def83c444cb1afc3f184edac
6d9dcf5eb8a6e280e32d9cc763b9f5084469fd95
41c72f2b29f65b4bb3852499e0d58d8fa58fe1d2
f4e4e8d5b292dc94468b6f88223cac4f55c03713
(END)
```

Figure 2.53: String format

```
git log --pretty=format:"%n %an %ae %n %s %n %b"
```

```
4022ba20657c7b0a9bc955cc927bc6e64b844240
 Move scientific module

00c6e2f59f8831ba92ceea30873acb07f999a2b4
 Rename scientific module

165cc3ffe636904943aa31eed1f1d2f6b0bb78ed
 Add scientific module

432c801fec7eb40f8b1fe68d9b74eda0bc8bde09
 Remove scientific module

474b5caaf480f7a367c1c456a53868c7fe32b9df
 Add scientific module

718e5cc5fc3eb5c1afa1461cd98f81d6ebe138e2
 Add subtraction support
```

Figure 2.54: Modifying the scientific module

Amending Commits

Consider a scenario where you have made changes and persisted them through `git commit`, and you now need to reword a commit message or the files in a commit. How can you edit the commit messages and their respective contents? In this section, we will explore how Git allows you to edit commits.

Amending a Single Most Recent Commit

The most recent commit can be edited by using `--amend` in the `git commit` command.

Exercise 17: Editing the Most Recent Commit

To edit the commit referenced by **HEAD**, that is, the most recent commit on a branch, follow these steps:

1. Launch the terminal and navigate to the location of the `abacus` repository.

2. Open the last commit message for editing by using the following command:

```
git commit --amend
```

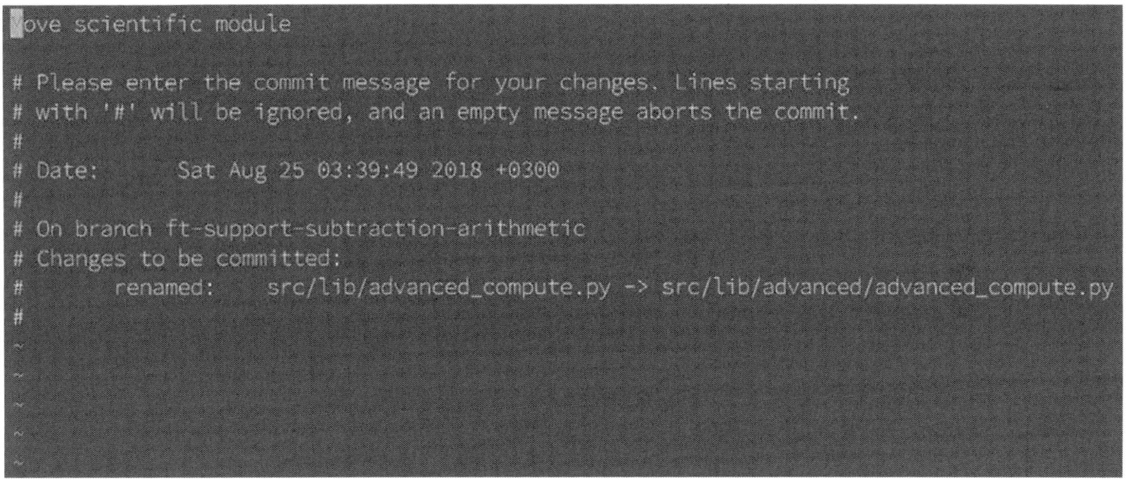

```
ove scientific module

# Please enter the commit message for your changes. Lines starting
# with '#' will be ignored, and an empty message aborts the commit.
#
# Date:      Sat Aug 25 03:39:49 2018 +0300
#
# On branch ft-support-subtraction-arithmetic
# Changes to be committed:
#       renamed:    src/lib/advanced_compute.py -> src/lib/advanced/advanced_compute.py
#
~
~
~
~
```

Figure 2.55: Editing the last commit

3. Press *i* to switch to INSERT mode.

4. Edit the message accordingly.

5. Press Esc to exit INSERT mode.

6. Press : and type wq to save the changes and exit the editor:

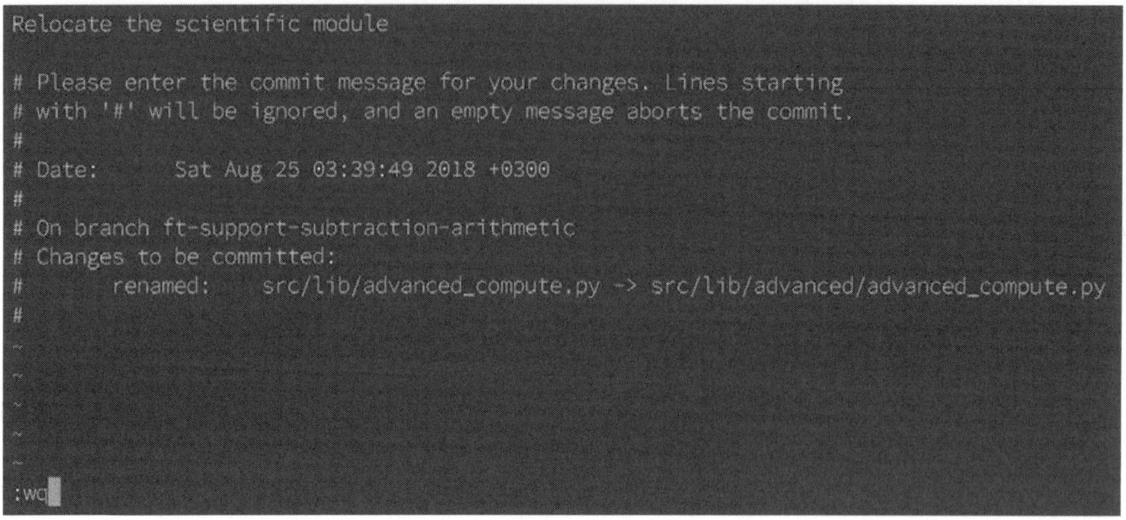

Figure 2.56: Saving the changes

7. Press *Return* to execute the wq command.

Outcome

Through following this exercise, the most recent commit message should have been updated. An example of this is shown in the following screenshot:

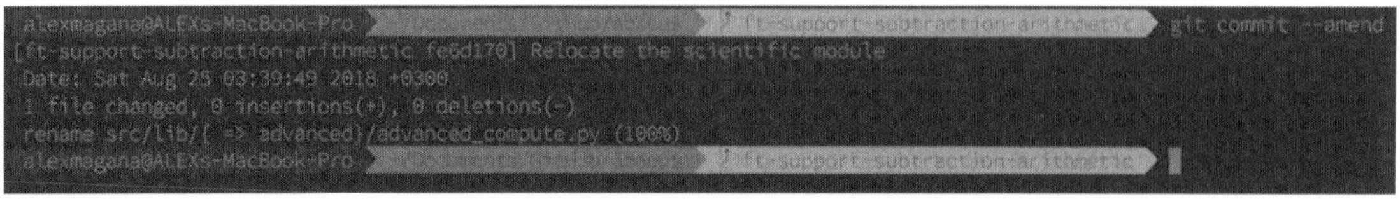

Figure 2.57: Displaying the commit message

Amending Multiple Commits

The `git rebase` command provides the reword and edit options to edit the commits. The reword option allows you to edit a message, while the edit option supports editing a commit message, as well as the contents of a commit.

Introduction to Versioning Commits | 99

Exercise 18: Editing Commits Using the reword Command

To edit a message using the `reword` command, follow these steps:

1. Launch the terminal and navigate to the location of the `abacus` repository.
2. Retrieve the last four commits by using the `git rebase -i HEAD~4` command:

```
pick 432c801 Remove scientific module
pick 731cdba Add scientific module
pick acce227 Rename scientific module
pick 3305a3a Relocate the scientific module

# Rebase 474b5ca..3305a3a onto 474b5ca (4 commands)
#
# Commands:
# p, pick = use commit
# r, reword = use commit, but edit the commit message
# e, edit = use commit, but stop for amending
# s, squash = use commit, but meld into previous commit
# f, fixup = like "squash", but discard this commit's log message
# x, exec = run command (the rest of the line) using shell
# d, drop = remove commit
#
```

Figure 2.58: Retrieving the last four commits

> **Note**
>
> The commits are listed from the earliest/oldest (at the top of the list) to the most recent (the last on the list).

3. Press **i** to switch to INSERT mode.
4. Pick the desired message accordingly.
5. Press *Esc* to exit INSERT mode.
6. Press : and type `wq` to save the changes and exit the editor.
7. Press *return* to execute the `wq` command.

8. Edit the message in the next prompt.

Before editing the commit:

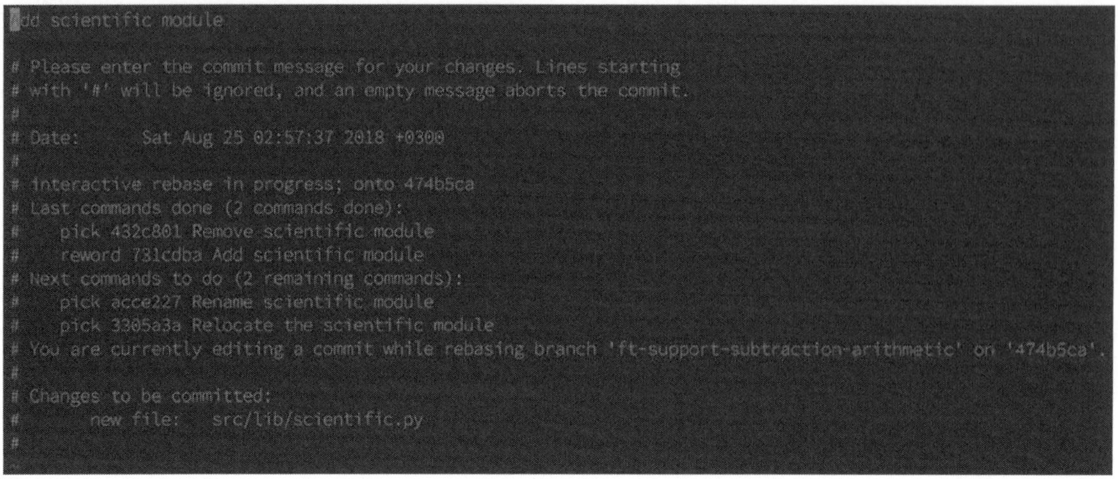

Figure 2.59: Before editing the commit

After editing the commit:

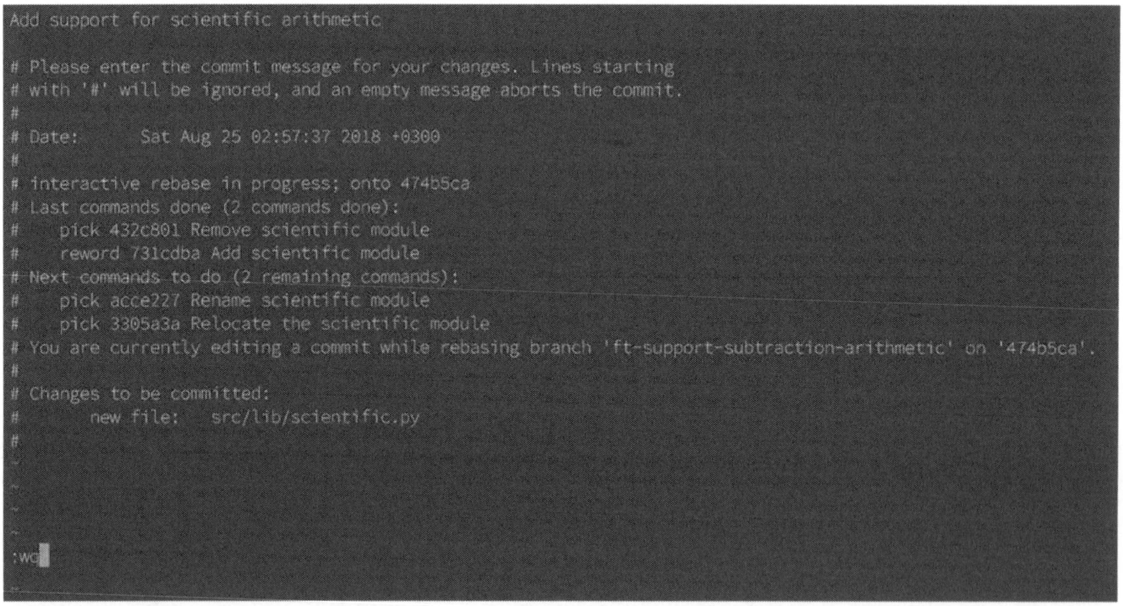

Figure 2.60: After editing the commit

Introduction to Versioning Commits | 101

9. Make sure that these changes were made by using the `git log -4` command:

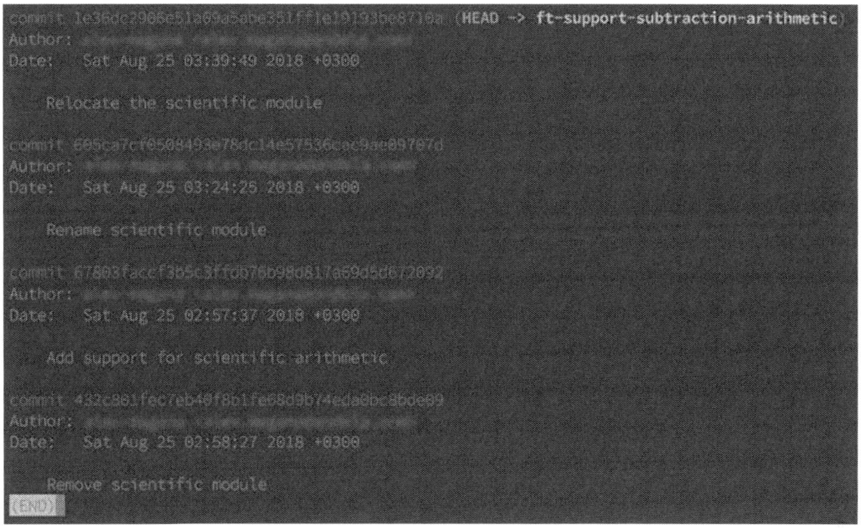

Figure 2.61: Confirming the changes

Outcome

Through following this exercise, the changes to the commit should now be reflected in the output.

Exercise 19: Editing Commits Using the edit Command

To edit a message using the `edit` command, follow these steps:

1. Launch the terminal and navigate to the location of the `abacus` repository.
2. Retrieve the last three commits by using the `git rebase -i HEAD~3` command:

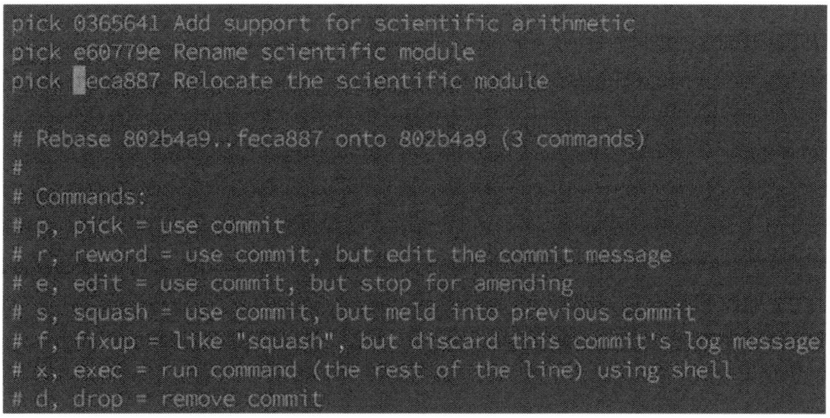

Figure 2.62: Retrieving the last three commits

3. Press *i* to switch to INSERT mode.
4. Pick the desired message accordingly.

> **Note**
>
> Here, we will edit the commit with the hash `feca887`.

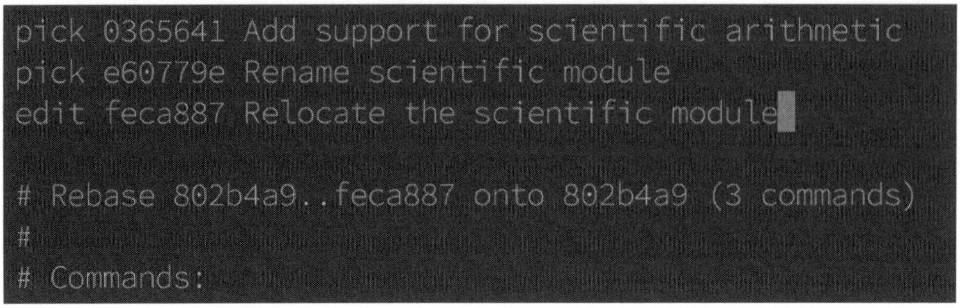

```
pick 0365641 Add support for scientific arithmetic
pick e60779e Rename scientific module
edit feca887 Relocate the scientific module

# Rebase 802b4a9..feca887 onto 802b4a9 (3 commands)
#
# Commands:
```

Figure 2.63: Editing the commit with the hash

5. Press **Esc** to exit INSERT mode.
6. Press : and type *wq* to save the changes and exit the editor.
7. Press **Return** to execute the *wq* command.
8. The rebase process pauses to allow for edits:

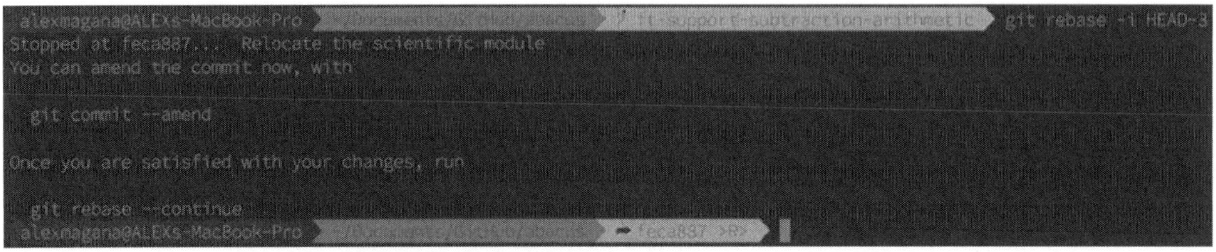

```
alexmagana@ALEXs-MacBook-Pro                    ft-support-subtraction-arithmetic   git rebase -i HEAD~3
Stopped at feca887...  Relocate the scientific module
You can amend the commit now, with

  git commit --amend

Once you are satisfied with your changes, run

  git rebase --continue
alexmagana@ALEXs-MacBook-Pro                    feca887
```

Figure 2.64: Using the rebase process

Introduction to Versioning Commits | 103

9. Change the file in **src/lib/advanced/advanced_compute.py**, as shown in the following screenshot:

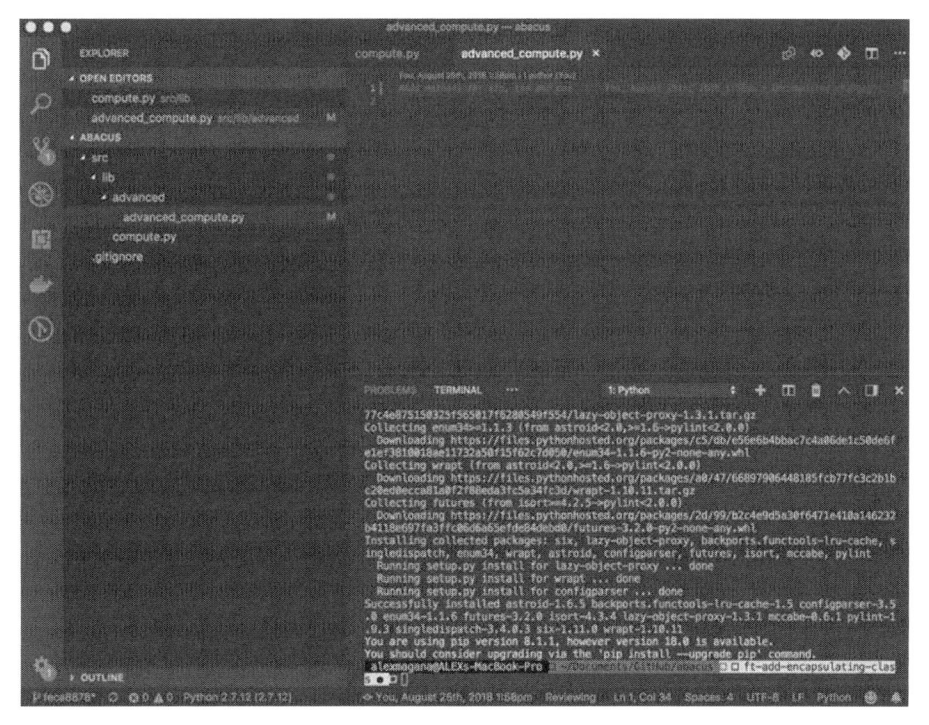

Figure 2.65: Making changes to the compute.py file

10. Add the file to the index and commit the changes by using the following commands:

```
git add src/lib/advanced/advanced_compute.py
git commit --amend
```

Figure 2.66: Committing the changes

11. In the editor, in the next prompt, press Esc to exit editing.

12. Press : and type wq to save the changes and exit the editor. The following screenshot shows the result that should be expected in the Terminal:

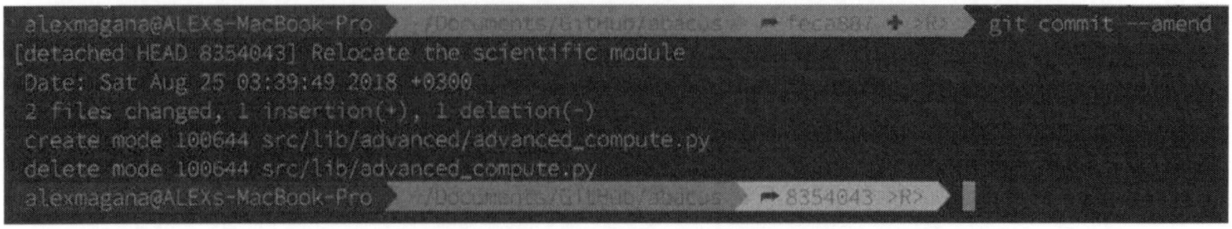

Figure 2.67: Result in the Terminal

13. Proceed with the rebase process and finish making any changes:

git rebase --continue

Figure 2.68: Rebase process

Outcome

The change to the commit has been reflected in the output via the use of the edit command.

Activity 2: Tracking Files

Suppose that you have been tasked with adding support for addition operations to the abacus application. The application should define a function that accepts a set of numbers and computes the sum of the numbers.

Your task is to implement file tracking commands and navigate the repository history.

To get started, you need to have the Git command-line tool installed on your computer. Additionally, you need to have an account on https://github.com/ and you need to be logged into your account on GitHub. Finally, you should have the abacus application repository on GitHub and your computer:

1. Launch the terminal and navigate to the location of the abacus directory.

2. Navigate to the required branch of the abacus application by using the required code.

3. Create a branch for the feature that you'll develop off the ft-support-subtraction-arithmetic branch by using the required code.

4. Add the required code lines to **src/lib/compute.py** and save the changes.
5. Check the status of the files on the branch.
6. Retrieve the alterations made to **src/lib/compute.py**.
7. Add the changed file to the index and commit the changes.
8. Create a file for recording the application logs.
9. Check the status of the branch.
10. Add the file to the index and commit it.
11. Remove the log file from the working tree and the index.
12. Retrieve the formatted details of the branch history for the five most recent commits.
13. Edit the last commit.
14. Edit the commit messages using the **rebase** utility:

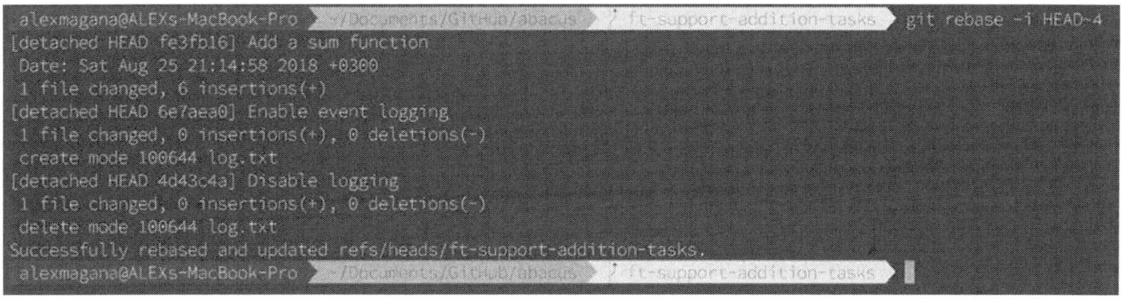

![Figure 2.69 terminal screenshot showing git rebase -i HEAD~4 output with detached HEAD commits for Add a sum function, Enable event logging, and Disable logging, ending with "Successfully rebased and updated refs/heads/ft-support-addition-tasks."]

Figure 2.69: Viewing the changes

Outcome

You have successfully implemented file tracking commands and navigated the repository history.

> **Note**
>
> For detailed steps regarding this activity, please refer to the **Appendix** section on page 276.

Summary

In this chapter, you explained the need for versioning commits. Then, you compared commits, branches, indexes, and working trees, and how they relate to each other. Next, you defined the various Git commands and stated their functions. Last but not least, you demonstrated how to amend commits, such as arbitrary commits.

In the next chapter, you will configure branch access and protection rules. You will also retrieve and incorporate changes in a repository.

3

Fetching and Delivering Code

Learning Objectives

By the end of this chapter, you will be able to:

- Configure connections to hosted repositories
- Configure branch access and protection rules
- Retrieve and incorporate change into a repository
- Reverse changes in a repository

This chapter describes the configuring of branches and handling changes in the repository.

Introduction

In the previous chapter, we covered the concept of versioning commits. Then, we compared commits, branches, indexes, and working trees, and how they relate to each other. Finally, we demonstrated how to amend commits, such as arbitrary commits.

Through exploring workflow terminology, the GitHub UI, and Git toolkit commands, you developed skills for the implementation of version control using Git and GitHub. You established the states that a file exists in, from the point that it's created and untracked in the working directory to when it's tracked and all of the changes in the file that are monitored and persisted through a commit.

In this chapter, we'll explore how to configure local repositories to communicate with the hosted repository. To regulate the process of accepting local changes, we'll implement restrictions that enforce benchmarks that, once achieved, will ensure the prevention of error causing changes. We'll look at how we can utilize the connection setup to retrieve changes from the shared hosted repository and make local changes available to the hosted repository.

Fetching the Code

As we discussed in the previous chapter, in distributed version control, the code base is hosted at a central point from which contributors can retrieve the code, make local changes to the code base on their computers, and publish the changes to the central host.

To develop a sound grasp of the distributed fashion in which Git implements version control, we will look at some terms that are commonly used to describe the link between the code that is modified locally and the source code that is hosted on GitHub:

Upstream

Upstream refers to the hosted repository. This is the repository (and the subsequent branch that is hosted on GitHub) from which contributors can clone the repository to their local environments, make changes, and publish changes to it.

In regard to forking, upstream refers to the repository that originates from a forked repository. This is the repository from which you create a fork to your account.

Downstream

This refers to the repository that is situated in your local environment. The downstream repository is obtained through the `git clone` command, which creates a copy of the hosted repository.

Remote

Remote refers to a named reference to a hosted repository. The remote connection is configured at the local repository level in order to enable pushing and pulling information to and from the hosted repository. Remote branches are prefixed by the remote they belong to, so that they don't mix with local branches.

Origin

This is the default `remote` that's configured on a repository. The `origin` is created when a repository is cloned by executing the `git clone` command.

git remote

With the terminology having been covered, we will proceed to look at the `git remote` utility, to explore how we can manage the connection between the local and upstream repositories.

The `git remote` utility includes commands that help with managing the remote/upstream repositories that are associated with a local repository.

Exercise 20: Configuring the Remote Repository

To set up, view, and modify the tracked repository, follow these steps:

1. Launch the Terminal.

2. Create a directory for the application by using the `mkdir remote-demo` command:

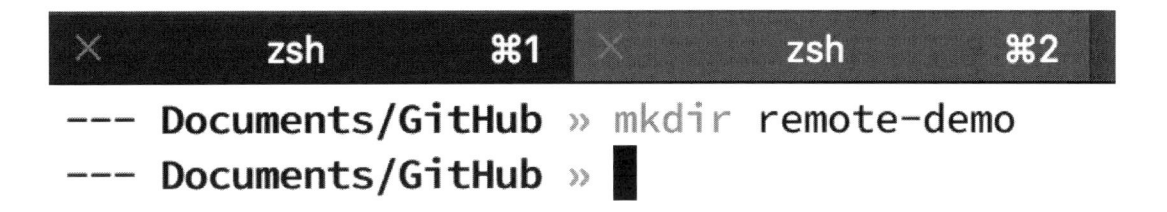

```
--- Documents/GitHub » mkdir remote-demo
--- Documents/GitHub »
```

Figure 3.1: Making the directory

3. Change the working directory to the project directory by using the `cd remote-demo` command:

```
--- Documents/GitHub » cd remote-demo
--- GitHub/remote-demo »
```

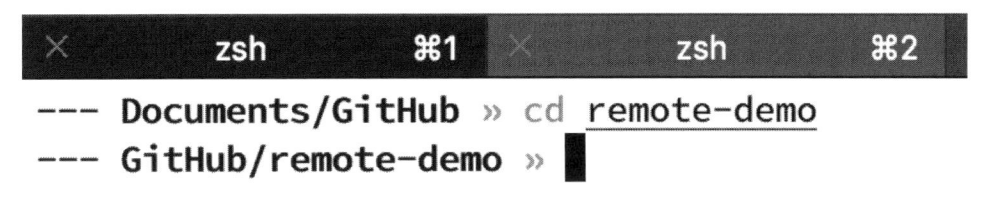

Figure 3.2: Changing the directory

4. Initialize the repository by using the `git init` command:

```
--- GitHub/remote-demo » git init
Initialized empty Git repository in /Users/alexmagana/Documents/GitHub/remote-demo/.git/
```

Figure 3.3: Initializing the repository

5. Go to https://github.com/ and create a repository with the name **remote-demo**.
6. Run `git remote` to view the currently tracked remote repository:

```
--- GitHub/remote-demo ‹master› » git remote
--- GitHub/remote-demo ‹master› »
```

Figure 3.4: Viewing the currently tracked remote repository

> **Note**
>
> This does not return a repository, since the remote tracked repository hasn't been set yet.

7. Retrieve the repository URL, as shown in the following screenshot, and add the remote tracked repository by using the `git remote add origin git@github.com:kifeh-polyswarm/remote-demo.git` command where **[kifeh-polyswarm]** is replaced with your user name on GitHub as seen in the following screenshot:

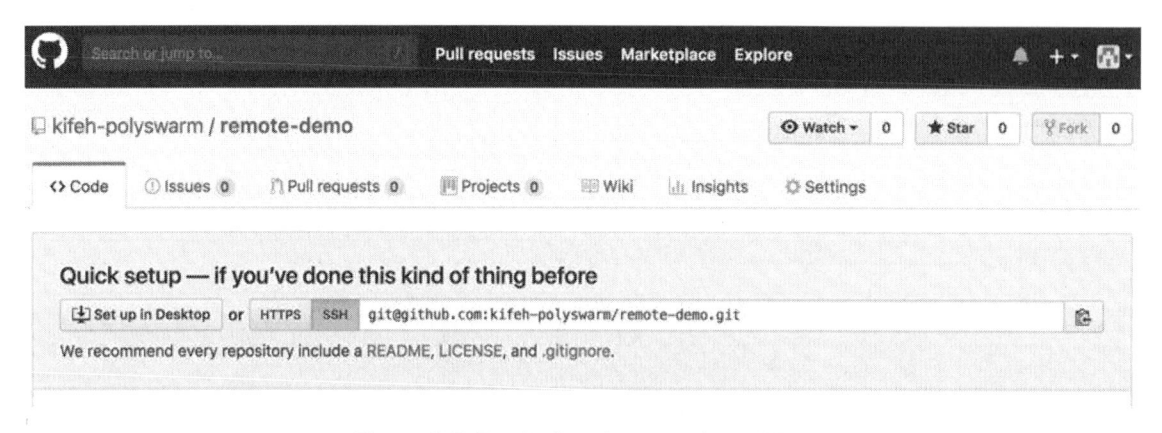

Figure 3.5: Retrieving the repository URL

8. View the remote configuration by using the `git remote -v` command

```
--- GitHub/remote-demo <master> » git remote -v
origin   git@github.com:kifeh-polyswarm/remote-demo.git (fetch)
origin   git@github.com:kifeh-polyswarm/remote-demo.git (push)
--- GitHub/remote-demo <master> »
```

Figure 3.6: Viewing the remote configuration

9. Rename the remote configuration from `origin` to `source-truth` by using the `git remote rename origin source-truth` command

```
--- GitHub/remote-demo <master> » git remote rename origin source-truth
--- GitHub/remote-demo <master> » git remote -v
source-truth   git@github.com:kifeh-polyswarm/remote-demo.git (fetch)
source-truth   git@github.com:kifeh-polyswarm/remote-demo.git (push)
--- GitHub/remote-demo <master> »
```

Figure 3.7: Rename the remote configuration

10. Add a **README.md** file by using the `echo "# remote-demo" >> README.md` command.

11. Commit the change and push the files to GitHub by using the following code:

```
git add README.md
git commit -m "Initial commit"
git push -u source-truth master
```

12. View the specifics of the `source-truth` remote by using the `git remote show source-truth` command:

```
--- GitHub/remote-demo <master> » git remote show source-truth
* remote source-truth
  Fetch URL: git@github.com:kifeh-polyswarm/remote-demo.git
  Push  URL: git@github.com:kifeh-polyswarm/remote-demo.git
  HEAD branch: master
  Remote branch:
    master tracked
  Local branch configured for 'git pull':
    master merges with remote master
  Local ref configured for 'git push':
    master pushes to master (up to date)
--- GitHub/remote-demo <master> »
```

Figure 3.8: Viewing the specifics of the source-truth remote

Outcome

By following the steps outlined in this section, you should be able to use `git remote` to configure a remote repository for a given local repository.

> **Note**
>
> The **prune** command removes local branches that correspond to branches that have been deleted from the remote repository:

```
git remote prune source-truth
```

```
 alex_magana_ext@i...  ⌘1             zsh            ⌘2            less            ⌘3
--- GitHub/remote-demo ‹master› » git remote prune source-truth
--- GitHub/remote-demo ‹master› »
```

Figure 3.9: Viewing the specifics of the prune-truth remote

The configured remote can be removed by using the `remove` command. For example, to remove the `source-truth` remote, run `git remote remove source-truth`:

```
 alex_magana_ext@i...  ⌘1             zsh            ⌘2            less            ⌘3
--- GitHub/remote-demo ‹master› » git remote remove source-truth
--- GitHub/remote-demo ‹master› » git remote -v
--- GitHub/remote-demo ‹master› »
```

Figure 3.10: Viewing the specifics of the remove source-truth remote

Default and Protected Branches

GitHub supports the enforcement of restrictions with respect to merging and pushing code to the branches that are protected.

These restrictions ensure that the code that is held in a particular branch remains void of as many errors as possible.

Additionally, to ensure and promote correctness, GitHub allows you to set a certain repository as the **default** branch. The default branch serves the purpose of providing a single source of truth on a repository. Pull requests are merged to this branch by default.

Exercise 21: Configuring the Base Branch and Branch Protection

To set up branch access restrictions, follow these steps:

1. In your browser, go to the https://github.com/[user_name]/abacus page.
2. Click on the **Settings** tab.
3. Select the **Branches** tab, as shown in the following screenshot:

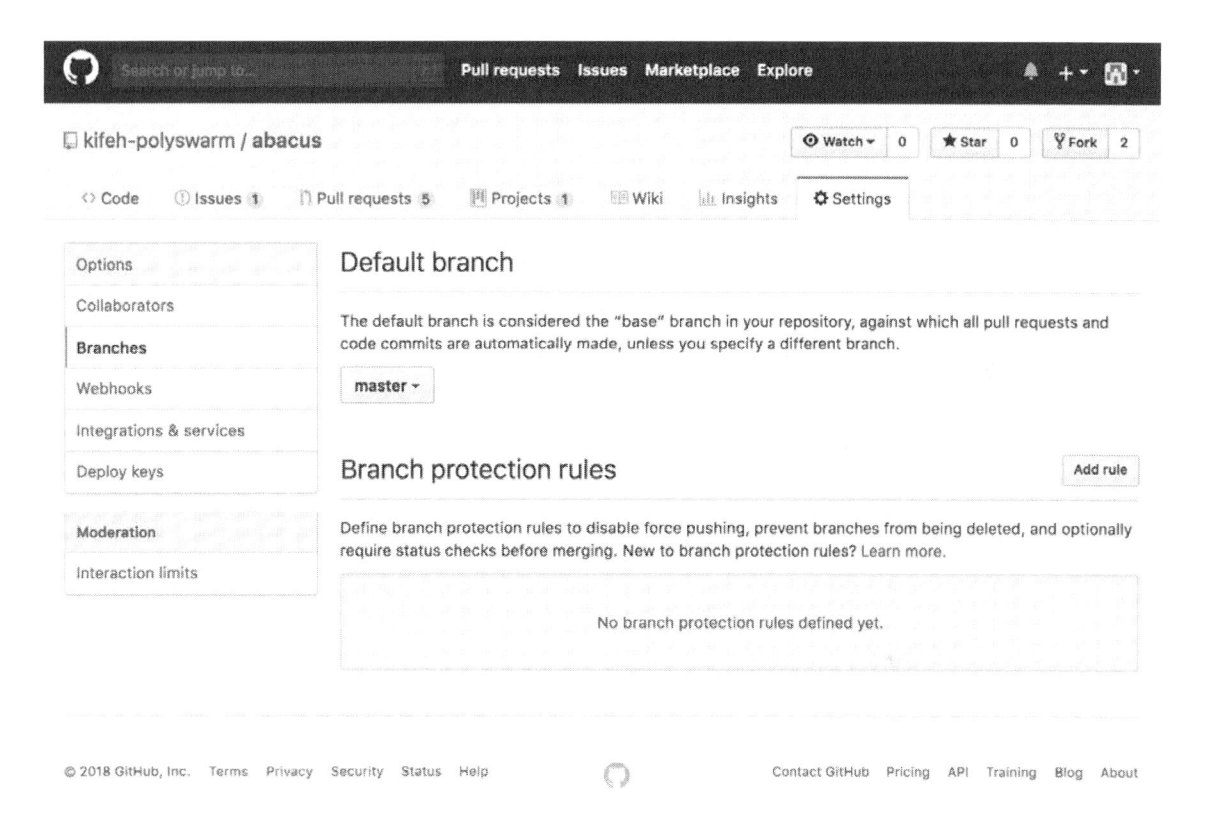

Figure 3.11: Selecting the branches

4. Select the desired branch from the drop-down menu in the previous screenshot to set it as the default branch. In this exercise, you will set the **master** branch.
5. To add a restriction on a specific branch in the repository, click on the **Add rule** button situated to the right of **Branch protection rules**.

6. Set a rule to indicate the branches that this rule applies to.

> **Note**
>
> The following rules support the condition forming character sets:
>
> `*` : Matches all branches.
>
> `*feature` : Matches branches ending with the text `feature`.
>
> `feature*` : Matches branches that start with the text `feature`.
>
> `*feature*`: Matches branches that have the text `feature` in them.
>
> `\` : Escapes the character that follows it. For example, `\*feature` will match branches that bear the text `*feature`.

7. Select the preferred protection settings. In the following diagram, the **Require branches to be up to date before merging** option should correspond to a status handling facility. This refers to **Continuous Integration (CI)** tools that run checks on commits that are pushed to the repository. The CI tool runs tests on the target branch and reports the results of the execution of tests. In *Chapter 6*: *Automated Testing and Release Management*, we will set up a CI tool on the repository, in order to ensure seamless change integration:

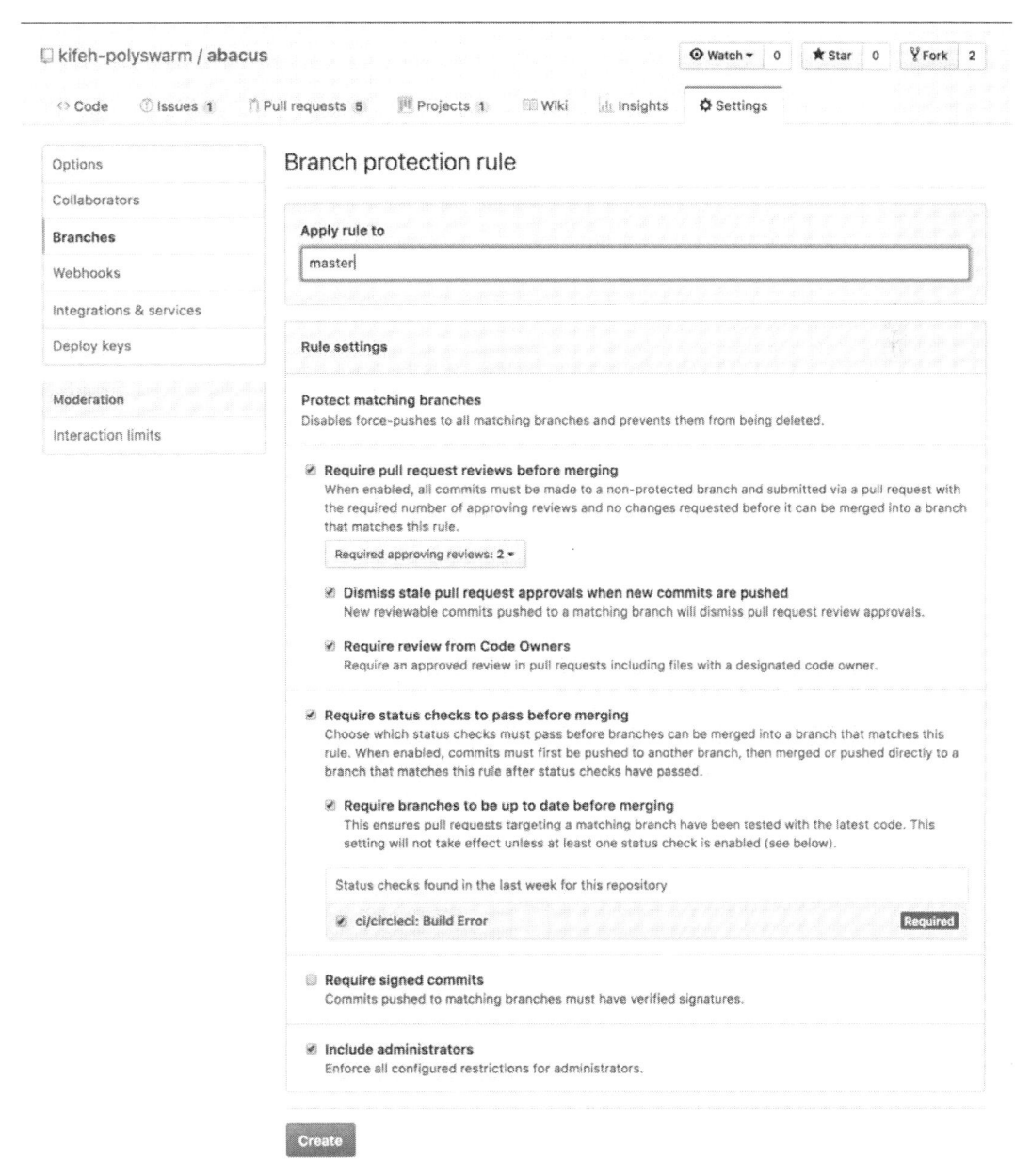

Figure 3.12: Creating branch protection rules

8. Click on the **Create** button and provide a password to conclude the configuration.

Outcome

By executing the preceding steps, you should be able to enforce restrictions on how changes are merged in a repository.

Fetching, Pushing, and Pulling Changes

To enable collaboration in a distributed version control system, Git provides the means to retrieve and publish your contributions to the shared repository. To demonstrate this, we will explore `git fetch`, `git push`, and `git pull`.

git fetch

To navigate changes that were made to a repository, you need to utilize references to the changes made to the repository, and consequently a branch. This command allows you to explore the changes before integrating them into your work.

The `git fetch` command downloads remote-tracking branches and tags from the remote repository. These branches and tags indicate changes that have been made to the remote repository.

The content retrieved by this command is isolated from the content in the local repository, and, when you do this, the work that is being undertaken locally isn't affected by the downloaded content.

> **Note**
>
> Remote-tracking branches keep track of changes occurring on the branches in the remote repository. Remote-tracking branches can be viewed by using the `git branch -r` command. The `refs` for remote-tracking branches are stored in `/.git/refs/remotes/[remote_name]`; for example, `/.git/refs/remotes/origin`.

Common usage of `git fetch` takes the following forms:

`git fetch`

You can fetch the branches of the default `origin` remote defined for the repository, or you can use the upstream configured for the current branch (if any) by using `git fetch [remote]`.

You can retrieve or download all of the branches of the repository specified by `[remote]` with `git fetch [remote]` e.g. `git fetch origin`:

`git fetch [remote] [branch]`

You can fetch the [branch] from the upstream repository specified by [remote] with `git fetch origin master`:

```
git fetch --all
```

You can fetch branches from all of the remote connections defined for a repository. For example, if you have a remote `origin` and `upstream`, as you will see in the *Chapter 4: Branches*, this command will fetch branches from the two repositories identified by `origin` and `upstream`:

```
git fetch --depth=[depth]
```

You can fetch the [depth] number of commits from the tip of each remote branch with `git fetch --depth=5`:

```
git fetch --prune
```

You can remove remote-tracking references that have ceased to exist in the remote repository, and then proceed to fetch the branches and their corresponding commits, files, and `refs` with: `+refs/heads/*:refs/remotes/origin/*`.

> **Note**
>
> The `git fetch` command uses the `refspec` defined in the repository-level config. This is defined in the `remote.[remote_name].fetch` config value. The `refspec` can be retrieved by running the `git config --local --list` command.

The `refspec` dictates that `refs` stored in the remote repository in `refs/heads/` are tracked locally, under `refs/remotes/origin/`.

The `+` indicates that references should be updated, including in scenarios where the commit is not a **fast-forward**.

The fast-forward mode is applied in scenarios where:

- Two or more individuals are working on the same branch and pushing changes to it.

- Two or more individuals create branches off a similar branch, (for example, the master,) and then seek to merge their respective branches to the common branch:

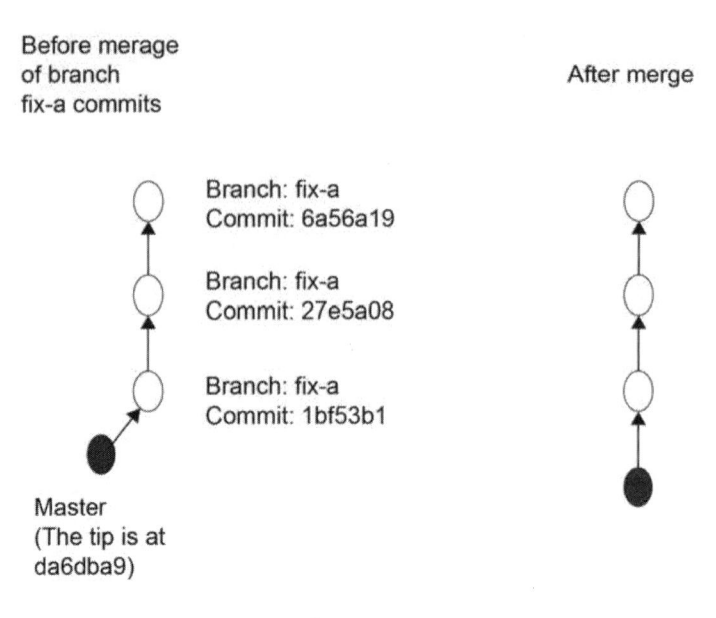

Figure 3.13: Before and after a merge

Exercise 22: Retrieving Changes

To demonstrate fetching changes using `git fetch`.

1. Navigate to the remote-demo repository by using `cd [path]/remote-demo`.
2. If, you are not on the branch master, switch to it by using `git checkout master`.
3. Create a branch off of the branch master by using `git checkout -b ft-new-carousel`.
4. Switch back to the branch master by using `git checkout master`.
5. Add introductory text to the README.md file as follows:

`echo "\n This is a sample repository" >> README.md`

6. Commit the changes and push the changes to the branch master:

`git add README.md`
`git commit -m "Add introduction text"`
`git push origin master`

```
--- GitHub/remote-demo ‹master* M› » git add README.md
--- GitHub/remote-demo ‹master* M› » git commit -m "Add introduction text"
[master 7da0b09] Add introduction text
 1 file changed, 2 insertions(+)
--- GitHub/remote-demo ‹master› » git push origin master
Counting objects: 3, done.
Writing objects: 100% (3/3), 289 bytes | 289.00 KiB/s, done.
Total 3 (delta 0), reused 0 (delta 0)
To github.com:kifeh-polyswarm/remote-demo.git
   df2bc21..7da0b09  master -> master
--- GitHub/remote-demo ‹master› »
```

Figure 3.14: Committing the changes

7. Switch to the branch ft-new-carousel by using git checkout ft-new-carousel.

8. Retrieve the branch master from the repository on GitHub by using git fetch origin master.

9. Check the differences between the branch master and ft-new-carousel by using the following code: git diff ft-new-carousel origin/master

```
diff --git a/README.md b/README.md
index d705571..bedeeea 100644
--- a/README.md
+++ b/README.md
@@ -1 +1,3 @@
 # remote-demo
+
+ This is a sample repository
(END)
```

Figure 3.15: Checking the differences between branches

10. Merge the changes from the branch `master` to `ft-new-carousel`:

`git merge origin/master`

```
--- GitHub/remote-demo <ft-new-carousel> » cat README.md
# remote-demo
--- GitHub/remote-demo <ft-new-carousel> » git merge origin/master
Updating df2bc21..7da0b09
Fast-forward
 README.md | 2 ++
 1 file changed, 2 insertions(+)
--- GitHub/remote-demo <ft-new-carousel> » cat README.md
# remote-demo

This is a sample repository
--- GitHub/remote-demo <ft-new-carousel> »
```

Figure 3.16: Merging the changes

Outcome

Having gone over the steps outlined in this exercise, you should now be able to fetch changes from an upstream branch, conduct a comparison between the two branches, and merge the desired changes.

git push

As demonstrated in the previous topic, the `git fetch` command enables you to retrieve changes from the remote repository. The downloaded changes can then be merged, in order to integrate the changes into the local repository and keep it up-to-date.

The `git push` command picks local commits and updates the remote branch with the local commits. By default, the `git push` command only supports pushing commits in a fast-forward mode. If the commits being pushed are non-fast-forward, you're required to either push changes by force, or update the local repository by merging the commits from the remote branch.

This command takes the form of `git push [remote_name]`

You can push commits from the current branch to the remote branch configured on the repository with `git push origin`

```
git push
```

This is similar to `git push [remote_name]`

    git push [remote_name] [branch_name]

This variant will push commits from the local branch to the specified branch on the specified remote repository. You can use `git push origin develop` for this:

    git push HEAD:[branch_name]

HEAD, as you may recall, refers to the tip of the current branch. This variant of `git push` uploads the commits of the current branch to the remote branch specified by `[branch_name]`; for example, `git push HEAD:develop`:

    git push origin [local_branch]:[remote_branch]

This command creates a new remote branch, bearing the commits in the `[local_branch]`. This command is useful when the local branch and the remote branch do not have matching names. You can use `git push origin feature-video:video-experiment`:

    git push origin :[branch_name]

This variant deletes the specified branch. You can use `git push origin :bug-logout-mobile` for this.

There are several options that are commonly used with the `git push` command. These include the following options:

The `--all` local branches. These branches are the branches that correspond to the heads stored in `.git/refs/heads/`. You can use `git push --all` for this:

    --dry-run

This option simulates the changes that would be implemented. The changes are not uploaded to the remote branch. You can use `git push --dry-run origin master` for this:

    --force or -f

This forces `git push` to update the remote branch in the event non-fast-forward changes are encountered. You can use `git push -f origin master` for this:

    git push --force origin master

> **Note**
>
> The use of this option may result in a loss of commits in the destination branch, and, as such, caution should be exercised when using this option.

You can set a tracking reference to the upstream branch for the current branch by using `git push -u origin master`.

Dealing with Non-Fast-Forward Commits

As we explained earlier, `git push` utilizes a fast-forward mode to merge commits. Non-fast-forward commits are therefore rejected, in order to avoid the loss of source code. To deal with this, it's advised that you use `git fetch` to retrieve the updated remote branch, and then run `git merge [remote_name]/[branch_name]` to merge the changes from the remote branch. Finally, run `git push` to upload your changes to the remote branch.

The `git rebase` command can also be used to integrate changes from the remote branch.

git pull

The `git pull` command is an alternative to using the `git fetch` mechanism to retrieve and integrate changes in the remote repository.

The `git pull` command, in its default mode, runs a combination of `git fetch` and `git merge`. The `git pull` utility may use a `rebase` mechanism, if it's specified as the synchronization mechanism in the place of a `merge`.

The `git pull` syntax is as follows:

```
git pull [options] [remote_name] [branch_name or refspec]
```

```
git pull [remote]
```

The preceding code retrieves changes from the remote branch that's been configured as the remote-tracking branch for the current branch and merges the changes into the local branch. This can be done with `git pull origin`.

```
git pull
```

This is similar to `git pull origin`.

```
git pull [remore_name] [origin]
```

You can fetch the remote branch `develop` and merge it into the current branch with `git pull origin develop`.

The `git push` command supports dictating how to conduct a merge of the content downloaded from the remote branch. This is achieved, by using merger-related options, which can be used with the `git pull` command:

```
--commit
```

The changes to the remote repository are merged, and a commit is performed; for example, `git pull --commit origin master`.

`--no-commit`

This option instructs `git merge` to integrate the changes from the remote repository, and to not perform a commit; for example, `git merge --no-commit origin master`.

> **Note**
>
> In the event that the commits being merged are resolved to be fast-forward, the `--no-ff` option should be used to override the default behavior, which is to update the branch pointer without creating a merge commit; for example, `git merge --no-commit --no-ff origin master`.

`--no-ff`

This option creates a merge commit, including in a scenario where commits resolve as being fast-forward; for example, `git merge --no-ff origin master`.

`--ff`

This is the opposite of `--no-ff`. It updates the branch pointer of the current branch to the tip of the branch with the incoming changes commits resolved as being fast-forward; for example, `git merge --ff origin master`.

`--edit`

The `git pull` command fetches and merges the changes, and launches an editor to allow for the editing of the automatically generated commit message; for example, `git merge --edit --no-ff origin master`.

`--no-edit`

This instructs the fetch and merge process of `git pull` to accept the auto-generated commit message; for example: `git merge --no-edit --no-ff origin master--strategy=[strategy]`.

This option specifies the merge strategy to be used for the `git merge` step of `git pull`.

The strategies used by git are `resolve`, `recursive`, `octopus`, `ours`, and `subtree`.

`--strategy-option=[option]`

This sets a strategy option that's specific to the strategy specified by the `--strategy` command option. The options for the `recursive` strategy include `ours`, `theirs`, `no-renames`, `ignore-all-space`, `ignore-space-at-eol`, and `ignore-cr-at-eol`.

Reversing Commits

Git provides multiple approaches to reversing changes that have been introduced to a file.

git revert

The `git revert` command reverses changes introduced by the given commit. `git revert` creates a commit to cause this reversal. Examining the commit created by `git revert` should indicate the modifications that have been reversed.

The `git revert` command uses the following syntax:

> `git revert [options] [commit(s)]`

The options supported by `git revert` are as follows:

`--edit`

This option provides support for editing the commit message for a given reversal; for example, `git revert --edit [commit hash]`.

`--no-edit`

The `--no-edit` option overrides the `--edit` option. It performs the revert with the default auto-generated commit message.

`--no-commit`

With this option, the `git revert` command makes changes to the index and the working tree, in order to reverse the modifications made by the given commit. It does this without creating a commit for the reversal.

`--mainline [parent-number]`

Two sets of changes exist in a merge commit, referenced by each of the two parents that constitute a merge commit. This option dictates which of the two sets should be used in the reversal process. We will explore this further in the cherry-pick section.

Exercise 23: Reversing Changes

To demonstrate change reversal using `git revert`, follow these steps:

1. Launch the terminal and navigate to the location of the `abacus` repository.
2. Create a branch off of `ft-support-subtraction-arithmetic` for the feature of division arithmetic that you will add to the application:

`git checkout ft-support-subtraction-arithmetic`

`git checkout -b ft-support-division-arithmetic`

```
--- GitHub/abacus <master> » git checkout ft-support-subtraction-arithmetic
Switched to branch 'ft-support-subtraction-arithmetic'
--- GitHub/abacus <ft-support-subtraction-arithmetic> » git checkout -b ft-support-division-arithmetic
Switched to a new branch 'ft-support-division-arithmetic'
--- GitHub/abacus <ft-support-division-arithmetic> »
```

Figure 3.17: Creating a branch

3. Open compute.py in a text editor.
4. Add the following lines to the compute.py file and save the changes:

Live Link for file exercise_4_step_4.py: https://bit.ly/2BmTcqa

```python
def division(self):
    quotient = 1
    for item in self.operands:
        quotient /= item
    print(quotient)
```

5. Stage the change to add the feature and commit it:

```
git status
git add src/lib/compute.py
git commit -m "Add support for division"
```

```
--- GitHub/abacus <ft-support-division-arithmetic> » git status
On branch ft-support-division-arithmetic
Changes not staged for commit:
  (use "git add <file>..." to update what will be committed)
  (use "git checkout -- <file>..." to discard changes in working directory)

        modified:   src/lib/compute.py

no changes added to commit (use "git add" and/or "git commit -a")
--- GitHub/abacus <ft-support-division-arithmetic* M> » git add src/lib/compute.py
--- GitHub/abacus <ft-support-division-arithmetic* M> » git commit -m "Add support for division"
[ft-support-division-arithmetic dae772b] Add support for division
 1 file changed, 6 insertions(+)
--- GitHub/abacus <ft-support-division-arithmetic> »
```

Figure 3.18: Staging the change to add the feature

6. Upon the realization that `1n2₁. quotient /= item` is incorrect, you need to revert the previous commit, in order to fix this issue. Obtain the commit hash of the last commit by using the `git log --oneline -n 2` command:

```
less
6bf23f3 (HEAD -> ft-support-division-arithmetic) Add support for division
8354043 (origin/ft-support-subtraction-arithmetic, ft-support-subtraction-arithmetic) Relocate the scientific module
(END)
```

Figure 3.19: Adding support for division

7. Reverse the commit in question by using `git revert --edit 6bf23f3`.

8. In the opened editor, switch to INSERT mode by pressing I. Add the desired commit message to reflect the change or reversal being made:

```
vim
Revert "Add support for division"

This reverts commit 6bf23f33ea6ccd361e550962220a701216f8a90e.

# Please enter the commit message for your changes. Lines starting
# with '#' will be ignored, and an empty message aborts the commit.
#
# On branch ft-support-division-arithmetic
# Changes to be committed:
#       modified:   src/lib/compute.py
#
```

Figure 3.20: Adding support for division

```
vim
Correct the operand arrangement

This reverts commit 6bf23f33ea6ccd361e550962220a701216f8a90e.

# Please enter the commit message for your changes. Lines starting
# with '#' will be ignored, and an empty message aborts the commit.
#
# On branch ft-support-division-arithmetic
# Changes to be committed:
#       modified:   src/lib/compute.py
#
~
~
```

Figure 3.21: Correcting the operand

9. Exit the **Insert** mode, save the change using the following :wq combination, and press the **Enter** key:

```
--- GitHub/abacus ‹ft-support-division-arithmetic› » git revert --edit 6bf23f3
[ft-support-division-arithmetic d41fe27] Correct the operand arrangement
 1 file changed, 6 deletions(-)
--- GitHub/abacus ‹ft-support-division-arithmetic› »
```

Figure 3.22: Saving the changes

10. The **division** method that you added in **src/lib/compute.py** should now be absent.

11. Change the **division** method so that it reads **quotient = item / quotient**:

Live Link for file exercise_4_step_11.py: https://bit.ly/2Tviv73

```
20    def division(self):
21        quotient = 1
22        for item in self.operands:
23            quotient = item / quotient
24        print(quotient)
25
```

Figure 3.23: Changing the division method

12. Stage the change and commit it:

        git add src/lib/compute.py

        git commit -m "Correct the division operation"

```
--- GitHub/abacus ‹ft-support-division-arithmetic* M› » git add src/lib/compute.py
--- GitHub/abacus ‹ft-support-division-arithmetic* M› » git commit -m "Correct the division operation"
[ft-support-division-arithmetic ff3afa9] Correct the division operation
 1 file changed, 6 insertions(+)
--- GitHub/abacus ‹ft-support-division-arithmetic› »
```

Figure 3.24: Stage the change and commit it

Outcome

Having executed the preceding steps, you should be able to revert changes using the **git revert** utility.

Other Possible Uses

```
git revert [least_recent_commit_hash]..[most_recent_commit_hash]
```

The preceding code shows how the `git revert` command is a forward-moving **undo** operation that provides an effective means of undoing changes.

git reset

The `git reset` command is used to roll back a file, directory, or repository at large to a given point in its history. This entails updating the `index`, `working tree`, and `commit history` of a repository where applicable, based on the options passed in the command.

Objects

Git uses objects to track changes throughout the history of a repository. To achieve this tracking, Git uses four types of objects. The objects are `commits`, `trees`, `blobs`, and `tags`. These objects are stored in `.git/objects`.

The following is a file and directory listing of a repository, as well as the history of the branch master. Using this, we will explore these object types, in order to gain a picture of what a reset entails:

```
--- GitHub/reset-demo <master> » ls -al
total 16
drwxr-xr-x    5 alexmagana  staff   170 10 Oct 03:38 .
drwxr-xr-x@  43 alexmagana  staff  1462 10 Oct 05:19 ..
drwxr-xr-x   12 alexmagana  staff   408 10 Oct 17:45 .git
-rw-r--r--    1 alexmagana  staff    36 10 Oct 03:39 test.txt
-rw-r--r--    1 alexmagana  staff    21 10 Oct 03:37 test.txt-e
--- GitHub/reset-demo <master> »
```

Figure 3.25: Using the master branch

```
220da08 (HEAD -> master) Adding the word 'stream'
11b8b15 Adding the word 'the'
5d2045c Adding the word 'down'
892a587 Changing the word 'boat' to 'car'
ab30a24 Adding the word 'gently'
4655b2d Adding the word 'boat'
744effe Adding the word 'your'
337a25f Adding first row
(END)
```

Figure 3.26: Adding words individually

Commit

A commit object stores the hash of the directory tree object that the commit corresponds to, the parent commit hash, the author, the committer date and time, and the commit message:

```
git cat-file -t 11b8b15
```

```
--- GitHub/reset-demo <master> » git cat-file -t 11b8b15
commit
--- GitHub/reset-demo <master> »
```

Figure 3.27: Using the commit command

Take a look at the following code:

```
git cat-file -p 11b8b15
```

```
--- GitHub/reset-demo <master> » git cat-file -p 11b8b15
tree 5dda013cf02f598b3063f5fb12c383f1e30816ae
parent 5d2045c33b22cf6b7134317855ad9ed6264a1d42
author alex-magana <alex.magana@andela.com> 1539131933 +0300
committer alex-magana <alex.magana@andela.com> 1539131933 +0300

Adding the word 'the'
--- GitHub/reset-demo <master> »
```

Figure 3.28: Using the commit command

Trees

A **tree** holds references to blobs and subtrees. It acts as a representation of the directory structure of a repository at a given point in its history. As such, a blob refers to files, and a tree refers to a directory.

A tree object lists the permissions of constituent blobs or trees, the object type, the object hash, and the object's name. The object type may be a **tree** or a **blob a**s seen in the following code snippets:

```
git cat-file -t 5dda013cf02f598b3063f5fb12c383f1e30816ae
```

```
--- GitHub/reset-demo <master> » git cat-file -t 5dda013cf02f598b3063f5fb12c383f1e30816ae
tree
--- GitHub/reset-demo <master> »
```

Figure 3.29: Using trees

132 | **Fetching and Delivering Code**

```
git cat-file -p 5dda013cf02f598b3063f5fb12c383f1e30816ae
```

```
--- GitHub/reset-demo <master> » git cat-file -p 5dda013cf02f598b3063f5fb12c383f1e30816ae
100644 blob 2aa9d75994066fb54c4db4245c5256ceef409879    test.txt
100644 blob 4841d176958e185dd66bb7f7b2534037f5e6a5c1    test.txt-e
--- GitHub/reset-demo <master> »
```

Figure 3.30: Using trees

BLOBs

Git uses blobs to store the contents of a file at a given point in time. A blob is a **Binary Large OBject (BLOB)**. It's Git's methodology of storing the contents of a file at a given point in its lifetime. A blob is created when we commence the tracking of a file by using the `git add` command:

```
git cat-file -t 2aa9d75994066fb54c4db4245c5256ceef409879
```

```
--- GitHub/reset-demo <master> » git cat-file -t 2aa9d75994066fb54c4db4245c5256ceef409879
blob
```

Figure 3.31: Using blobs

Take a look at the following code:

```
git cat-file -p 2aa9d75994066fb54c4db4245c5256ceef409879
```

```
--- GitHub/reset-demo <master> » git cat-file -p 2aa9d75994066fb54c4db4245c5256ceef409879
row
your
car
gently
down
the
--- GitHub/reset-demo <master> »
```

Figure 3.32: Using blobs

Comparing the blob hash `2aa9d75994066fb54c4db4245c5256ceef409879` to a previous blob hash, `c2b35620a2db369bcd59e266de5d8e17d7a045c0`, we are able to see the differences in the content of `test.txt` at the two given times:

```
git cat-file -p 744effe
```
```
git cat-file -p 826f5e89e5d6dac1b27175f7a0723c4e9e5154cb
```
```
git cat-file -p c2b35620a2db369bcd59e266de5d8e17d7a045c0
```

```
--- GitHub/reset-demo (master) » git cat-file -p 744effe
tree 826f5e8915d6dac1b27175f7a0723c4e9e5154cb
parent 337a25faeb302fee7f8d49262f99b775268a8ccc
author alex-magana <alex.magana@andela.com> 1539131829 +0300
committer alex-magana <alex.magana@andela.com> 1539131829 +0300

Adding the word 'your'
--- GitHub/reset-demo (master) » git cat-file -p 826f5e8915d6dac1b27175f7a0723c4e9e5154cb
100644 blob c2b35620a2db369bcd59e266de5d8e17d7a045c0    test.txt
--- GitHub/reset-demo (master) » git cat-file -p c2b35620a2db369bcd59e266de5d8e17d7a045c0
row
your
--- GitHub/reset-demo (master) »
```

Figure 3.33: Using blobs

Tags

A **tag** is a pointer to a specific commit. The tag object contains the hash of the tagged object, the type of the object that the tag was created for, the tag name, and the the author details, such as the author name, date, and message:

> git tag -a v1.4 ab30a24 -m "This is demo commit"
>
> git cat-file -t f333f6b574af3d0443ac185b8de96a9475b922ef
>
> git cat-file -p f333f6b574af3d0443ac185b8de96a9475b922ef

```
--- GitHub/reset-demo (master) » git cat-file -t f333f6b574af3d0443ac185b8de96a9475b922ef
tag
--- GitHub/reset-demo (master) » git cat-file -p f333f6b574af3d0443ac185b8de96a9475b922ef
object ab30a24cd5ffbf979a67d3d860d3a14ebc7e282e
type commit
tag v1.4
tagger alex-magana <alex.magana@andela.com> 1539188275 +0300

This is demo commit
--- GitHub/reset-demo (master) »
```

Figure 3.34: Using tags

The `git reset` syntax follows the following form:

> git reset [tree-ish] [path(s)]
>
> git reset [mode] [commit]

To demonstrate how `git reset` works, we will explore the aforementioned variants and how each works to examine and establish how each affects a repository:

> git reset [tree-ish] [path(s)]

In Git, `tree-ish` refers to identifiers that reference a tree object, that is, a directory or subdirectory at a given point in a repository's history.

This variant of `git reset` resets the `[path(s)]` index to its state at `[tree-ish]`. The files and directories in the working tree are not affected:

For example. `git reset master:./test.txt test.txt`

`git reset 5d2045c test.txt`

`git reset HEAD:README README`

`git reset :/Adding the word 'boat' -- test.txt`

The text Adding the word 'boat' represents a commit message.

--patch

The `--patch` option allows you to choose portions of the differences between the index and `[tree-ish]` to reset to their respective states at `[tree-ish]`; for example, `git reset --patch 5d2045c test.txt`.

`git reset [mode] [commit]`

This variant resets the head of the current branch to the state at `[commit]`. Additionally, the index and working tree are reset, depending on the mode used to conduct the reset.

The supported modes are as follows:

--soft

This resets the head to `[commit]`. The index and the working tree are not altered by this option.

--hard

The `--hard` mode resets the head to `[commit]`. The index and working tree are reset to `[commit]`. Changes introduced to the working tree are discarded.

--mixed

This mode resets the head to `[commit]`. Additionally, it resets, the index to `[commit]`. The changes made to the working tree are not altered or discarded.

Activity 3: Handling Changes and Enforcing Branch Restrictions

Suppose that you're a release engineer, and you have been tasked with consolidating deliverables scheduled for the release of abacus, the utility your department has been building. You need to obtain work done by the other team that you've been collaborating with, in order to deliver the goals set for the now-concluded two week work period. With the work now consolidated, you are required to implement branch protection, to ensure that any fixes introduced to the branch with the code being released are tested and reviewed.

Our aim is to demonstrate the retrieval and reversal of changes and enforcing checks on branches for successful merging.

To get started, you must have the Git command-line tool installed on your computer. You will need to have an account at https://github.com/, and you should be logged in to your account on GitHub. Finally, you should have the abacus application repository on GitHub and your computer. Follow these steps to complete this activity:

1. Navigate to the location of the `abacus` repository.
2. Add a remote to reference the `abacus-team-b` repository.
3. Switch to the `ft-support-addition-tasks` branch, in order to create the consolidation branch.
4. Create and switch to the consolidation branch.
5. Retrieve the work that delivers the area calculation function.
6. Integrate the retrieved changes into the current directory.
7. Retrieve and merge the work that delivers the perimeter calculation function.
8. Retrieve and merge the volume computation branch.
9. In the process of establishing a consensus on what features were rolled out, it's decided that the volume feature isn't required. Reverse the addition of the volume function to the release-candidate branch.
10. To proceed with the rollout, you need to make a change to the perimeter method to support triangles. Reset the head to the point where we merged the perimeter function.
11. Edit the `util.py` file to support the computation of the perimeter for triangles.
12. Stage and commit the changes made to on `src/lib/util/util.py`.
13. Push the branch to the remote `origin`.

14. To protect the branch against untested quick fixes, so that you will be ready to ship the features, you need to add restrictions to the `release-candidate` branch.

15. Click the **Branches** option and select **Add rule.**

16. Specify the branch and the appropriate restriction options, and click on the **Create** button.

17. Provide the account password in the prompt that follows.

18. Save the changes by clicking on **Save changes**. This will put the rules into effect:

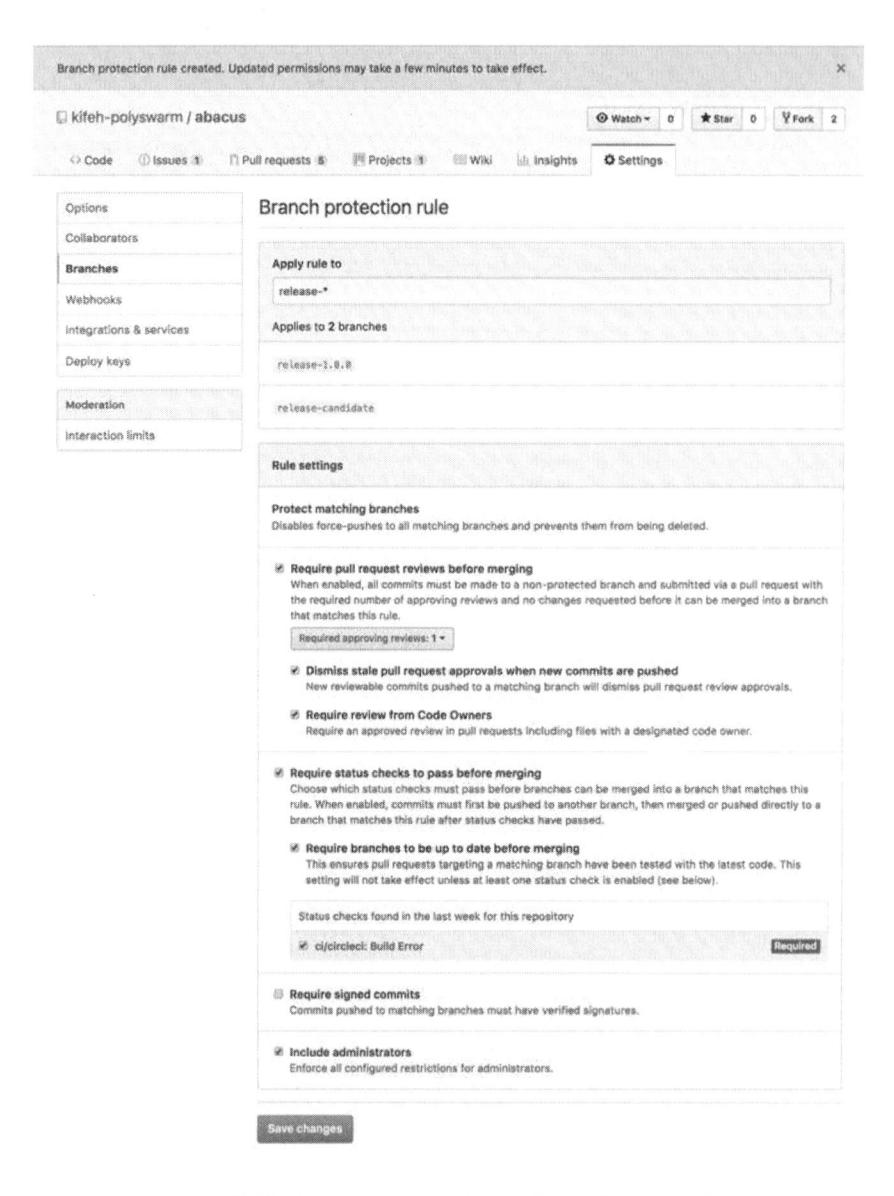

Figure 3.35: Saving changes in the branch protection

Outcome

Through completing this activity, a branch release-candidate with changes integrated into it and protection restrictions has been defined.

> **Note**
>
> For detailed steps for this activity, refer to the **Appendix** section on page 283.

Summary

In this chapter, we explored how local repositories can connect to the remotely hosted repository. In regard to branch protection, we implemented checks to police the integration of changes, by laying down measures that are taken into account when merging work into the repository's branch. We covered the `git push`, `git fetch`, and `git pull` commands, which facilitate the retrieval of changes and uploading the changes to the shared repository. Finally, we explored the `git revert` and `git reset` commands, which rescind changes.

In the next chapter, you will create, navigate, and delete branches. You will also merge changes and resolve issues via pull requests.

4
Branches

Learning Objectives

By the end of this chapter, you will be able to:

- Explain the feature-branch workflow
- Create, navigate, and delete branches
- Manage changes in the working directory
- Merge changes through pull requests
- Identify and resolve issues with pull requests

This chapter describes the working of branches, workflows and conflict resolution.

Introduction

In the previous chapter, we explored how local repositories are able to connect to a remotely hosted repository. We covered the `git push`, `git fetch`, and `git pull` commands, which facilitate the retrieval of changes and uploading of changes to the shared repository. Lastly, we explored the `git revert` and `git reset` commands, which rescind changes.

In this chapter, we'll look at a common workflow that's utilized in version control, the feature-branch workflow. In doing so, we will also learn about branches and how changes are affected through the merging of branches and shipping the work to the user-facing product on your live environment. The topics covered in this chapter are geared toward demonstrating how version control fits into the picture, from when you start building a feature to when it's shipped.

Utilizing Workflows

Workflows refer to the approach a team takes to introduce changes to a code base. A workflow is characterized by a distinct approach in the use of branches, or lack thereof, to introduce changes into a repository.

Gitflow Workflow

This uses two branches: **master** and **develop**. The master branch is used to track the release history, while the develop branch is used to track feature integration into the product.

To introduce a feature, first, you must create a feature branch from the develop branch and then make changes in the created branch and commit those changes. Next, you should push the changes to the remote feature branch. Additionally, you must raise a pull request against the develop branch, and then follow up by resolving the feedback provided in the pull request. Afterward, merge the feature branch to the develop branch and create a release branch once an agreed number of features are merged to develop. Next, you should raise a pull request against the master. Lastly, you need to merge the pull request once it's been approved.

Hotfix workflow

To make a hotfix, first you must create a branch off the branch master, make changes, and commit them. Next, you can push the changes to the remote hotfix branch. Follow this up by raising a pull request against the master. Lastly, merge the pull request once it's been approved.

Centralized Workflow

This approach uses the master branch as the default development branch. The changes are committed to the master branch. It's a suitable workflow for small size teams and teams transitioning from Apache Subversion. In Apache Subversion, the trunk is the equivalent of the master branch.

Creating a Centralized Workflow

To commission work and conduct development on a project, you need to initialize the central repository, host the central repository on GitHub, and clone the central repository. The next step is to make the desired changes and commit. Finally, push the changes to the central repository and manage the emergent conflicts by using the rebase utility of Git.

Feature Branch Workflow

In this workflow, feature development is carried out in a dedicated branch. The branch is then merged with the master once the intended changes are approved.

To introduce a feature into an application, you should first initialize a repository with the default master branch. Then, you must clone the repository or pull changes from the remote master branch in the event that you have the repository locally. Next, create a new branch, make changes, and commit the changes. Then, push the feature branch to the remote repository and raise a pull request. Lastly, resolve the feedback provided in the pull request review and merge the pull request.

Forking Workflow

A **forking workflow** takes the following approach in the development of features or in the general introduction of a change to the code base. Initially, you must fork an official product repository to your account on GitHub and clone the forked repository to your local environment. Then, create a new branch for the feature, make changes, and commit the changes. Next, you should push the changes to the remote cloned repository and raise a pull request against the official repository. Finally, resolve the feedback provided and merge the PR into the original/official repository. Merging is done by an authorized repository owner.

Feature-Branch Workflow

In this workflow, feature and maintenance-oriented development is carried out in a dedicated branch. The branch is then merged to the master once the intended changes are approved.

To ensure ease in the tracking of changes being introduced to the branch `master`, a naming convention is required for the branches that are created off of the branch `master`. The branch name should have an appropriate description, in a manner that indicates the change being introduced by a branch.

The following sample notation demonstrates the form a branch name assumes:

`branch_type-task_description`

Given that a project is undertaken using an issue tracking tool such as **Jira**, **Trello**, or **PivotalTracker**, the branch name should be suffixed by the issue number corresponding to the change the branch seeks to introduce.

Branch types include `feature`, `bug`, `fix`, and `chore`. Take a look at their abbreviations in the following table:

Branch Type	Abbreviation
feature	`ft`
bug	`bg`
fix	`fx`
chore	`ch`

To introduce a feature into an application, you should initialize a repository with the default master branch. Then, clone the repository or pull changes from the remote master branch in the event that the repository is local. Next, you need to create a new branch, make changes, and commit those changes. Then, follow up by pushing the feature branch to the remote repository and raising a pull request. Finally, round up by resolving the feedback provided in the pull request review and merge the pull request.

Exercise 24: Feature-Branch Workflow-Driven Delivery

To roll out a feature using the feature-branch workflow, follow these steps:

1. Navigate to the abacus repository of your GitHub account, as shown in the following screenshot:

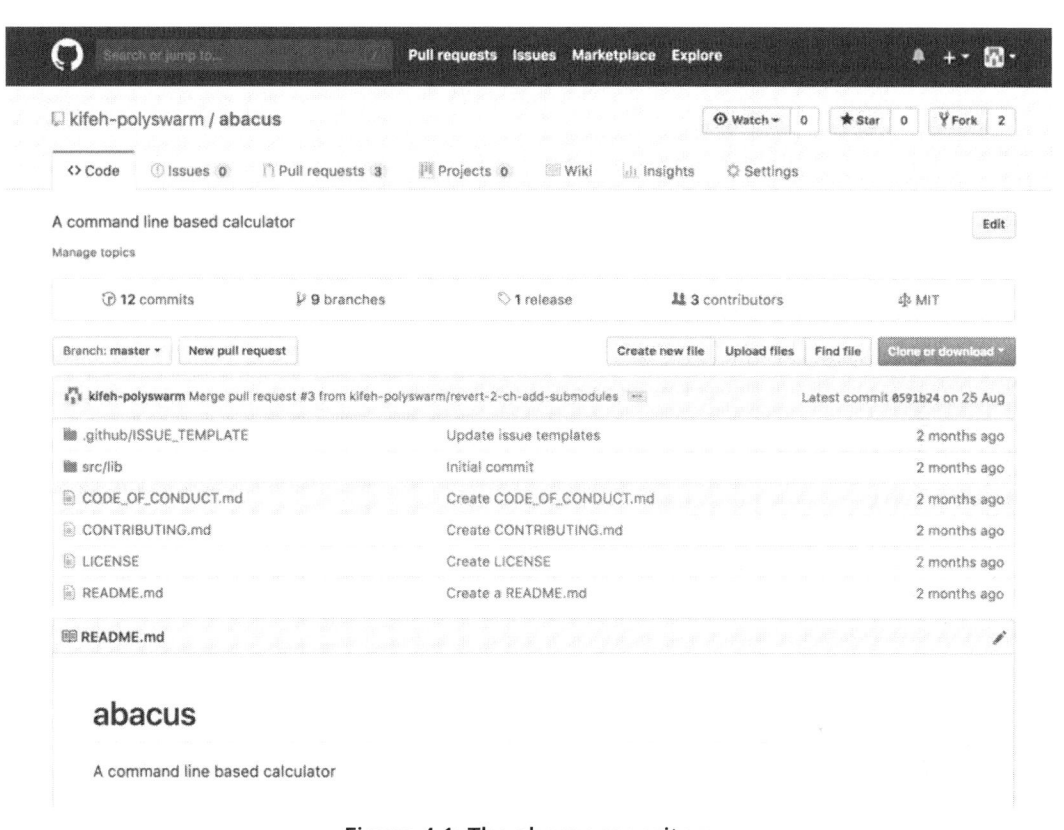

Figure 4.1: The abacus repository

2. Select the **Projects** tab and click the **Create a project** button in the window you're directed to, as shown in the following screenshot:

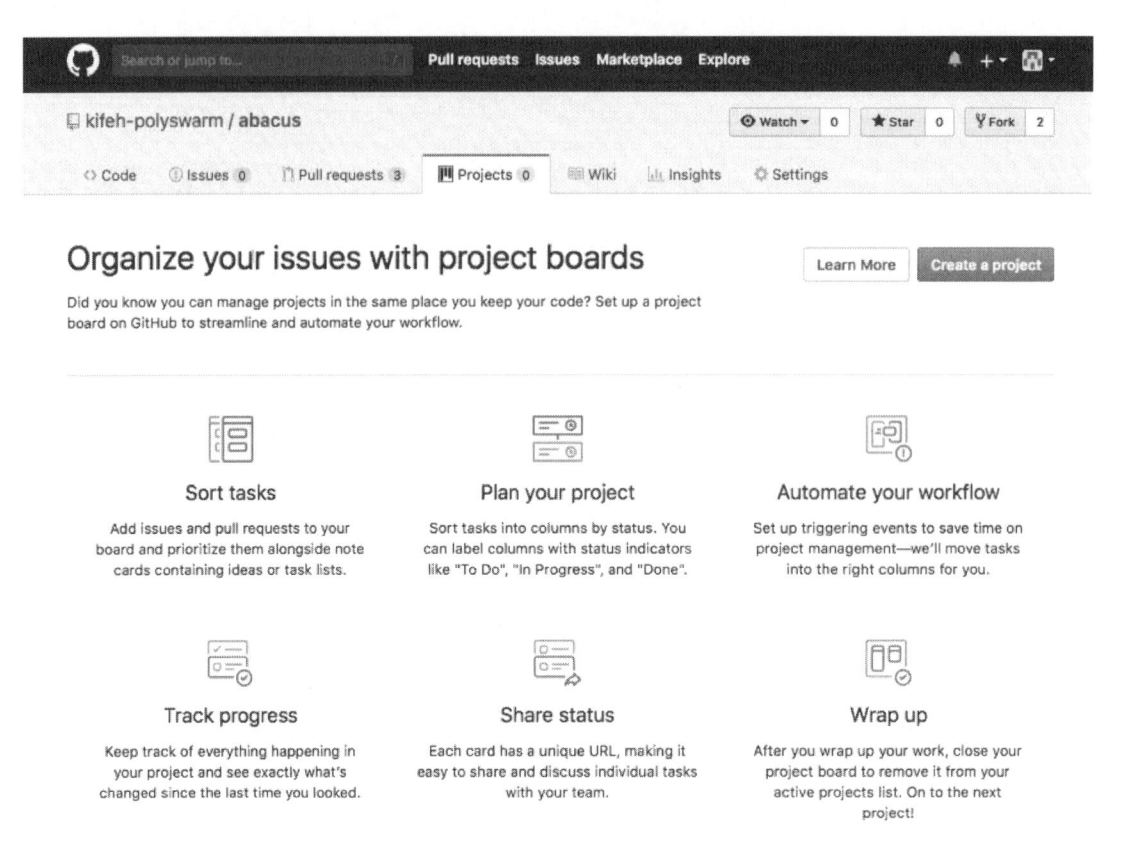

Figure 4.2: Organizing your issues

3. In the resultant window, specify a name and description for the project's issue tracking board, as shown in the following screenshot:

> **Note**
>
> Templates for task organization are available and may be used for scenarios where a bespoke ordering of tasks isn't required. For the purpose of this demonstration, we shall use the `Basic kanban` template.

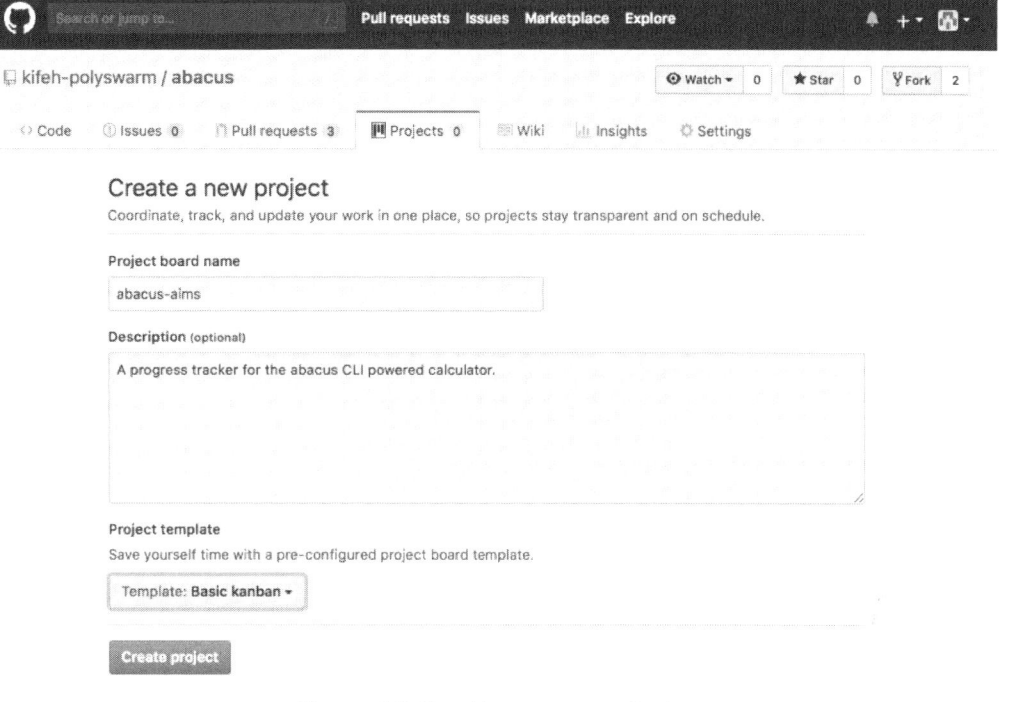

Figure 4.3: Creating a new project

4. Click the **Create project** button pictured in step **3**. The result is the board shown in the following screenshot:

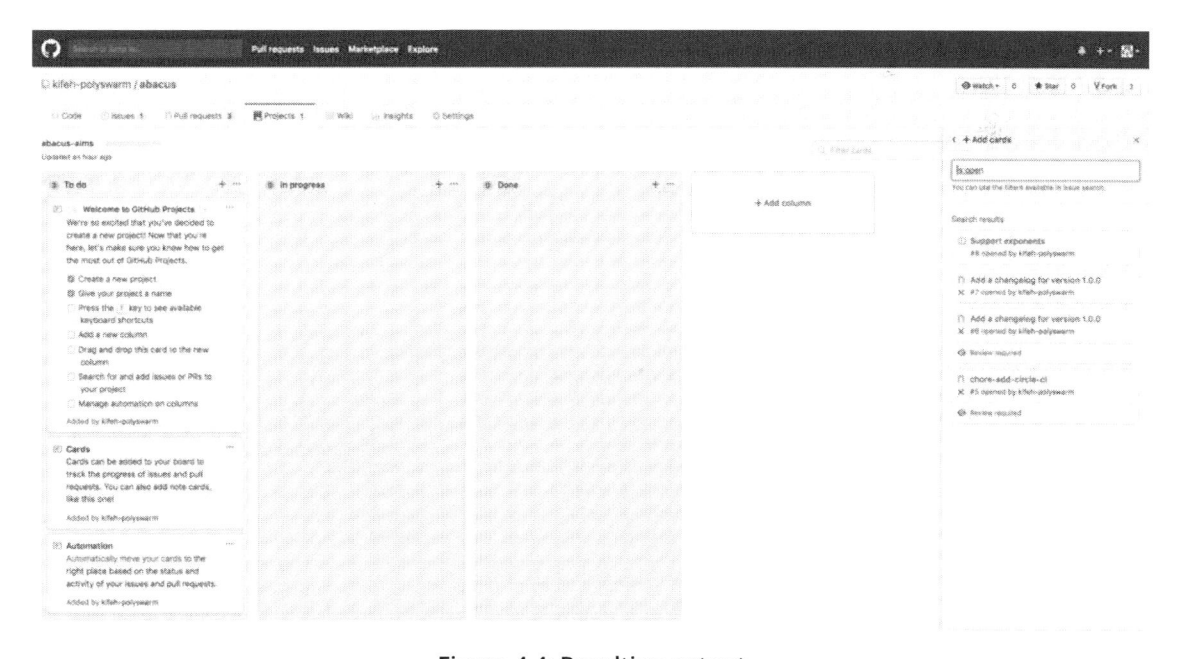

Figure 4.4: Resulting output

5. Create an issue to add support for exponents arithmetic operations by selecting the **Issues** tab and clicking the **New Issue** button to create a feature request, as shown in the following screenshot:

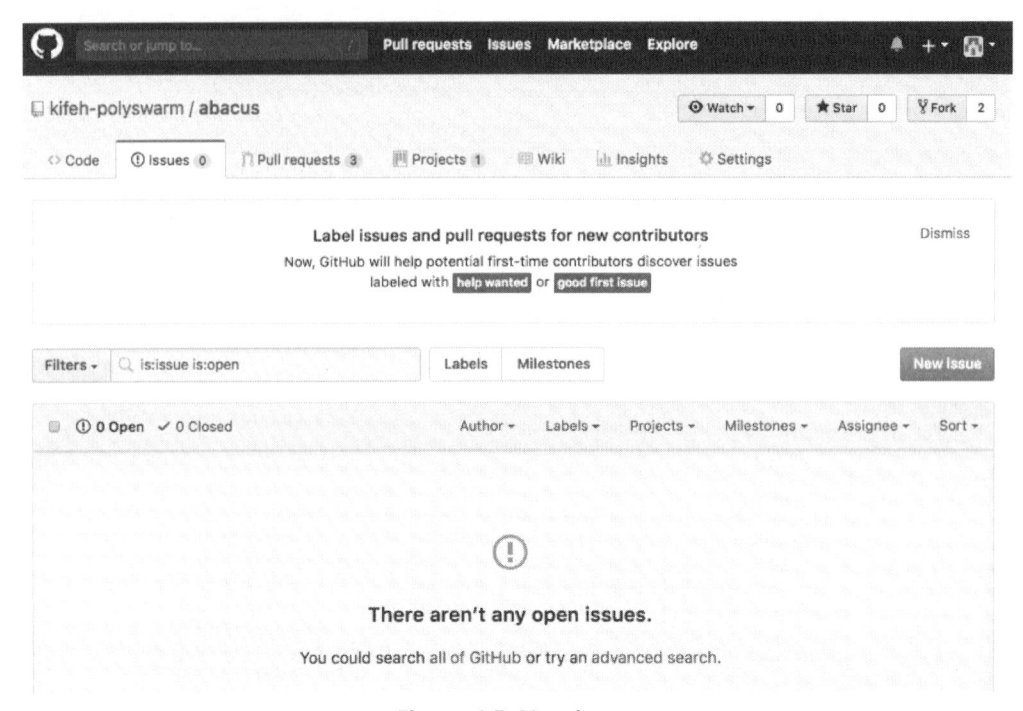

Figure 4.5: New issue

6. We will now utilize the issues templates we configured earlier. Click the **Get started** button to the right of the **Feature request** text, as shown in the following screenshot:

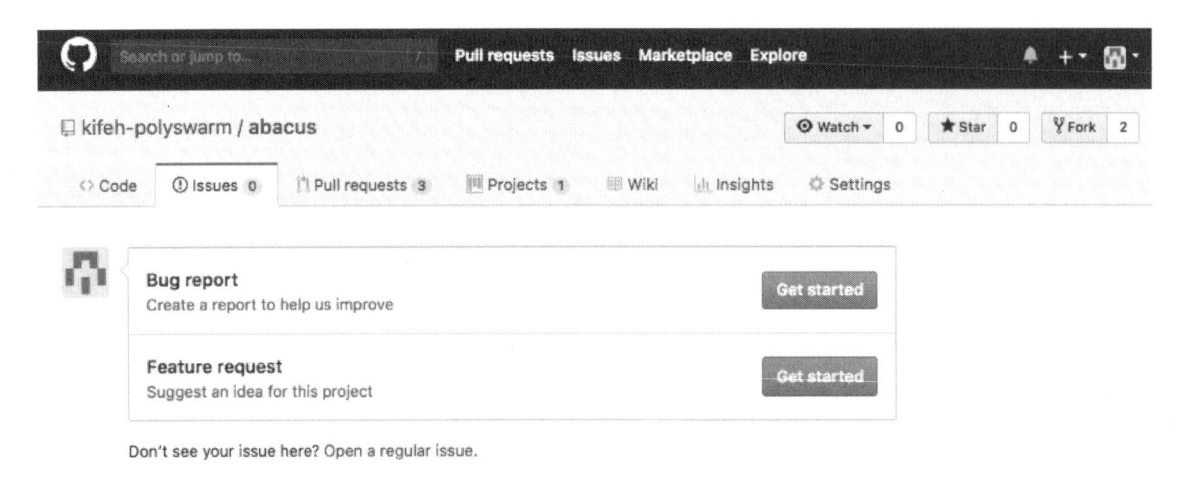

Figure 4.6: Getting started

Utilizing Workflows | 147

7. Provide the feature request specification and click **Submit new issue**, as shown in the following screenshot:

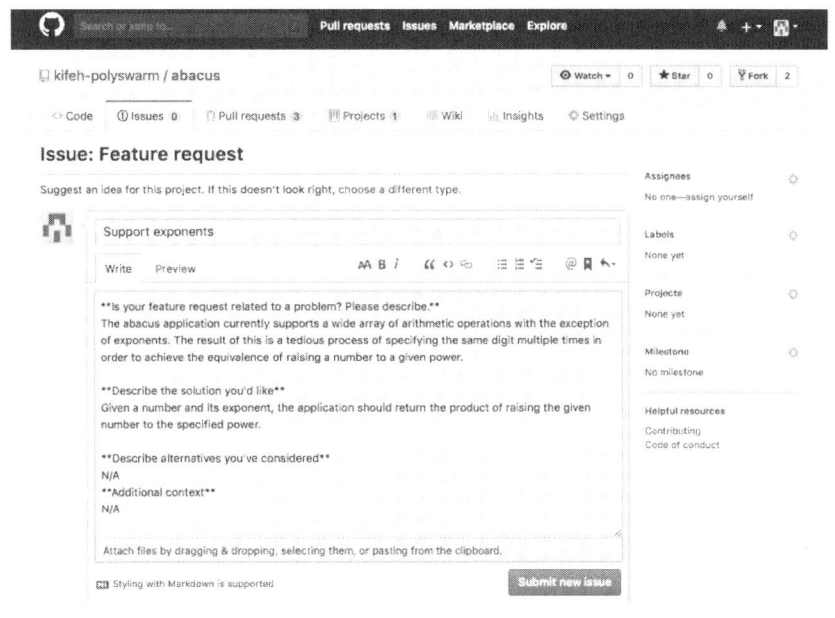

Figure 4.7: Submitting a new issue

8. Navigate to the `abacus-aims` board and click the **Add cards** option on the top pane of the board, as shown in the following screenshot:

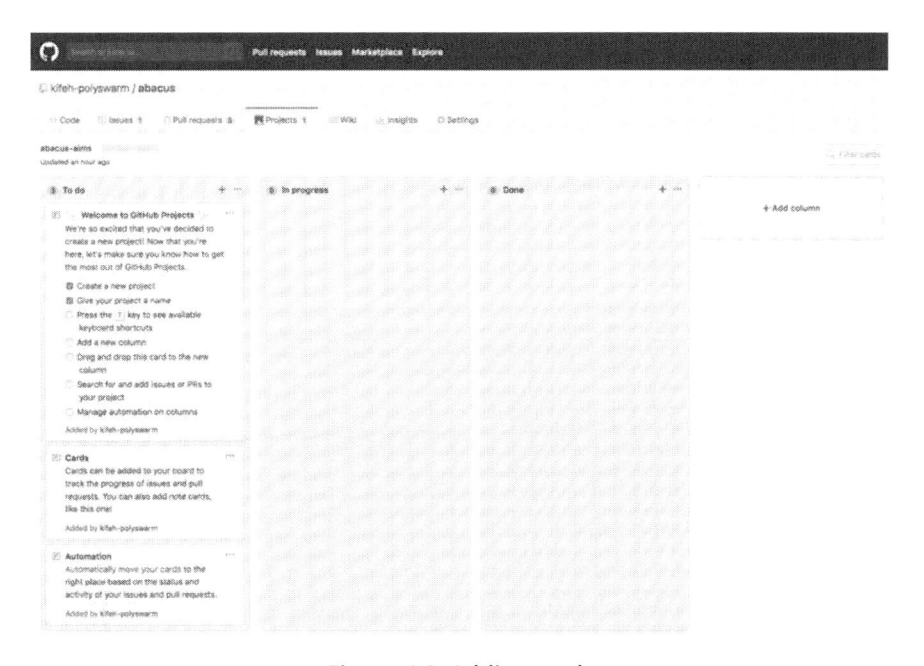

Figure 4.8: Adding cards

9. On the resultant panel, click the **Support exponents** issue:

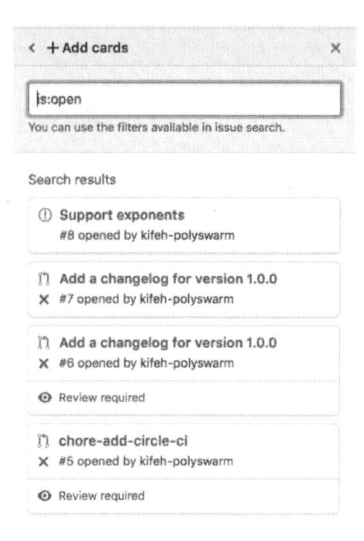

Figure 4.9: Support exponents issue

10. Allot an assignee and project to the issue and click **Back to Add cards**, as shown in the following screenshot:

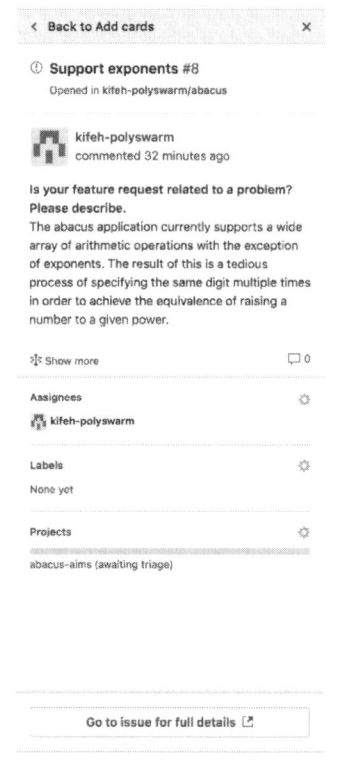

Figure 4.10: Back to Add cards

11. Click and drag the issue to the To do column and to In progress thereafter.
12. Launch the terminal and navigate to the location of the abacus repository.
13. Create a branch off ft-support-subtraction-arithmetic for the feature of the exponents arithmetic that you will add to the application, as seen in the following screenshot:

```
git branch ft-support-exponents
git checkout ft-support-exponents
```

```
--- GitHub/abacus <ft-support-subtraction-arithmetic> » git branch ft-support-exponents
--- GitHub/abacus <ft-support-subtraction-arithmetic> » git checkout ft-support-exponents
Switched to branch 'ft-support-exponents'
--- GitHub/abacus <ft-support-exponents> »
```

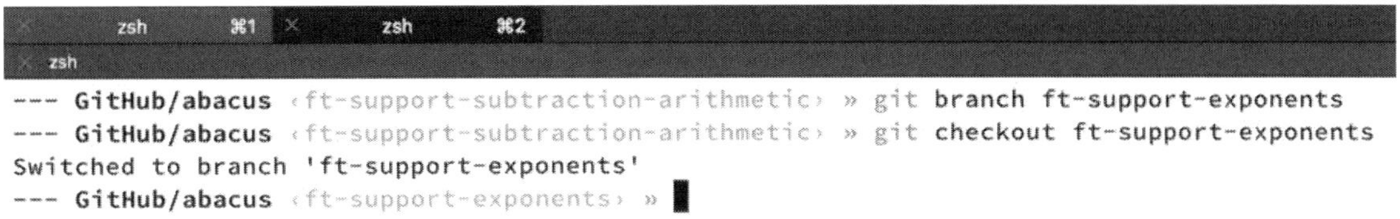

Figure 4.11: Creating a branch

14. Add the following function to support exponents using the following code, and as seen in the following screenshot:

Live Link for file exercise_1_step_14.py: https://bit.ly/2QgnNRa

```python
def exponent(self):
    num_exponent = self.operands[0] ** self.operands[1]
    print(num_exponent)
```

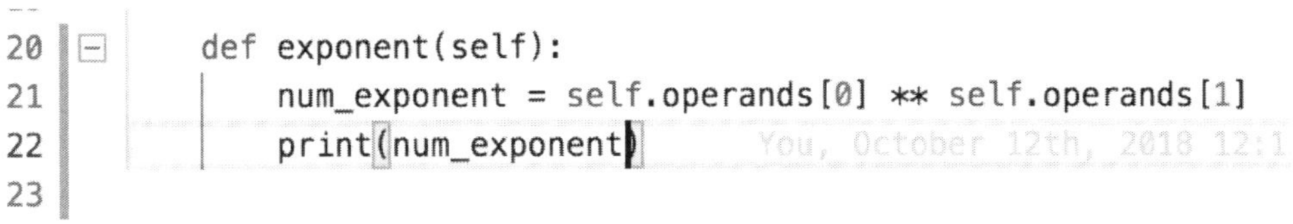

```
20    def exponent(self):
21        num_exponent = self.operands[0] ** self.operands[1]
22        print(num_exponent)
23
```

Figure 4.12: Adding the function

150 | Branches

15. Persist the change and push it to a remote branch using the following code, and as seen in the following screenshots:

```
git add src/lib/compute.py
git commit -m "Add support for exponents"
git push origin ft-support-exponents
```

```
--- GitHub/abacus ‹ft-support-exponents* M› » git add src/lib/compute.py
--- GitHub/abacus ‹ft-support-exponents* M› » git commit -m "Add support for exponents"
[ft-support-exponents 0ec3284] Add support for exponents
 1 file changed, 4 insertions(+)
```

Figure 4.13: Persisting the change

```
--- GitHub/abacus ‹ft-support-exponents› » git push origin ft-support-exponents
Counting objects: 5, done.
Delta compression using up to 4 threads.
Compressing objects: 100% (4/4), done.
Writing objects: 100% (5/5), 503 bytes | 503.00 KiB/s, done.
Total 5 (delta 1), reused 0 (delta 0)
remote: Resolving deltas: 100% (1/1), completed with 1 local object.
remote:
remote: Create a pull request for 'ft-support-exponents' on GitHub by visiting:
remote:      https://github.com/kifeh-polyswarm/abacus/pull/new/ft-support-exponents
remote:
To github.com:kifeh-polyswarm/abacus.git
 * [new branch]      ft-support-exponents -> ft-support-exponents
--- GitHub/abacus ‹ft-support-exponents› »
```

Figure 4.14: Pushing to a remote branch

16. Raise a pull request to merge the change and navigate to the new pull request page, as seen in the following screenshot. Use the following template as an example: https://github.com/[username]/abacus/pull/new/ft-support-exponents. My page link is as follows: https://github.com/TrainingByPackt/Version-Control-with-Git-and-GitHub:

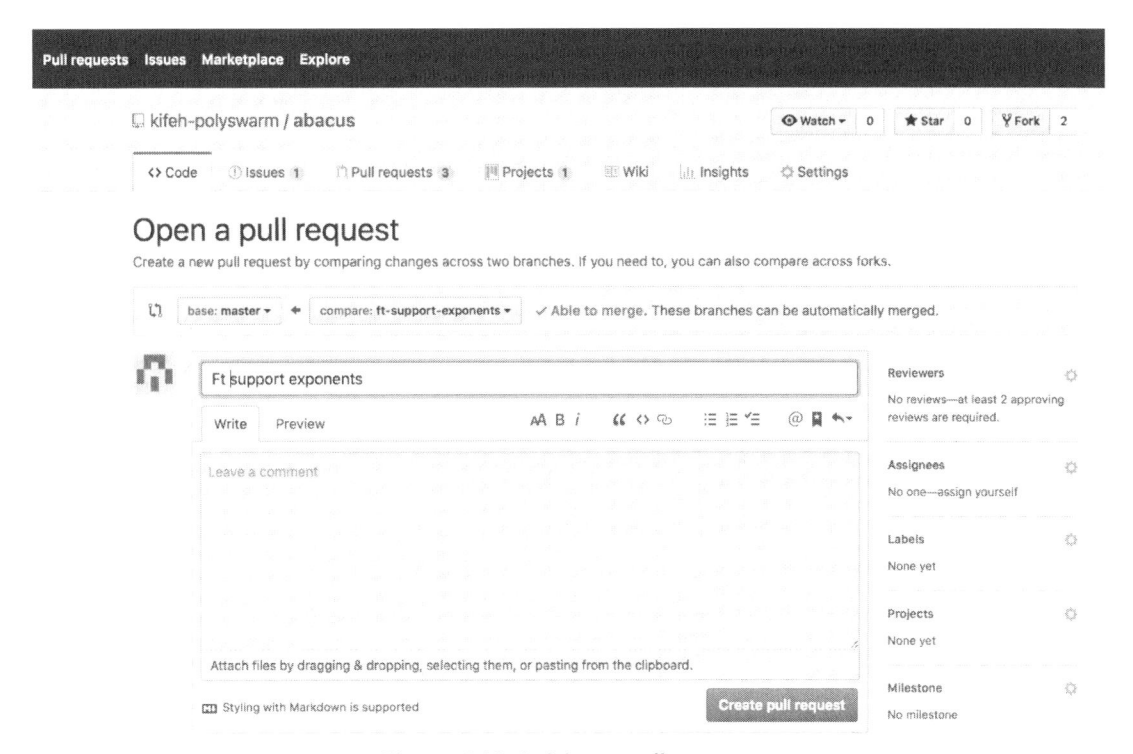

Figure 4.15: Raising a pull request

> **Note**
>
> Add an apt title and description. In the description, indicate the issue that the pull request (PR) is meant to resolve. GitHub establishes the issue number when the said digit(s) is prefixed with a #. Conclude the process by clicking the **Create pull request** button, as shown in the following screenshot:

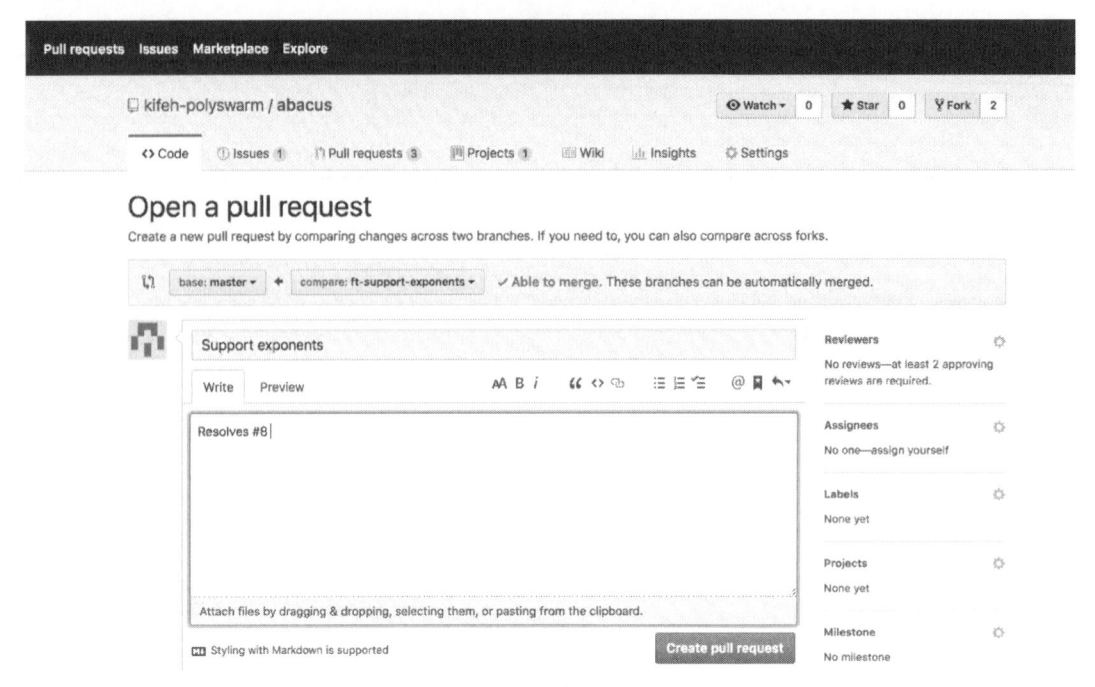

Figure 4.16: Raising a pull request

17. Merge the changes to the branch master by clicking the **Merge pull request** button presented in the window you're directed to.

Outcome

By using the steps outlined in this exercise, you should be able to demonstrate the feature-branch process of change incorporation.

Creating, Renaming, Deleting, and Listing Branches

In `git reset`, we examined how Git stores a commit and the contents of a commit. The commit object stores a snapshot of the directories and files that constitute a repository at a given point in time. In addition, the commit specifies auxiliary information, which includes the parent commit of the created commit, the author, the committer date and time, and the commit message:

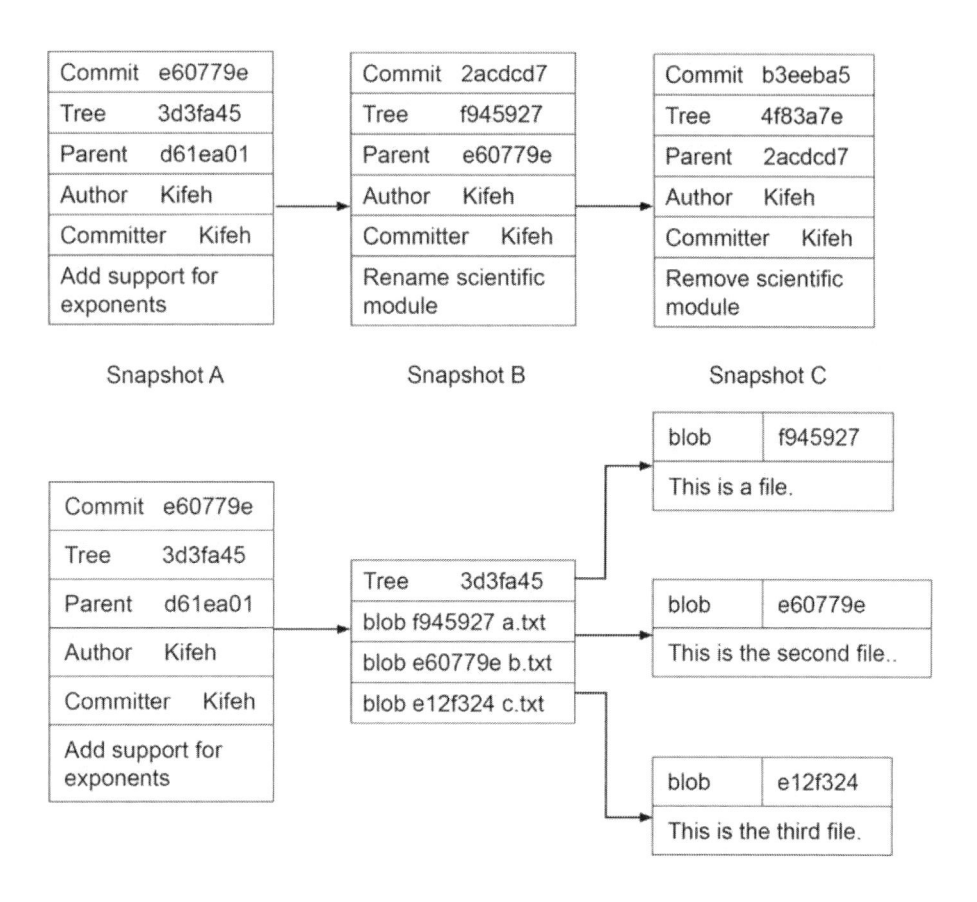

Figure 4.17: Snapshots of repository branches

A branch is therefore a pointer to a snapshot of the repository. This pointer refers to the commit at the tip of the branch. These tips are the commit hashes stored in `.git/refs/heads/`. HEAD is the pointer that references the commit at the tip of the current branch. This commit is imperative because it's based on the fact that git is able to navigate the history of a repository with the help of the parent-child association between commits. The creation of a branch, in turn, creates a pointer and the head, which bears a branch's name. Navigating from one branch to another updates the HEAD to refer to the tip of the branch you switch to – or in Git terms, check out to.

154 | Branches

Creating:
```
git branch [branch_name]
git branch --set-upstream-to [remote_branch_name]
e.g. git branch --set-upstream-to origin/ft-support-exponents
git branch --unset-upstream [branch_name]
git branch [branch_name] [start_point]
```

Renaming:
```
git branch -m [old_branch_name] [new_branch_name]
git branch -M [old_branch_name] [new_branch_name]
```
This is similar to invoking `git branch` with the `--move` and `--force` options.
```
git branch -c [old_branch_name] [new_branch_name]
```

Copy:
```
git branch -C [old_branch_name] [new_branch_name]
```
This is similar to invoking `git branch` with the `--copy` and `--force` options.

Deleting:
```
git branch -d [branch_name]
```
Delete a branch, granted that it's fully merged into its upstream branch or the HEAD, in the event that the upstream branch is not specified.
```
git branch -D [branch_name]
```
This forces the deletion of a branch.

It's similar to using `--delete --force`.

Listing:
```
git branch --list
git branch --list [pattern]
```
For example, you can use `git branch --list 'ft*'`.
```
git branch --contains [commit]
```
For example, you can use `git branch --contains 8354043`.
```
git branch --no-contains [commit]
git branch --merged [commit]
```
For example, you can use `git git branch --merged 8354043`.

This lists branches that have been merged into a given commit, that is, commits whose tip is reachable from the given commit.

`git branch --no-merged [commit]`

This is used for branches that are not merged into the given commit.

`git branch -a`

This is used to get all branches:

`git branch -r`

This is used for the remote tracking of branches.

Switching to New and Existing Branches

The process of moving from one branch to another is done by switching to [branch] and then setting the files in the index and working tree to reflect [branch]'s latest commit. Lastly, you must set the HEAD to branch:

> **Note**
>
> Modifications to the working tree are retained in case you wish to commit them in [branch].

`git checkout [branch_name]`

`git checkout -b [branch_name]`

`git branch -B [branch_name] [start_point]`

Create a new branch and set its tip to [start_point]. If the branch exists, then reset it to [start_point].

Switching to a Detached Head

Consider a rookie-day-one branch with the commits a-->b-->c. Commit a is the initial/first commit.

HEAD refers to a named branch. In this case, branch rookie-day-one refers to commit c.

a-->b-->c-->d

156 | Branches

In adding a new commit, d, to the branch, HEAD refers to branch rookie-day-one, which is updated to refer to commit d:

Example:

```
git checkout b
```

HEAD now points to commit b:

```
echo 'Test HEAD' >> a.txt
git add a.txt && git commit -m "Test"
echo 'Test HEAD' >> a.txt
git add a.txt && git commit -m "Test 2"
```

Adding changes and commits by extension changes HEAD to refer to commit f.

```
git checkout rookie-day-one
```

```
  e-->f
```


a-->b-->c-->d

The preceding command shifts HEAD back to a named branch, rookie-day-one.

As such, changes in commits e and f are discarded, given that no reference is created to point to the commit, for example, via the following:

```
git checkout -b sample
git branch sample
git tag v1.0
git checkout [commit_hash]
git checkout [tag]
git checkout --detach [branch]
```

This detaches HEAD from the specified branch and switches to the specified branch.

```
git checkout --detach [commit]
```

The preceding code detaches HEAD from the [commit] and updates the working tree and index to match the state at [commit].

Switching to a Specific Version of a File

When switching, the git check out command takes the following syntax:

```
git checkout [commit] -- [path]
```

Other uses of `git checkout` are as follows:

```
git checkout -b --orphan [new_branch] [start_point]
```

This creates a branch whereby the first commit has no parent. This is necessary when certain information contained in the repository's history needs to remain unexposed for privacy reasons.

Incorporating Changes with Stashing

In the book of development work, emerging requests are a typical occurrence, including in scenarios where you are attending a planned work stream over a specific period of time. The book of action in this scenario, normally, is to put aside what you're working on and attend to this request, be it an emergency or not.

How does Git enable you to "put away" what you're working on without losing the progress you'd achieved on a certain task? Ask no more.

In comes `git stash`. The `git stash` command temporarily moves staged, unstaged, or untracked modifications made to a repository, to and from the index and working directory.

To achieve this with `git stash`, use the following subcommands:

```
git stash push -m [message] or git stash push —message [message]
```

This saves modifications to a stash list and reverts the index and the working tree to the state reflected by HEAD.

The –keep-index option retains changes made to the index. This means that the modifications in the index are not reverted.

The –include-untracked option includes untracked files in the stash entry made to the stash list.

The –all option stashes ignored files in the stash entry made to the stash list.

> **Note**
>
> `git stash save` was deprecated in favor of this command.

git stash list

This command lists the entries in the stash list. These are all of the created stashes:

`Git stash show [stash_id]`

This command displays the changes introduced by the stash identified by `[stash_id]`.

`git stash apply [stash_id]`

This updates the working directory with the changes stored in `[stash_id]`.

`git stash pop [stash_id]`

This updates the working directory with the stash `[stash_id]` and removes it from the stash list.

`git stash drop [stash_id]`

This removes the specified stash from the stash list.

`git stash clear`

This removes all stashes from the stash list.

`git stash branch [branchname] [stash_id]`

> **Note**
> The stash list is available from every branch.

Merging

The order that the introduction of a change to a repository entails is as follows:

1. Creating a change branch off the main branch
2. Building the change
3. Unifying the change with the main branch

The exercise of merging is one of unifying the change into the main branch. This involves reconciling the divergent histories of the change branch and the feature branch, and creating a snapshot referenced by a commit to indicate the emergent result of incorporating the change branch.

A merge takes one of two modes, namely:
1. **Fast-forward merge**
2. **Three-way merge**

Where a merge is required from, branch-a to split, branch-b; in the event that there have been no changes in branch-a, Git adds the commits from branch-a to branch-b and updates the tip of branch-b (HEAD) to be the commit at the tip of branch-a. This is a fast-forward merge.

In merging two branches, that is, branch-a into branch-b, where there have been changes introduced into branch-b in the form of commits since branch-a was created off branch-b, that is, their shared ancestor, Git does the following:

1. Compares the files in the two branches from the point where they diverged
2. Reconciles the changes from both branches and merges incoming changes into the current branch by updating the index and working directory
3. Retains changes from both branches where differences cannot be resolved for the purpose of merge conflict resolution
4. Once the merge conflict (if any) is resolved, a merge commit is created to represent the incoming changes

This is a Three-way merge.

Merging is achieved by using the `git merge` command. This command uses the following syntax:

```
git merge [options] [branch_name]
```

`--no-commit`

This option merges changes into the current branch. However, the command does not create a merge commit in order to leave room for evaluating the result of the merge.

`--edit`

This option launches the editor to allow for editing of the generated commit message.

`--no-edit`

This conducts the merge using the message generated by the command.

`--no-ff`

This option creates a merge commit in all merge scenarios, including when the merge resolves to a fast-forward merge.

`--squash`

This option instructs `git merge` to update the index and working directory to reflect the incoming changes without creating a commit. Using this option enables you to create a commit as part of the current branch, thus referencing the incoming changes. With this option, the `HEAD` is not changed and the `MERGE_HEAD` ref is not recorded. As a result, the subsequent commit is not a merge commit.

`--strategy=[strategy]`

This specifies the merge strategy to be used for the merge.

The supported [strategy] includes

`--strategy-option=[strategy_option]`

This sets the option that's specific to the provided strategy.

Cherry-Pick

The `git cherry-pick` command takes a commit from one branch and applies the specified commit to another branch.

`git cherry-pick` is useful when you wish to check the effects of certain changes that have been introduced to a branch you're working on.

The syntax of the `git cherry-pick` command is a follows:

`git cherry-pick [options] [commit]`.

`git cherry-pick` supports options that dictate how the introduced commits are handled. This includes the following:

`-x`: This option adds a standardized message to the commit of the form "`cherry picked from commit ...`" to specify the commit that introduces the incoming change.

`--edit`: This allows you to edit the commit message for the incoming changes.

`--no-commit`: You may wish to integrate changes from a specific commit without creating a corresponding commit. The `--no-commit` command integrates changes from a commit without creating a commit.

`--mainline [parent_number]`: Since a parent commit possesses two parents, running a cherry-pick against a merge commit requires that a parent is specified. The given parent is compared to the merge tree of the merge commit and the resulting difference is introduced into the branch where `git cherry-pick` is invoked from.

Consider two branches, namely `branch-1` and branch-2.

Branch-1 implements the add-to-cart feature, while branch-2 implements a system-wide refactor.

From branch-1, you can merge branch-2:

```
git checkout branch-1
git merge branch-2
```

This creates a **merge commit.**

The merge commit corresponds to a merge tree that combines the changes implemented by branch-1 and the changes introduced by branch-2. This merge commit, as is the case with all merge commits, has two parents. Each parent represents the series of changes implemented in each branch.

The `--mainline` option requires that a parent is specified in order to indicate which of the two sets of changes should be incorporated when a merge commit is specified:

parent-1 is the last commit made in branch-1, that is, the add-to-cart implementation.

`parent-2` is the last commit made in branch-2, that is, the refactor.

Consider branch-3.

In this branch, we would like to test the effects of changes introduced by the merge commit in git check out branch-3.

Scenario 1

```
git cherry-pick -m 1 merge_commit
```

By specifying -m 1, we choose parent-1.

This is the difference, or `diff` in Git terms, between the merge tree of `merge_commit` and commit parent-1. This is the refactor.

As such, this command will introduce the changes that refactor the code base in branch-3.

Scenario 2

```
git cherry-pick -m 2 merge_commit
```

By specifying -m 2, we choose parent-2.

This is the difference, or diff in Git terms, between the merge tree of `merge_commit` and commit parent-2. This is the add-to-cart implementation.

162 | Branches

As such, this command will introduce, the changes that add the add-to-cart feature in branch-3.

Pull Request (PR)

A **pull request (PR)** is the culmination of a piece of work undertaken on a branch. A PR is an intent to merge. Pull requests are intended to avail the forum where changes that are to be made to a repository's main branch are accorded scrutiny. Consensus is arrived upon the completion of a satisfactory discussion on the modifications that are borne by the branch that seeks to introduce changes.

To gain a clear picture of the changes that a PR seeks to introduce, we need to check the diff between two branches. Let's take a look at how you can achieve this.

Exercise 25: Examining Branch Differences

To compare branches to establish impending changes, follow these steps:

1. Navigate to the abacus repository of your GitHub account, as shown in the following screenshot:

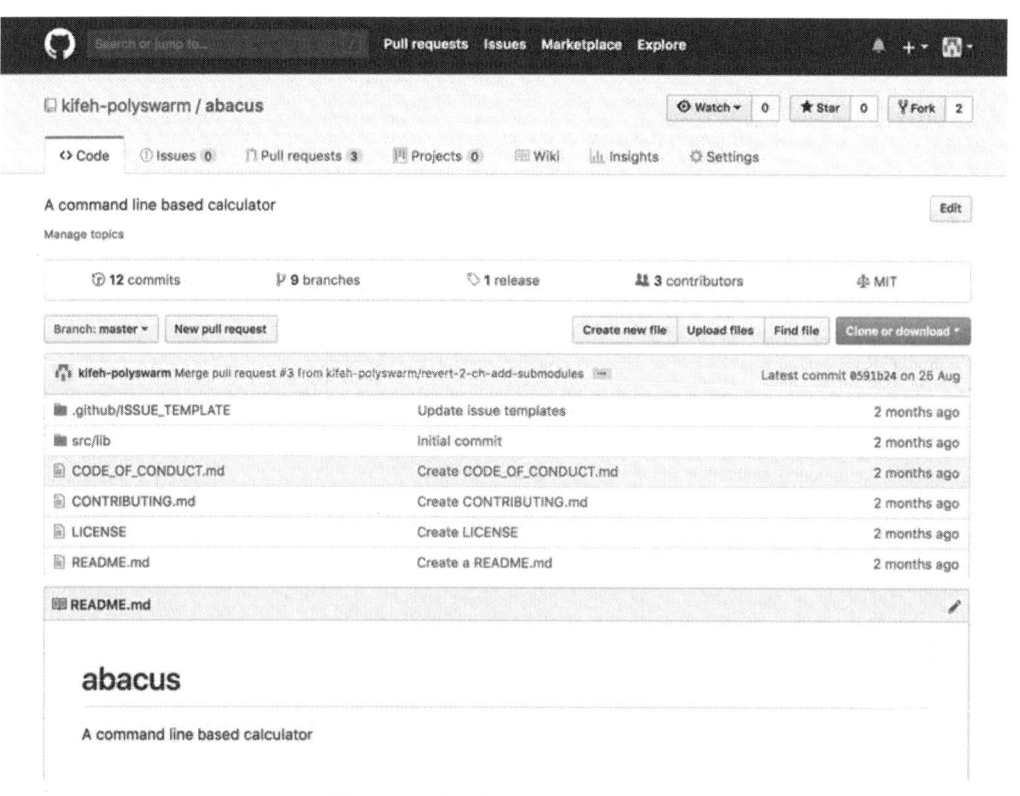

Figure 4.18: Abacus repository

2. On the branch selection drop down, select the ft-support-addition-tasks branch, as shown in the following screenshot:

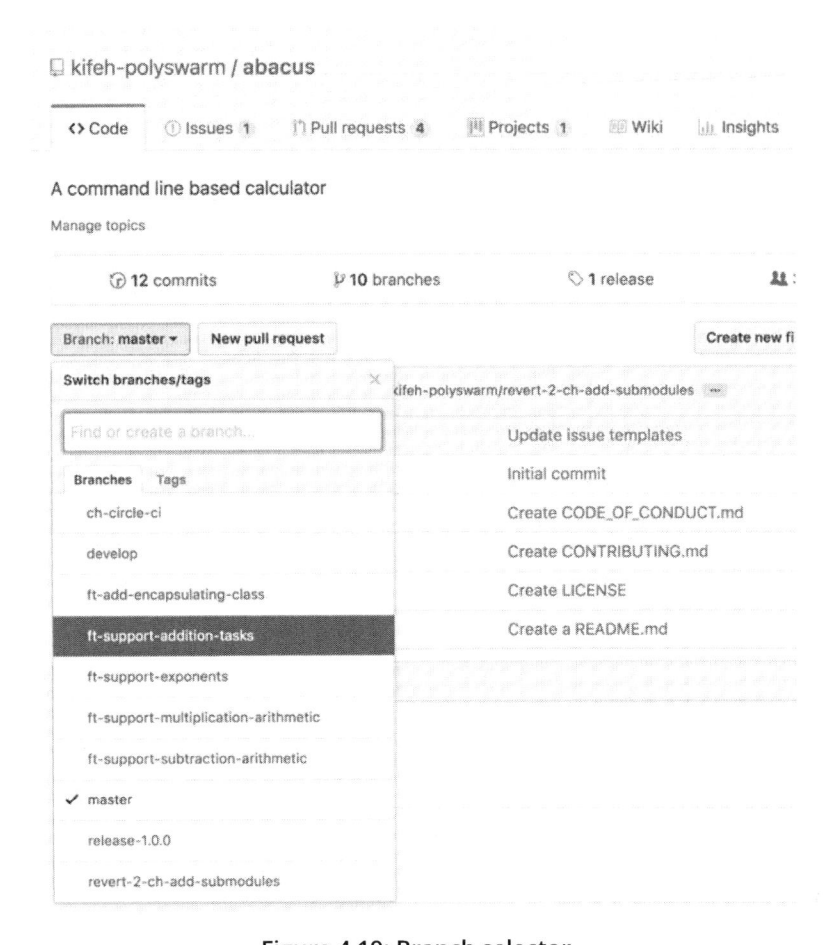

Figure 4.19: Branch selector

3. Click the **New pull request** button.

4. GitHub will redirect you to https://github.com/TrainingByPackt/Version-Control-with-Git-and-GitHub.

164 | Branches

5. GitHub will display additions using the + sign and deletions using the - sign, as shown in the following screenshot:

Figure 4.20: Branch selector

Outcome

By following the preceding steps, you should be able to identify the changes that a branch introduces into another branch through a merged pull request.

Pull Request Templates

In *Chapter 1-Introduction to Version Control*, we looked at the usage of **issue templates** to aid in the contribution process by setting a guideline for the process of the resolution of bug and feature requests. To ensure the seamless integration of changes being introduced to the primary branch of a repository, GitHub supports standardized pull requests by providing means for stating a format for pull requests. A template seeks to ensure that each pull request raised on the repository is clear in communicating what the potential change seeks to resolve. This lends itself to the appropriate discourse and comprehensive scrutiny, which in turn ensures that the result of the PR review process is a change that has been agreed upon by the relevant stakeholders. We shall now proceed and define a template that is to be used for raising a pull request.

> **Note**
>
> The pull request template must adhere to the following canons:
>
> 1. The template should be stored in a repository's default branch.
>
> 2. The template should be stored in the repository's `root` directory, the `docs` directory, or the hidden `.github` directory.

Exercise 26: Standardizing Procedures through Ordered Templates

To demonstrate the usage of templates in raising pull requests and organizing the application's pipeline, follow these steps:

1. Navigate to the `abacus` repository on your computer and check out to the branch master.

2. Create a branch called `ch-add-pr-template` and switch to it using the following code:

```
git branch ch-add-pr-template
git checkout ch-add-pr-template
```

3. Add the template to the root directory by using the `touch PULL_REQUEST_TEMPLATE.md` command:

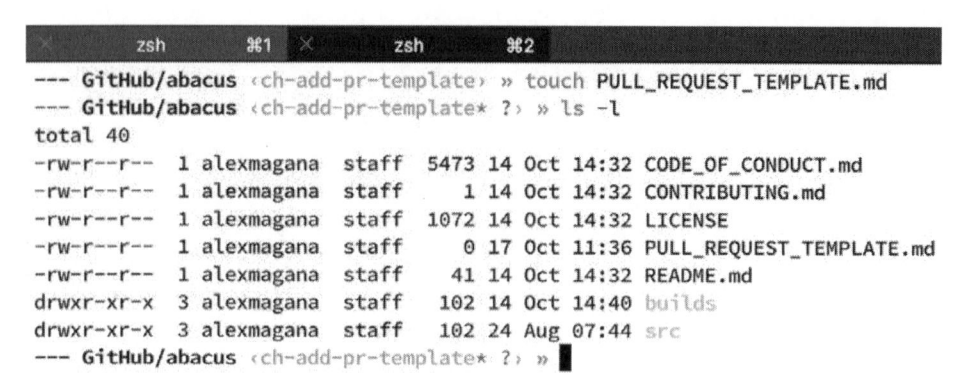

```
   x        zsh       ⌘1   X       zsh       ⌘2
--- GitHub/abacus ‹ch-add-pr-template› » touch PULL_REQUEST_TEMPLATE.md
--- GitHub/abacus ‹ch-add-pr-template* ?› » ls -l
total 40
-rw-r--r--  1 alexmagana  staff  5473 14 Oct 14:32 CODE_OF_CONDUCT.md
-rw-r--r--  1 alexmagana  staff     1 14 Oct 14:32 CONTRIBUTING.md
-rw-r--r--  1 alexmagana  staff  1072 14 Oct 14:32 LICENSE
-rw-r--r--  1 alexmagana  staff     0 17 Oct 11:36 PULL_REQUEST_TEMPLATE.md
-rw-r--r--  1 alexmagana  staff    41 14 Oct 14:32 README.md
drwxr-xr-x  3 alexmagana  staff   102 14 Oct 14:40 builds
drwxr-xr-x  3 alexmagana  staff   102 24 Aug 07:44 src
--- GitHub/abacus ‹ch-add-pr-template* ?› »
```

Figure 4.21: Branch selector

4. Open the `PULL_REQUEST_TEMPLATE.md` template on your editor of choice.
5. Add the earlier template text to the file and save it.

> **Note**
>
> What issue does this pull request correspond to?
>
> What is the acceptance criteria for the proposed solution?
>
> #### Merging Checklist
>
> - [ ] PR approved
>
> - [ ] All checks pass
>
> - [ ] Manual tests approved

6. Stage the file, and commit and push it to the remote branch using the following code:

```
git add PULL_REQUEST_TEMPLATE.md
git commit -m "Add pull request template"
git push origin ch-add-pr-template
```

```
--- GitHub/abacus ‹ch-add-pr-template* ?› » git add PULL_REQUEST_TEMPLATE.md
--- GitHub/abacus ‹ch-add-pr-template* A› » git commit -m "Add pull request template"
[ch-add-pr-template 082b752] Add pull request template
 1 file changed, 8 insertions(+)
 create mode 100644 PULL_REQUEST_TEMPLATE.md
--- GitHub/abacus ‹ch-add-pr-template› » git push origin ch-add-pr-template
Counting objects: 14, done.
Delta compression using up to 4 threads.
Compressing objects: 100% (12/12), done.
Writing objects: 100% (14/14), 1.64 KiB | 839.00 KiB/s, done.
Total 14 (delta 5), reused 0 (delta 0)
remote: Resolving deltas: 100% (5/5), completed with 3 local objects.
remote:
remote: Create a pull request for 'ch-add-pr-template' on GitHub by visiting:
remote:      https://github.com/kifeh-polyswarm/abacus/pull/new/ch-add-pr-template
remote:
To github.com:kifeh-polyswarm/abacus.git
 * [new branch]      ch-add-pr-template -> ch-add-pr-template
--- GitHub/abacus ‹ch-add-pr-template› »
```

Figure 4.22: Staging the file

7. Raise a pull request and merge it as shown in the following screenshots:

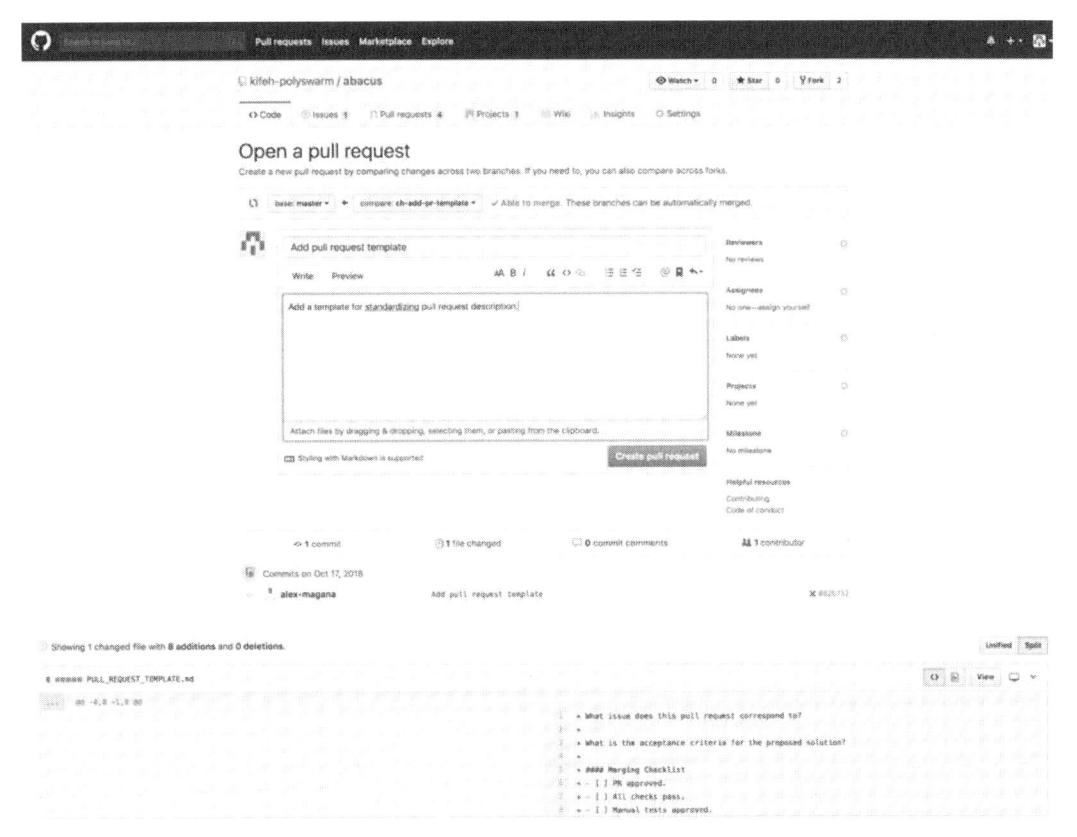

Figure 4.23: Raising a pull request

168 | Branches

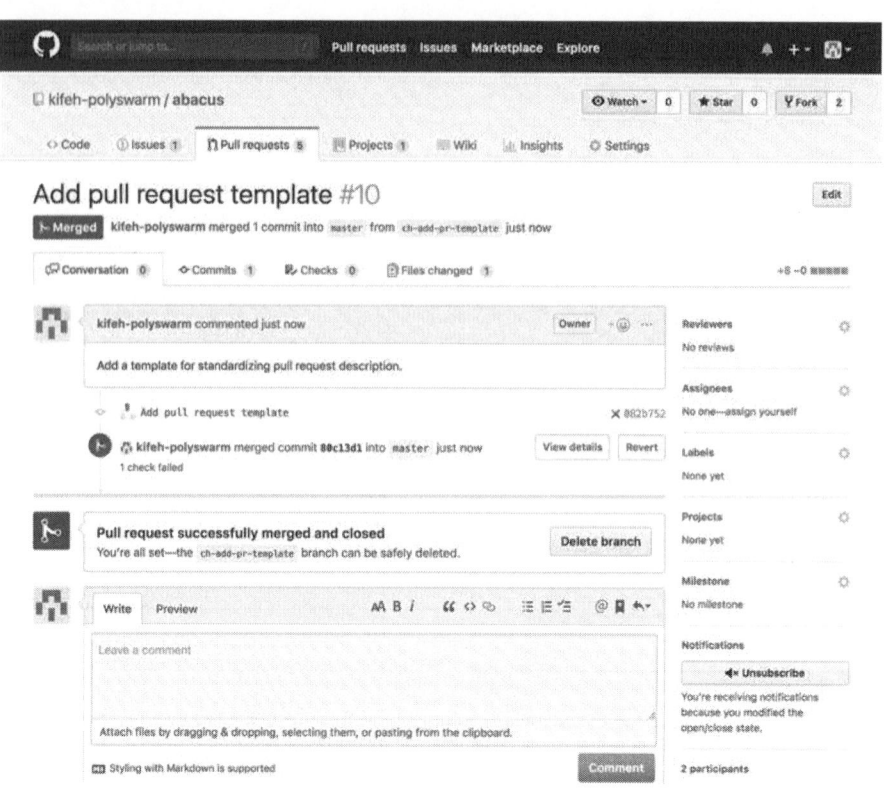

Figure 4.24: Adding a pull request

8. To observe the template in action, retrieve the changes from the remote branch `master`, check out a new branch, and make the following edit in the `README.md` file using the following code:

```
git checkout master
git pull origin master
git checkout -b ch-add-usage-instructions
```

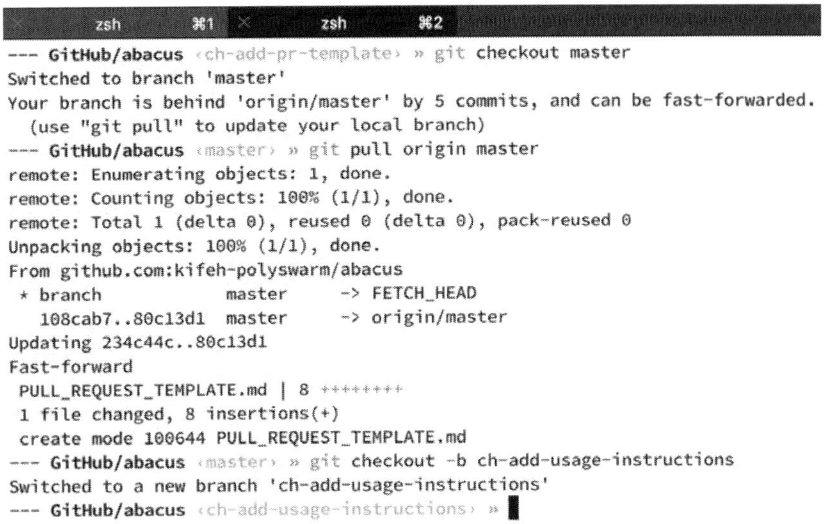

Figure 4.25: Adding a pull request

9. Use the following sub-steps:

> **Note**
> Getting started:
>
> 1. git clone git@github.com:[username]/abacus.git.
>
> 2. Navigate to the repository location.
>
> 3. Run python bin/runner.py.

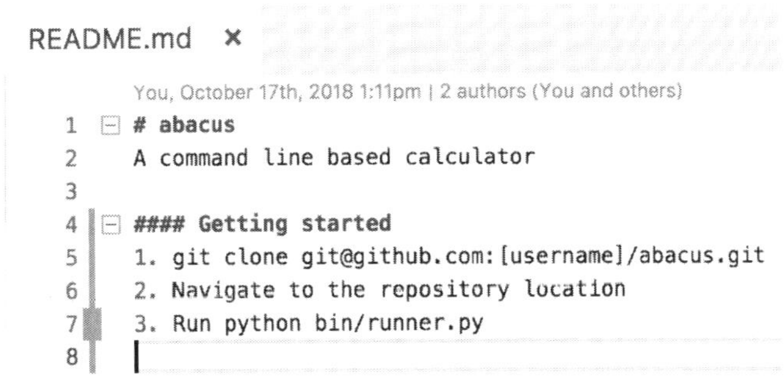

Figure 4.26: The README.md file

170 | Branches

10. Stage the change, and commit and push it to the remote branch using the following code:

    git add README.md

    git commit -m "Add usage instructions"

    git push origin ch-add-usage-instructions

```
--- GitHub/abacus (ch-add-usage-instructions) » git add README.md
--- GitHub/abacus (ch-add-usage-instructions* M) » git commit -m "Add usage instructions"
[ch-add-usage-instructions 31a1bd9] Add usage instructions
 1 file changed, 5 insertions(+)
--- GitHub/abacus (ch-add-usage-instructions) » git push origin ch-add-usage-instructions
Counting objects: 3, done.
Delta compression using up to 4 threads.
Compressing objects: 100% (3/3), done.
Writing objects: 100% (3/3), 404 bytes | 404.00 KiB/s, done.
Total 3 (delta 1), reused 0 (delta 0)
remote: Resolving deltas: 100% (1/1), completed with 1 local object.
remote:
remote: Create a pull request for 'ch-add-usage-instructions' on GitHub by visiting:
remote:      https://github.com/kifeh-polyswarm/abacus/pull/new/ch-add-usage-instructions
remote:
To github.com:kifeh-polyswarm/abacus.git
 * [new branch]      ch-add-usage-instructions -> ch-add-usage-instructions
--- GitHub/abacus (ch-add-usage-instructions) »
```

Figure 4.27: Staging the change

11. Raise a pull request. On the page where you provide details of the pull request, add the usage instructions, as seen in the screenshots below:

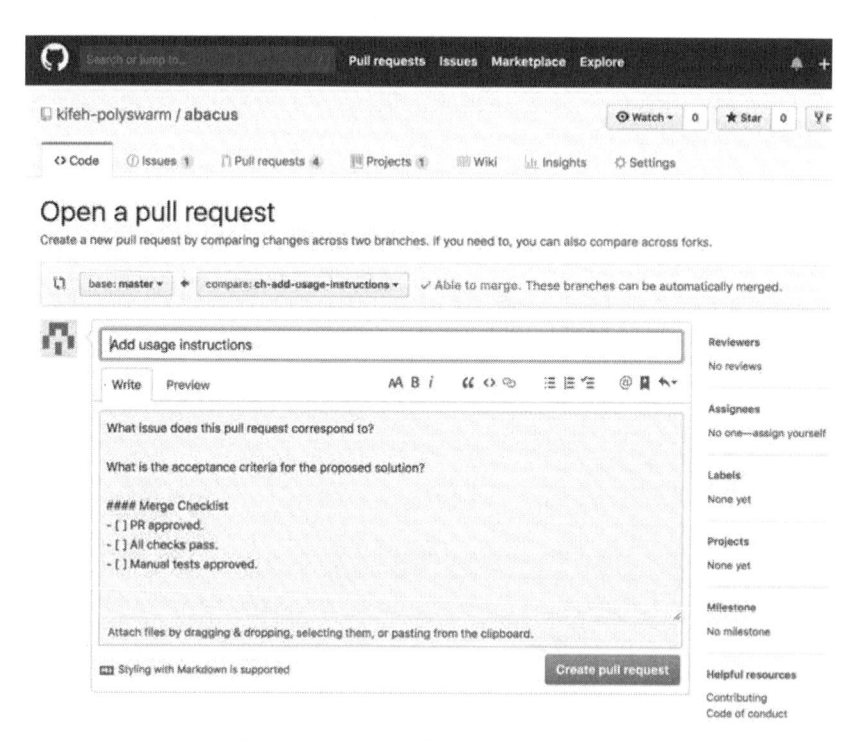

Figure 4.28: Opening a pull request

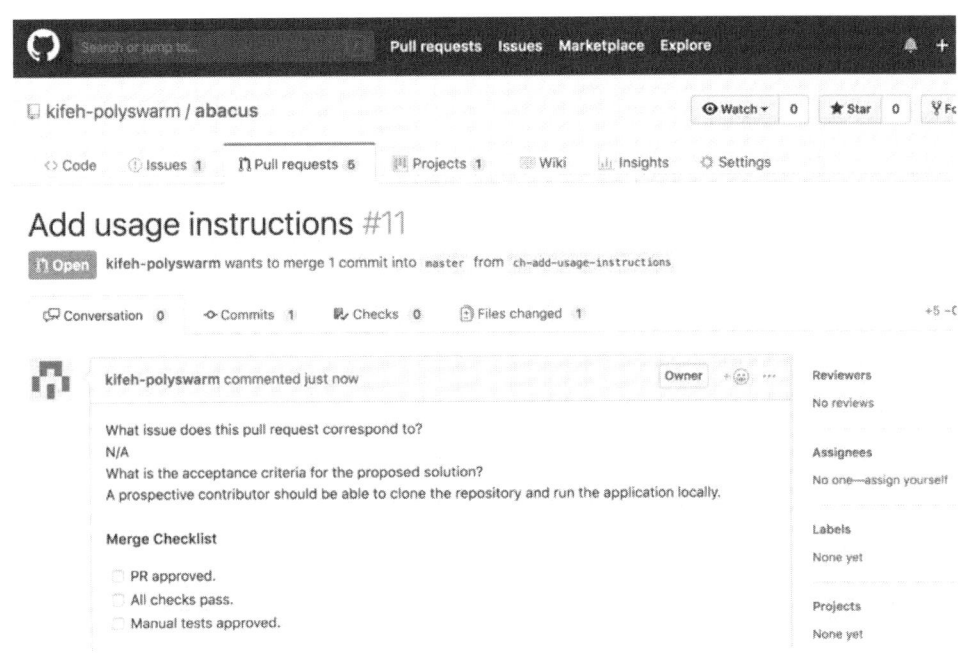

[Figure 4.29: Adding usage instructions]

Outcome

By following this exercise, you should be able to outline the steps that need to be adhered to for a pull request to be merged. Additionally, you should be able to lay out the format that a pull request's description follows.

Identifying and Fixing Merge Issues

As part of incorporating changes, certain checks need to pass for a pull request to be merged. These checks vary from repository to repository. In this section, we will explore failed status checks and merge conflicts.

Failed Status Checks

A PR may execute unit tests as part of a pre-merge sanity check. To proceed with the merging of PR, you need to ensure that the set checks pass. In this scenario, this means ensuring that unit and integration tests pass in the CI/CD builds.

As demonstrated in the following screenshot, failed checks need to pass for a merge to be conducted:

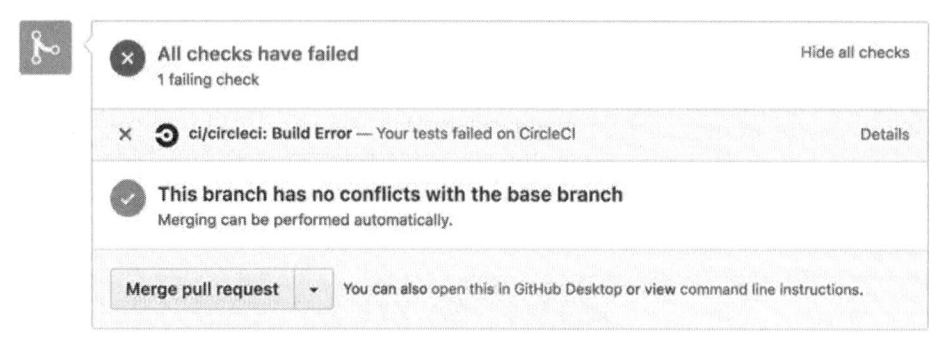

Figure 4.30: Failed check status

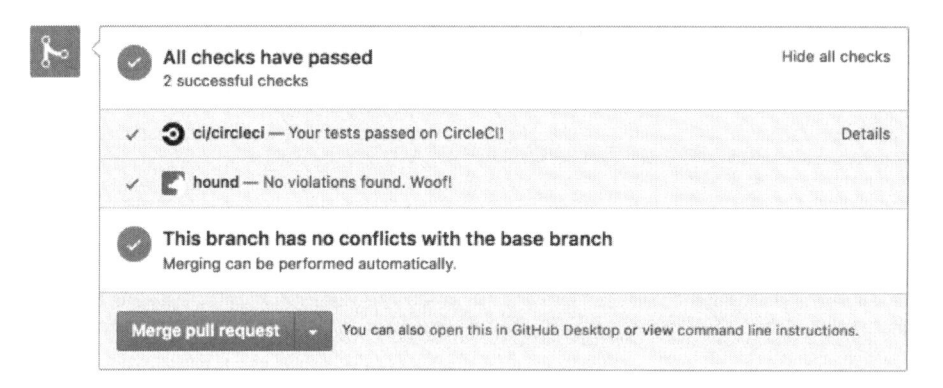

Figure 4.31: Passed check status

In *Chapter 6: Automated Testing and Release Management*, we will look into configuring tests that are to be triggered when we create pull requests and rectify failed builds when they occur.

Merge Conflicts

A **merge conflict** is a term that depicts an issue whereby modifications made in separate branches can't be amalgamated into one unit of change or modification.

A merge conflict will occur when:

1. Modifications are made on the same line of a file.

2. Changes are made to a file on one branch and the same file is deleted on another branch.

Merge conflict resolution encompasses picking which of the differing sets of changes should be used in a merge process.

Exercise 27: Merge Conflict Resolution

To demonstrate merge conflicts that are the result of multiple contributors changing the same line in a file, follow these steps:

1. Navigate to the location of the abacus repository. Ensure that you are on the master branch.

2. Create a branch and check out to it using the `git checkout -b conflict-branch-1` command, as shown in the following screenshot:

```
--- GitHub/abacus ‹master› » git checkout -b conflict-branch-1
Switched to a new branch 'conflict-branch-1'
--- GitHub/abacus ‹conflict-branch-1› »
```

Figure 4.32: Creating a branch

3. Open the `PULL_REQUEST_TEMPLATE.md` file and add the following text between line 7 and line 8. Line 8 should read - **[ ] Architecture changes approved**:

```
1     What issue does this pull request correspond to?
2
3     What is the acceptance criteria for the proposed solution?
4
5     #### Merging Checklist
6     - [ ] PR approved.
7     - [ ] All checks pass.
8     - [ ] Architecture changes approved.
9     - [ ] Manual tests approved.
10
```

Figure 4.33: Opening the pull request template

4. Stage and commit the change using the following code:

git add PULL_REQUEST_TEMPLATE.md

git commit -m "Add PR instructions"

```
--- GitHub/abacus ‹conflict-branch-1› » git add PULL_REQUEST_TEMPLATE.md
--- GitHub/abacus ‹conflict-branch-1* M› » git commit -m "Add PR instructions"
[conflict-branch-1 f36a6fd] Add PR instructions
 1 file changed, 1 insertion(+)
```

Figure 4.34: Staging and committing the change

5. Switch to the branch master. Create a branch called conflict-branch-2 and check out to this branch using the following code:

git checkout master

git checkout -b conflict-branch-2

```
--- GitHub/abacus ‹conflict-branch-1› » git checkout master
Switched to branch 'master'
Your branch is up to date with 'origin/master'.
--- GitHub/abacus ‹master› » git checkout -b conflict-branch-2
Switched to a new branch 'conflict-branch-2'
--- GitHub/abacus ‹conflict-branch-2› »
```

Figure 4.35: Switching to the branch master

6. Open the PULL_REQUEST_TEMPLATE.md file and edit line 8 to read "- [ ] Manual tests approved and test screenshots attached" as follows:

```
1    What issue does this pull request correspond to?
2
3    What is the acceptance criteria for the proposed solution?
4
5    #### Merging Checklist
6    - [ ] PR approved.
7    - [ ] All checks pass.
8    - [ ] Manual tests approved and test screenshots attached.
9
```

Figure 4.36: Opening the pull request

7. Stage and commit the change using the following code:

```
git add PULL_REQUEST_TEMPLATE.md
git commit -m "Modify PR checklist"
```

```
--- GitHub/abacus ‹conflict-branch-2› » git add PULL_REQUEST_TEMPLATE.md
--- GitHub/abacus ‹conflict-branch-2* M› » git commit -m "Modify PR checklist"
[conflict-branch-2 b74fed2] Modify PR checklist
 1 file changed, 1 insertion(+), 1 deletion(-)
--- GitHub/abacus ‹conflict-branch-2› »
```

Figure 4.37: Staging and committing the change

8. Switch to the conflict-branch-1 branch and merge the changes from conflict-branch-2 using the following code:

```
git checkout conflict-branch-1
git merge conflict-branch-2
```

> **Note**
>
> On the terminal, you will see the following message, indicating conflicting sets of changes:

```
--- GitHub/abacus ‹conflict-branch-2› » git checkout conflict-branch-1
Switched to branch 'conflict-branch-1'
--- GitHub/abacus ‹conflict-branch-1› » git merge conflict-branch-2
Auto-merging PULL_REQUEST_TEMPLATE.md
CONFLICT (content): Merge conflict in PULL_REQUEST_TEMPLATE.md
Automatic merge failed; fix conflicts and then commit the result.
--- GitHub/abacus ‹conflict-branch-1* UU› »
```

Figure 4.38: Switching to the branch

176 | Branches

9. Open `PULL_REQUEST_TEMPLATE.md` in your editor, as shown in the following screenshot:

```
 1    What issue does this pull request correspond to?
 2
 3    What is the acceptance criteria for the proposed solution?
 4
 5    #### Merging Checklist
 6    - [ ] PR approved.
 7    - [ ] All checks pass.
                  Accept Current Change | Accept Incoming Change | Accept Both Changes | Compare Changes
 8    <<<<<<< HEAD (Current Change)
 9    - [ ] Architecture changes approved.
10    - [ ] Manual tests approved.
11    =======
12    - [ ] Manual tests approved and test screenshots attached.
13    >>>>>>> conflict-branch-2 (Incoming Change)
14
```

Figure 4.39: Opening the pull request template

> **Note**
>
> Take a look at the format to be used:
>
> <<<<<<< HEAD
>
> Content in current branch
>
> =======
>
> Content from the incoming branch
>
> \>>>>>>>

10. Edit the file to accept either of the sets of changes or both sets of changes, shown as follows:

```
1     What issue does this pull request correspond to?
2
3     What is the acceptance criteria for the proposed solution?
4
5     #### Merging Checklist
6     - [ ] PR approved.
7     - [ ] All checks pass.
8     - [ ] Architecture changes approved.
9     - [ ] Manual tests approved and test screenshots attached.
10
```

Figure 4.40: Editing the file

11. Stage the file and commit the change using the following code:

```
git add PULL_REQUEST_TEMPLATE.md
git commit -m "Merge conflicting edits"
```

```
--- GitHub/abacus ‹conflict-branch-1* UU› » git add PULL_REQUEST_TEMPLATE.md
--- GitHub/abacus ‹conflict-branch-1* M› » git commit -m "Merge conflicting edits"
[conflict-branch-1 dc43a83] Merge conflicting edits
--- GitHub/abacus ‹conflict-branch-1› » 
```

Figure 4.41: Staging the file

Outcome

Having followed these steps, you should be able to resolve a merge conflict that encompasses competing changes on the same line of a single file.

Exercise 28: Resolving Conflicts

To demonstrate merge conflicts that are the result of the removal of a file in one branch and the changing of a file's content in another branch, follow these steps:

1. Navigate to the location of the abacus repository. Ensure that you are on the master branch.

2. Create a new branch and check out to it using `git checkout -b conflict-branch-3` as shown in the following screenshot:

```
--- GitHub/abacus <master> » git checkout -b conflict-branch-3
Switched to a new branch 'conflict-branch-3'
--- GitHub/abacus <conflict-branch-3> »
```

Figure 4.42: Staging the file

3. Open the `PULL_REQUEST_TEMPLATE.md` file and add the following text between line 7 and line 8. Line 8 should read "- [ ] Architecture changes approved":

```
1     What issue does this pull request correspond to?
2
3     What is the acceptance criteria for the proposed solution?
4
5     #### Merging Checklist
6     - [ ] PR approved.
7     - [ ] All checks pass.
8     - [ ] Architecture changes approved.
9     - [ ] Manual tests approved.
10
```

Figure 4.43: opening and pulling the request template

4. Stage and commit the change using the following code:

`git add PULL_REQUEST_TEMPLATE.md`

`git commit -m "Add PR instructions"`

```
--- GitHub/abacus <conflict-branch-3> » git checkout master
Switched to branch 'master'
Your branch is up to date with 'origin/master'.
--- GitHub/abacus <master> » git checkout -b conflict-branch-4
Switched to a new branch 'conflict-branch-4'
--- GitHub/abacus <conflict-branch-4> »
```

Figure 4.44: Opening the pull request template

5. Switch to the branch master. Create a branch called `conflict-branch-3` and check out to this branch using the following code:

```
git checkout master
git checkout -b conflict-branch-4
```

```
--- GitHub/abacus ‹conflict-branch-4› » git rm PULL_REQUEST_TEMPLATE.md
rm 'PULL_REQUEST_TEMPLATE.md'
--- GitHub/abacus ‹conflict-branch-4* D› » git commit -m "Remove pull request template"
[conflict-branch-4 b9b8a04] Remove pull request template
 1 file changed, 8 deletions(-)
 delete mode 100644 PULL_REQUEST_TEMPLATE.md
--- GitHub/abacus ‹conflict-branch-4› »
```

Figure 4.45: Switching to the branch master

6. Stage and commit the change using the following code:

```
git checkout conflict-branch-3
git merge conflict-branch-4
```

> **Note**
>
> In the Terminal, you will see the following message, indicating conflicting sets of changes:

```
--- GitHub/abacus ‹conflict-branch-4› » git checkout conflict-branch-3
Switched to branch 'conflict-branch-3'
--- GitHub/abacus ‹conflict-branch-3› » git merge conflict-branch-4
CONFLICT (modify/delete): PULL_REQUEST_TEMPLATE.md deleted in conflict-branch-4 and modified in HEAD. Version HEAD of PULL_REQUEST_TEMPLATE.md left in tree.
Automatic merge failed; fix conflicts and then commit the result.
--- GitHub/abacus ‹conflict-branch-3*› » git status
On branch conflict-branch-3
You have unmerged paths.
  (fix conflicts and run "git commit")
  (use "git merge --abort" to abort the merge)

Unmerged paths:
  (use "git add/rm <file>..." as appropriate to mark resolution)

        deleted by them: PULL_REQUEST_TEMPLATE.md

no changes added to commit (use "git add" and/or "git commit -a")
--- GitHub/abacus ‹conflict-branch-3*› »
```

Figure 4.47: Switching the branch

7. Stage the file and commit the change using the following code, and as seen in the following screenshot:

```
git add PULL_REQUEST_TEMPLATE.md
or    git rm PULL_REQUEST_TEMPLATE.md
then       git commit -m "Merge conflicting edits"
```

```
--- GitHub/abacus ‹conflict-branch-3*› » git rm PULL_REQUEST_TEMPLATE.md
PULL_REQUEST_TEMPLATE.md: needs merge
rm 'PULL_REQUEST_TEMPLATE.md'
--- GitHub/abacus ‹conflict-branch-3* D› » git commit -m "Merge conflicting edits"
[conflict-branch-3 7956c7f] Merge conflicting edits
--- GitHub/abacus ‹conflict-branch-3› » ▮
```

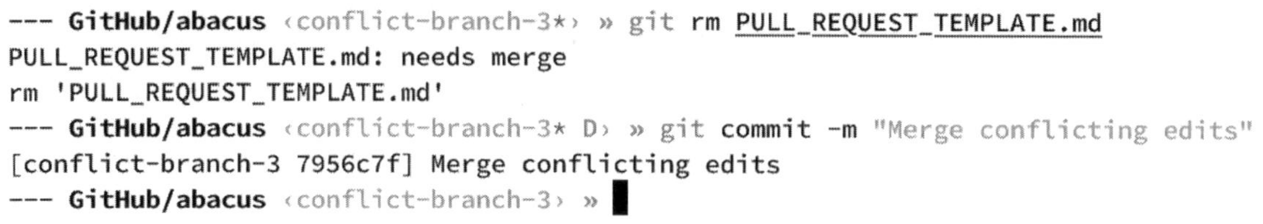

Figure 4.48: Stage the file

Outcome

Following the preceding steps should enable you to resolve a merge conflict where the competing changes are the removal of a file in one branch and the modification of the same file in another branch.

Merging and Reverting Pull Requests

With the prospective changes approved and all of the checks having been successful, a PR may be merged.

There are three modes available for merging pull requests, as shown in the following screenshot:

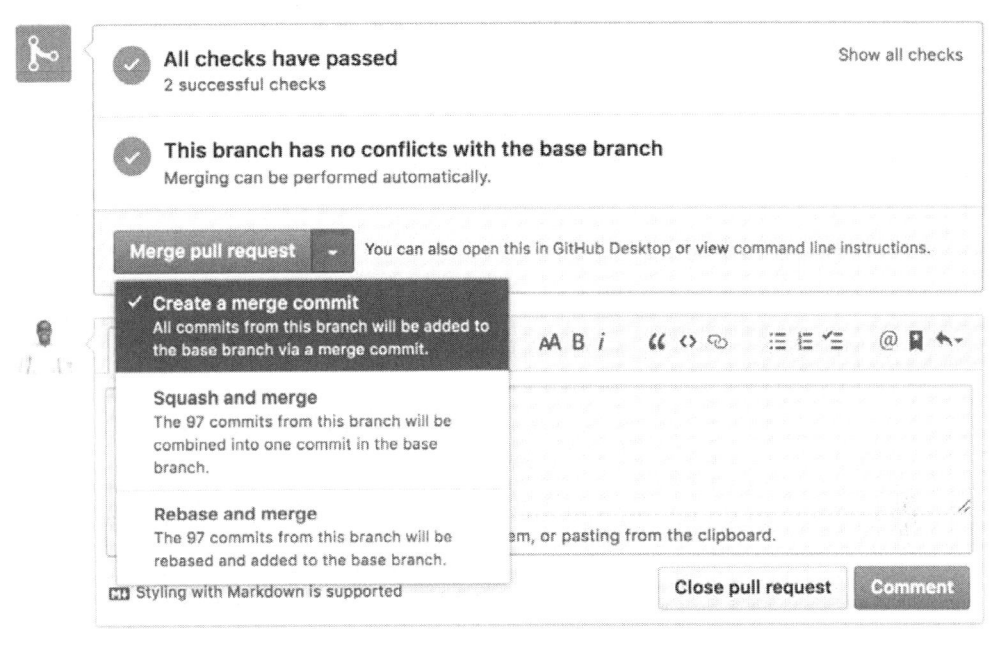

Figure 4.49: Available modes

Consider a PR merging the feature-1 branch to the master branch:

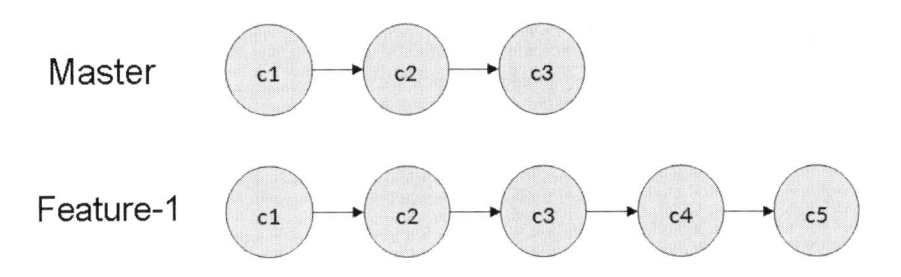

Figure 4.50: PR Merging

Merge Commit

This mode adds commits c4 and c5 to the branch master using a unifying commit, c6, referred to as a merge commit. This is a non-fast-forward mode:

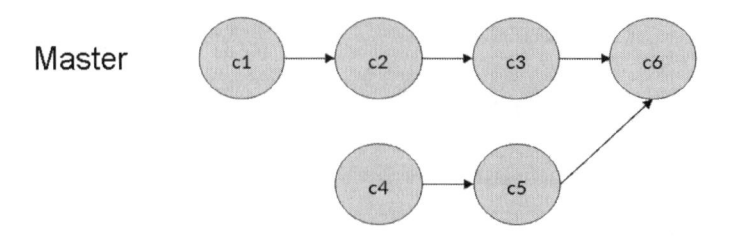

Figure 4.51: Merge Commit

Squash and Merge

Commits c4 and c5 are combined into a single commit, c6. The c6 command is then merged in the fast-forward mode:

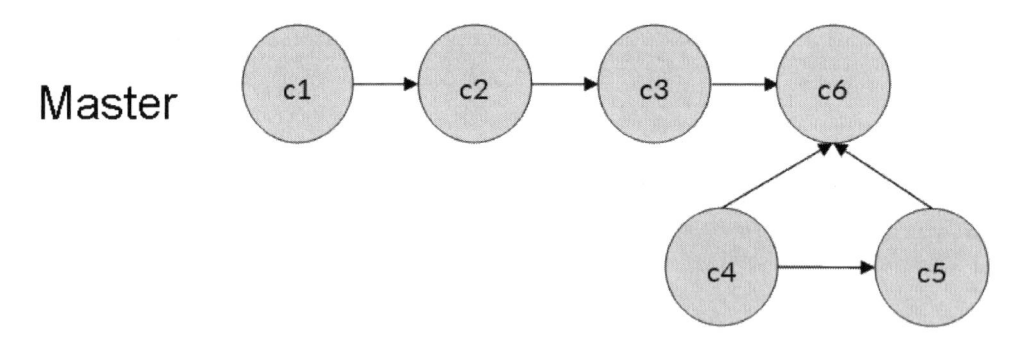

Figure 4.52: Squash and Merge

Rebase and Merge

In this mode, each commit from the feature-1 branch is added to the branch master without the use of a merge commit:

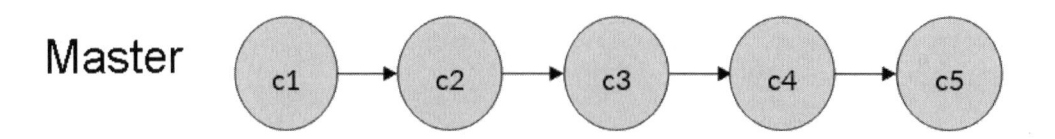

Figure 4.53: Rebase and Merge

Exercise 29: Pull Request Reversal

To establish the process of reversing a merged pull request, follow these steps:

1. Navigate to the location of the abacus repository locally.

2. Switch to the conflict-branch-1 branch and push the branch to the remote repository using the following code:

   ```
   git checkout conflict-branch-1
   git push origin conflict-branch-1
   ```

```
--- GitHub/abacus <master> » git checkout conflict-branch-1
Switched to branch 'conflict-branch-1'
--- GitHub/abacus <conflict-branch-1> » git push origin conflict-branch-1
Counting objects: 9, done.
Delta compression using up to 4 threads.
Compressing objects: 100% (9/9), done.
Writing objects: 100% (9/9), 812 bytes | 812.00 KiB/s, done.
Total 9 (delta 7), reused 0 (delta 0)
remote: Resolving deltas: 100% (7/7), completed with 2 local objects.
remote:
remote: Create a pull request for 'conflict-branch-1' on GitHub by visiting:
remote:      https://github.com/kifeh-polyswarm/abacus/pull/new/conflict-branch-1
remote:
To github.com:kifeh-polyswarm/abacus.git
 * [new branch]      conflict-branch-1 -> conflict-branch-1
--- GitHub/abacus <conflict-branch-1> »
```

Figure 4.54: Switching the branch

184 | Branches

3. In your browser, go to https://github.com/kifeh-polyswarm/abacus/compare/conflict-branch-1?expand=1 to raise a pull request:

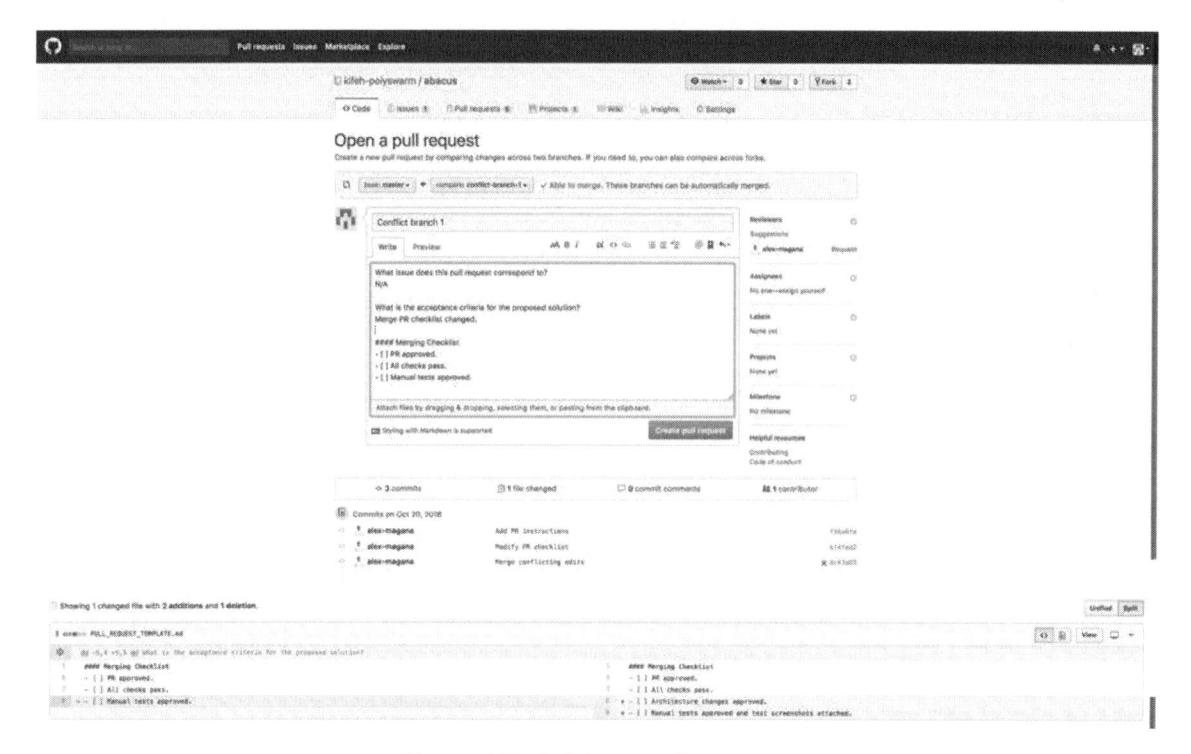

Figure 4.55: Raising a pull request

4. Merge the pull request.
5. To revert the pull request, go to a pull request. In this case, this is https://github.com/kifeh-polyswarm/abacus/pull/12.

6. Click the **Revert** button, as shown in the following screenshot:

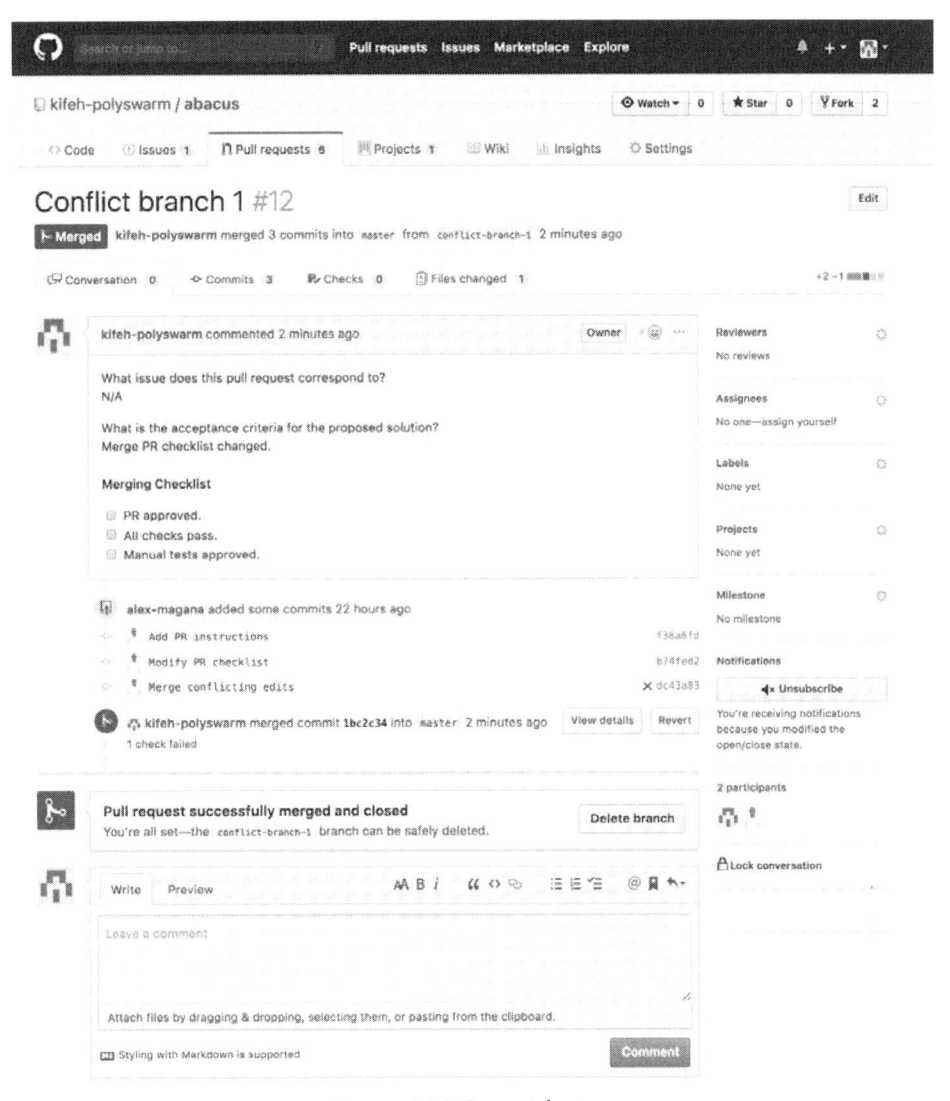

Figure 4.56: Revert button

> **Note**
>
> Clicking this button redirects you to a page so that you can create a revert commit.

7. Create the revert PR and merge it as shown in the following screenshot:

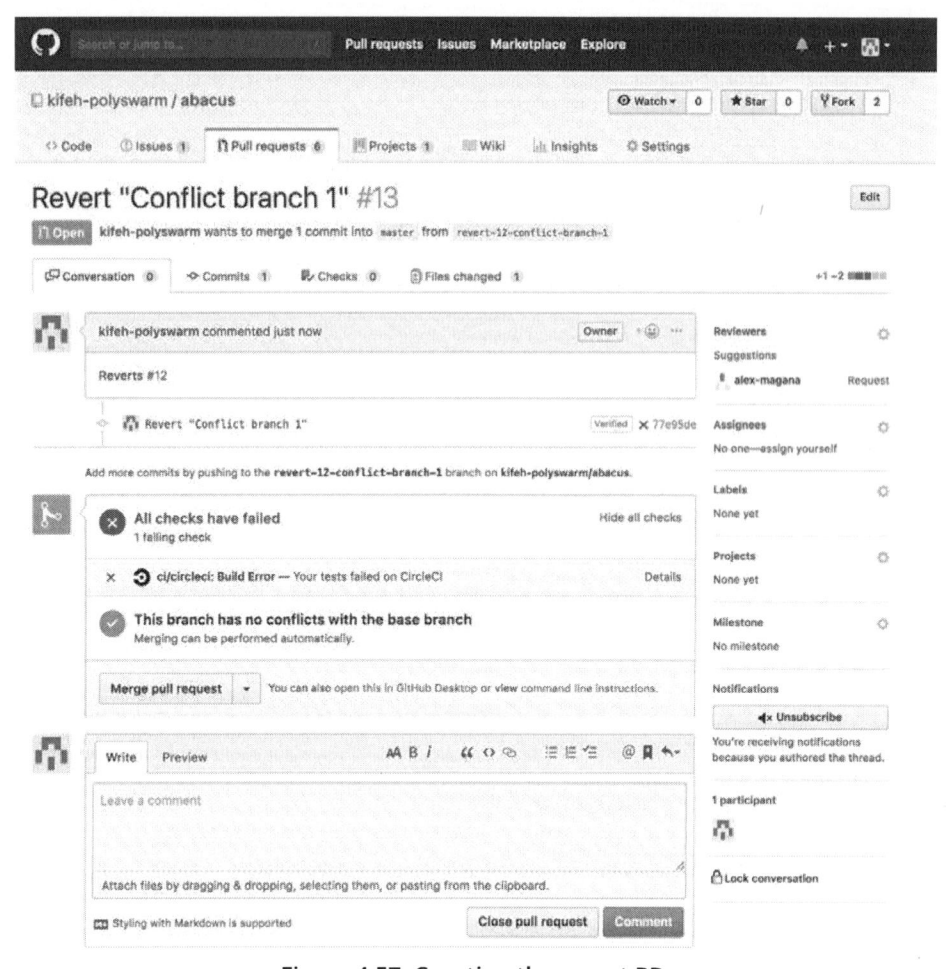

Figure 4.57: Creating the revert PR

Outcome

Having followed these steps, you should be able to create a pull request and reverse changes once a pull request has been merged.

Activity 4: Managing Branches and Experimentation with Selective Changes

You have been tasked with adding capabilities for computing speed and distance to your company's application. The features need to be handled separately and merged as a single work stream. You need to raise a pull request of the `release-candidate` branch you created in the activity in *Topic 1: Utilizing Workflows*. Merge the pull request once the changes have been approved. This is required since the tasks in this activity are a continuation of the work done in the activity in *Topic 1: Utilizing Workflows*.

The aim of this activity is to demonstrate being able to handle branches.

To start this activity, you need to have the Git command-line tool installed on your computer. Then, you need to have an account on https://github.com/. You should be logged into your account on GitHub. Lastly, you should have the **abacus** application repository on GitHub and your computer:

1. Open the browser and navigate to the abacus repository to raise a pull request.
2. Provide the appropriate description of the purpose of the pull request.
3. Edit the rule associated with the branch **master** and save the changes.
4. Merge the pull request on the page you're directed to.
5. Open the terminal on your computer and navigate to the location of the abacus repository.
6. Retrieve the changes for the remote master branch.
7. Create a branch called **ft-speed** to implement the speed computation feature.
8. Edit the speed method as required.
9. Stage the changes made on **src/lib/util/util.py /** and commit the changes.
10. Create a branch to compute the distance, given a speed and time.
11. Retrieve the available stash list entries and apply the changes of the relevant stash to the working directory.
12. Delete the stash from the stash entry.
13. Stage the changes and commit them.
14. List the branches to obtain the names
15. Switch to the **ft-compute-speed** branch and create a branch called **bg-speed-calc** to resolve the bug and switch to the branch.
16. Edit the **speed** method.
17. Switch to the **ft-compute-distance** branch and create a branch called **ft-distance-arguments** to resolve the bug and switch to the branch.
18. Edit the **distance** method.
19. Rename **bg-speed-calc** and **fx-distance-arguments**.
20. Delete the **ft-compute-distance** and **ft-compute-speed** branches.

21. To explore the difference in the `distance` method, check out to the revision prior to the point at which you introduced the fix in the method.
22. Switch back to the `ft-compute-calc` branch and create a branch named `util-milestone`.
23. In `src/lib/util/util.py`, edit the file as required.
24. Integrate the functionality to compute speed.
25. Resolve the merge conflict by editing `src/lib/util/util.py` to adopt the incoming change.
26. Merge the changes.
27. To conclude this task, we need to include a function to calculate time.
28. Stage the changes and commit them.
29. Obtain the hash commit for use in the next step.
30. Push the change to the remote repository.
31. Visit https://github.com/ [username]/abacus/compare/util-milestone?expand=1 to raise a pull request.

Outcome

The activity in the culmination of this topic should enable you to navigate branches as well as the snapshots represented by their respective commits.

> **Note**
>
> For detailed steps for this activity, refer to the **Appendix** section on page 294.

Summary

In this chapter, you used the feature-branch workflow to implement units of work through branches. This workflow has also introduced you to the naming convention utilized to identify the nature of work a branch delivers. Using the `git branch` command, you've created, listed, and deleted branches. We've explored how to navigate different revisions of a repository and utilized the same revisions to selectively integrate changes into branches. We then looked at how to manage unstaged changes in the working directory. Lastly, we shipped the changes we've introduced by comparing branches, raising pull requests to merge desired changes, and reverting the changes where necessary.

In the next chapter, you will develop collaboratively on a remote repository, build application artifacts, and automate testing on GitHub. Additionally, you will develop new software version releases.

5
Collaborative Git

Learning Objectives

By the end of this chapter, you will be able to:

- Develop collaboratively on a remote repository, among other contributors
- Test and inspect code effectively
- Build application artifacts and automate testing on GitHub
- Develop new software version releases

This chapter describes the forking of repositories, rebasing and utilizing Gitmodules.

192 | Collaborative Git

Introduction

In the previous chapter, we went over a variety of fundamental Git modules and workflows, ranging from setting up repositories to making pull requests.

In this chapter, we are going to delve deeper into more Git commands and collaborative workflows. As an individual, you may have encountered public repositories, some labeled open source and some just belonging to different developers. This chapter provides an overview of housekeeping, and explains how to effectively work with highly engaging distributed teams.

Forking the Workflow

The following diagram displays an example of a fork:

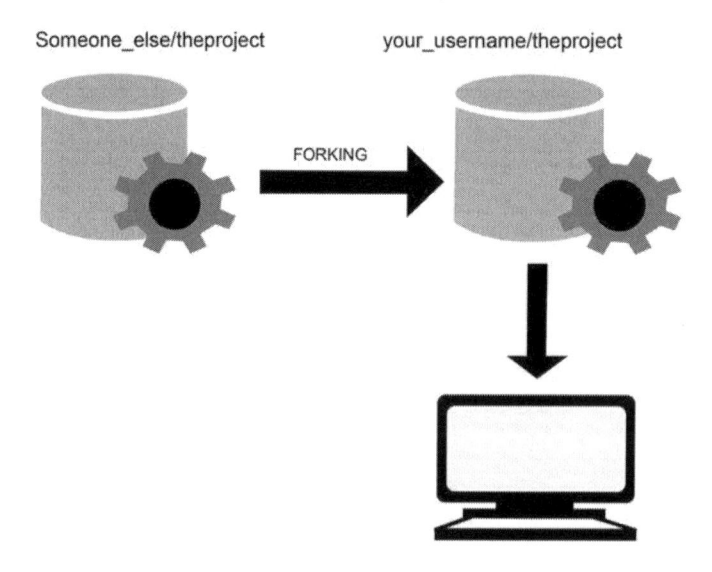

Figure 5.1: Fork example

Exercise 30: Forking a Repository

To set up a fork in the GitHub repository.

1. Open your favorite browser and go to https://github.com/mrmuli/fork-demo:

    > **Note**
    >
    > The following screenshot shows what an original repository would look like on the top-right corner; notice the **Fork** button.

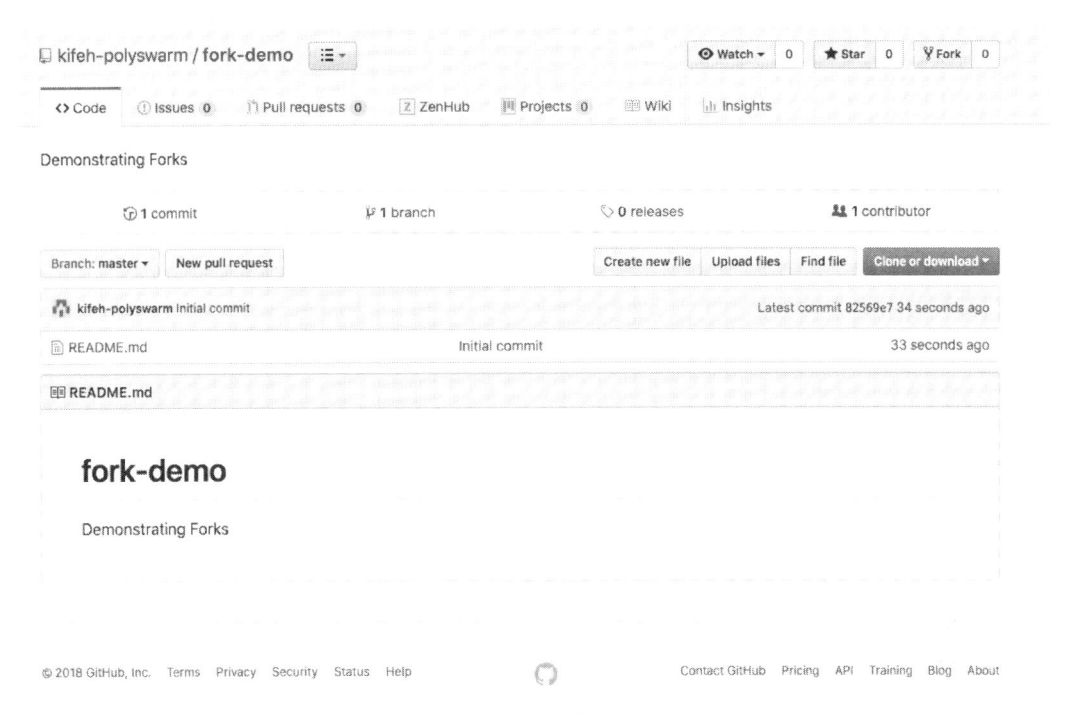

Figure 5.2: Fork demo

2. Select the **Fork** button, and GitHub should show the following prompt:

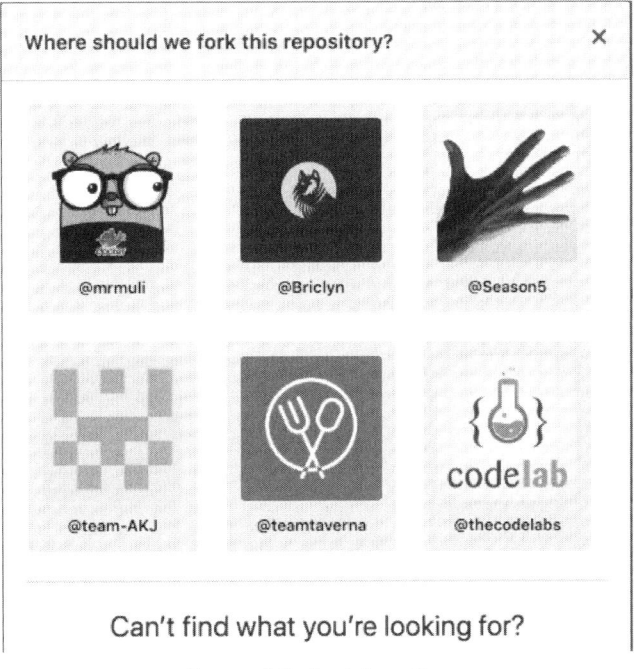

Figure 5.3: Fork location

3. Select your profile, and GitHub should immediately start the process.

> **Note**
>
> This should automatically direct you to the fork you just made.

Outcome

From the repository name, GitHub will show the fork icon, the repository name, and the upstream (origin), as shown in the following screenshot:

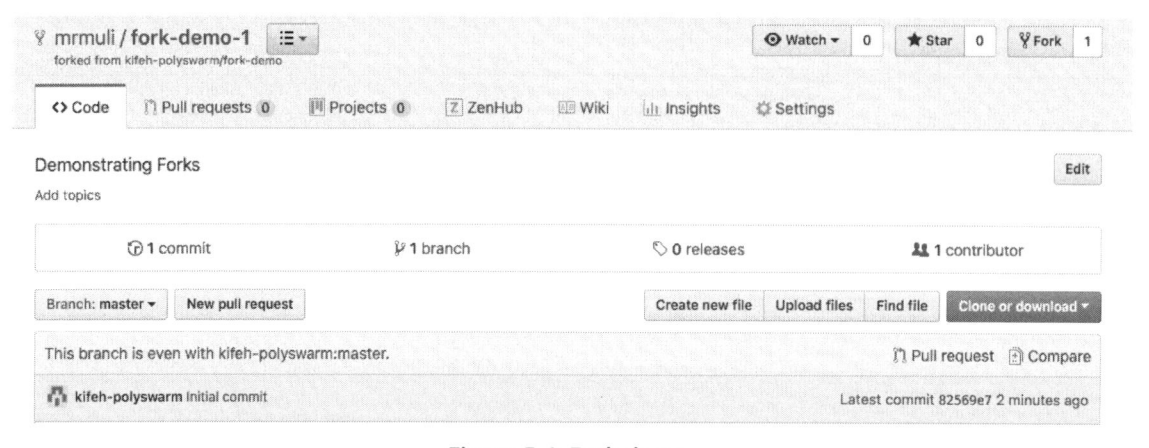

Figure 5.4: Fork demo

Why Do We Fork Repositories?

There are a number of reasons why forking repositories is important, and, no, it's not because it's a click away. Among these reasons are the following ones:

- Forks allow contributions to other repositories through pull requests in cases where the individual is not added as a contributor to those repositories. In the following screenshot, notice that GitHub informs us of the master branch on our repository being even with `kifeh-polyswarm:master`:

Figure 5.5: Branch master

- Forks also help avoid loss when the upstream repository is taken down, especially in situations where the code on the repository is a dependency for an ongoing project.

> **Note**
>
> The purpose of forking will not always be technical; it could be used as a "save for later and I do not want to clone" kind of situation. However, with every fork, you should beware of changes from upstream, which must be done manually.

In this chapter, we are going to explore forking with contribution intent.

Embedding Upstream Changes

We recently used the term **upstream** a number of times. In relation to forked repositories, upstream refers to the original repository a fork is made out of. When working with active forked repositories, changes are going be implemented almost every hour, and within a short period, your fork will be outdated. Let's demonstrate how to tackle this.

Assuming that your fork's master has had no new changes introduced to it, change your current working directory to your local project. If you haven't cloned it, this would be the best time to do so.

Git status shows that there are no new changes and that my **master** branch is also up to date with **origin/master**. **Origin/master** represents the forked repository on my GitHub profile; take note of this:

```
josephmuli at Friday in ~/Repositories/writing/fork-demo-1 on master
$ git status
On branch master
Your branch is up to date with 'origin/master'.

nothing to commit, working tree clean
```

Figure 5.6: Branch master

Also note that we currently only have one origin according to `git remote -v`:

```
josephmuli at Friday in ~/Repositories/writing/fork-demo-1 on master
$ git remote -v
origin   git@github.com:mrmuli/fork-demo-1.git (fetch)
origin   git@github.com:mrmuli/fork-demo-1.git (push)
```

Figure 5.7: Using git remote -v

When more changes are introduced to the upstream repository, our repository automatically identifies this status and reports it on GitHub.

> **Note**
>
> Notice how the fork reports being one commit behind upstream, as shown in the following screenshot:

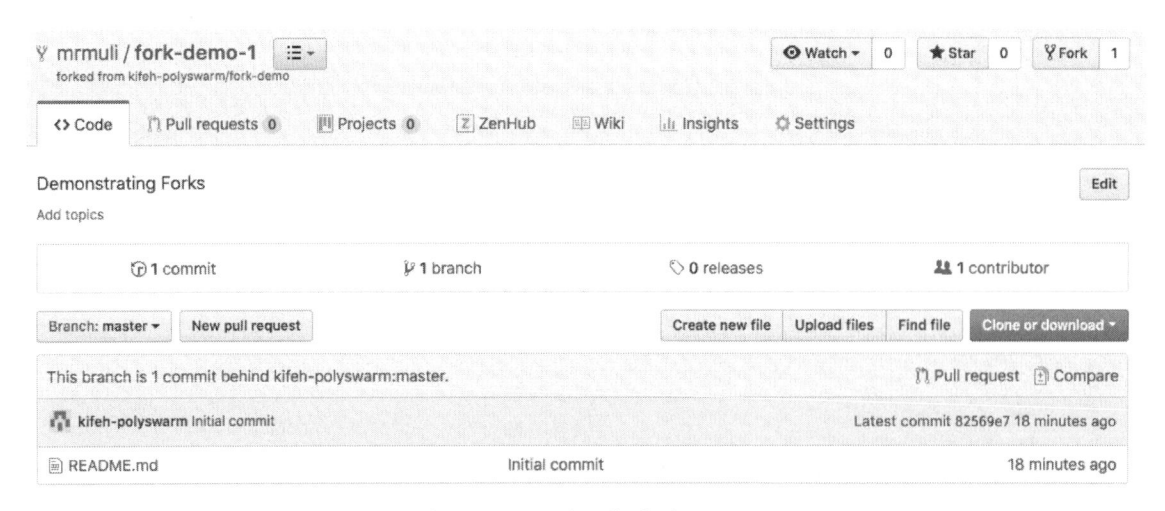

Figure 5.8: Using fork-demo-1

To even out the changes on forked repositories, you will need to add the upstream repository remote address and pull changes from it. Let's demonstrate this in the following exercise.

Exercise 31: Modifying the Upstream Repository Remote Address

To add the upstream repository remote address and pull changes from it.

1. On your terminal, add a new upstream repository by using the following command syntax in the following screenshot:

```
git remote add upstream <upstream clone url>
```

```
josephmuli at Friday in ~/Repositories/writing/fork-demo-1 on master
$ git remote add upstream https://github.com/kifeh-polyswarm/fork-demo.git
```

Figure 5.9: Adding a new upstream repository

2. Take a quick glance at our remote URLs to check that we now have upstream set up, as seen in this screenshot:

```
josephmuli at Friday in ~/Repositories/writing/fork-demo-1 on master
$ git remote -v
origin    git@github.com:mrmuli/fork-demo-1.git (fetch)
origin    git@github.com:mrmuli/fork-demo-1.git (push)
upstream          https://github.com/kifeh-polyswarm/fork-demo.git (fetch)
upstream          https://github.com/kifeh-polyswarm/fork-demo.git (push)
```

Figure 5.10: Upstream repository setup

3. If you are not on the master branch, then checkout to the master branch. Notice the branch that I am currently on, as shown in the following screenshot:

```
josephmuli at Friday in ~/Repositories/writing/fork-demo-1 on master
$ git branch
* master
```

Figure 5.11: Git branch

4. Run the following command to fetch changes from the upstream repository, as shown in the following screenshot:

```
josephmuli at Friday in ~/Repositories/writing/fork-demo-1 on master
$ git fetch upstream
remote: Counting objects: 3, done.
remote: Compressing objects: 100% (2/2), done.
remote: Total 3 (delta 0), reused 0 (delta 0), pack-reused 0
Unpacking objects: 100% (3/3), done.
From https://github.com/kifeh-polyswarm/fork-demo
 * [new branch]      master     -> upstream/master
```

Figure 5.12: Fetching changes from upstream repository

> **Note**
>
> We now have changes from `upstream` and, as a final step, Git still informs us that we need to update `origin` through `git status`:

```
josephmuli at Friday in ~/Repositories/writing/fork-demo-1 on master
$ git status
On branch master
Your branch is ahead of 'origin/master' by 1 commit.
  (use "git push" to publish your local commits)

nothing to commit, working tree clean
```

Figure 5.13: Branch master

Forking the Workflow | 199

5. As a final step, let's push our changes to origin through the use of the `git push origin master` command as shown in the following screenshot:

Figure 5.14: Pushing the changes

> **Note**
>
> Our fork should now be even with upstream; here's the result on GitHub:

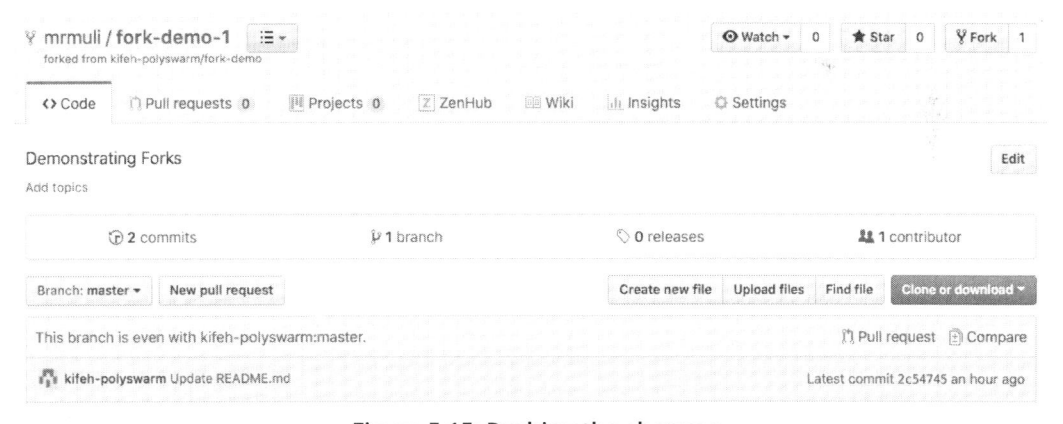

Figure 5.15: Pushing the changes

> **Note**
>
> Contributions in a forking workflow, as mentioned earlier, also work through pull requests.

200 | Collaborative Git

6. From your local repository, checkout to a new branch. Let's call it `patch-1`, as shown in the following screenshot:

```
josephmuli at Friday in ~/Repositories/writing/fork-demo-1 on master [$]
$ git checkout -b patch-1
Switched to a new branch 'patch-1'
```

Figure 5.16: Pushing the changes

7. Introduce the following change to the `README.md` file. Notice the changes highlighted by a green line on my editor. Preferably, use your name, as shown in the following screenshot:

```
README.md ×
1    # fork-demo
2    Demonstrating Forks
3
4    ## How to Use this fork
5    This fork as part of a lorem ipsum dolor sit amet, consectetur adipiscing elit, sed do ei
     veniam, quis nostrud exercitation ullamco laboris nisi ut aliquip ex ea commodo consequat
     eu fugiat nulla pariatur. Excepteur sint occaecat cupidatat non proident, sunt in culpa q
6
7    ## Fork contribution
8
9    Mr Muli added this line
```

Figure 5.17: Editing the README.md file

8. Stage and commit the change, as shown in the following screenshot:

```
josephmuli at Friday in ~/Repositories/writing/fork-demo-1 on patch-1 [!$]
$ git status
On branch patch-1
Changes not staged for commit:
  (use "git add <file>..." to update what will be committed)
  (use "git checkout -- <file>..." to discard changes in working directory)

        modified:   README.md

no changes added to commit (use "git add" and/or "git commit -a")

josephmuli at Friday in ~/Repositories/writing/fork-demo-1 on patch-1 [!$]
$ git add README.md

josephmuli at Friday in ~/Repositories/writing/fork-demo-1 on patch-1 [+$]
$ git commit -m"update README.md"
[patch-1 bcf613b] update README.md
 1 file changed, 4 insertions(+)

josephmuli at Friday in ~/Repositories/writing/fork-demo-1 on patch-1 [$]
$
```

Figure 5.18: Staging and committing the change

9. Push your changes to `origin` as shown in the following screenshot:

```
josephmuli at Friday in ~/Repositories/writing/fork-demo-1 on patch-1 [$]
$ git push origin patch-1
Enumerating objects: 5, done.
Counting objects: 100% (5/5), done.
Delta compression using up to 4 threads.
Compressing objects: 100% (2/2), done.
Writing objects: 100% (3/3), 322 bytes | 322.00 KiB/s, done.
Total 3 (delta 1), reused 0 (delta 0)
remote: Resolving deltas: 100% (1/1), completed with 1 local object.
To github.com:mrmuli/fork-demo-1.git
 * [new branch]      patch-1 -> patch-1
```

Figure 5.19: Pushing your changes to origin

10. Create a pull request on demo repository. The repository should already have a pull request popup, as shown in the following screenshot:

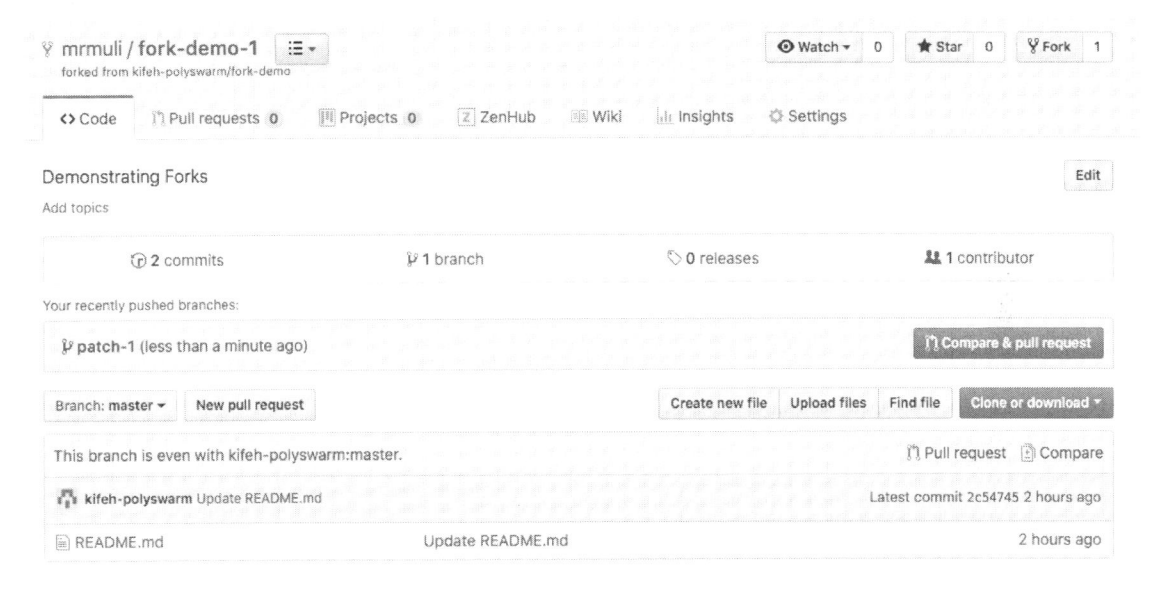

Figure 5.20: Creating a pull request on GitHub

11. Select the **Compare & pull request button,** which should lead to a merge-eligibility check between your fork and upstream's master branch, as shown in the following screenshot:

> **Note**
>
> The branch you seek to merge to may vary depending on your workflow.

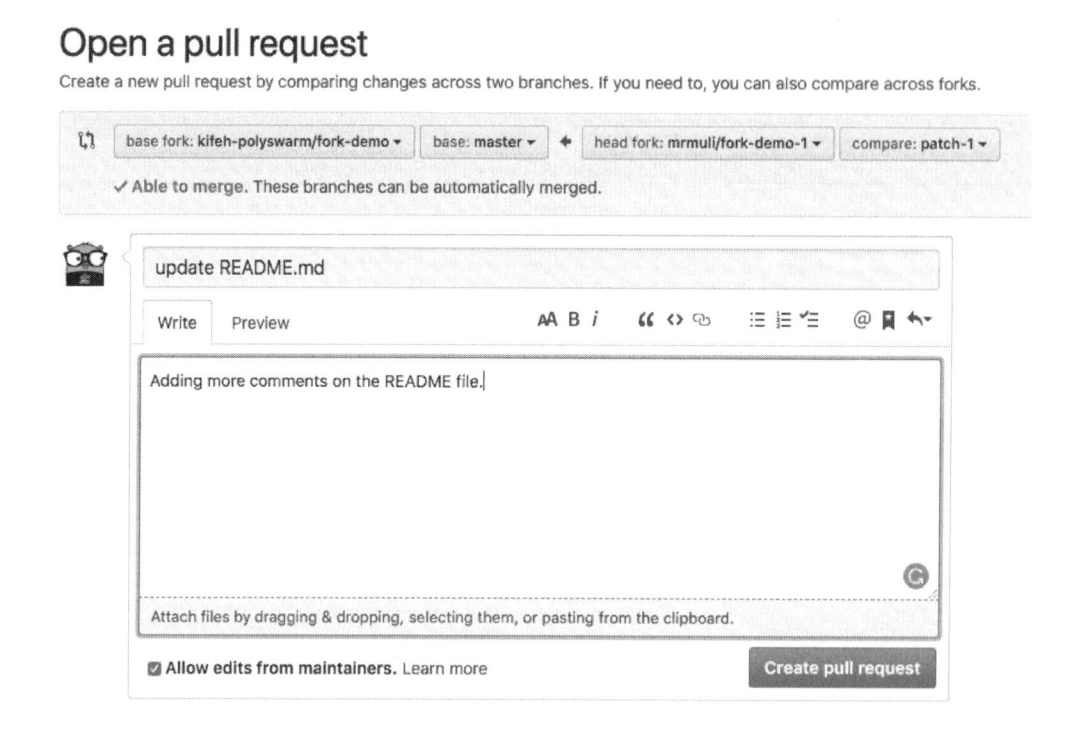

Figure 5.21: Opening a pull request

12. If you create a pull request to upstream, it should be displayed on upstream's pull request list, as shown in the following screenshot:

> **Note**
>
> Be sure to always add appropriate pull request names and comments. From the upstream repository, you can identify the pull request from the `Pull requests` tab. Do not create pull request on the author repository.

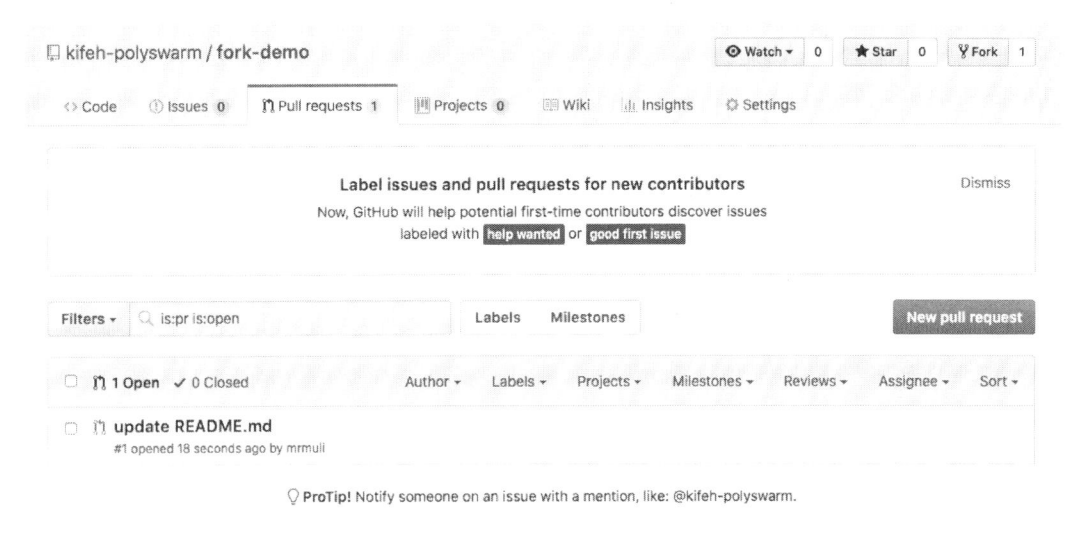

Figure 5.22: Creating the pull request

Outcome

The maintainer should be notified about the upstream repository remote address and if everything checks out, your pull request will be merged.

To keep track of the history we have added to, we'll create a merge commit to the base branch. (More on this will be covered in the next sub-topic):

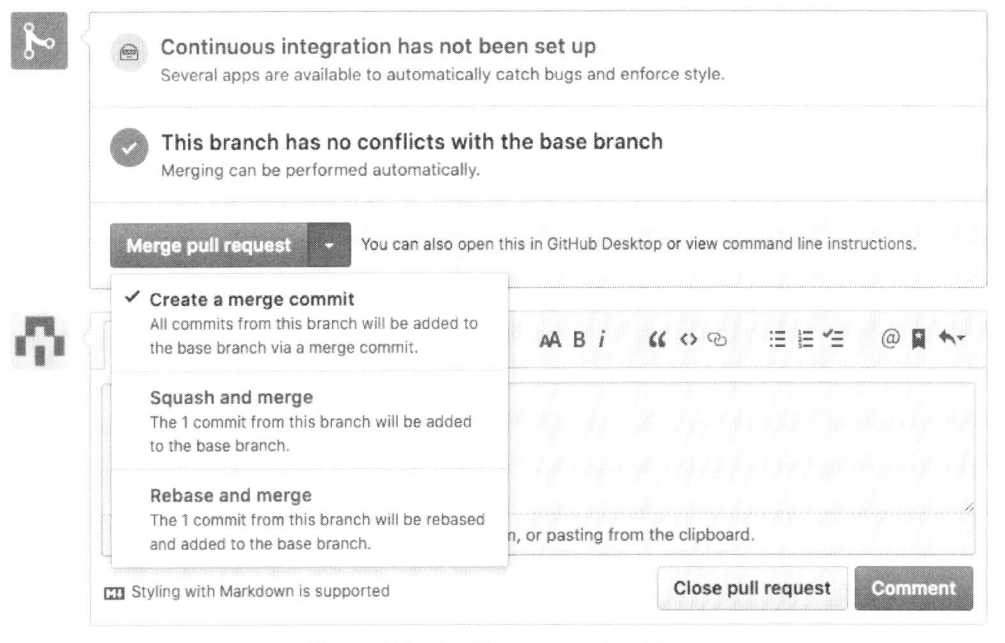

Figure 5.23: Pulling request options

If you are the maintainer, go ahead and merge via **Create a merge commit** and **confirm merge**.

From upstream, we can confirm that the changes were merged:

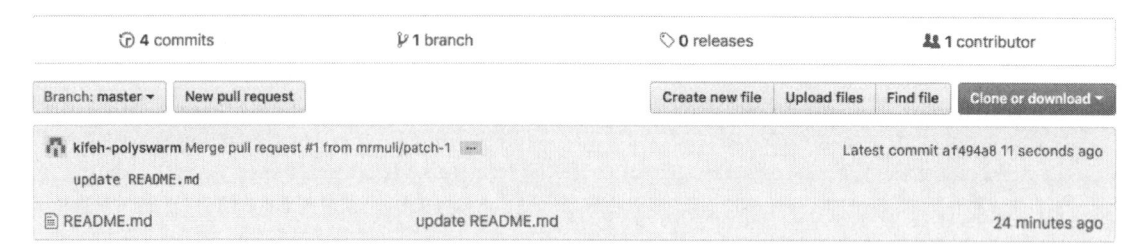

Figure 5.24: Confirming the changes

Rebasing

We recently covered how to merge changes into a base branch, both locally and through pull requests. It should be noted that merging is one of the ways changes on different branches can be incorporated. Let's recap what happens during a merge as we introduce rebasing.

The following diagram demonstrates a simple merge where we're checking out a new branch at commit **A** from the master, committing a new change at **C,** and then merging back by creating merge commit **D** from **C** and **B**:

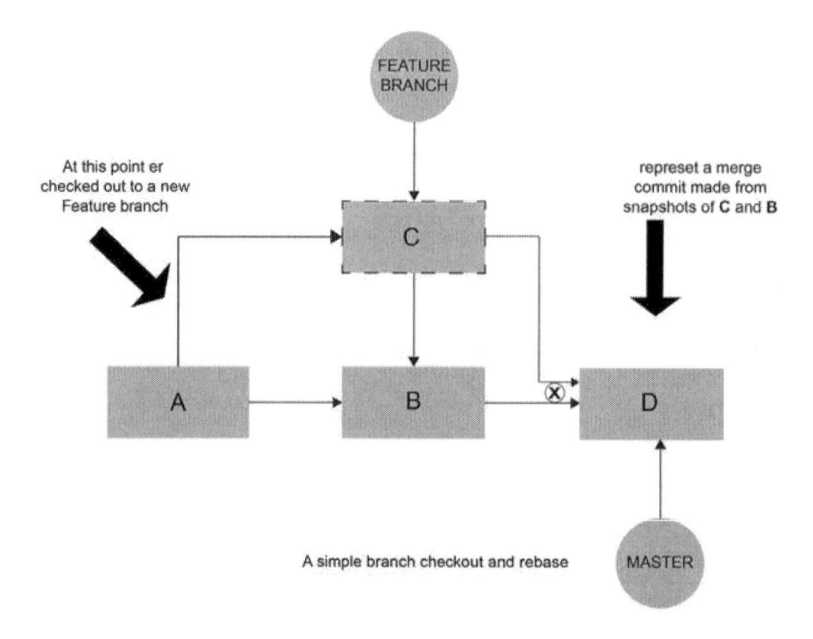

Figure 5.25: A simple branch checkout and merge

Similar to merging changes back to the base branch (master), the following is an illustration of what happens during a rebase as shown in the following figure:

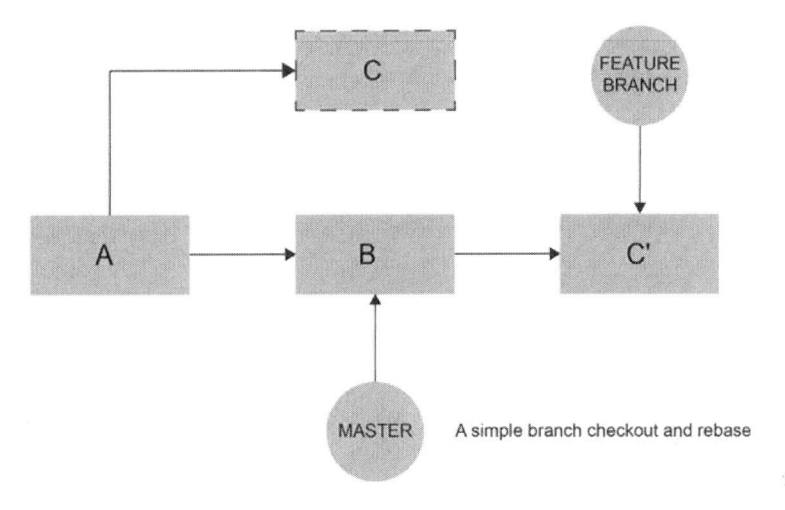

Figure 5.26: A simple branch checkout and rebase

> **Note**
> The **D** commit or **HEAD** on merge is similar to the **C** commit on the rebase diagram.

As seen in the merge diagram, a feature branch is merged back into a master or **base** branch, creating a **merge commit D**. On the other hand, rebasing alters **HEAD** by layering commit **C** on top of **B**. Note that this means **B** gets recreated. During the rebase, the feature branch is reset to the master's most recent commit (**B**) and is then added on top. This is why the feature branch ends up ahead of the master, according to the diagram. To even out the master, you would need to do a fast-forward feature branch merge into the master.

Picture a scenario where you have been working on a feature branch from the master, and your colleagues have been continuously merging new changes on to the master. To get the most recent commits and still maintain a clean history that will show that you have been working with the most recent changes, you must perform a **rebase**. Think of it this way: **you want to re-organize your branch's base with the most recent changes, your work being most recent**.

206 | Collaborative Git

Exercise 32: Rebasing in GitHub

To merge the branch being currently worked upon using the rebase command in GitHub.

1. Assuming you are still on the patch-1 branch, checkout to the master, as shown in the following screenshot:

```
josephmuli at Friday in ~/Repositories/writing/fork-demo-1 on patch-1 [$]
$ git status
On branch patch-1
nothing to commit, working tree clean

josephmuli at Friday in ~/Repositories/writing/fork-demo-1 on patch-1 [$]
$ git checkout master
Switched to branch 'master'
Your branch is up to date with 'origin/master'.
```

Figure 5.27: Checkout to the master

2. From our previous exercise, our master branch isn't up to date with merged changes on upstream. Run the `git pull upstream master` command to make this change, as shown in the following screenshot:

```
josephmuli at Friday in ~/Repositories/writing/fork-demo-1 on master [$]
$ git pull upstream master
remote: Counting objects: 1, done.
remote: Total 1 (delta 0), reused 0 (delta 0), pack-reused 0
Unpacking objects: 100% (1/1), done.
From https://github.com/kifeh-polyswarm/fork-demo
 * branch            master     -> FETCH_HEAD
   2c54745..af494a8  master     -> upstream/master
Updating 2c54745..af494a8
Fast-forward
 README.md | 4 ++++
 1 file changed, 4 insertions(+)
```

Figure 5.28: Pull request on master

> **Note**
>
> Keep in mind that our fork on GitHub also doesn't have these changes from upstream on the master.

3. While on the master, introduce the following changes to the README.md file, as shown in the following screenshot:

```
### changes on Master

these changes were added on the base (Master) branch
```

Figure 5.29: Changes to the README.md file

4. Stage the changes and commit, as shown in the following screenshot:

```
josephmuli at Friday in ~/Repositories/writing/fork-demo-1 on master [!$]
$ git add README.md

josephmuli at Friday in ~/Repositories/writing/fork-demo-1 on master [+$]
$ git commit -m"change introduced on master"
[master 98ea7cb] change introduced on master
 1 file changed, 5 insertions(+), 1 deletion(-)

josephmuli at Friday in ~/Repositories/writing/fork-demo-1 on master [$]
$ git status
On branch master
Your branch is ahead of 'origin/master' by 3 commits.
  (use "git push" to publish your local commits)

nothing to commit, working tree clean
```

Figure 5.30: Staging the changes and commit

5. Notice that we now have three commits more than our origin repository: two from the upstream and the one we just added.

6. Checkout to **patch-1** and create a new file, introducing a new change, as shown in the following screenshot:

```
josephmuli at Friday in ~/Repositories/writing/fork-demo-1 on master [$]
$ git checkout patch-1
Switched to branch 'patch-1'

josephmuli at Friday in ~/Repositories/writing/fork-demo-1 on patch-1 [$]
$ git status
On branch patch-1
nothing to commit, working tree clean

josephmuli at Friday in ~/Repositories/writing/fork-demo-1 on patch-1 [$]
$ touch sample.txt
```

Figure 5.31: Checkout to patch-1

208 | Collaborative Git

7. Stage and commit your new change, as shown in the following screenshot:

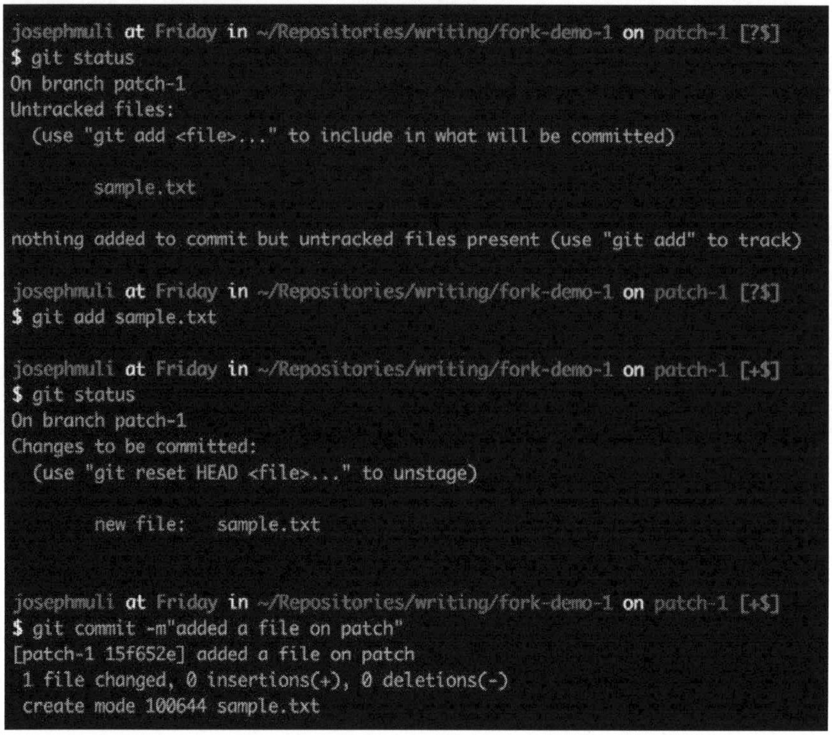

```
josephmuli at Friday in ~/Repositories/writing/fork-demo-1 on patch-1 [?$]
$ git status
On branch patch-1
Untracked files:
  (use "git add <file>..." to include in what will be committed)

        sample.txt

nothing added to commit but untracked files present (use "git add" to track)

josephmuli at Friday in ~/Repositories/writing/fork-demo-1 on patch-1 [?$]
$ git add sample.txt

josephmuli at Friday in ~/Repositories/writing/fork-demo-1 on patch-1 [+$]
$ git status
On branch patch-1
Changes to be committed:
  (use "git reset HEAD <file>..." to unstage)

        new file:   sample.txt


josephmuli at Friday in ~/Repositories/writing/fork-demo-1 on patch-1 [+$]
$ git commit -m"added a file on patch"
[patch-1 15f652e] added a file on patch
 1 file changed, 0 insertions(+), 0 deletions(-)
 create mode 100644 sample.txt
```

Figure 5.32: Staging and committing your new change

> **Note**
>
> Notice how the README.md file doesn't have the changes on the master.

8. To keep your branch up to date, rebase with the master, as shown in the following screenshot:

```
josephmuli at Friday in ~/Repositories/writing/fork-demo-1 on patch-1 [$]
$ git rebase master
First, rewinding head to replay your work on top of it...
Applying: added a file on patch
```

Figure 5.33: Rebase with the master

> **Note**
>
> Take note of the following message: rewind the head to replay your work on top of it then apply changes from the patch. Internally, Git resets your branch, creates new commits, and applies them on top of the base (master). This reason makes it a very bad idea to rebase a public branch on a repository you are contributing to. While you're still on the feature branch patch-1, notice that the README.md file has changes from the master on it:

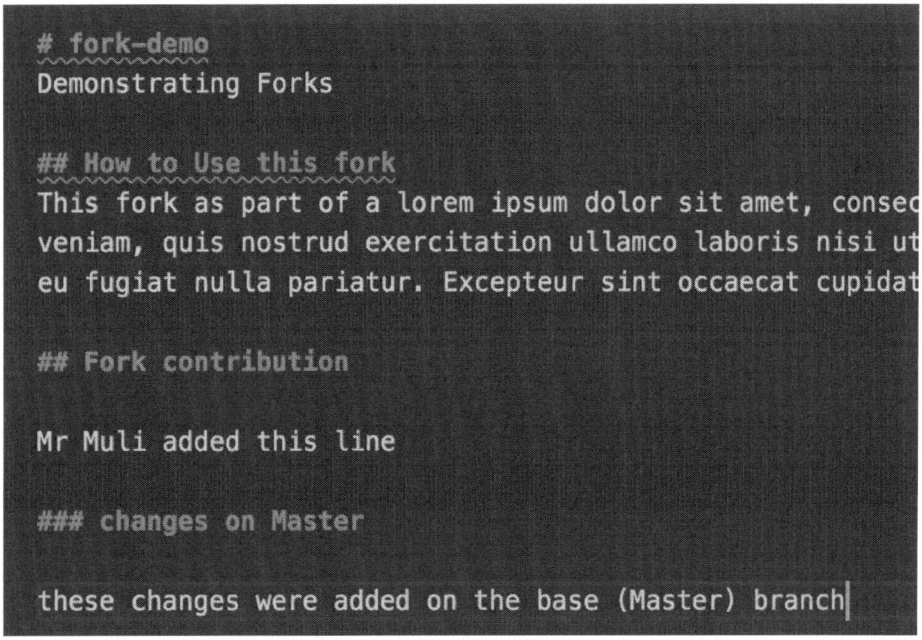

```
# fork-demo
Demonstrating Forks

## How to Use this fork
This fork as part of a lorem ipsum dolor sit amet, consec
veniam, quis nostrud exercitation ullamco laboris nisi ut
eu fugiat nulla pariatur. Excepteur sint occaecat cupidat

## Fork contribution

Mr Muli added this line

### changes on Master

these changes were added on the base (Master) branch
```

Figure 5.34: Changes on the Master

9. To prove that our rebase only affected the feature branch, switch to the master and notice that the file we created on **patch-1** as **sample.txt** doesn't exist, as shown in the following screenshot:

```
josephmuli at Friday in ~/Repositories/writing/fork-demo-1 on patch-1 [$]
$ git checkout master
Switched to branch 'master'
Your branch is ahead of 'origin/master' by 3 commits.
  (use "git push" to publish your local commits)

josephmuli at Friday in ~/Repositories/writing/fork-demo-1 on master [$]
$ ls
README.md
```

Figure 5.35: Switching to Master

> **Note**
> Take heed that we are working on a forked repository, where we have modified the base branch.

Outcome

You have successfully merged the branch using the **git rebase** command.

Fixup and Squash Commits

Consider a scenario where you made a typo on a previous commit, or even missed something. Normally, fixing and adding a new commit would be an ideal option to use on both a public or feature branch. If this happened solely on a feature branch, Git presents an option to fixup and autosquash the previous commits. The reason this shouldn't be done on public branches is because that Git rewrites commits, as this is also a rebase operation. Rewriting history on a public branch will cause conflicts and data loss to other contributors. Let's demonstrate this.

Exercise 33: Utilizing the Autosquash Feature

To `fixup` the previous commits using the autosquash facility in GitHub.

1. Switch back to your `patch`-1 branch, as shown in the following screenshot:

```
josephmuli at Friday in ~/Repositories/writing/fork-demo-1 on patch-1 [$]
$ git branch
  master
* patch-1
```

Figure 5.36: Switching to the patch-1 branch

> **Note**
>
> Due to a new environment requirement, you are required to update all text files to markdown (md). Remember that on a previous commit, a file with a text extension was committed.

2. To quickly `fixup` this change, we'll update the file and later modify the commit, as shown in the following screenshot:

```
josephmuli at Friday in ~/Repositories/writing/fork-demo-1 on patch-1 [$]
$ ls
README.md  sample.txt

josephmuli at Friday in ~/Repositories/writing/fork-demo-1 on patch-1 [$]
$ mv sample.txt sample.md

josephmuli at Friday in ~/Repositories/writing/fork-demo-1 on patch-1 [!?$]
$ ls
README.md sample.md
```

Figure 5.37: Updating the file

> **Note**
>
> In the preceding example, we modified the `sample.txt` file through the `mv` command to `sample.md`.

212 | Collaborative Git

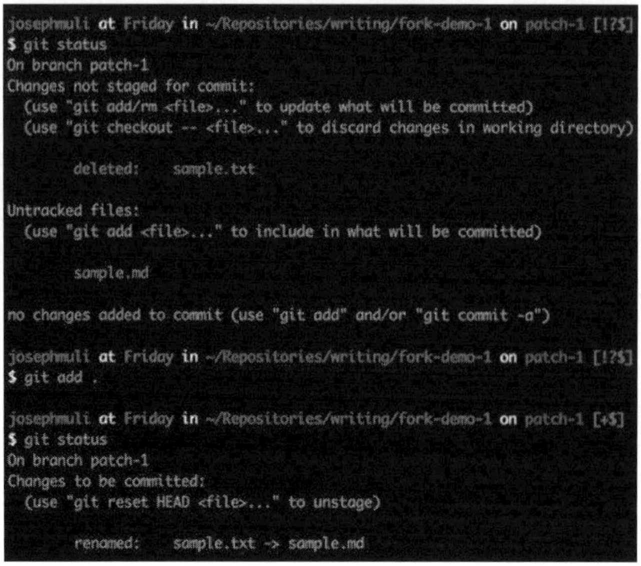

3. Go ahead and stage the new changes, as shown in the following screenshot:

Figure 5.38: Staging the new changes

4. Instead of a normal commit, include a `--fixup` argument and a commit hash to the command as follows: `git commit --fixup dd4b896`

5. To get the hash, run the `git log` command, as shown in the following screenshot:

> **Note**
>
> The hash to use belongs to the commit that added a file on patch. In my case, it's the first one.

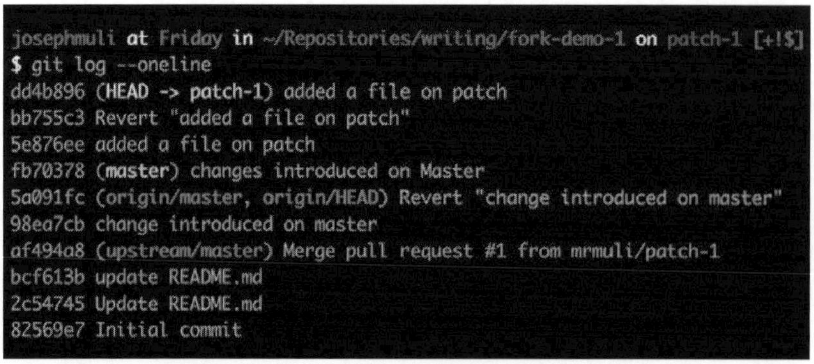

Figure 5.39: Running the Git log command

```
josephmuli at Friday in ~/Repositories/writing/fork-demo-1 on patch-1 [+!$]
$ git commit --fixup dd4b896
[patch-1 521964e] fixup! added a file on patch
 1 file changed, 0 insertions(+), 0 deletions(-)
 create mode 100644 sample.md
```

Figure 5.40: Running the Git commit command

6. Run the `git log --oneline` command to show our new commit, as shown in the following screenshot:

```
josephmuli at Friday in ~/Repositories/writing/fork-demo-1 on patch-1 [!$]
$ git log --oneline
521964e (HEAD -> patch-1) fixup! added a file on patch
dd4b896 added a file on patch
bb755c3 Revert "added a file on patch"
5e876ee added a file on patch
fb70378 (master) changes introduced on Master
5a091fc (origin/master, origin/HEAD) Revert "change introduced on master"
98ea7cb change introduced on master
af494a8 (upstream/master) Merge pull request #1 from mrmuli/patch-1
bcf613b update README.md
2c54745 Update README.md
82569e7 Initial commit
```

Figure 5.41: Running the Git log command

7. To clean this up, rebase and autosquash the commit, as shown in the following screenshot:

```
josephmuli at Friday in ~/Repositories/writing/fork-demo-1 on patch-1 [$]
$ git rebase -i --autosquash 5e876ee
Successfully rebased and updated refs/heads/patch-1.
```

Figure 5.42: Rebasing and autosquashing the commit

> **Note**
>
> Be sure to select the commit hash that's just before the commit you want to autosquash.

Outcome

Running `git log` shows that the `fixup` commits have been merged, as shown in the following screenshot:

```
josephmuli at Friday in ~/Repositories/writing/fork-demo-1 on patch-1 [$]
$ git log --oneline
1e38c47 (HEAD -> patch-1) added a file on patch
bb755c3 Revert "added a file on patch"
5e876ee added a file on patch
fb70378 (master) changes introduced on Master
5a091fc (origin/master, origin/HEAD) Revert "change introduced on master"
98ea7cb change introduced on master
af494a8 (upstream/master) Merge pull request #1 from mrmuli/patch-1
bcf613b update README.md
2c54745 Update README.md
82569e7 Initial commit
```

Figure 5.43: Rebasing and autosquashing the commit

Drop Commits

In the previous example, we demonstrated how to `fixup` commits. Earlier in the book, we covered how to cherry-pick. Sometimes, the need to get rid of unwanted changes comes up for instance changes that introduce bugs during a root cause analysis.

A lot of approaches can be taken toward this, including resetting HEAD to a commit just before the problematic commit or explicitly dropping the problematic commit. Resetting HEAD may not be a viable option in a case where the commit is back in the history. To be safe, especially with no proper rebase option, reset the HEAD when the commit is most recent. This topic, however, will focus on rebasing.

Forking the Workflow | 215

Back on the terminal, you will have a random commit labelled `fixing stuff`. Let's assume that this commit was made a week ago when a team member was fixing some broken tests. To get rid of this, leverage on the following command:

`git rebase -i <a commit prior to the targeted commit>`

From my `git log`, my target commit is `0115bbb fix stuff`, so we'll work with `0ce2ad2`. Run `git log` as follows to get your hash:

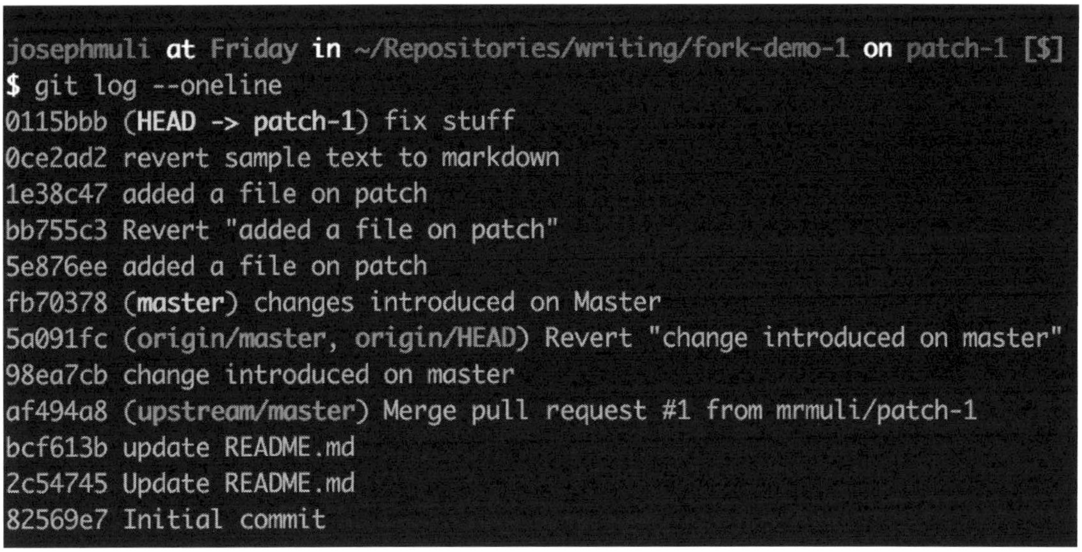

```
josephmuli at Friday in ~/Repositories/writing/fork-demo-1 on patch-1 [$]
$ git log --oneline
0115bbb (HEAD -> patch-1) fix stuff
0ce2ad2 revert sample text to markdown
1e38c47 added a file on patch
bb755c3 Revert "added a file on patch"
5e876ee added a file on patch
fb70378 (master) changes introduced on Master
5a091fc (origin/master, origin/HEAD) Revert "change introduced on master"
98ea7cb change introduced on master
af494a8 (upstream/master) Merge pull request #1 from mrmuli/patch-1
bcf613b update README.md
2c54745 Update README.md
82569e7 Initial commit
```

Figure 5.44: Running Git log

Exercise 34: Dropping Commits

To get rid of unwanted changes or commits in GitHub.

1. Run the rebase command, as shown in the following screenshot:

Figure 5.45: Running the git rebase command

> **Note**
>
> Git should automatically open the interactive rebase prompt, as shown in the following screenshot:

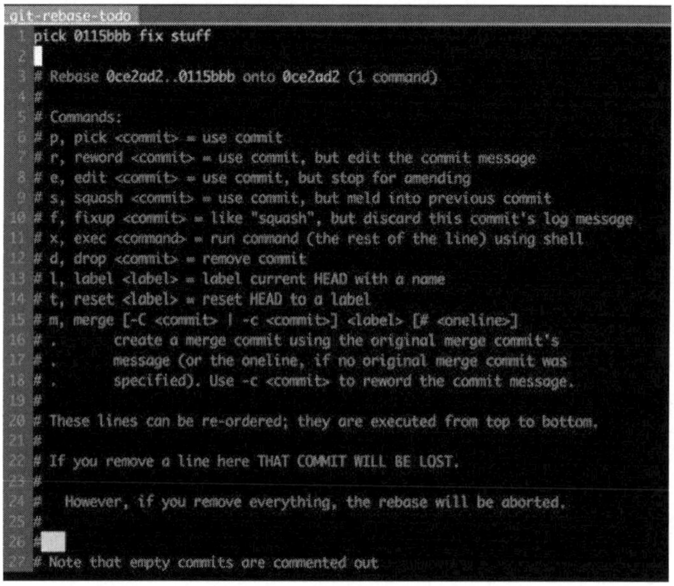

Figure 5.46: Running the git rebase command

> **Note**
>
> The terminal editor will vary according to your computer's settings; mine is **VIM**. The prompt lists all of the commits from the point selected and just below that, actions that can be applied to the commits. To drop the commit, there are two ways we can handle this: clearing the line or, as advised in the prompt, using the keyword drop. Let's take the second option:

Forking the Workflow | 217

```
git-rebase-todo
 1 drop 0115bbb fix stuff
 2
 3 # Rebase 0ce2ad2..0115bbb onto 0ce2ad2 (1 command)
 4 #
 5 # Commands:
 6 # p, pick <commit> = use commit
 7 # r, reword <commit> = use commit, but edit the commit message
 8 # e, edit <commit> = use commit, but stop for amending
 9 # s, squash <commit> = use commit, but meld into previous commit
10 # f, fixup <commit> = like "squash", but discard this commit's log message
11 # x, exec <command> = run command (the rest of the line) using shell
12 # d, drop <commit> = remove commit
13 # l, label <label> = label current HEAD with a name
14 # t, reset <label> = reset HEAD to a label
15 # m, merge [-C <commit> | -c <commit>] <label> [# <oneline>]
16 # .       create a merge commit using the original merge commit's
17 # .       message (or the oneline, if no original merge commit was
18 # .       specified). Use -c <commit> to reword the commit message.
19 #
20 # These lines can be re-ordered; they are executed from top to bottom.
21 #
22 # If you remove a line here THAT COMMIT WILL BE LOST.
23 #
24 #   However, if you remove everything, the rebase will be aborted.
25 #
26 #
27 # Note that empty commits are commented out
```

Figure 5.47: Using the drop command

2. If you are running VIM as I am, select **I** on your keyboard to use the **Insert** option and edit the command. To drop and escape and select :wq without the quotes to write and quit, as shown in the following screenshot:

```
NORMAL  +0 ~0 -0  patch-1  git-rebase-todo[+]    gitrebase
:wq
```

Figure 5.48: Using the wq command

> **Note**
>
> This will start the rebase. When this is done, the following should be your terminal message:

```
josephmuli at Friday in ~/Repositories/writing/fork-demo-1 on patch-1 [$]
$ git rebase -i 0ce2ad2
Successfully rebased and updated refs/heads/patch-1.
```

Figure 5.49: Running Git rebase

Outcome

Checking the logs, we shouldn't have the commit on the list, as shown in the following screenshot:

```
josephmuli at Friday in ~/Repositories/writing/fork-demo-1 on patch-1 [$]
$ git log --oneline
0ce2ad2 (HEAD -> patch-1) revert sample text to markdown
1e38c47 added a file on patch
bb755c3 Revert "added a file on patch"
5e876ee added a file on patch
fb70378 (master) changes introduced on Master
5a091fc (origin/master, origin/HEAD) Revert "change introduced on master"
98ea7cb change introduced on master
af494a8 (upstream/master) Merge pull request #1 from mrmuli/patch-1
bcf613b update README.md
2c54745 Update README.md
82569e7 Initial commit
```

Figure 5.50: Checking the logs

Submodules

Git submodules, often referred to as gitmodules, enable the **separation of concern** toward project dependencies. In other words, they help organize code based on a **single responsibility principle**.

Consider a scenario where a project in development requires deployment dependencies. While the dependencies are handled by a DevOps team, the Dev team needs to maintain focus on the product. This can get a little messy if both teams work on the same repository, even though ultimately the product will require that dependencies are run through pipelines and eventually deploy to other environments.

To enhance the efficacy, dependencies can be migrated to a different repository and included as a submodule of the product repository, thereby separating both teams' concerns and still maintaining mutual exclusiveness.

Submodules are tracked through a `.gitmodules` file, and, just like any other dependency, you need to clone them into their parent repositories. For instance, Node.js applications require a package manager such as npm to install dependencies to a `node_modules` directory, through a `package.json` file. Submodules require a `.gitmodules` file and dependencies to be installed through the `git submodule` command.

Before we demonstrate this, here are the steps to take when handling submodules:

When handling submodules for the first time, be sure to do the following:

- Add submodules through the `git submodule add <repository url>` command.
- Initialize the submodules through the `git submodule init` command.

Exercise 35: Utilizing Gitmodules

This demo will make use of abacus, the repository we set up earlier in this book as the product. A different repository exists, holding all maintenance and deployment scripts. Go ahead and set up yours, as shown in the following screenshot:

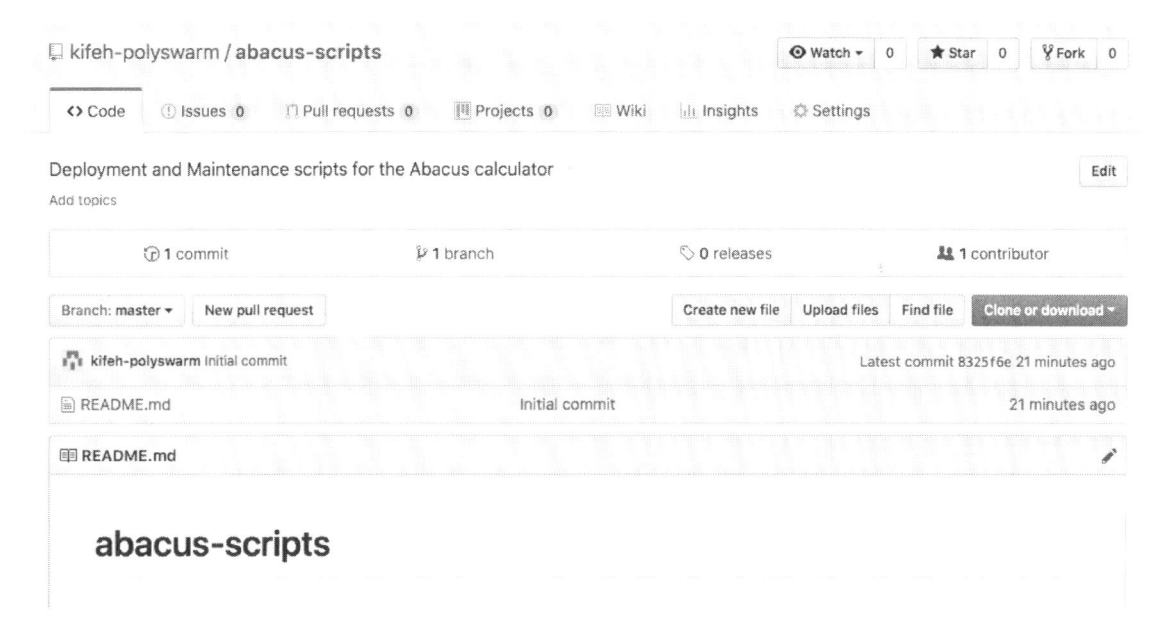

Figure 5.51: Using the abacus repository

As a contributor to the DevOps team, I have a forked copy on my profile, where all changes will be contributed through. You do not need to fork if the repository belongs to an organization you are part of or has been added as a contributor, as shown in the following screenshot:

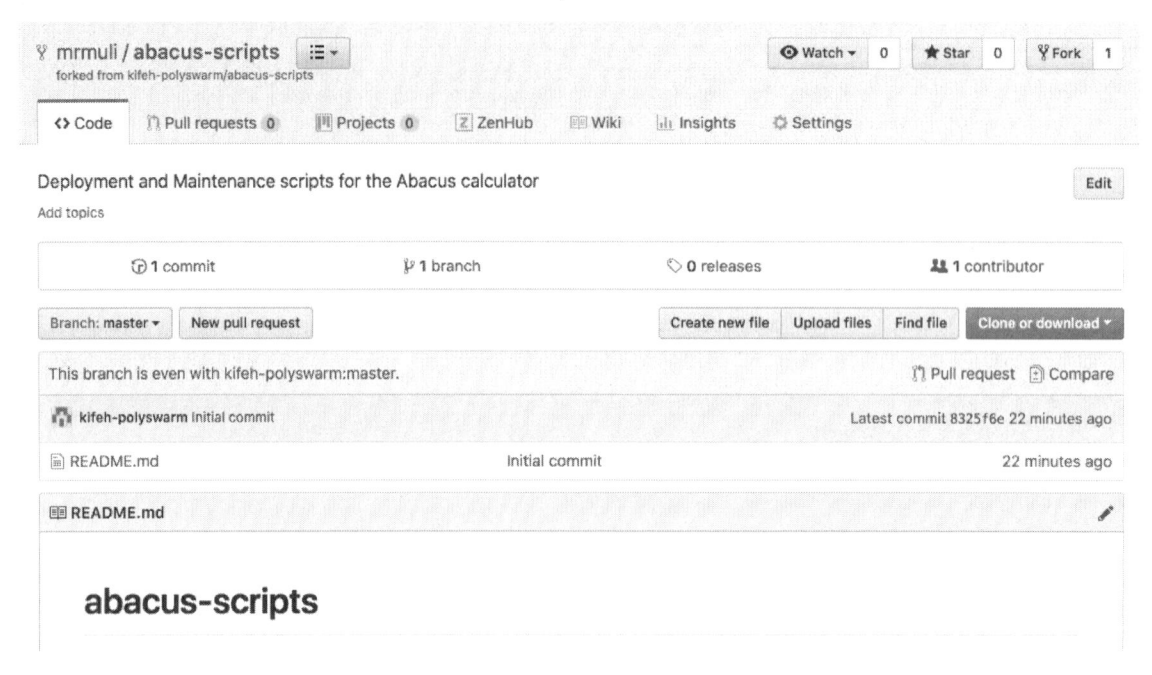

Figure 5.52: Using the abacus repository

To create submodules using abacus.

1. On your terminal, change directories to the abacus repository. Checkout to a new branch, as shown in the following screenshot:

Figure 5.53: Changing directories to the abacus repository

2. Run the following command to add abacus scripts as a submodule in a builds directory. If the path already exists, the following message will be given as output:

```
josephmuli at Friday in ~/Repositories/writing/abacus on ch-add-submodules
$ git submodule add https://github.com/kifeh-polyswarm/abacus-scripts.git builds/abacus-scripts
'builds/abacus-scripts' already exists in the index
```

Figure 5.54: Adding abacus scripts as a submodule

3. Notice the new `.gitmodules` file in the path, entailing a path and remote URL to the abacus-scripts repository, as shown in the following screenshot:

```
.gitmodules ×
1   [submodule "builds/abacus-scripts"]
2       path = builds/abacus-scripts
3       url = https://github.com/kifeh-polyswarm/abacus-scripts.git
4
```

Figure 5.55: URL to the abacus-scripts repository

4. If you also run `git status`, you'll notice the `.gitmodules` file and an abacus-scripts path, as shown in the following screenshot:

```
Changes to be committed:
    (use "git reset HEAD <file>..." to unstage)

        new file:   .gitmodules
        new file:   builds/abacus-scripts
```

Figure 5.56: Running git status

5. Finally, commit the new changes and push to origin as shown in the following screenshot:

```
josephmuli at Friday in ~/Repositories/writing/abacus on ch-add-submodules [+]
$ git commit -m"update submodule remote url"
[ch-add-submodules 7666210] update submodule remote url
 1 file changed, 1 insertion(+), 1 deletion(-)

josephmuli at Friday in ~/Repositories/writing/abacus on ch-add-submodules
$ git push origin ch-add-submodules
Enumerating objects: 5, done.
Counting objects: 100% (5/5), done.
Delta compression using up to 4 threads.
Compressing objects: 100% (3/3), done.
Writing objects: 100% (3/3), 326 bytes | 326.00 KiB/s, done.
Total 3 (delta 2), reused 0 (delta 0)
remote: Resolving deltas: 100% (2/2), completed with 2 local objects.
To github.com:mrmuli/abacus.git
   da6dba9..7666210  ch-add-submodules -> ch-add-submodules
```

Figure 5.57: Committing the new changes

6. Raise a pull request, and once the changes are reviewed and merged, you should have submodule symbolic links on the abacus repository, as shown in the following screenshot:

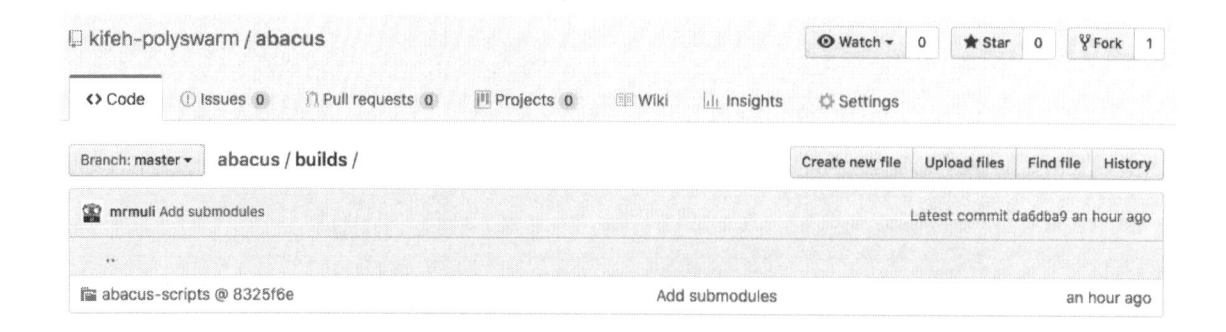

Figure 5.57: Raising a pull request

Outcome

On that note, we should now be able to create and version submodules.

Let's have a look at working with repositories that already have submodules.

Forking the Workflow | 223

Additional Steps:

1. `git submodule update` will fetch submodules that are not present in your project path, as shown in the following screenshot:

```
josephmuli at Friday in ~/Repositories/writing/abacus on ch-add-submodules
$ ls
total 48
drwxr-xr-x  10 josephmuli  staff   320 Aug 25 17:50 ./
drwxr-xr-x   6 josephmuli  staff   192 Aug 25 17:50 ../
drwxr-xr-x  12 josephmuli  staff   384 Aug 25 17:51 .git/
drwxr-xr-x   3 josephmuli  staff    96 Aug 25 17:50 .github/
-rw-r--r--   1 josephmuli  staff   127 Aug 25 17:50 .gitmodules
-rw-r--r--   1 josephmuli  staff  5473 Aug 25 17:50 CODE_OF_CONDUCT.md
-rw-r--r--   1 josephmuli  staff     1 Aug 25 17:50 CONTRIBUTING.md
-rw-r--r--   1 josephmuli  staff  1072 Aug 25 17:50 LICENSE
-rw-r--r--   1 josephmuli  staff    41 Aug 25 17:50 README.md
drwxr-xr-x   3 josephmuli  staff    96 Aug 25 17:50 src/

josephmuli at Friday in ~/Repositories/writing/abacus on ch-add-submodules
$ git submodule update
Cloning into '/Users/josephmuli/Repositories/writing/abacus/builds/abacus-scripts'...
Submodule path 'builds/abacus-scripts': checked out '8325f6e9672f0d00cc713a8e3aee99d90599b2a7'
```

Figure 5.58: Updating submodules

2. `git clone --recurse-submodules: https:github.com/<username>/abacus-scripts` clones the repository and submodules defined in a `.gitmodules` file.

Outcome

You have successfully fetched submodules that are not present in your project path and cloned the repository and submodules.

Activity 5: Rebasing

You have been tasked with squashing and dropping select commits.

The aim of this activity is to demonstrate forking a workflow and rebasing.

Ensure that you have a GitHub account:

1. Fork https://github.com/mrmuli/track-it.
2. Checkout to a new branch by using `ch-implement-feedback`.

3. Rebase and squash the following commits:

    a. `parse input`

    b. `add extra functions`

    Rebase and drop the commits with the message `remove unused methods`.

Outcome

You have successfully forked the workflow and removed the used commits and methods.

> **Note**
>
> For detailed steps for this activity, refer to the **Appendix** section on page 313.

Debugging and Maintenance

In the previous topic, we covered a number of concepts that are helpful in day-to-day version control operations. We have been able to rewrite history through rebasing, understand and implement a forking workflow, and make external contributions.

This topic presents a similar focus, except now we'll be looking more into ways that Git can handle root cause analysis and housekeeping operations.

At this point, you can now confidently collaborate on any public repository. That, however, is not all that is required. Developing involves more than just building, and the crucial part of this process is how to handle problems or put out fires. Git presents numerous ways of conducting root-cause analysis, and in this topic, we will cover this through the following commands:

- `git blame`
- `git bisect`
- `git reflog`

Furthermore, we will learn about a number of best practices, including how to trigger and react to events such as commits through Git hooks.

git blame

`git blame` helps identify and present occurrences from a revision that has modified a block of code. Usually, this is done line by line. This means that through the command, we can identify who made a change, the commit used, and what line(s) were affected. This also makes Git a very effective audit tool.

Let's demonstrate this command's basic usage. We'll run this from the abacus repository. Change directories for this project.

Exercise 36: Identifying Revisions Using Git Blame

To find out the most recent revision that occurred on the README.md file.

1. Run a blame on the README.md file:

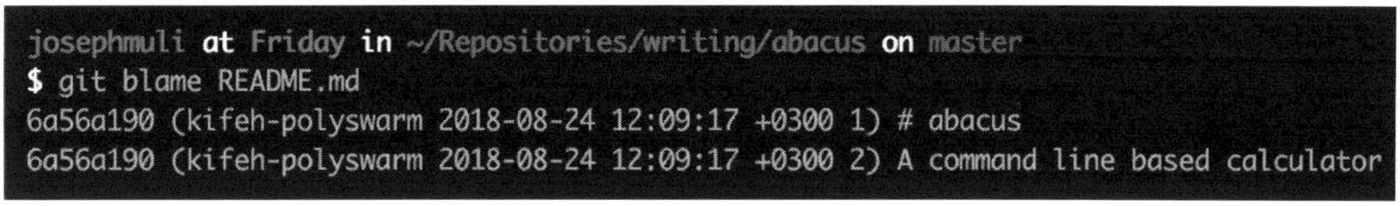

```
josephmuli at Friday in ~/Repositories/writing/abacus on master
$ git blame README.md
6a56a190 (kifeh-polyswarm 2018-08-24 12:09:17 +0300 1) # abacus
6a56a190 (kifeh-polyswarm 2018-08-24 12:09:17 +0300 2) A command line based calculator
```

Figure 5.59: Using git blame

> **Note**
>
> From the result, there are a few points to note:
>
> a. The commit hash
>
> b. The Author
>
> c. A time stamp, that is, when the commits were done
>
> d. The actual change implemented

2. Run another example of the README.md file on a different repository.
3. Change directories to the track-it repositories.

4. Run a blame on `todo.py`, as shown in the following screenshot:

```
josephmuli at Friday in ~/Repositories/writing/track-it on master [$]
$ git blame todo.py
86e9310b (mrmuli 2018-08-25 18:26:36 +0300  1) #!/usr/bin/env python3
86e9310b (mrmuli 2018-08-25 18:26:36 +0300  2)
86e9310b (mrmuli 2018-08-25 18:26:36 +0300  3) class todo(object):
86e9310b (mrmuli 2018-08-25 18:26:36 +0300  4)     def init(self):
86e9310b (mrmuli 2018-08-25 18:26:36 +0300  5)         pass
5450a266 (mrmuli 2018-08-25 18:33:37 +0300  6)
5450a266 (mrmuli 2018-08-25 18:33:37 +0300  7)     def read_data(self, input):
5450a266 (mrmuli 2018-08-25 18:33:37 +0300  8)         return "get some input from x"
38017125 (mrmuli 2018-08-25 18:41:14 +0300  9)
38017125 (mrmuli 2018-08-25 18:41:14 +0300 10) # helper method
38017125 (mrmuli 2018-08-25 18:41:14 +0300 11) def parse_input(input):
38017125 (mrmuli 2018-08-25 18:41:14 +0300 12)     return "parse input for the read_data method"
86e9310b (mrmuli 2018-08-25 18:26:36 +0300 13)
86e9310b (mrmuli 2018-08-25 18:26:36 +0300 14) def main():
86e9310b (mrmuli 2018-08-25 18:26:36 +0300 15)     tdo = todo()
86e9310b (mrmuli 2018-08-25 18:26:36 +0300 16)     pass
86e9310b (mrmuli 2018-08-25 18:26:36 +0300 17)
86e9310b (mrmuli 2018-08-25 18:26:36 +0300 18) if __name__ == "__main__":
86e9310b (mrmuli 2018-08-25 18:26:36 +0300 19)     main()
```

Figure 5.60: Using git blame

> **Note**
>
> Just like before, we get the same content, but this time with more detail. Notice how there is a repetition of commits, showing all changes staged and committed through that hash.

Outcome

`git blame` includes several other options, such as showing the filename in the original commit, whereby the default filename is displayed if a change comes from a different file, with a different name, as shown in the following screenshot:

```
josephmuli at Friday in ~/Repositories/writing/track-it on master [$]
$ git blame -f todo.py
86e9310b todo.py (mrmuli 2018-08-25 18:26:36 +0300  1) #!/usr/bin/env python3
86e9310b todo.py (mrmuli 2018-08-25 18:26:36 +0300  2)
86e9310b todo.py (mrmuli 2018-08-25 18:26:36 +0300  3) class todo(object):
86e9310b todo.py (mrmuli 2018-08-25 18:26:36 +0300  4)     def init(self):
86e9310b todo.py (mrmuli 2018-08-25 18:26:36 +0300  5)         pass
5450a266 todo.py (mrmuli 2018-08-25 18:33:37 +0300  6)
5450a266 todo.py (mrmuli 2018-08-25 18:33:37 +0300  7)     def read_data(self, input):
5450a266 todo.py (mrmuli 2018-08-25 18:33:37 +0300  8)         return "get some input from x"
38017125 todo.py (mrmuli 2018-08-25 18:41:14 +0300  9)
38017125 todo.py (mrmuli 2018-08-25 18:41:14 +0300 10) # helper method
38017125 todo.py (mrmuli 2018-08-25 18:41:14 +0300 11) def parse_input(input):
38017125 todo.py (mrmuli 2018-08-25 18:41:14 +0300 12)     return "parse input for the read_data method"
86e9310b todo.py (mrmuli 2018-08-25 18:26:36 +0300 13)
86e9310b todo.py (mrmuli 2018-08-25 18:26:36 +0300 14) def main():
86e9310b todo.py (mrmuli 2018-08-25 18:26:36 +0300 15)     tdo = todo()
86e9310b todo.py (mrmuli 2018-08-25 18:26:36 +0300 16)     pass
86e9310b todo.py (mrmuli 2018-08-25 18:26:36 +0300 17)
86e9310b todo.py (mrmuli 2018-08-25 18:26:36 +0300 18) if __name__ == "__main__":
86e9310b todo.py (mrmuli 2018-08-25 18:26:36 +0300 19)     main()
```

Figure 5.61: git blame outcome

git bisect

`git bisect`, as described on Git's official documentation, is used to find a commit that has introduced an anomaly through a binary search. This is most helpful when trying to identify a commit to test a failing feature after previous success.

Consider a scenario where at commit 1, feature **A** was working perfectly.
However, at the current commit, 9, something happened, and suddenly the feature doesn't work anymore. At this point, you have established the faulty code, but not when it was introduced, and this is where `git bisect` comes in. A binary search would run as follows:

1. Sort the commits (in our case, numbers) in ascending order.

2. Get the median of 1 and 9, which is **5** ((n + 1) / 2).

3. Recommend the commit at position 5. After a run and no success, `git bisect` is going to lean toward the beginning half, run a median, and recommend until it either identifies the commit or phases the half out; then move to the other half.

Assuming that we are at **HEAD** or the most recent commit, `track-it` is giving a 404 error on loading the web page. We manage to trace the issue to the `list_todos` method that is missing, but we're really not sure when this change was introduced. Moreover, it was working perfectly when we introduced the `parsing` method:

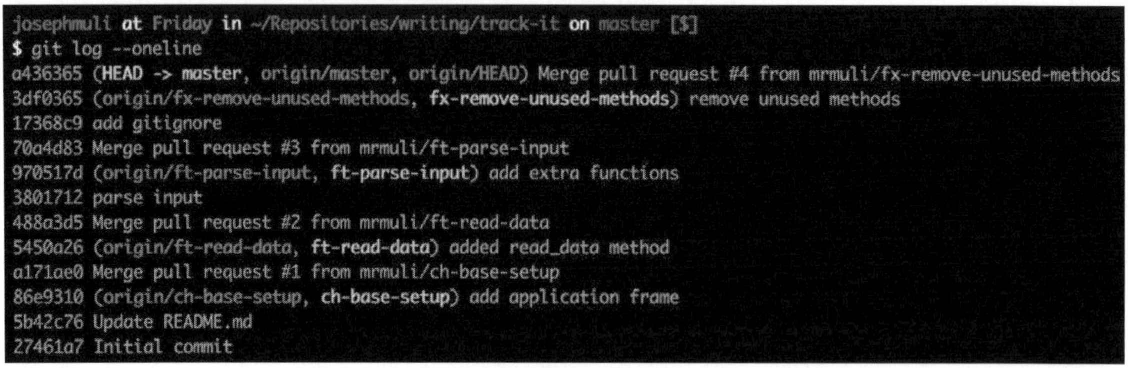

```
josephmuli at Friday in ~/Repositories/writing/track-it on master [$]
$ git log --oneline
a436365 (HEAD -> master, origin/master, origin/HEAD) Merge pull request #4 from mrmuli/fx-remove-unused-methods
3df0365 (origin/fx-remove-unused-methods, fx-remove-unused-methods) remove unused methods
17368c9 add gitignore
70a4d83 Merge pull request #3 from mrmuli/ft-parse-input
970517d (origin/ft-parse-input, ft-parse-input) add extra functions
3801712 parse input
488a3d5 Merge pull request #2 from mrmuli/ft-read-data
5450a26 (origin/ft-read-data, ft-read-data) added read_data method
a171ae0 Merge pull request #1 from mrmuli/ch-base-setup
86e9310 (origin/ch-base-setup, ch-base-setup) add application frame
5b42c76 Update README.md
27461a7 Initial commit
```

Figure 5.62: Using git log

Exercise 37: Finding Commits using Git Bisect

To run `git bisect` to find commits.

1. Run the `git bisect` command, as shown in the following screenshot:

```
josephmuli at Friday in ~/Repositories/writing/track-it on master [$]
$ git bisect start
```

Figure 5.63: Using git bisect

2. Introduce the good commit hash (where it last worked) and the bad commit hash, that is, the current **HEAD**, as shown in the following screenshots:

> **Note**
>
> Git rebase is going to recommend a commit, which in terms of a binary search is the median. Still on that point, notice that bisect has moved the branch to a detached HEAD on that commit. Here, we are using `todo.py`, and we still don't have `list_todos`, which means this isn't the commit.

Debugging and Maintenance | 229

```
josephmuli at Friday in ~/Repositories/writing/track-it on master [$]
$ git bisect good 70a4d83

josephmuli at Friday in ~/Repositories/writing/track-it on master [$]
$ git bisect bad a436365
Bisecting: 0 revisions left to test after this (roughly 1 step)
[3df0365cc836387330bc16a7a3389396d3e93100] remove unused methods
```

Figure 5.64: Using git bisect

```
josephmuli at Friday in ~/Repositories/writing/track-it on 3df0365 [$]
$ cat todo.py
#!/usr/bin/env python3

class todo(object):
    def init(self):
        pass

    def read_data(self, input):
        return "get some input from x"

# helper method
def parse_input(input):
    return "parse input for the read_data method"

def main():
    tdo = todo()
    pass

if __name__ == "__main__":
    main()
```

Figure 5.65: Using git bisect

3. Run `git bisect bad` to inform that this isn't the commit we are looking for. Immediately after, a new commit is recommended and we're moved to another detached HEAD as shown in the following screenshot:

```
josephmuli at Friday in ~/Repositories/writing/track-it on 3df0365 [$]
$ git bisect bad
Bisecting: 0 revisions left to test after this (roughly 0 steps)
[17368c976900fc17f40a6812c7b086d3e6cfbf1b] add gitignore
```

Figure 5.66: Using git bisect bad

4. Listing the content shows `list_todos`, thus identifying the commit as `add gitignore` as shown in the following screenshot:

```
josephmuli at Friday in ~/Repositories/writing/track-it on 17368c9 [$]
$ cat todo.py
#!/usr/bin/env python3

class todo(object):
    def init(self):
        pass

    def read_data(self, input):
        return "get some input from x"

    def delete_todos(self, input):
        pass

    def list_todos(self, input):
        pass

# helper method
def parse_input(input):
    return "parse input for the read_data method"

def main():
    tdo = todo()
    pass

if __name__ == "__main__":
    main()
```

Figure 5.67: Listing the content

5. Run `git bisect good` to inform the bisect of the success. The following output is displayed as seen in the following screenshot, listing:

- The timestamp
- Commit message
- The Author

```
josephmuli at Friday in ~/Repositories/writing/track-it on 17368c9 [$]
$ git bisect good
3df0365cc836387330bc16a7a3389396d3e93100 is the first bad commit
commit 3df0365cc836387330bc16a7a3389396d3e93100
Author: mrmuli <jayjaymuli00@gmail.com>
Date:   Sat Aug 25 18:48:32 2018 +0300

    remove unused methods

:100644 100644 058713349b6693d8b05bbf5c8ec381fc2434b64d 0b87707ad4efc96b7a0bc4f616a41829baae176b M      todo.py
```

Figure 5.68: Using git bisect good

6. To end the wizard, run `git bisect reset`, as shown in the following screenshot:

```
josephmuli at Friday in ~/Repositories/writing/track-it on 17368c9 [$]
$ git bisect reset
Previous HEAD position was 17368c9 add gitignore
Switched to branch 'master'
Your branch is up to date with 'origin/master'.
```

Figure 5.69: Using git bisect reset

Outcome

You have successfully used the `git bisect` command to identify the timestamp, commit message, and author.

git reflog

`git reflog` is short for Git **reference logs**. Reflogs keep track of changes to HEAD over a defined period of time. These changes can be best defined as events, as they are saturated, which is basically all activities, that is, checking out branches, rebase events, and branch updates from remote URLs.

By default, reflog doesn't traverse, as it consists of a list of all activities occurring on HEAD, which also includes activities from unreachable branches and lost commits through operations such as a rebase. However, a default period of 30 days exists before the data expires. Entries belonging to reachable branches also have an expiration period of 90 days by default.

232 | Collaborative Git

The basic usage of `git reflog` involves the following:

The `git reflog` both shows and outputs HEAD reference logs, as shown in the following screenshots:

```
josephmuli at Friday in ~/Repositories/writing/track-it on master [$]
$ git reflog
a436365 (HEAD -> master, origin/master, origin/HEAD) HEAD@{0}: checkout: moving from 17368c976900fc17f40a6812c7b086d3e6cfbf1b to master
17368c9 HEAD@{1}: checkout: moving from 3df0365cc836387330bc16a7a3389396d3e93100 to 17368c976900fc17f40a6812c7b086d3e6cfbf1b
3df0365 (origin/fx-remove-unused-methods, fx-remove-unused-methods) HEAD@{2}: checkout: moving from master to 3df0365cc836387330bc16a7a3389396d3e93100
a436365 (HEAD -> master, origin/master, origin/HEAD) HEAD@{3}: checkout: moving from master to master
a436365 (HEAD -> master, origin/master, origin/HEAD) HEAD@{4}: checkout: moving from master to master
a436365 (HEAD -> master, origin/master, origin/HEAD) HEAD@{5}: checkout: moving from ch-implement-feedback to master
0d66b22 (origin/ch-implement-feedback, ch-implement-feedback) HEAD@{6}: rebase -i (finish): returning to refs/heads/ch-implement-feedback
0d66b22 (origin/ch-implement-feedback, ch-implement-feedback) HEAD@{7}: rebase -i (start): checkout HEAD~2
6834a55 HEAD@{8}: rebase -i (finish): returning to refs/heads/ch-implement-feedback
6834a55 HEAD@{9}: rebase -i (pick): remove unused methods
0d66b22 (origin/ch-implement-feedback, ch-implement-feedback) HEAD@{10}: rebase -i (pick): add gitignore
```

Figure 5.70: Using git reflog

The commit hashes show where HEAD is and was **n** number of times ago. For instance, the following commits show that HEAD was at **6834a55**, **8** and **9** moves ago, as shown in the following screenshot:

```
6834a55 HEAD@{8}: rebase -i (finish): returning to refs/heads/ch-implement-feedback
6834a55 HEAD@{9}: rebase -i (pick): remove unused methods
```

Figure 5.71: Using git rebase

To get the reflog on a specific branch, pass the branch name as an argument, as shown in the following screenshot:

```
josephmuli at Friday in ~/Repositories/writing/track-it on master [$]
$ git branch
  ch-base-setup
  ch-implement-feedback
  ft-parse-input
  ft-read-data
  fx-remove-unused-methods
* master

josephmuli at Friday in ~/Repositories/writing/track-it on master [$]
$ git reflog show ft-read-data
5450a26 (origin/ft-read-data, ft-read-data) ft-read-data@{0}: commit: added read_data method
a171ae0 ft-read-data@{1}: branch: Created from HEAD
```

Figure 5.72: Using git reflog

Housekeeping

In this subtopic, we will highlight a number of best practices that can be applied toward maintaining a clean and operable repository through the following commands:

- `git clean`
- `git gc`
- `git prune`

git clean

`git clean` recursively removes untracked files from a working tree. This emphasizes that any file that is not staged to be tracked or reset is rid of, maintaining a versioned only directory. Normally, `git clean` purges files through a list defined from a `.gitignore` file, but in special cases, these rules can be ignored and any untracked file is cleared.

Let's complete the following exercise to understand the basic usage of `git clean`.

Exercise 38: Removing Untracked Files using Git Clean

To remove untracked files from a working tree using `git clean`, follow these steps:

1. From the `track-it` repository, add a new file that collects output data for development, as shown in the following screenshot:

```
josephmuli at Friday in ~/Repositories/writing/track-it on master [$]
$ touch output.json
```

Figure 5.73: Adding a new file for output data

2. By default, `Output.json` is untracked, if not staged. Adding a new file and staging it changes the status to tracked, as identified through `git status`, as shown in the following screenshot:

```
josephmuli at Friday in ~/Repositories/writing/track-it on master [?$]
$ touch input.json

josephmuli at Friday in ~/Repositories/writing/track-it on master [?$]
$ git add input.json

josephmuli at Friday in ~/Repositories/writing/track-it on master [+?$]
$ git status
On branch master
Your branch is up to date with 'origin/master'.

Changes to be committed:
  (use "git reset HEAD <file>..." to unstage)

        new file:   input.json

Untracked files:
  (use "git add <file>..." to include in what will be committed)

        output.json
```

Figure 5.74: Using git status

3. Executing `git clean` will get rid of `output.json`, as shown in the following screenshot:

> **Note**
>
> However, it's advisable to perform a dry run; just to be sure of what to expect. Just as suspected, `output.json` will be removed. The `-n option` will enable a dry run accompanying `git clean`, as shown in the following screenshot:

```
josephmuli at Friday in ~/Repositories/writing/track-it on master [+?$]
$ git clean -n
Would remove output.json
```

Figure 5.75: Using git clean

4. To remove the file, the `-f` and `-i` options can be utilized, as shown in the following screenshot:

> **Note**
>
> The `-i` option presents an interactive mode that presents an interactive session.

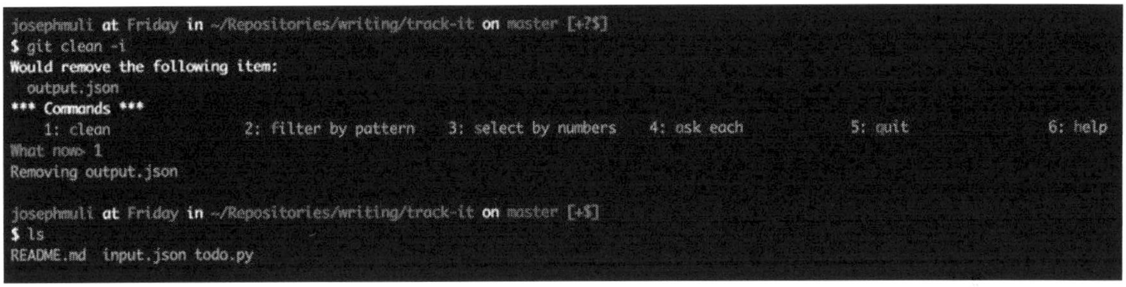

```
josephmuli at Friday in ~/Repositories/writing/track-it on master [+?$]
$ git clean -i
Would remove the following item:
  output.json
*** Commands ***
    1: clean            2: filter by pattern    3: select by numbers   4: ask each         5: quit             6: help
What now> 1
Removing output.json

josephmuli at Friday in ~/Repositories/writing/track-it on master [+$]
$ ls
README.md  input.json todo.py
```

Figure 5.76: Using git clean

> **Note**
>
> A similar result can be achieved through the `-f` option, as demonstrated in the following screenshot:

```
josephmuli at Friday in ~/Repositories/writing/track-it on master [+?$]
$ git clean -f
Removing output.json

josephmuli at Friday in ~/Repositories/writing/track-it on master [+$]
$ ls
README.md  input.json todo.py
```

Figure 5.77: Using git clean -f

Outcome

You have successfully used the `git clean` command to remove the untracked `output.json` file.

git gc

`git gc` is responsible for garbage collection on targeted repositories. This process handles the deletion of staged and committed objects from unreachable branches, particularly those holding a reflog. Depending on the repository activity, `git gc` helps optimize disk space and maintains a decent repository.

As mentioned previously, running `git gc` depends on how heavy the repository's usage is. With multiple contributors, you may want to run it frequently, that is, at least twice a week. This can also be automated through a cron job to maintain focus on the product.

To verify whether any housekeeping is required, `git gc` appends the `--auto` option and if not necessary, no output shall be displayed, as demonstrated in the following screenshot:

```
josephmuli at Friday in ~/Repositories/writing/track-it on master [+$]
$ git gc --auto
```

Figure 5.78: Using git gc

To proceed without necessarily requiring housekeeping, run the following command, and optionally append `--force`, as shown in the following screenshot:

```
josephmuli at Friday in ~/Repositories/writing/track-it on master [+$]
$ git gc
Enumerating objects: 46, done.
Counting objects: 100% (46/46), done.
Delta compression using up to 4 threads.
Compressing objects: 100% (38/38), done.
Writing objects: 100% (46/46), done.
Total 46 (delta 15), reused 6 (delta 0)
```

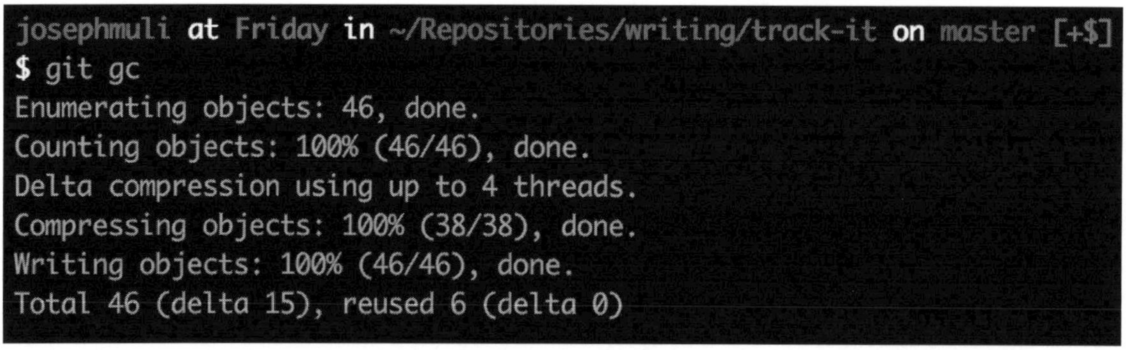

Figure 5.79: Using git gc

git prune

The `git prune` command, similar to `git gc`, gets rid of all unreachable objects, that is, basically objects without references, such as ones from deleted branches. According to the documentation, it's best to go for `git gc`. which calls `git prune`, killing two birds with one stone.

Removing Merged Local and Remote Branches

Getting rid of a branch after the feature is merged into a base branch is highly advisable and one of Git's best practices.

To deal with this issue of clutter, Git and GitHub present two solutions:

1. Deleting the branch from the GitHub UI after a successful merge and then a local fetch.
2. Manual deletion locally.

   Before we start taking out branches, we need to be aware of merged and not unmerged branches. The following commands help us identify this:

   ```
   josephmuli at Friday in ~/Repositories/writing/track-it on master [+$]
   $ git branch --merged
     ch-base-setup
     ft-parse-input
     ft-read-data
     fx-remove-unused-methods
   * master

   josephmuli at Friday in ~/Repositories/writing/track-it on master [+$]
   $ git branch --no-merged
     ch-implement-feedback
   ```

   Figure 5.80: Using git branch --merged

With that in mind, we can be assured of not losing changes that are not present on the base branch, which is the master. Now, to delete these branches individually, run the following command:

```
josephmuli at Friday in ~/Repositories/writing/track-it on master [+$]
$ git branch -d fx-remove-unused-methods
Deleted branch fx-remove-unused-methods (was 3df0365).
```

Figure 5.81: Using git branch

Exercise 39: Deleting Branches

To demonstrates the manual deletion of branches.

1. To delete the remote branch reference, run the following command:

   ```
   josephmuli at Friday in ~/Repositories/writing/track-it on master [+$]
   $ git push --delete origin fx-remove-unused-methods
   To github.com:mrmuli/track-it.git
    - [deleted]         fx-remove-unused-methods
   ```

   Figure 5.82: Deleting the remote branch reference

2. To delete a branch that is not merged, run the command with a -D option, as shown in the following screenshot:

```
josephmuli at Friday in ~/Repositories/writing/track-it on master [+$]
$ git branch -D ch-implement-feedback
Deleted branch ch-implement-feedback (was 0d66b22).
```

Figure 5.83: Deleting the unmerged branch

Outcome

You have successfully deleted the branches that are not merged.

Pre-commit hooks

Pre-commit hooks, as client-side Git hooks, are custom scripts that are triggered before certain actions occur, such as commits and merges, hence the name prefix. They can be customized to any team's workflow, and in most scenarios, teams use pre-commit hooks to achieve the following:

- Running language linters and standardization checks before commits
- Verifying that sensitive keys aren't being versioned
- Verifying compatibility and portability of the code in play

Hooks generally reside within the hooks directory, under `.git.` which is present in all repositories. The following screenshot shows you a glance at the hooks directory:

```
josephmuli at Friday in ~/Repositories/writing/track-it/.git/hooks on master
$ ls
applypatch-msg.sample    fsmonitor-watchman.sample  pre-applypatch.sample  pre-push.sample     pre-receive.sample         update.sample
commit-msg.sample        post-update.sample         pre-commit.sample      pre-rebase.sample   prepare-commit-msg.sample
```

Figure 5.84: Using the ls command

To create custom hooks, include the scripts as executables in your repository's `.git/hooks` directory, or remove the `.sample` extension from the currently existent hook scripts. Be sure to edit them appropriately.

Activity 6: Utilizing Pre-Commit Hooks for Housekeeping

To have a clean, effective, and resource-friendly repository, you have been tasked with getting rid of merged local and remote branches on `track-it`.

The aim of this activity is to demonstrate using pre-commit hooks to remove the merged remote branches on `track-it`.

Ensure that you have a cloned `track-it` repository from the previous activity:

1. Update the `prepare-commit-msg.sample` script.
2. Run the required command to update its name.
3. Finally, make the script executable.
4. Back on the root directory, stage a new file.
5. Commit the file through the `git commit` command to observe the changes.
6. Identify all merged branches using the required commands
7. For each branch, delete the required commands.

Outcome

You have successfully utilized pre-commit hooks to remove the merged remote branches on `track-it`.

> **Note**
>
> For detailed steps for this activity, refer to the **Appendix** section on page 315.

Summary

In this chapter, we described and implemented a forked workflow. Then, we demonstrated how to rewrite history with Git and explained how Git approaches root-cause analysis. Lastly, we identified numerous ways that Git handles housekeeping.

In the next chapter, we will automate the testing and building of application releases on GitHub and version software releases.

6

Automated Testing and Release Management

Learning Objectives

By the end of this chapter, you will be able to:

- Automate the testing and building of application releases on GitHub
- Version software releases

This chapter describes utilizing webhooks, CircleCi and tagging and releasing with Git.

Introduction

You have recently gone over a variety of Git modules, workflows, and operations ranging from versioning commits to collaboratively forking and rebasing commits. You can now comfortably contribute to any desired repository, abiding by the necessary best practices.

This chapter will introduce a new perspective on handling code and operations on your repositories. We will walk through and implement test automation and release management, which are crucial practices and processes that enable product delivery. Even though they can be related to DevOps, this knowledge is crucial to all developers, regardless of their stacks.

Test Automation

Simply put, this is the use of software or tools to control the testing of applications. Test automation enables processes such as **Continuous Integration**, **Continuous Delivery**, and **Continuous Deployment**. Usually, it's the first step of any of the aforementioned processes, and practically what happens on a Continuous Integration pipeline. You may have come across a badge such as the one shown in the following screenshot on a repository and wondered why and how it's there. We'll be answering these questions and setting them up on our repositories later:

Figure 6.1: GitHub badge

Webhooks and GitHub Applications

As we build on our knowledge of test automation, let's take a minute to understand what webhooks and GitHub applications are, and how they affect this process. **Webhooks** are callbacks that intercept events and implement actions. In this context, webhooks enable GitHub applications to subscribe to events such as pushed commits and the creation of pull requests. For instance, you could be running a Jenkins server and need to run tests on new branch changes. Jenkins would use a webhook to listen for push events and run tests every time branches are updated.

Test Automation | 243

Exercise 40: Setting up a Webhook

To set up a webhook on a GitHub repository.

Use the abacus repository from GitHub for this exercise:

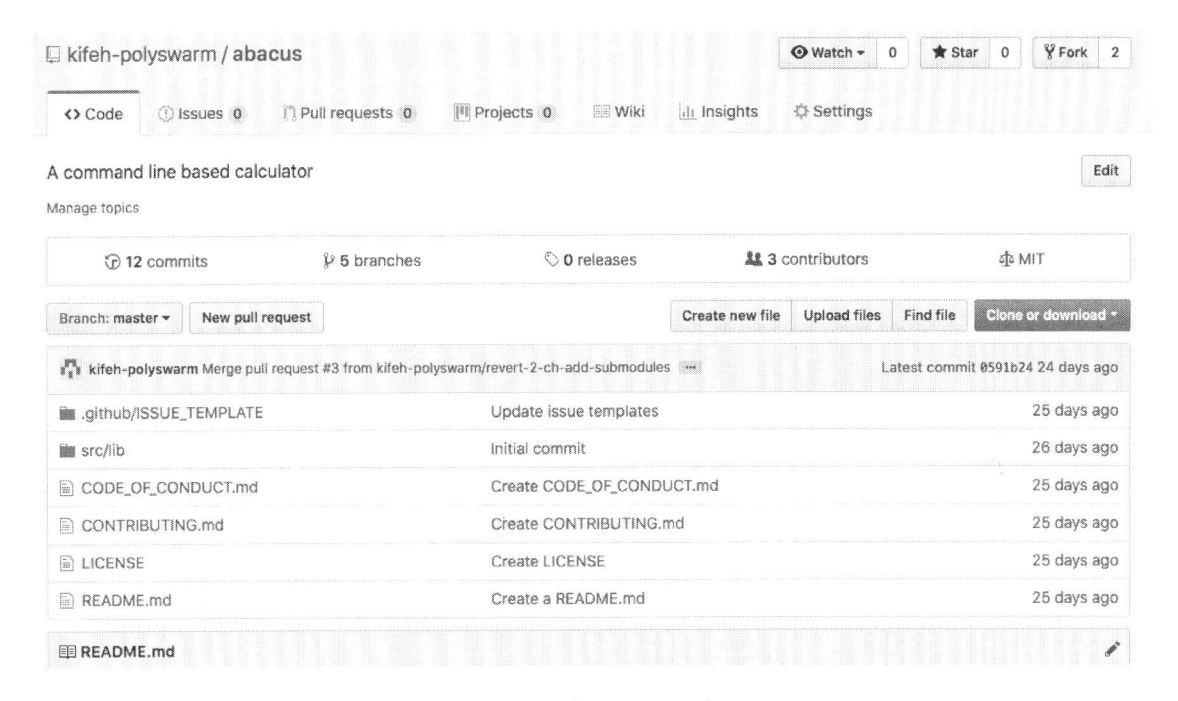

Figure 6.2: Abacus repository

1. Select **Webhooks** under the settings menu, as shown in the following screenshot:

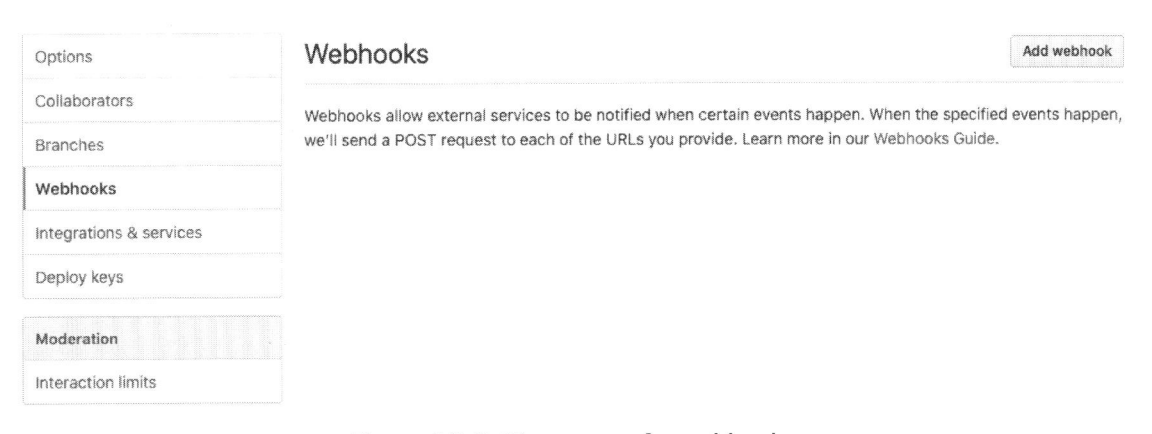

Figure 6.3: Settings menu for webhooks

244 | Automated Testing and Release Management

2. Select **Add webhook**, authorize it, and GitHub should redirect you to the following page:

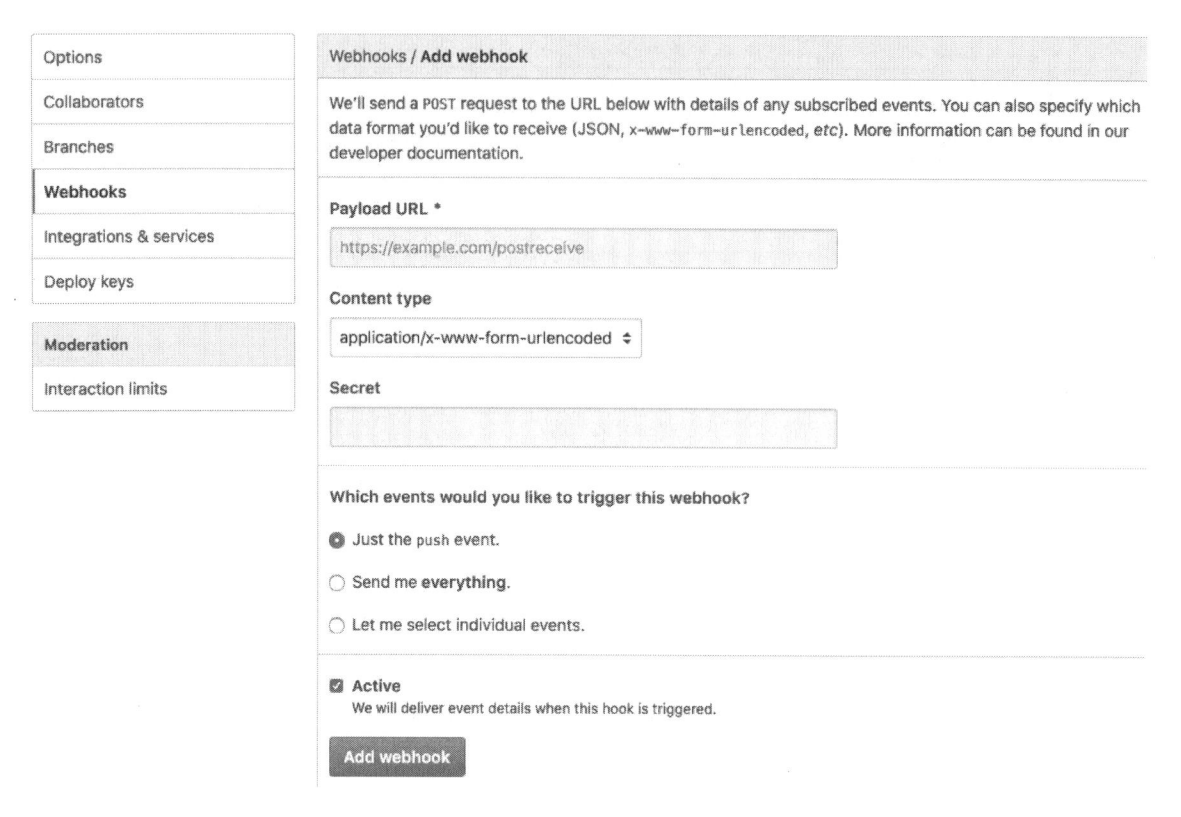

Figure 6.4: Adding webhooks

> **Note**
>
> The **Payload URL** dictates the link to your **hosted** service, such as a Jenkins server. If you are running it in a private subnetwork, be sure to provide a public gateway IP address or web address.
>
> The **Content type** dictates the data format you expect to receive, and **Secret** is a random value that helps validate request sources; specifically, it ensures that the requests are from GitHub. Here is a sample setup:

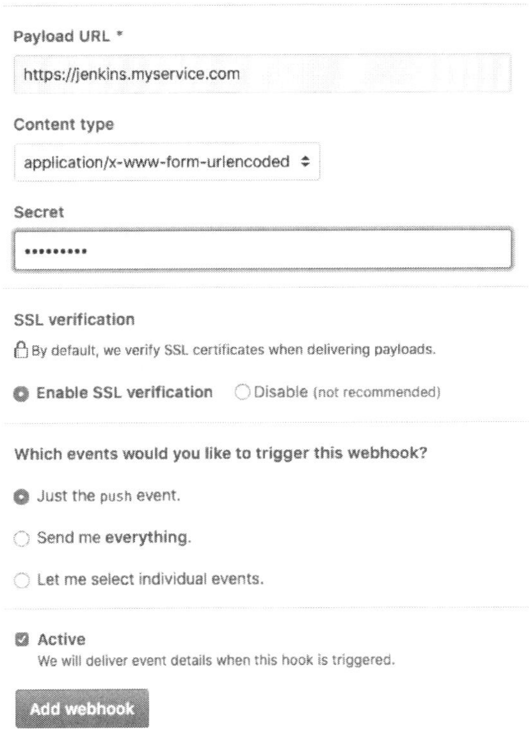

Figure 6.5: Webhook settings

3. Once you have finished filling in the required fields, select **Add webhook**, as shown in the preceding screenshot.

Outcome

You have successfully set up a webhook on a GitHub repository. GitHub will immediately try reaching the service and if it's up, all should be well. This is a demo, hence the warning sign next to the webhook.

GitHub Applications

GitHub applications are services that enable a variety of operations such as the testing, building, and deployment of applications, and are accessible from the GitHub marketplace. They entail, but are not limited to, the following service types:

- **Continuous Integration**
- **Code Quality**
- **Monitoring**
- **Project Management**
- **Deployment**

This chapter will particularly focus on Continuous Integration (CI) through **CircleCi** so that we can build on our test automation knowledge. CircleCi is a platform for CI and Continuous Delivery (CD) that simplifies the quick build and release of software in teams of various sizes.

Exercise 41: Setting Up CircleCi CI

To set up a CircleCi CI pipeline.

1. Select **Marketplace** from your GitHub repository or profile. Under **Continuous Integration**, select **CircleCi**:

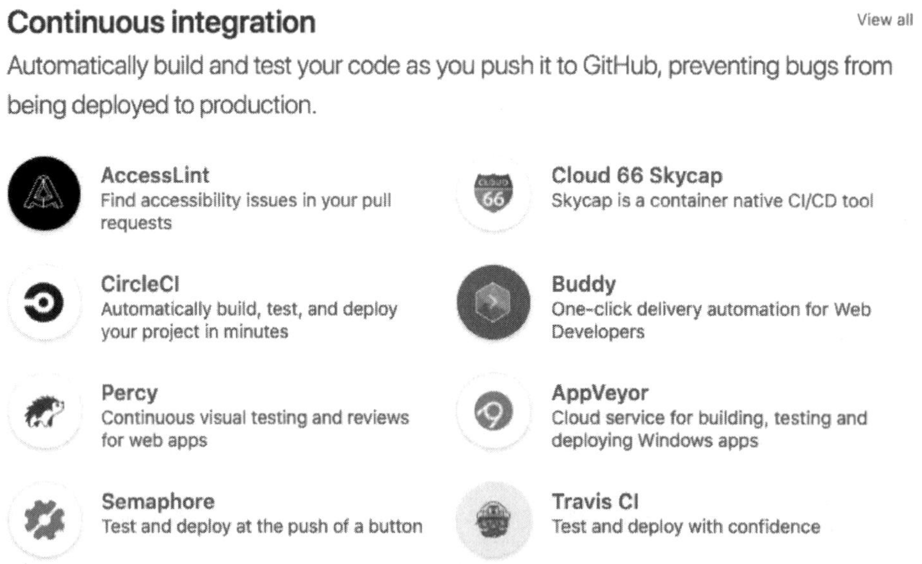

Figure 6.6: Continuous Integration options

2. Select **Set up a plan**, as shown in the following screenshot. For now, we will work with the free plan:

> **Note**
>
> Paid plans are recommended according to your team's size as they provide better flexibility and scalability.

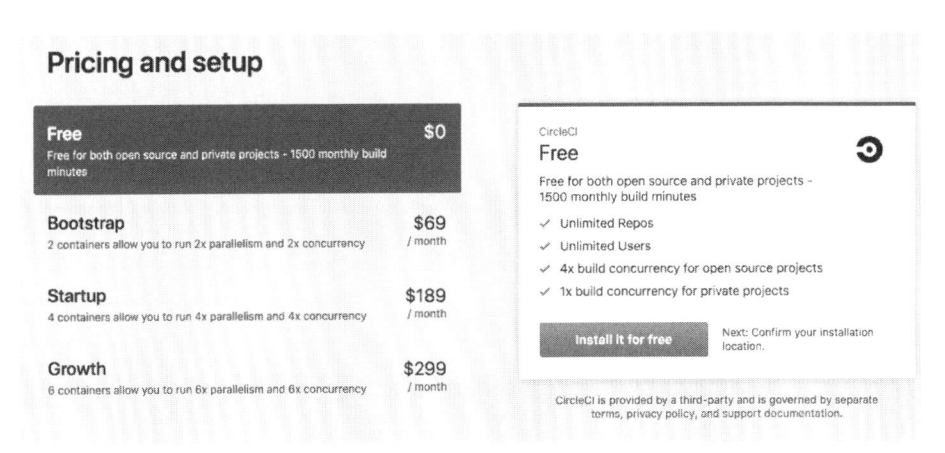

Figure 6.7: Pricing for CircleCI

3. Complete the order, begin the installation, and you should be redirected to **circleci.com** after you authorize.

4. Remember to authorize your organizations to use the service if you are setting this up for collaborative purposes, as shown in the following screenshot:

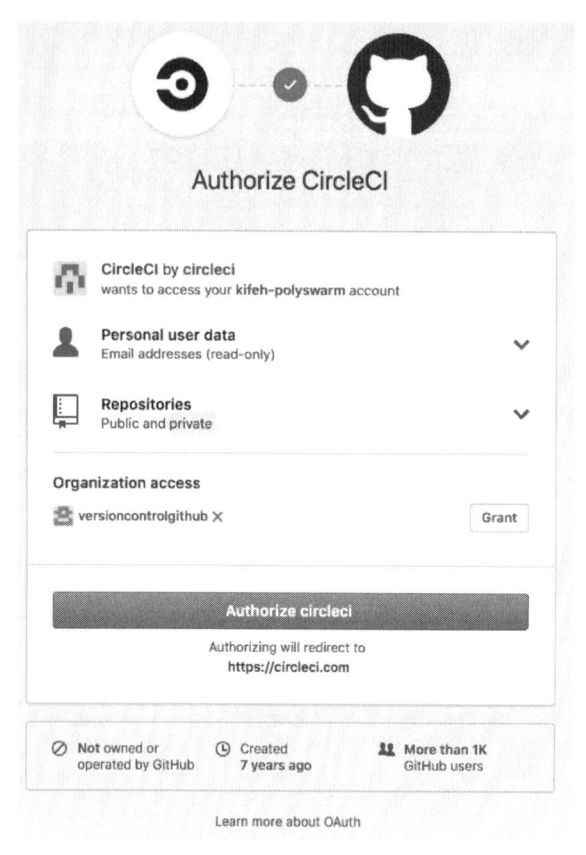

Figure 6.8: Authorizing CircleCI

> **Note**
>
> From your dashboard, notice the flexibility provided by CircleCi, which enables processes such as build insights and workflows.

5. Add a project from the **Jobs** window, as shown in the following screenshot:

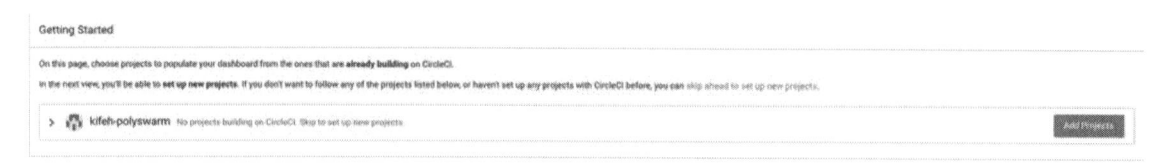

Figure 6.9: Adding a project

6. From the repository list, select **abacus** and **Set Up Project**, as shown in the following screenshot:

Figure 6.10: Setting up a project

> **Note**
>
> CircleCI will automatically redirect you to the project definition page.

7. Complete the setup by selecting **Python** as the language. As per the instructions, you are required to have the CircleCi configuration versioned on the repository, as shown in the following screenshot:

> **Note**
>
> If you attempt to build the project without a config file, the job will still run, and a summary will be presented, as shown in the following screenshot:

Figure 6.11: Setting up the test summary

8. From the abacus repository, create a new branch called **ch-circle-ci** or a name of your choice.

9. Create a **.circleci** folder and a **config.yml** file in the folder, as advised by CircleCi as shown in the following screenshot:

Live Link for file config.yml: https://bit.ly/2DC6aC5

> **Note**
>
> My config file is in the following screenshot. This is also present at https://github.com/TrainingByPackt/Version-Control-with-Git-and-GitHub/blob/master/Lesson%206-Automated%20Testing%20and%20Release%20Management/config.yml.

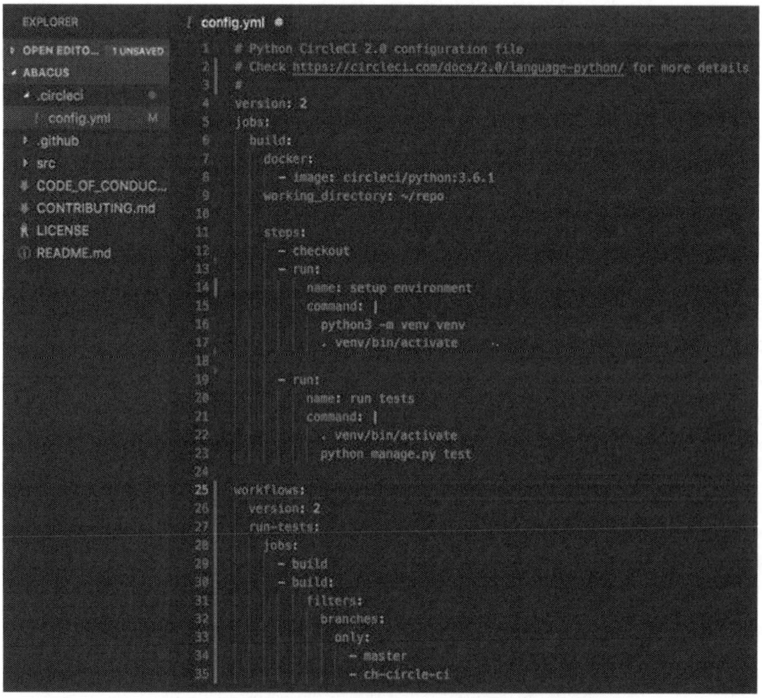

Figure 6.12: Creating the config.yml file

> **Note**
>
> Notice that the configuration identifies and filters the job to run on defined branches, the application-specific commands to be run, the setup of the virtual environment, and runs tests.

10. Stage your changes, and then commit and push them to GitHub, as shown in the following screenshot:

> **Note**
>
> Back on CircleCi, the build should automatically start, and if it doesn't, go ahead and rebuild the previous one:

Figure 6.13: Job failure

> **Note**
>
> The job failed because no tests have been defined and the wrong command is in use, according to the job log:

Figure 6.14: Test failure

11. Add a build badge to the GitHub repository.

252 | Automated Testing and Release Management

12. From the CircleCI jobs dashboard, select the gear button next to the project name, as shown in the following screenshot:

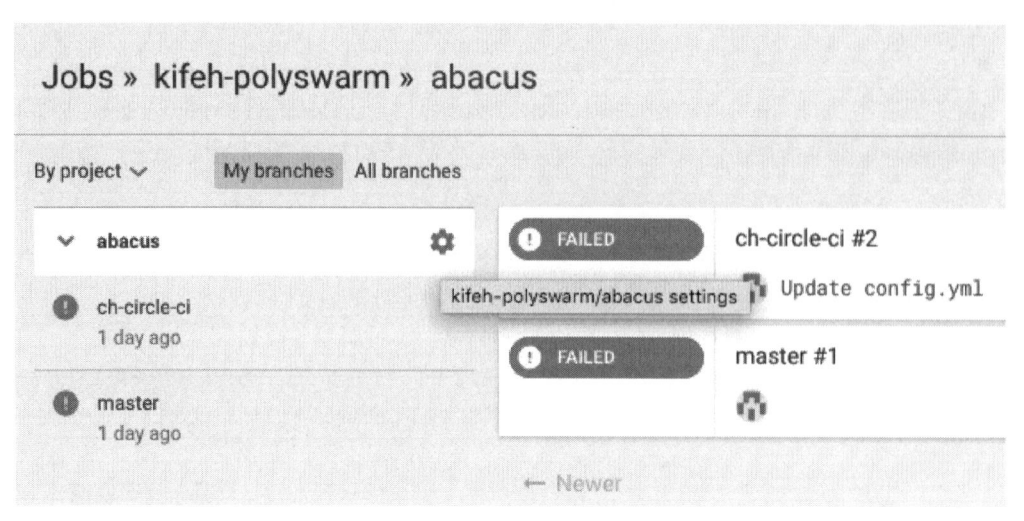

Figure 6.15: Job failure

13. Navigate to **status badges** under notifications, as shown in the following screenshot:

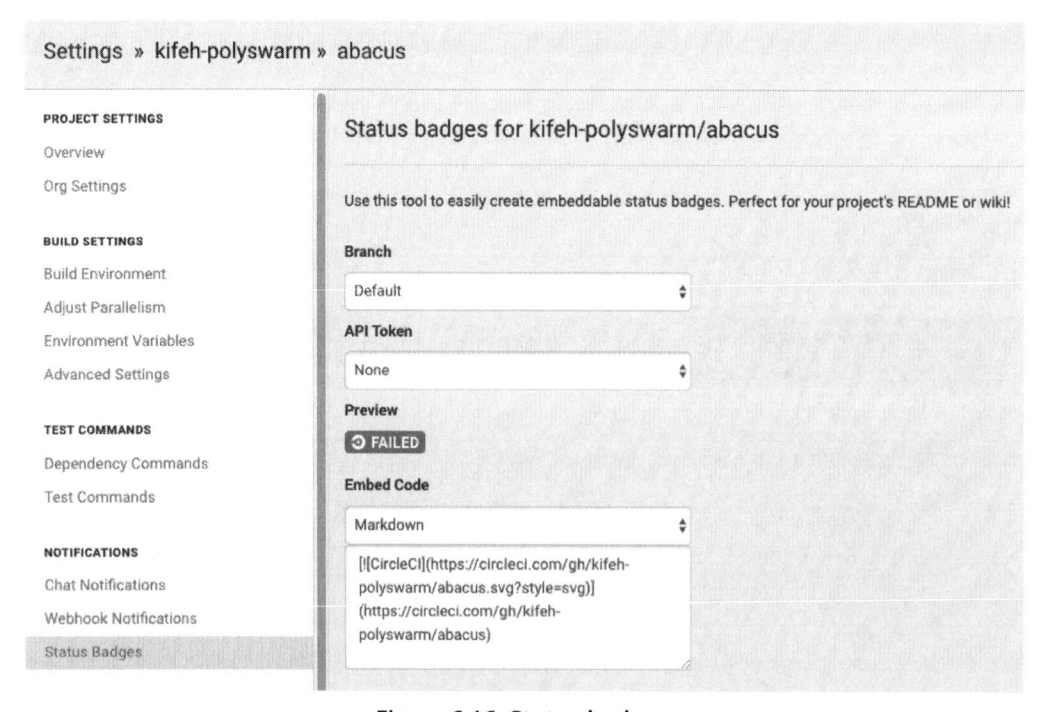

Figure 6.16: Status badges

14. Copy the markdown under **Embed Code** and paste it into your README.md file, just under the repository name.

> **Note**
>
> Because this is a markdown, add two line spaces on the same line as the embedded code, as shown in the following screenshot. Notice the cursor position:

Figure 6.17: The README.md file

15. Stage, commit, and push your changes so that you should now have a badge that informs you of the repository's build status, as shown in the following screenshot:

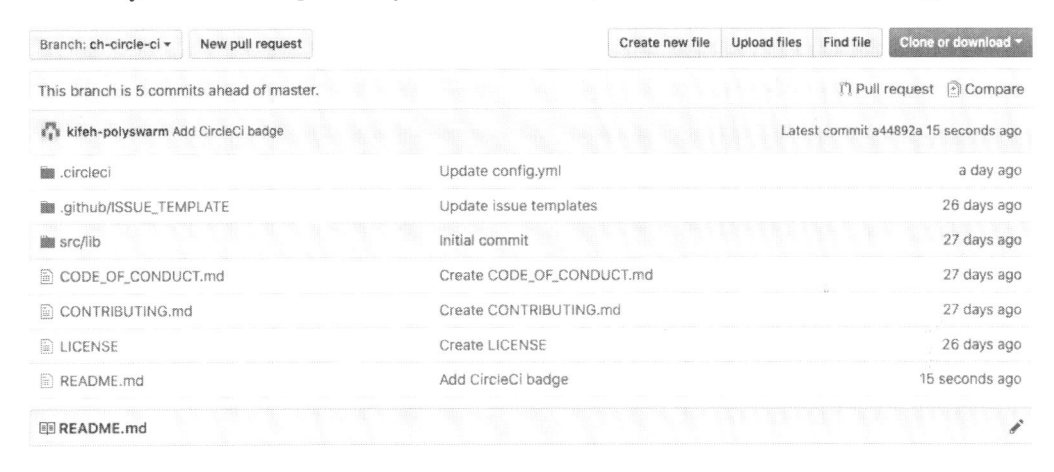

Figure 6.18: Build status

Outcome

You have successfully set up a CircleCi CI pipeline.

Automated Pull Requests

You have recently gone through and implemented pull requests. While the procedure still remains the same, this subtopic introduces a better and efficient way of effecting code integrity on pull requests. Here, we get to demonstrate and implement how to prevent branch merges before certain conditions are met.

We have recently pushed changes to a new branch and added configuration files for a build pipeline, and it would be best if all of the branches are based on this. In order to achieve this, a pull request needs to be set up and merged against the master branch.

Exercise 42: Utilizing Automated Pull Requests

To set up an automated pull request and merge against the master branch.

1. Open your abacus GitHub repository. Since the changes you just made were the most recent updates, you will get a **Compare & pull request** pop up, as shown in the following screenshot:

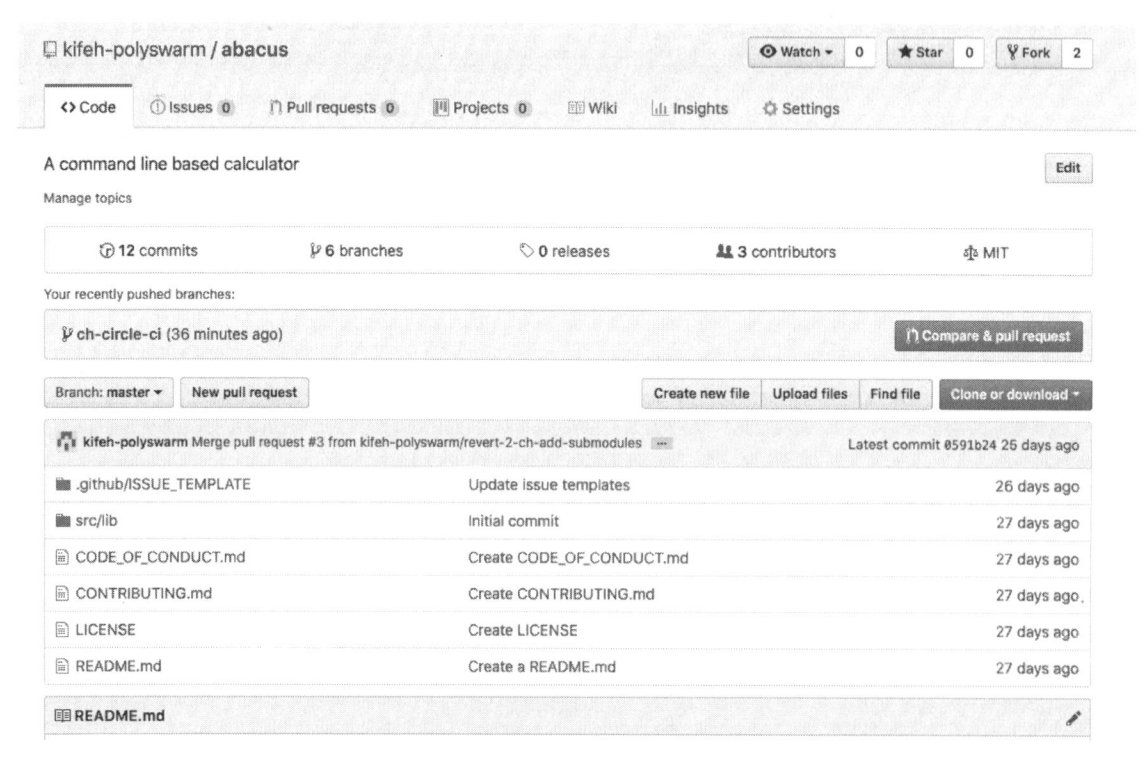

Figure 6.19: Abacus repository

2. Select **Compare** and create a **pull request**, as shown in the following screenshot:

Open a pull request

Create a new pull request by comparing changes across two branches. If you need to, you can also compare across forks.

base: master ← compare: ch-circle-ci ✓ Able to merge. These branches can be automatically merged.

chore-add-circle-ci

This change introduces CircleCi base configurations

Reviewers
No reviews—at least 2 approving reviews are required.

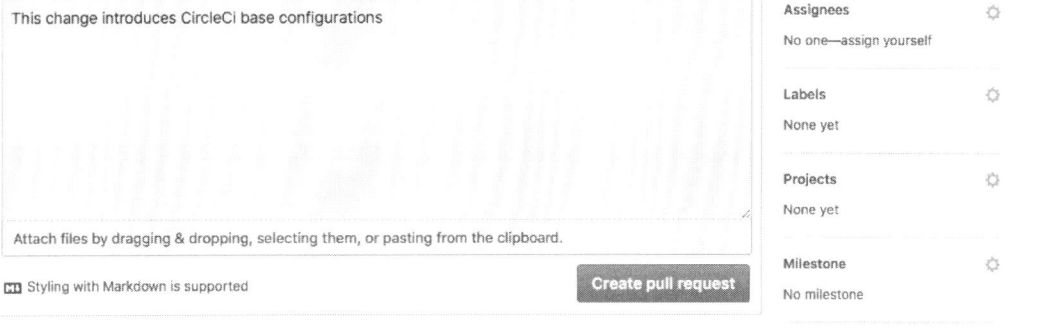

Assignees
No one—assign yourself

Labels
None yet

Projects
None yet

Milestone
No milestone

Figure 6.20: Creating a pull request

> **Note**
>
> On the far right under **reviewers**, GitHub is already hinting at the rules we set for the master branch earlier in this book; there are **at least two approving reviewers**.

3. Go ahead and create the pull request, as shown in the following screenshot:

> **Note**
>
> Notice the various conditions required for a merge into master branch, and, among them, a CircleCi build.

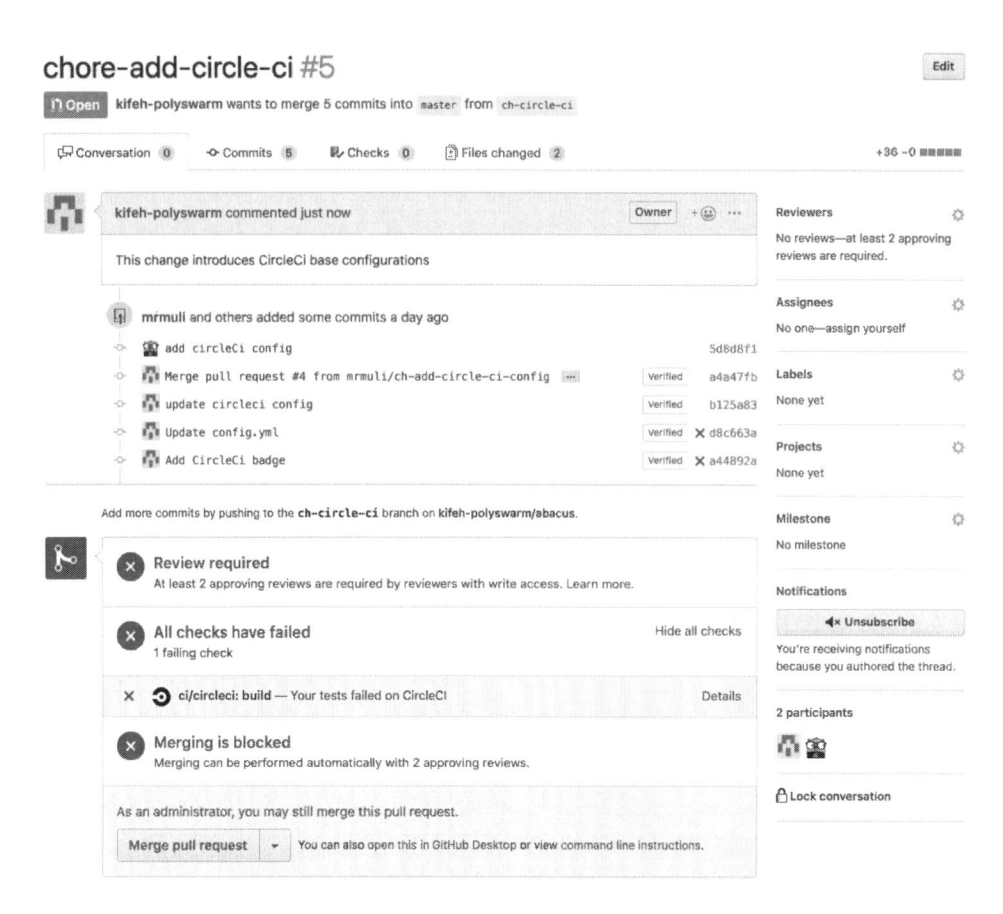

Figure 6.21: Merging against the master branch

Outcome

You have successfully set up an automated pull request and merged against the master branch.

Activity 7: Integrating a Build Pipeline on CircleCi

You have been instructed to set up a repository and build a pipeline for a new Python API that will serve as a gateway for your current infrastructure. To start this, the first requirement is setting up the project's base, involving its repository and pipeline.

To create build pipelines and integrate them with GitHub applications, follow these steps:

1. Create the repository on GitHub, and clone it locally.
2. Ensure that you have a **master branch** and **develop** branches with README.md files.

3. Checkout from the develop branch into a feature branch.
4. Create a **.circleci** folder.
5. Push your changes to GitHub.
6. Add the backend-API project and run the first build.
7. Add a **config.yml** file and include the required configuration.

Outcome

You have successfully set up build pipelines and integrated them with GitHub applications.

> **Note**
> For detailed steps for this activity, refer to the **Appendix** section on page 317.

Release Management

We have recently demonstrated automated testing and building on CircleCi. We also concluded that the two processes are building blocks of CI pipelines, which is a critical process that occurs on a software development life cycle. This chapter will demonstrate the role Git plays in software delivery, more specifically, in release management and as a final stage of software delivery.

Release management can be simply put as the process of scheduling and controlling software builds across different environments. This means that it is the process through which teams can unify and organize application releases toward production for customers or any other environments they run.

Git plays a critical role in this process through **tags**. We previously went through tag definition, and, at this point, you should be able to identify and create different types of tags, namely:

- **Lightweight**
- **Annotated**

In this chapter, we will be identifying and demonstrating a number of practices that can be used to facilitate an effective release-management process. Let's start by understanding tags better.

Tagging

As we discussed previously, tagging involves the creation of markers to correspond to software versions. To simulate a real-world scenario, we will be working with annotated instead of lightweight tags.

To affect a release process, the first step would be to introduce and standardize a release branch. Depending on your team's workflow, the branch can be temporary. As a best practice, you should always get rid of this branch as soon as changes have been merged to the base branch and deployed to production.

In our case, and on my computer, you are currently on the **ch-circle-ci** branch. **Master** is our base branch, and, because of a lack of multiple environments for our application, we do not have a **develop** or **qa** branch as other teams would:

```
josephmuli at Friday in ~/Desktop/abacus on ch-circle-ci
$ git branch
* ch-circle-ci
  master
```

Figure 6.22: CircleCI branch

This also means in this context and example that all deployed and production changes are dictated by what is on the master. In a real-world scenario, the following branches would present an ideal environment and release-friendly workflow:

- A **Base** branch, that is, a **master** where each commit represents a release that's been made and deployed, and what is running in production.

- A **Testing**, **QA,** and **development branch**, commonly named **develop**, which, as suggested, dictates what is running on the development, staging, and QA environments

- A **Feature** branch. This would be branched from **develop** by all repository collaborators and merged back with new changes. This is commonly adopted in feature branch workflows, as we previously discussed.

- A **Release** branch. This branch is based or branched from the develop branch after feature delivery, testing, and quality assurance has been carried out. The branch is then tagged, merged into the base branch, and deleted.

For demonstration purposes, you created a **develop** branch based on the **master**, where all of the features shall not be merged into, and finally released to the **master** through release branches. To implement this, we need to complete the following exercise.

Exercise 43: Creating Tags

To create automated tags to identify changes on the file version.

1. Ensure that you have committed any pending changes, as shown in the following screenshot:

```
josephmuli at Friday in ~/Desktop/abacus on master
$ git status
On branch master
Your branch is up to date with 'origin/master'.

nothing to commit, working tree clean
```

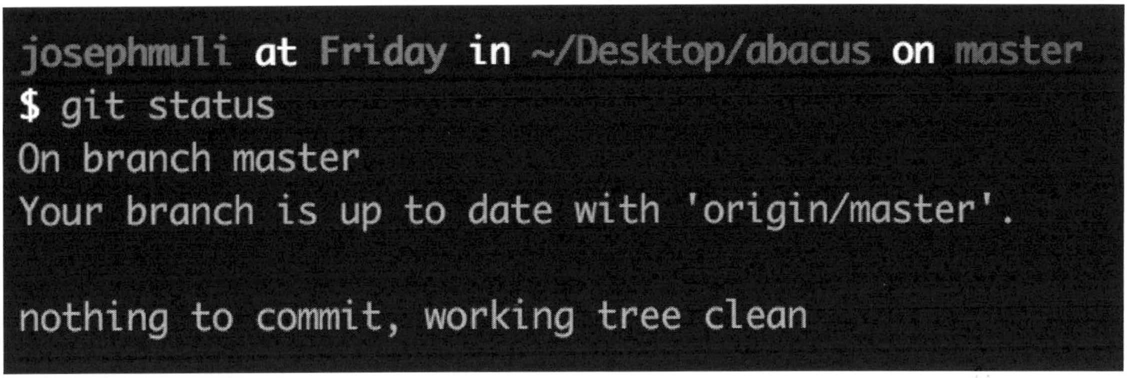

Figure 6.23: Branch master

2. Checkout to master the branch as shown in the following screenshot:

```
josephmuli at Friday in ~/Desktop/abacus on ch-circle-ci
$ git checkout master
Switched to branch 'master'
Your branch is up to date with 'origin/master'.
```

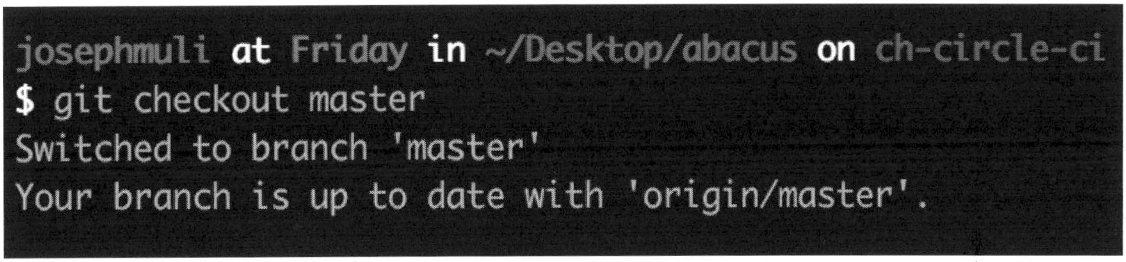

Figure 6.24: Checkout to the master branch

3. Create a new branch and name it **develop**, as shown in the following screenshot:

```
josephmuli at Friday in ~/Desktop/abacus on master
$ git checkout -b develop
Switched to a new branch 'develop'
```

Figure 6.25: Creating a new branch

4. Push the branch to **Origin** as shown in the following screenshot:

```
josephmuli at Friday in ~/Desktop/abacus on develop
$ git push origin develop
Total 0 (delta 0), reused 0 (delta 0)
remote:
remote: Create a pull request for 'develop' on GitHub by visiting:
remote:      https://github.com/kifeh-polyswarm/abacus/pull/new/develop
remote:
To github.com:kifeh-polyswarm/abacus.git
 * [new branch]      develop -> develop
```

Figure 6.26: Pushing the branch to Origin

> **Note**
>
> From this point onward, develop should be even to the base branch. From the develop branch, checkout to a new branch called **release-1.0.0**, as shown in the following screenshot:

```
josephmuli at Friday in ~/Desktop/abacus on develop [?]
$ git checkout -b release-1.0.0
Switched to a new branch 'release-1.0.0'
```

Figure 6.27: Switching to a new branch

> **Note**
>
> The naming convention on the branch name is **release-1.0.0**. This is in accordance with the Semver standard, where builds should be versioned according to the following change types:
>
> Major releases
>
> Minor releases
>
> Patches
>
> However, the release would have to be **v1.0.0** to fully align with Semver standards.

Release Management | 261

5. While you are still on the release branch, create a file and name it **Changelog.md**:

> **Note**
>
> This file can be a central point for any version and dependency change on your applications.

```
josephmuli at Friday in ~/Desktop/abacus on ch-release-one
$ touch Changelog.md
```

Figure 6.28: Touch changelog

6. Take a look at what the Changelog looks like:

```
Changelog.md

### Abacus Changelog

This file Entails All Abacus versions and dependency updates. Please run the most recent and stable releases unless advised otherwise.
```

Figure 6.29: Changelog

7. Stage the changes, as shown in the following screenshot:

```
josephmuli at Friday in ~/Desktop/abacus on release-1.0.0 [+]
$ git add Changelog.md
```

Figure 6.30: Staging the changes

8. Commit your changes, as shown in the following screenshot:

```
josephmuli at Friday in ~/Desktop/abacus on release-1.0.0 [+]
$ git commit -m"Add a changelog for version 1.0.0"
[release-1.0.0 3897c06] Add a changelog for version 1.0.0
 1 file changed, 5 insertions(+)
 create mode 100644 Changelog.md
```

Figure 6.31: Committing the changes

9. Create an annotated tag, identifying the changes we have made on this version, as shown in the following screenshot:

```
josephmuli at Friday in ~/Desktop/abacus on release-1.0.0
$ git tag -a v1.0.0 -m"Initial Abacus release"
```

Figure 6.32: Creating an annotated tag

10. Push your changes to **origin**, as shown in the following screenshot:

```
josephmuli at Friday in ~/Desktop/abacus on release-1.0.0
$ git push origin release-1.0.0
Enumerating objects: 5, done.
Counting objects: 100% (5/5), done.
Delta compression using up to 4 threads.
Compressing objects: 100% (4/4), done.
Writing objects: 100% (4/4), 541 bytes | 541.00 KiB/s, done.
Total 4 (delta 1), reused 0 (delta 0)
remote: Resolving deltas: 100% (1/1), completed with 1 local object.
To github.com:kifeh-polyswarm/abacus.git
 * [new branch]      release-1.0.0 -> release-1.0.0
 * [new tag]         v1.0.0 -> v1.0.0
```

Figure 6.33: Pushing your changes to Origin

11. Open your repository on GitHub, and notice that the release number has increased to 1.

Outcome

You have successfully created automated tags to identify the changes on the file version. Take a look at the following screenshot to see how change in the commits appear:

A command line based calculator

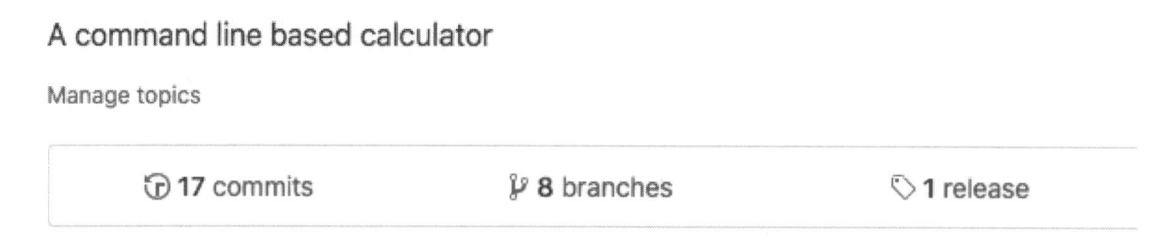

Manage topics

17 commits   8 branches   1 release

Figure 6.34: Command line-based calculator

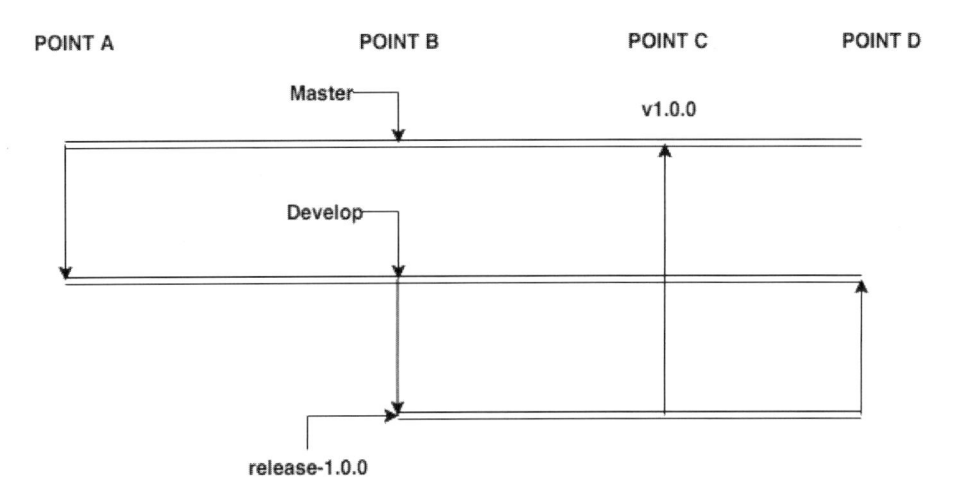

Figure 6.35: Branch stages

Let's explain what the preceding diagram is showing us:

- **Point A**: This is the initial stage, where we branched the develop branch off the master.

- **Point B**: At this point, we branched off develop into release-1.0.0 and added a Changelog.

- **Point C**: This is where we are currently, At this point, we created a new tag and pulled the request to the master. In a real-world scenario, a pull request to the master would trigger smoke tests and finally a deployment to your intended environments.

- **Point D**: At this point, we will merge release-1.0.0 into develop and delete the release branch, as it will no longer be needed.

Exercise 44: Publishing GitHub Releases

We will now create and publish GitHub releases.

1. Create a pull request to the master from the release branch and merge it, as shown in the following screenshot:

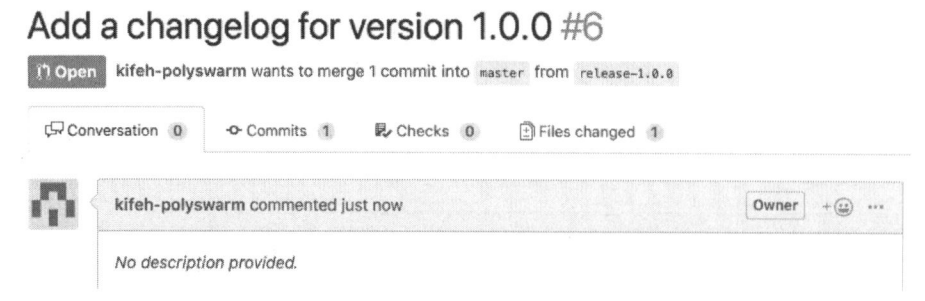

Figure 6.36: Creating a pull request to the master

2. Merge your release branch into **develop** through a pull request and ensure that the branch has been deleted. This will now make the **develop** branch even with the **master** branch, as shown in the following screenshot:

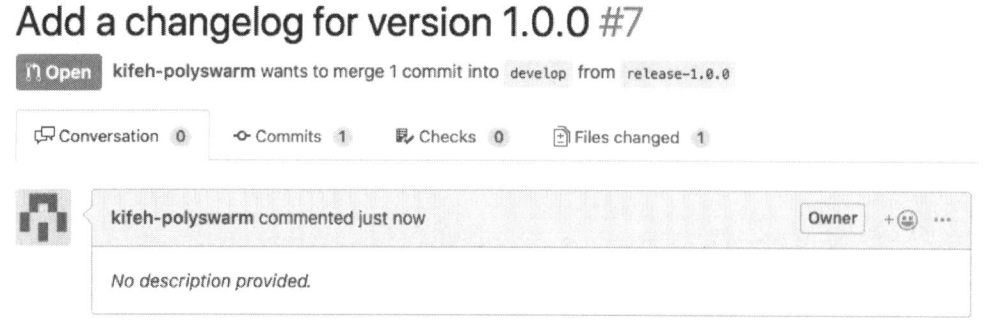

Figure 6.37: Merging your release branch

3. When you are not using a **Changelog file**, **GitHub releases** the enable tag and release documentation, as shown in the following screenshot:

> **Note**
>
> This feature is readily available on your repository and is a best practice to follow.

4. From the abacus repository, select the **Releases** tab, as shown in the following screenshot:

Figure 6.38: Selecting the Releases tab

> **Note**
> This should bring you to a **Releases** and **Tags** page, as shown in the following screenshot:

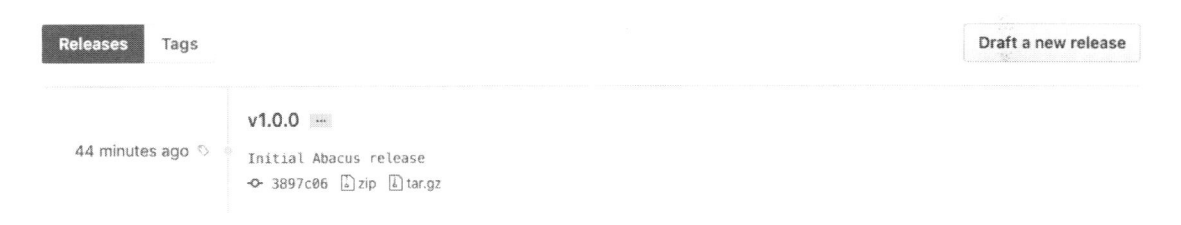

Figure 6.39: Releases and Tags

5. Select the tag number and GitHub will expand the annotated tag, listing details of the following:

- Who tagged the release
- The source code until that marker
- The release note

> **Note**
> GitHub allows tag editing to add more context to the release if the developer wasn't able to add context on the service, or in cases where the process is fully automated, or the message is templated.

266 | Automated Testing and Release Management

6. To achieve this, select the **Edit Tag** button, and GitHub will open the form, as shown in the following screenshot:

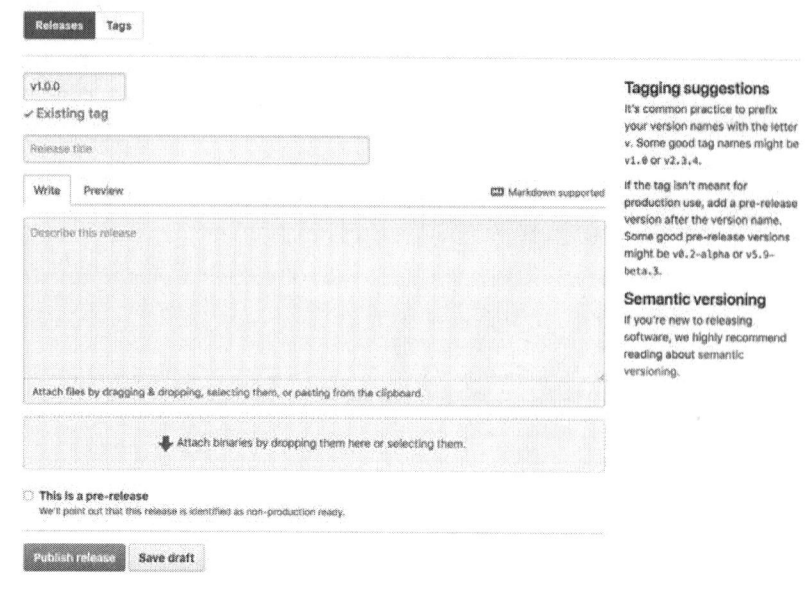

Figure 6.40: Pre-release

7. Update the tag number, include a more descriptive release note, and choose to either do a **pre-release** or publish the release as before.

8. Update the **Release title** and release notes, as shown in the following screenshot:

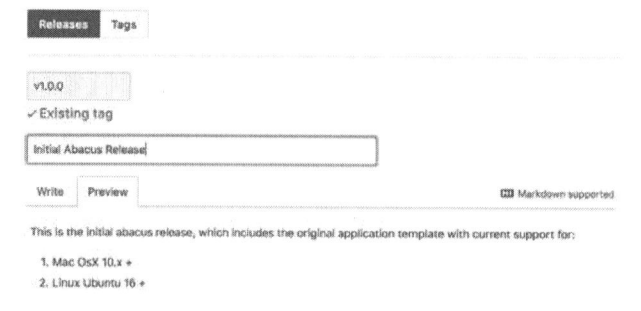

Figure 6.41: Existing tag

> **Note**
>
> As advised, you can also add application binaries on this form that are specific for different operating systems or according to the service and system you are designing for.

9. Once this is done, go ahead and select **Publish release.**

Outcome

GitHub will publish your release and redirect you to the **Releases** and **Tags** page, thus listing the updated tags:

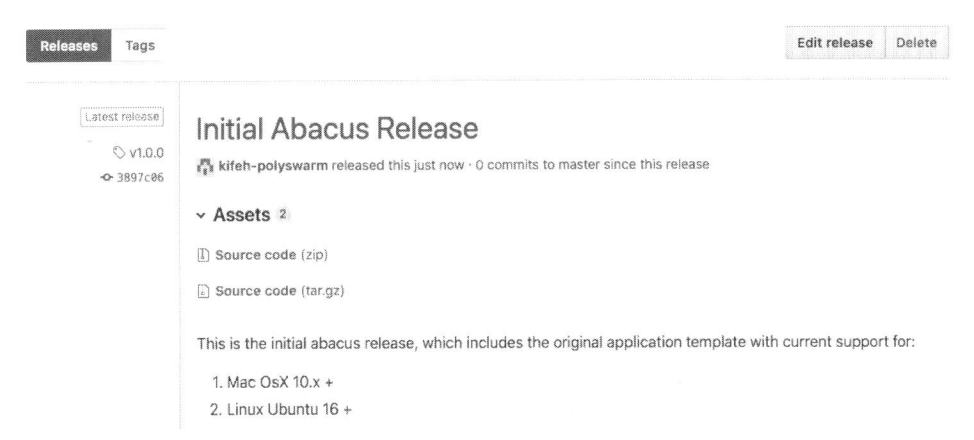

Figure 6.42: Initial abacus release

Git Archive

Apart from enabling release management through tagging, Git enables the packaging of source code as zipped and .tar files, making them available for downloads on release pages, and sometimes on download or installation pages. This is achieved through the `git archive` command.

Exercise 45: Packaging through GitHub Archive

To package source code using the `git archive` command.

1. From your terminal, ensure that you are on the **master** branch and that it is even with **origin**, as shown in the following screenshot:

Figure 6.43: Checkout of the master branch

2. Run the `git archive` command with the arguments shown in the following screenshot:

```
josephmuli at Friday in ~/Desktop/abacus on master [?]
$ git archive --format=tar --prefix=abacus-1.0.0/ v1.0.0 | gzip >abacus-v1.0.0.tar.gz
```

Figure 6.44: Git archive

> **Note**
> The arguments are basically creating a compressed tarball for the abacus **v1.0.0** release.

Outcome

Your path should now have the releases that can be uploaded or deployed to their respective pages, as shown in the following screenshot:

```
josephmuli at Friday in ~/Desktop/abacus on master [?]
$ ls
CODE_OF_CONDUCT.md   Changelog.md    README.md                src
CONTRIBUTING.md      LICENSE         abacus-v1.0.0.tar.gz  v1.0.0.tar.gz
```

Figure 6.45: Output

Activity 8: Tagging and Releasing with Git

You have been instructed to update the abacus documentation, tag the feature, and document the release changes. Tag at least one stage of abacus, branching off the develop branch, and document the tags in a Changelog.

To tag and release software with Git, follow these steps:

1. Make sure that you do not have any pending changes on the branch you are on.
2. Checkout to a feature branch, that is, **ch-update-readme.**
3. Add the changes demonstrated to the **README.md.**
4. Stage, commit, and push your changes to GitHub.
5. Create a pull request to the develop branch.
6. Create a release branch off of the develop branch.

7. Stage and commit the changes.
8. Tag the commit as demonstrated, following the conventions.
9. Push the changes to **origin**.
10. Create a pull request to the **master** and merge the release branch.
11. Finally, merge the release branch to develop and delete the release branch.
12. Update the release notes on GitHub.

Outcome

You have successfully tagged and released software with Git.

> **Note**
>
> For detailed steps for this activity, refer to the **Appendix** section on page 318.

Summary

In this chapter, we covered automated testing and builds through GitHub applications and automated pull requests through CircleCi. Then, we explored Git Tags and the Semver naming convention, as well as changelogs and release notes. Lastly, we examined archiving GitHub releases.

This rounds up the book. In this book, you implemented the best practices in version control, analyzed a Feature Branch Workflow, and implemented its features, such as submodules and rebasing. Lastly, you implemented CI with CircleCi and versioned software releases. Now you should be equipped with the tools to put what you have learned into practice in the real world. Thank you for choosing this book.

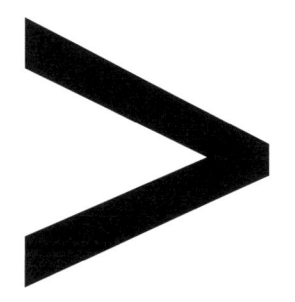

Appendix

About

This section is included to assist the students to perform the activities in the book. It includes detailed steps that are to be performed by the students to achieve the objectives of the book.

272 | Appendix

Chapter 1: Introducing Version Control

Activity 1: Repository Creation

You have been instructed to build an application that enables its users to order food from a restaurant and have it delivered. To commence this task, you need to build the application while leveraging version control. You need to create a repository that will host the application. This repository will be used to track task completion and the deployment of the application.

The aim of this chapter is to create a repository in GitHub.

To get started, you need to have the Git command-line tool installed on your computer. Then, you need to have an account on https://github.com/, and you should be logged into it:

1. Launch the terminal.

    a. On a Linux computer: Press *Ctrl* + *Alt* + *T*.

    b. On a macOS computer: Press ⌘ + *spacebar*, Type **Terminal** or **iTerm**, and then click the application logo to launch the terminal:

![Launching a terminal on macOS - iTerm search result]

Figure 1.72: Launching a terminal on macOS

   c. On a Microsoft Windows computer: Press *Win* + *R* on your keyboard to launch the **Run** window. Then, type **cmd.exe** and press *Enter* on your keyboard or click **OK** on the **Run** window.

2. Create a directory for the application by using the `mkdir dine-in` command as shown in the following screenshot:

![Terminal showing mkdir dine-in command]

Figure 1.73: Creating a directory

3. Navigate to the dine-in directory by using the `cd dine-in` command as shown in the following screenshot:

Figure 1.74: Navigating to the correct directory

4. Initialize the repository by using the `git init` command as shown in the following screenshot:

Figure 1.75: Navigating to the correct directory

5. Go to https://github.com/ to create a new repository with the name `dine-in`.
6. Obtain the HTTPS or SSH URL of the repository from GitHub.

For example: `git@github.com:kifeh-polyswarm/dine-in.git`.

7. Set the remote URL on the local repository as shown in the following screenshot, using the following code:

   `git remote add origin git@github.com:kifeh-polyswarm/dine-in.git`

Figure 1.76: Setting the remote URL

8. Create a README file using the following command as shown in the screenshot below:

   ```
   echo '#dine-in\nA food ordering application' > README.md
   ```

   Figure 1.77: Creating a README.md file

9. Create a .gitignore file using the following command as shown in the screenshot below:

   ```
   echo '.DS_Store' > .gitignore
   ```

   Figure 1.78: Creating a gitignore

10. Add the README file and the .gitignore file to the index using the following command as shown in the screenshot below: `git add README.md .gitignore`

    Figure 1.79: Adding the README.md file

11. Commit the files by using the `git commit -m "Initial commit"` command shown in the is screenshot below it:

    Figure 1.80: Committing the files

12. Push the files to the remote repository by using the `git push -u origin master` command shown is the screenshot:

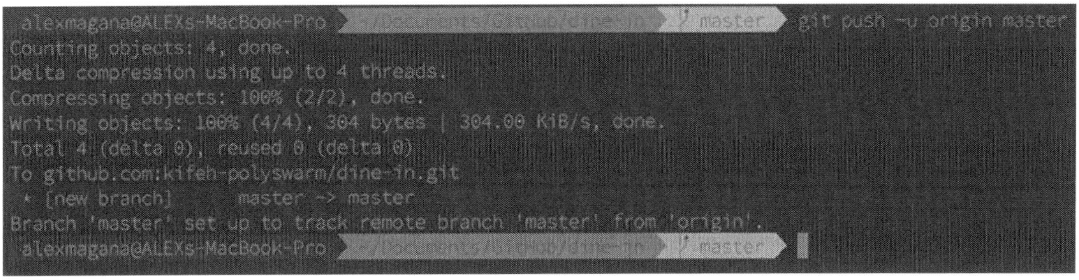

Figure 1.81: Setting the remote URL

Outcome

A repository was created on your GitHub account with the README.md and .gitignore files.

Chapter 2: Versioning Commits

Activity 2: Tracking Files

You are required to add support for addition operations to the **abacus** application. The application should define a function that accepts a set of numbers and computes the sum of the numbers.

The aim of this activity is to implement file tracking commands and navigate the repository's history.

To get started, you need to have the Git command-line tool installed on your computer. Then, you need to have an account on https://github.com/ and should be logged into it. Lastly, you should have the **abacus** application repository on GitHub and your computer:

1. Launch the terminal and navigate to the location of the **abacus** directory.

2. Navigate to the **ft-support-subtraction-arithmetic** branch of the **abacus** application using the following command: git checkout ft-support-subtraction-arithmetic.

3. Create a branch for the feature you'll develop off of the **ft-support-subtraction-arithmetic** branch using the git branch ft-support-addition-tasks. Use the following command as shown in the next screenshot: git checkout ft-support-addition-tasks:

Figure 2.70: Creating a branch for the feature

4. Add the following lines to **src/lib/compute.py** and save the changes shown in the screenshot below:

Live Link for file activity_step_4.py: https://bit.ly/2DPgh7j

```
def add(self):
    total = 1
    for item in self.operands:
        total -= item
    print(total)
```

Figure 2.71: Modifying the compute.py file

5. Check the status of the files on the branch by using the `git status` command shown in the is screenshot below:

Figure 2.72: Checking the status of the files

6. Retrieve the alterations made on src/lib/compute.py using the following command as shown in the next: screenshot: git diff src/lib/compute.py:

```
diff --git a/src/lib/compute.py b/src/lib/compute.py
index 00c3198..eb770c2 100644
--- a/src/lib/compute.py
+++ b/src/lib/compute.py
@@ -16,3 +16,9 @@ class Compute:
         for item in self.operands:
             difference -= item
         print(difference)
+
+    def add(self):
+        total = 0
+        for item in self.operands:
+            total += item
+        print(total)
(END)
```

Figure 2.73: Retrieving the alterations

7. Add the changed file to the index and commit the changes using the following code as shown in the next screenshot below:

git add src/lib/compute.py

git commit -m "Add support for summation"

Figure 2.74: Adding the changed file to the index

8. Create a file for recording application logs by using the touch logs.txt command shown in the screenshot below:

Figure 2.75: Creating an application log

9. Check the status of the branch by using the `git status command` shown in the screenshot below:

Figure 2.76: Checking the branch status

10. Add the file to the index and commit it using the following code as shown in the next screenshot below:

    `git add log.txt`

    `git commit -m "Add application logs"`

Figure 2.77: Adding the file to the index

11. Remove the log file from the working tree and the index. Commit the removal of the log file, `log.txt`: using the following code as shown in the screenshot below:

    `git rm log.txt`

    `git commit -m "Remove logs"`

Figure 2.78: Removing the log file

12. Retrieve the formatted details of the branch history for five of the most recent commits using the following code as shown in the next screenshot below:

```
git log -5 --pretty=format:"%n %an %ae %n %s %n %b"
```

```
c484aa20d803638f9322264183c30d1effe3612b alex-magana alex.magana@andela.com
 Remove logs

92a648a88533401832d07ff82c0ba27d7fd86354 alex-magana alex.magana@andela.com
 Add application logs

c968d39a7b94c0aabdf6533485b576096ec735fb alex-magana alex.magana@andela.com
 Add support for summation

8354043607e3d51f5f52f25056e3ceee6f17cc33 alex-magana alex.magana@andela.com
 Relocate the scientific module

e60779e4ba199137dc5e10479f80871982b0f69e alex-magana alex.magana@andela.com
 Rename scientific module

(END)
```

Figure 2.79: Branch history

13. Edit the last commit by using the `git commit --amend` command using the following code as shown in the screenshot below:

```
alexmagana@ALEXs-MacBook-Pro  /Documents/Github/shards  ft-support-addition-tasks  git commit --amend
[ft-support-addition-tasks 1da1ed6] Remove the application log file
 Date: Sat Aug 25 21:38:13 2018 +0300
 1 file changed, 0 insertions(+), 0 deletions(-)
 delete mode 100644 log.txt
alexmagana@ALEXs-MacBook-Pro  /Documents/Github/shards  ft-support-addition-tasks
```

Figure 2.80: Editing the last commit

```
Remove the application log file

# Please enter the commit message for your changes. Lines starting
# with '#' will be ignored, and an empty message aborts the commit.
#
# Date:        Sat Aug 25 21:38:13 2018 +0300
#
# On branch ft-support-addition-tasks
# Changes to be committed:
#       deleted:    log.txt
#
```

Figure 2.81: Removing the log file

14. Edit the commit messages using the rebase utility will the `git rebase -i HEAD~4` command using the following code as shown in the screenshots below:

```
pick 8354043 Relocate the scientific module
reword c968d39 Add support for summation
reword 92a648a Add application logs
reword 1da1ed6 Remove the application log file

# Rebase e60779e..1da1ed6 onto e60779e (4 commands)
#
# Commands:
# p, pick = use commit
# r, reword = use commit, but edit the commit message
# e, edit = use commit, but stop for amending
# s, squash = use commit, but meld into previous commit
# f, fixup = like "squash", but discard this commit's log message
# x, exec = run command (the rest of the line) using shell
# d, drop = remove commit
#
```

Figure 2.82: Editing commit messages

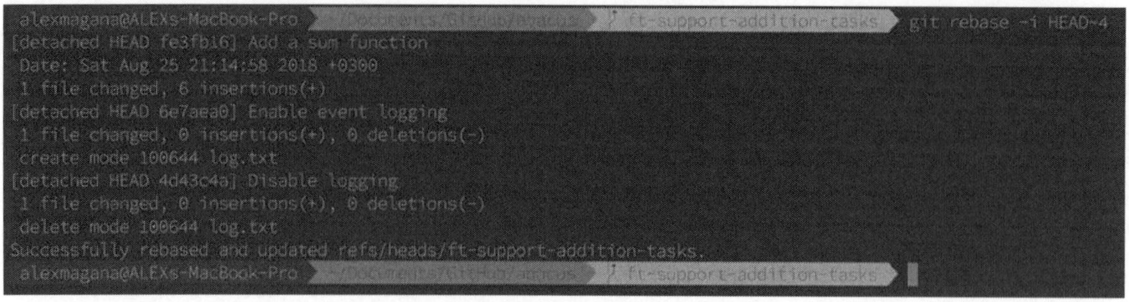

Figure 2.83: Viewing the changes

Outcome

You have successfully implemented file tracking commands and navigated the repository history.

Chapter 3: Fetching and Delivering Code

Activity 3: Handling Changes and Enforcing Branch Restrictions

You're a release engineer and have been tasked with consolidating deliverables scheduled for the release of abacus, the utility your department has been building. You need to obtain work done by the other team you've been collaborating with to deliver the goals set for the now-concluded 2-week work period. With the work consolidated, you are required to implement branch protection to ensure that any fixes introduced to the branch with the code being released are tested and reviewed.

The aim of this activity is to demonstrate the retrieval and reversal of changes and enforcing checks on branches for successful merging.

To get started, you need to have the Git command-line tool installed on your computer. You need to have an account on https://github.com/ and should be logged into it. Lastly, you should have the `abacus` application repository on GitHub and your computer. Follow these steps to complete this activity:

1. Navigate to the location of the `abacus` repository.

2. Add a remote to reference the `abacus-team-b` repository using the following code as seen in the screenshots below:

   ```
   git remote add origin-team-b git@github.com:kifeh-polyswarm/abacus-team-b.git
   ```

   > **Note**
   >
   > Please clone the repository at https://github.com/kifeh-polyswarm/abacus-team-b to https://github.com/TrainingByPackt for use in this step.

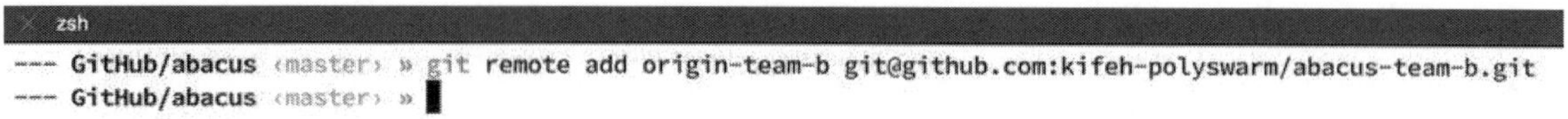

```
--- GitHub/abacus <master> » git remote add origin-team-b git@github.com:kifeh-polyswarm/abacus-team-b.git
--- GitHub/abacus <master> »
```

Figure 3.36: Adding a remote

3. Switch to the `ft-support-addition-tasks` branch to create the consolidation branch as seen in the screenshot below using the following code:

   `git checkout ft-support-addition-tasks`

```
--- GitHub/abacus <master> » git checkout ft-support-addition-tasks
Switched to branch 'ft-support-addition-tasks'
--- GitHub/abacus <ft-support-addition-tasks> »
```

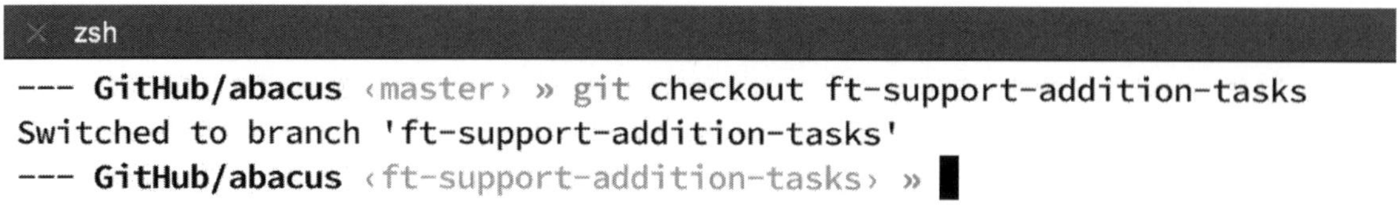

Figure 3.37: Creating the consolidation branch

4. Create and switch to the consolidation branch by using the `git checkout -b release-candidate command` as shown in the following screenshot:

```
--- GitHub/abacus <ft-support-addition-tasks> » git checkout -b release-candidate
Switched to a new branch 'release-candidate'
--- GitHub/abacus <release-candidate> »
```

Figure 3.38: Switching to the consolidation branch

5. Retrieve the work that delivers the area calculation function by using the `git fetch origin-team-b add-area-calc` command as shown in the following screenshot:

```
--- GitHub/abacus <release-candidate> » git fetch origin-team-b add-area-calc
remote: Enumerating objects: 22, done.
remote: Counting objects: 100% (20/20), done.
remote: Compressing objects: 100% (11/11), done.
remote: Total 16 (delta 3), reused 11 (delta 1), pack-reused 0
Unpacking objects: 100% (16/16), done.
From github.com:kifeh-polyswarm/abacus-team-b
 * branch            add-area-calc -> FETCH_HEAD
 * [new branch]      add-area-calc -> origin-team-b/add-area-calc
--- GitHub/abacus <release-candidate> »
```

Figure 3.39: Retrieving the work

> **Note**
>
> Examining the directory at this point, the incoming changes shouldn't be available:

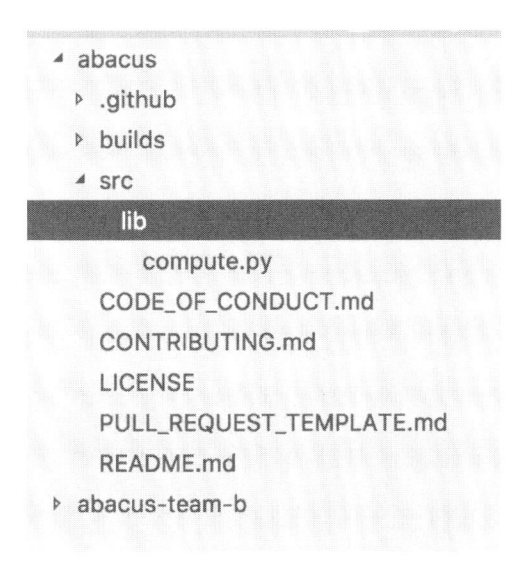

```
▲ abacus
   ▷ .github
   ▷ builds
   ▲ src
      lib
         compute.py
      CODE_OF_CONDUCT.md
      CONTRIBUTING.md
      LICENSE
      PULL_REQUEST_TEMPLATE.md
      README.md
   ▷ abacus-team-b
```

Figure 3.40: Examining the directory

286 | Appendix

6. Integrate the retrieved changes into the current directory by using the `git merge origin-team-b/add-area-calc` command as shown in the following screenshot:

```
--- GitHub/abacus ‹release-candidate› » git merge origin-team-b/add-area-calc
Merge made by the 'recursive' strategy.
 src/lib/util/util.py | 36 ++++++++++++++++++++++++++++++++++++++
 1 file changed, 36 insertions(+)
 create mode 100644 src/lib/util/util.py
--- GitHub/abacus ‹release-candidate› »
```

Figure 3.41: Integrating the retrieved changes

> **Note**
>
> `src/lib/util/util.py` should, at this point, host the `util class`:

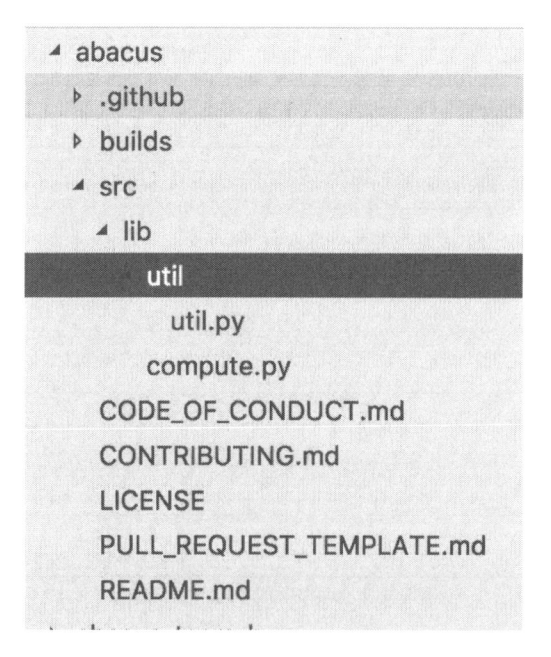

```
▲ abacus
  ▷ .github
  ▷ builds
  ▲ src
    ▲ lib
        util
          util.py
        compute.py
      CODE_OF_CONDUCT.md
      CONTRIBUTING.md
      LICENSE
      PULL_REQUEST_TEMPLATE.md
      README.md
```

Figure 3.42: Hosting the util

7. Retrieve and merge the work that delivers the perimeter calculation function by using the `git pull origin-team-b add-perimeter-calc` command as shown in the following screenshot:

```
x zsh
--- GitHub/abacus ‹release-candidate› » git pull origin-team-b add-perimeter-calc
remote: Enumerating objects: 11, done.
remote: Counting objects: 100% (11/11), done.
remote: Compressing objects: 100% (3/3), done.
remote: Total 6 (delta 1), reused 6 (delta 1), pack-reused 0
Unpacking objects: 100% (6/6), done.
From github.com:kifeh-polyswarm/abacus-team-b
 * branch            add-perimeter-calc -> FETCH_HEAD
 * [new branch]      add-perimeter-calc -> origin-team-b/add-perimeter-calc
Auto-merging src/lib/util/util.py
Merge made by the 'recursive' strategy.
 src/lib/util/util.py | 14 ++++++++++++--
 1 file changed, 12 insertions(+), 2 deletions(-)
--- GitHub/abacus ‹release-candidate› »
```

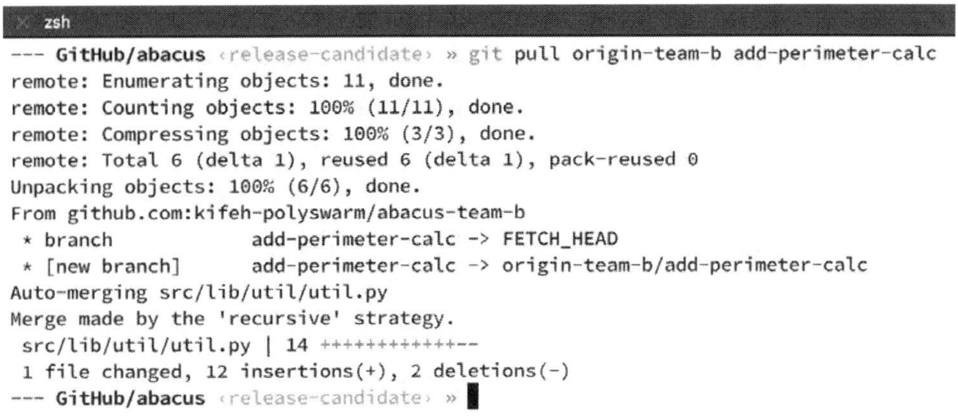

Figure 3.43: Retrieving and merging the work

> **Note**
>
> Unlike `git fetch`, you can see that the changes have been integrated into the `release-candidate` branch. This is the case since `git pull` combines `git fetch` and `git merge`.

8. Retrieve and merge the volume computation branch by using the `git pull origin-team-b add-volume-calc` command as shown in the following screenshot:

```
x zsh
--- GitHub/abacus ‹release-candidate› » git pull origin-team-b add-volume-calc
remote: Enumerating objects: 11, done.
remote: Counting objects: 100% (11/11), done.
remote: Compressing objects: 100% (3/3), done.
remote: Total 6 (delta 2), reused 4 (delta 1), pack-reused 0
Unpacking objects: 100% (6/6), done.
From github.com:kifeh-polyswarm/abacus-team-b
 * branch            add-volume-calc -> FETCH_HEAD
 * [new branch]      add-volume-calc -> origin-team-b/add-volume-calc
Auto-merging src/lib/util/util.py
Merge made by the 'recursive' strategy.
 src/lib/util/util.py | 6 ++++--
 1 file changed, 4 insertions(+), 2 deletions(-)
--- GitHub/abacus ‹release-candidate› »
```

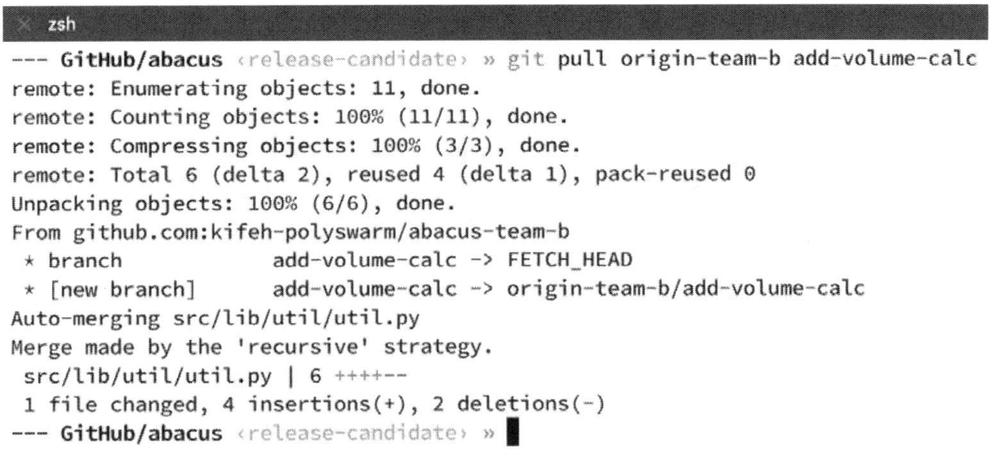

Figure 3.44: Retrieving and merging the volume

9. In the process of establishing a consensus on what features are to be rolled out, it's decided that the volume feature isn't required. Reverse the addition of the volume function to the release-candidate branch by using the `git revert --edit --mainline 1 64ccff0` command as shown in the following screenshots:

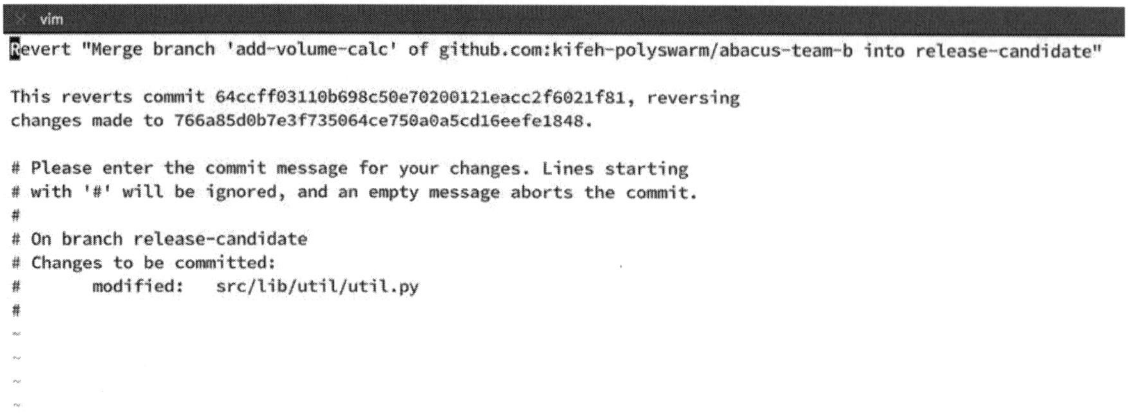

```
Revert "Merge branch 'add-volume-calc' of github.com:kifeh-polyswarm/abacus-team-b into release-candidate"

This reverts commit 64ccff03110b698c50e70200121eacc2f6021f81, reversing
changes made to 766a85d0b7e3f735064ce750a0a5cd16eefe1848.

# Please enter the commit message for your changes. Lines starting
# with '#' will be ignored, and an empty message aborts the commit.
#
# On branch release-candidate
# Changes to be committed:
#       modified:   src/lib/util/util.py
#
```

Figure 3.45: Reversing the addition of the volume function

```
--- GitHub/abacus <release-candidate> » git revert --edit --mainline 1 64ccff0
[release-candidate 0b65a92] Revert "Merge branch 'add-volume-calc' of github.com:kifeh-polyswarm/abacus-team-b into release-candidate"
 1 file changed, 2 insertions(+), 4 deletions(-)
--- GitHub/abacus <release-candidate> »
```

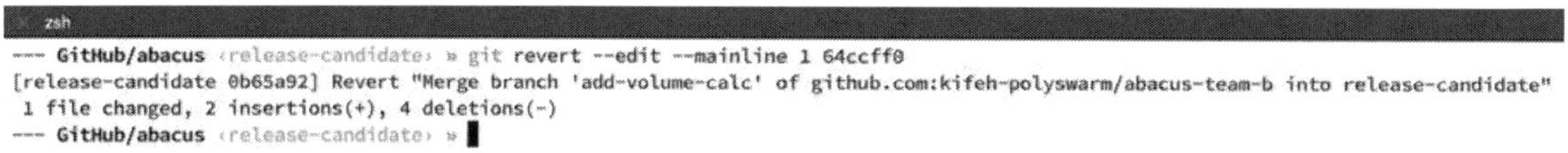

Figure 3.46: Reviewing the change

> **Note**
>
> By specifying `--mainline 1`, you indicate that you wish to revert to the changes that have been introduced to the repository by merging the `add-volume-calc` branch. Examining the object associated with commit `64ccff0`, we find that it is
>
>   git cat-file -p 64ccff03110b698c50e70200121eacc2f6021f81:

```
--- GitHub/abacus (release-candidate) » git cat-file -p 64ccff03110b698c50e70200121eacc2f6021f81
tree d63d440f48a8a8bad33bb16cd8127ae0ad3a8967
parent 766a85d0b7e3f735064ce750a0a5cd16eefe1848
parent 5f52489f0e34616ae96b6de5892385a30f7c2747
author alex-magana <alex.magana@andela.com> 1540411976 +0300
committer alex-magana <alex.magana@andela.com> 1540411976 +0300

Merge branch 'add-volume-calc' of github.com:kifeh-polyswarm/abacus-team-b into release-candidate
--- GitHub/abacus (release-candidate) »
```

Figure 3.47: Examining the object

> We can see that the merge commit has two parents, as should be the case. Therefore, `--mainline 1` means that we should reverse changes brought in by the second parent, that is, 5f52489f0e34616ae96b6de5892385a30f7c2747.

10. To proceed with the rollout, we need to make a change to the perimeter method to support triangles. Reset the head to the point where we merged the perimeter function using the following command as shown in the following screenshot: `git reset --soft 766a85d`

```
zsh
--- GitHub/abacus (release-candidate) » git reset --soft 766a85d
--- GitHub/abacus (release-candidate) »
```

Figure 3.48: Resetting the head to the point

11. Edit the `util.py` file to support the computation of the perimeter for triangles. Add lines 16 and 17, as shown in the code:

Live Link for file activity_step_11.py: https://bit.ly/2Qv14EC

```
elif shape == "triangle":
perimeter = reduce(lambda x, y: x+y, args)
```

Appendix

```
util.py  ×
1   import math
2
3   class Util(object):
4       def __init__(self):
5           self
6
7       @classmethod
8       def perimeter(cls, shape, *args):
9           perimeter = 0
10          if shape == "square":
11              perimeter = args[0] * 4
12          elif shape == "rectangle":
13              perimeter = reduce(lambda x, y: (2 * x) + (2 * y), args)
14          elif shape == "circle":
15              perimeter = 2 * math.pi * args[0]
16          elif shape == "triangle":
17              perimeter = reduce(lambda x, y: x+y, args)
18          else:
19              print "The shape, %s, is not supported" % (shape)
20          return perimeter
21
```

Figure 3.49: Editing the util.py file

12. Stage and commit the changes conducted on `src/lib/util/util.py` using the following code as shown in the following screenshot:

```
git add src/lib/util/util.py

git commit -m "Add support for triangles"
```

```
zsh
--- GitHub/abacus ‹release-candidate* M› » git add src/lib/util/util.py
--- GitHub/abacus ‹release-candidate* M› » git commit -m "Add support for triangles"
[release-candidate 8d22645] Add support for triangles
 1 file changed, 2 insertions(+), 1 deletion(-)
--- GitHub/abacus ‹release-candidate› »
```

Figure 3.50: Staging and committing the changes

13. Push the branch to the remote `origin` by using the `git push origin release-candidate` command as shown in the following screenshot:

```
x  zsh
--- GitHub/abacus <release-candidate> » git push origin release-candidate
Counting objects: 35, done.
Delta compression using up to 4 threads.
Compressing objects: 100% (24/24), done.
Writing objects: 100% (35/35), 3.41 KiB | 1.14 MiB/s, done.
Total 35 (delta 11), reused 0 (delta 0)
remote: Resolving deltas: 100% (11/11), completed with 1 local object.
remote:
remote: Create a pull request for 'release-candidate' on GitHub by visiting:
remote:      https://github.com/kifeh-polyswarm/abacus/pull/new/release-candidate
remote:
To github.com:kifeh-polyswarm/abacus.git
 * [new branch]      release-candidate -> release-candidate
--- GitHub/abacus <release-candidate> »
```

Figure 3.51: Pushing the branch to the remote origin

14. To protect the branch against untested quick fixes in readiness for shipping the features, we need to add restrictions to the `release-candidate` branch and click the **Settings** tab on the repository's page.

15. Click the **Branches** option and select **Add rule:** as shown in the following screenshot:

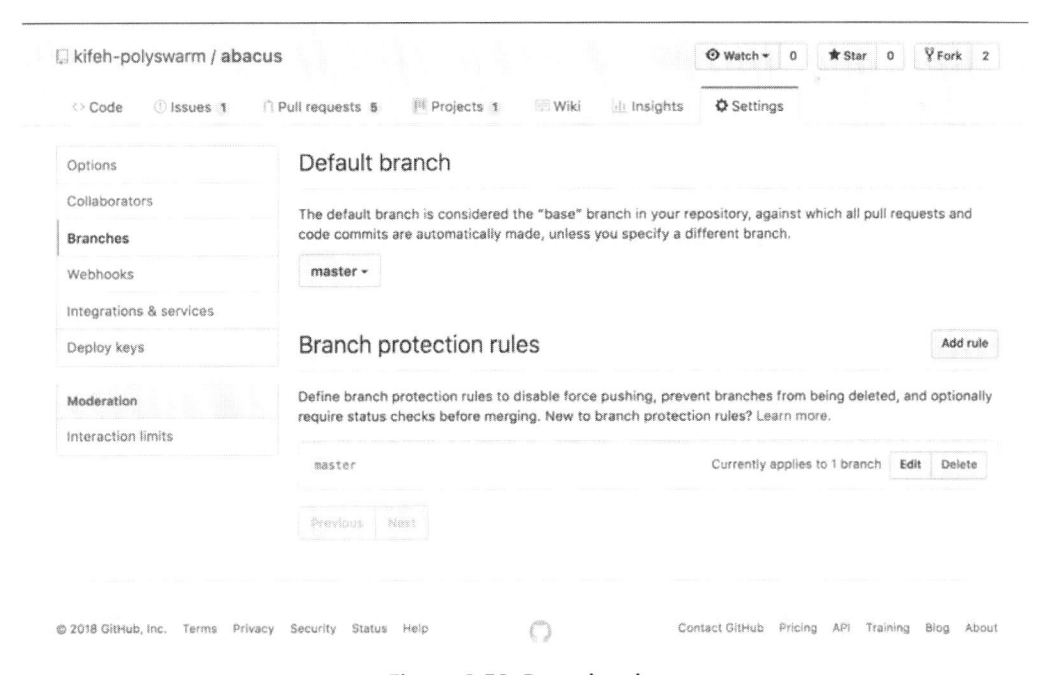

Figure 3.52: Branch rules

16. Specify the branch and appropriate restriction options and click the **Create** button as shown in the following screenshot:

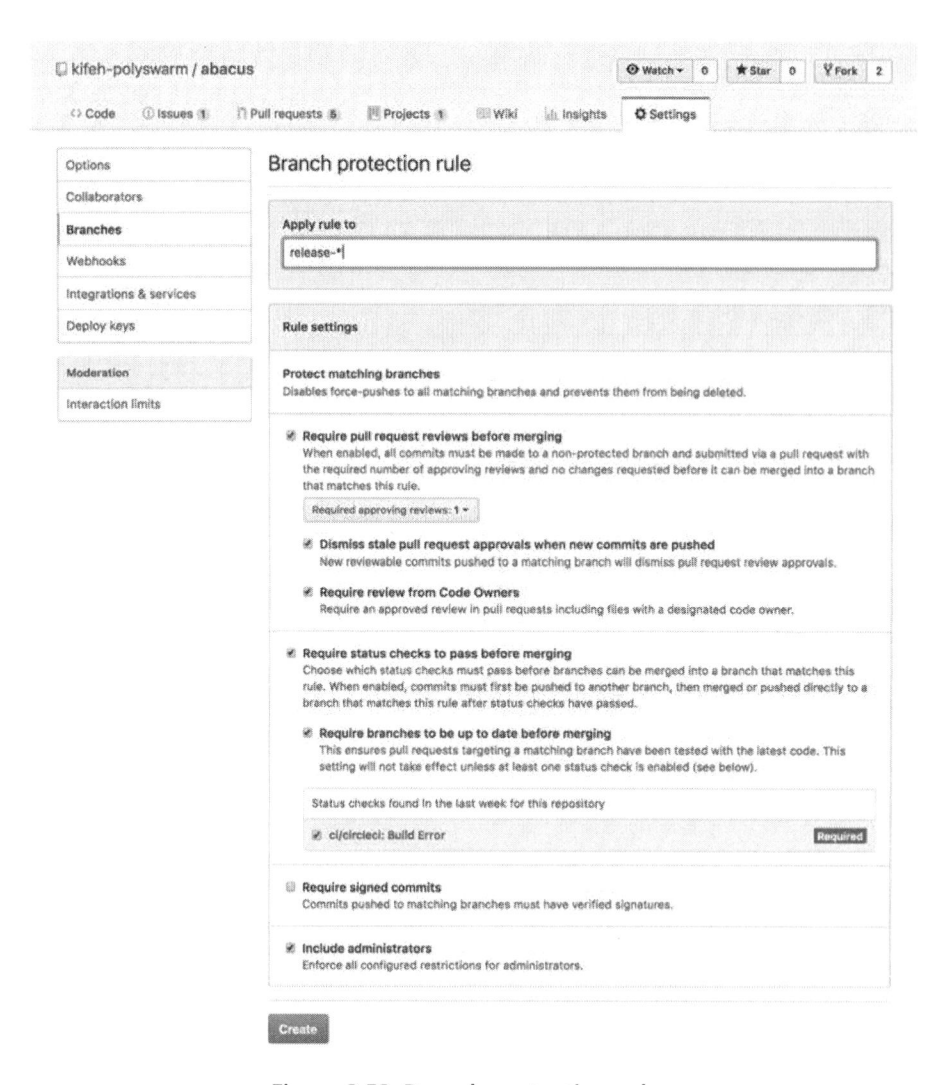

Figure 3.53: Branch protection rules

17. Provide the account password in the prompt that follows.

18. Save the changes by clicking **Save changes** to finalize getting the rules into effect as shown in the following screenshot:

Figure 3.54: Branch protection rules

Outcome

You have successfully created a branch release-candidate with changes integrated into it and protection restrictions defined.

Chapter 4: Branches

Activity 4: Managing Branches and Experimentation with Selective Changes

You have been tasked with adding capabilities for computing speed and distance to your company's application. The features need to be handled separately and merged as a single work stream. You need to raise a pull request of the release-candidate branch you created in the activity in Topic 1. Merge the pull request once the changes have been approved. This is required since the tasks in this activity are a continuation of the work done in the activity in *Topic 1: Utilizing Workflows*.

The aim of this activity is to demonstrate being able to handle branches.

To get started, you need to have the Git command-line tool installed on your computer. You need to have an account on https://github.com/ and should be logged into it. Lastly, you should have the abacus application repository on GitHub and your computer:

1. Open the browser and navigate to github.com/[username]/abacus/compare/release-candidate.

2. Click the **Create pull request** button as shown in the following screenshot:

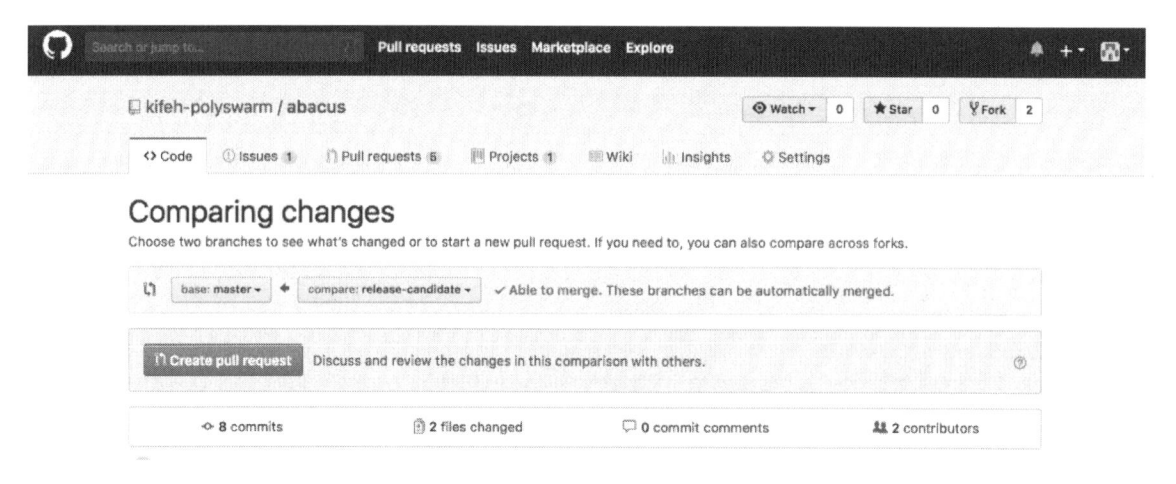

Figure 4.58: Creating a pull request

3. Provide the appropriate description of the purpose of the pull request and click **Create pull request**:

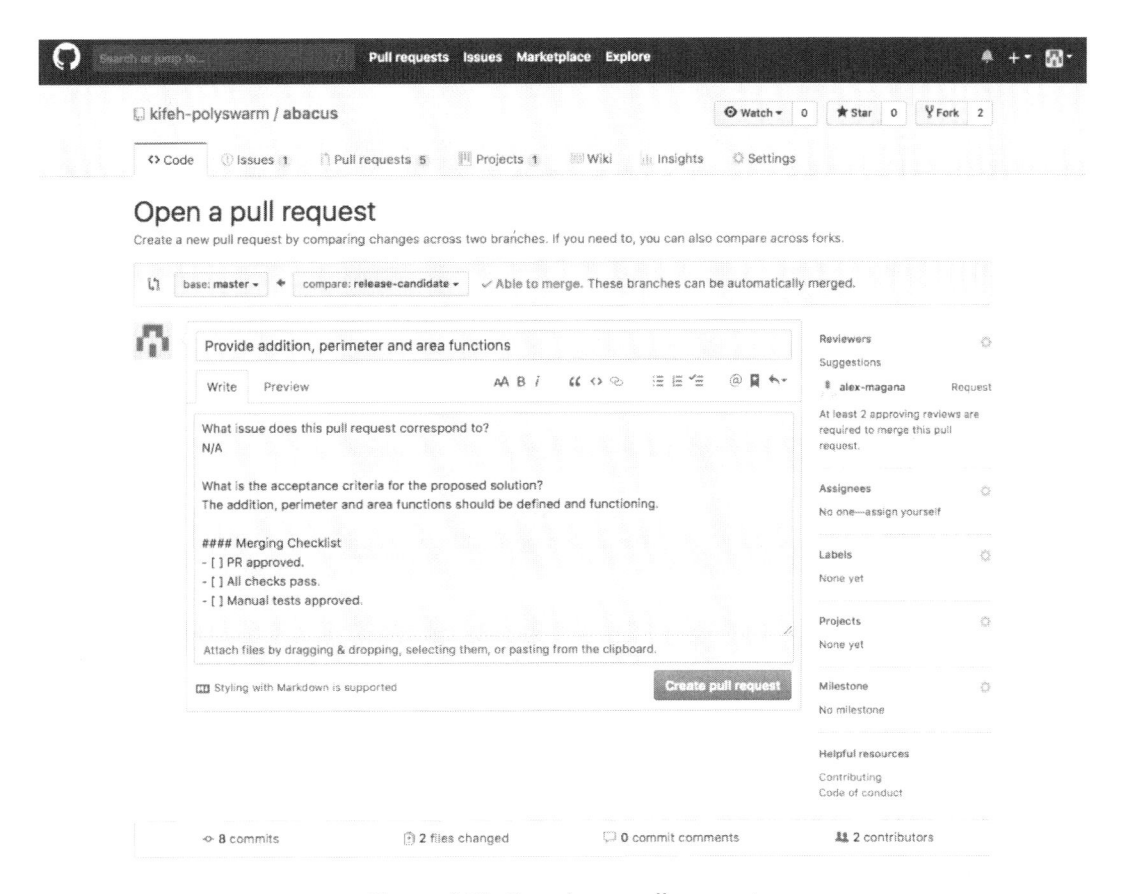

Figure 4.59: Opening a pull request

> **Note**
> With branch protection rules in place, merging the branch is not allowed. This is because we require at least one approval on the review:

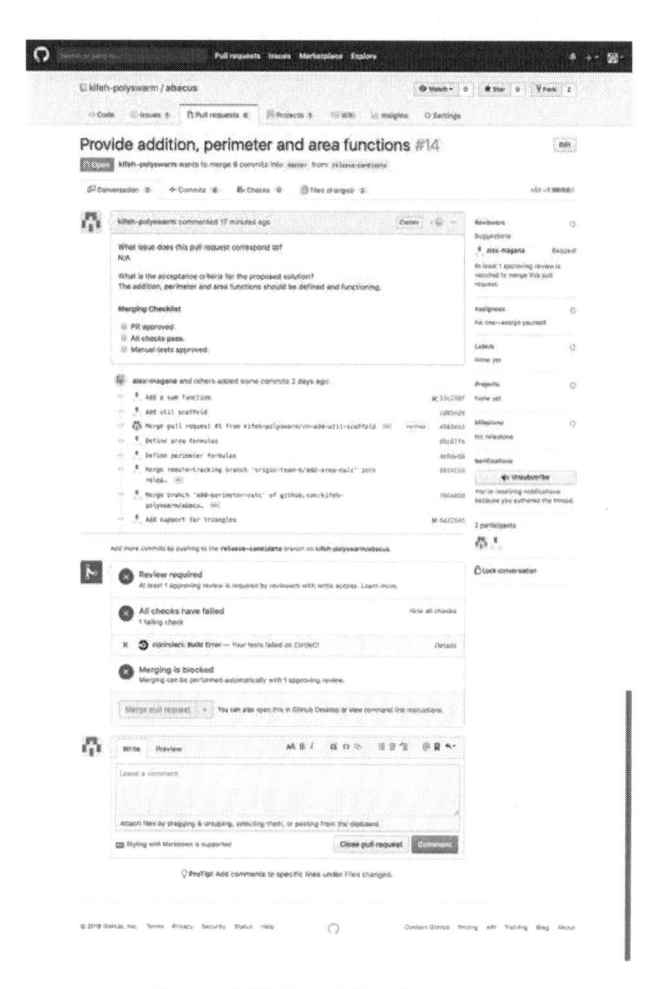

Figure 4.60: Providing functions

> **Note**
>
> For the purpose of this demonstration, you will need to disable a certain rule setting to enable the merging of the branch.

4. Click the **Settings** tab on the repository navigation bar.
5. Select the **Branches** settings on the pane on the left.
6. On the page you are directed to, select **Edit** on the rule associated with the branch **master** as shown in the following screenshot:

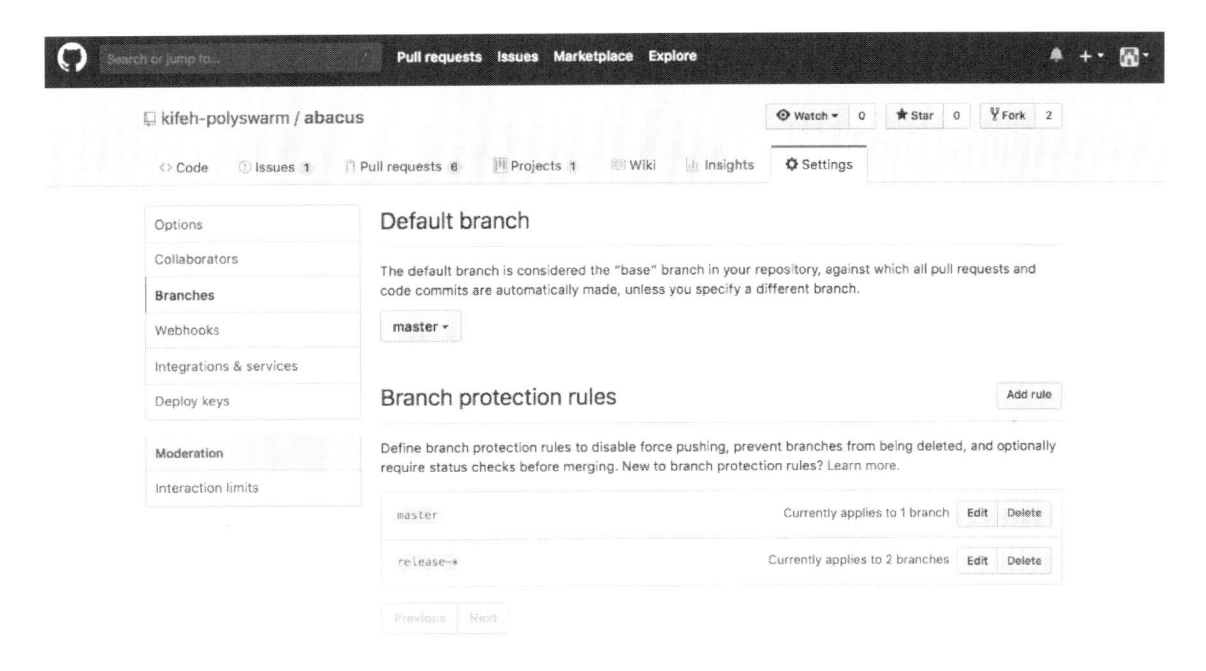

Figure 4.61: Branch protection rules

7. Deselect the **Require pull request reviews before merging** rule and click **Save changes** as shown in the following screenshot:

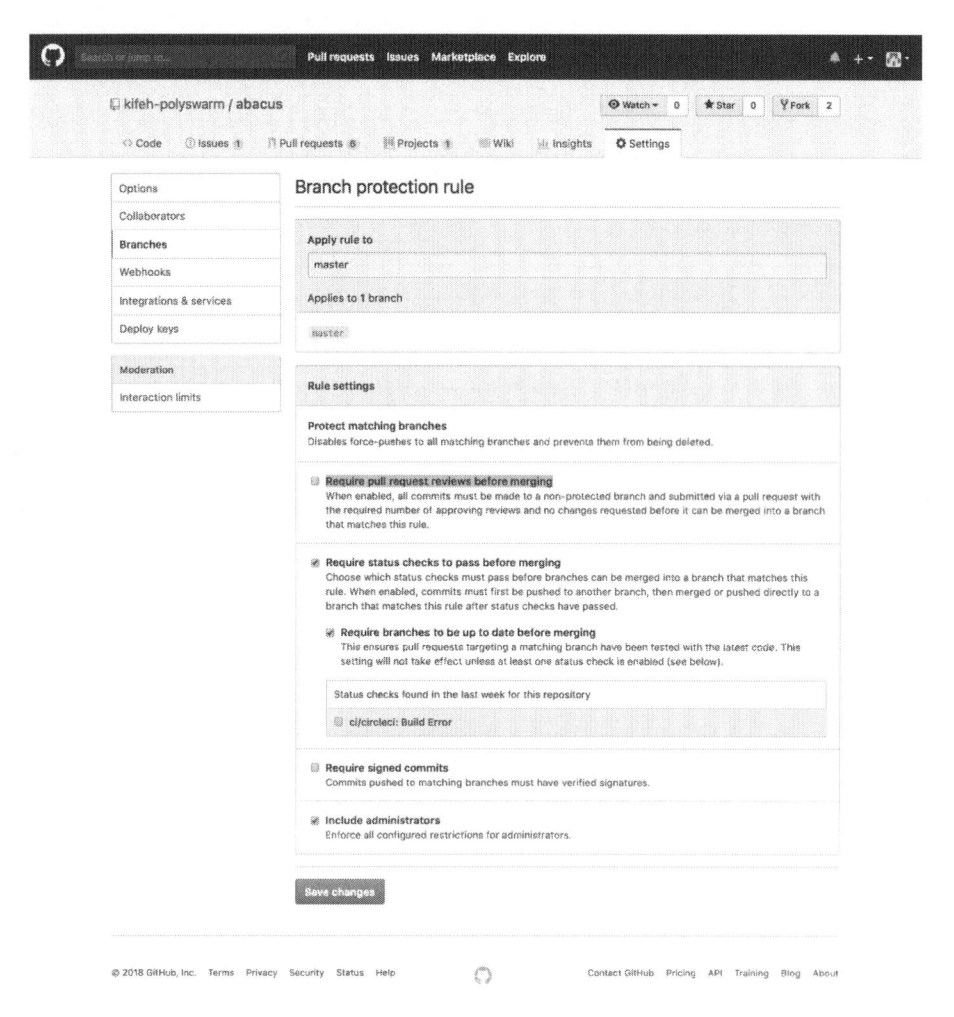

Figure 4.62: Saving the changes

8. Click the **Pull request** tab and select the pull request titled **Provide addition, perimeter, and area functions**.

9. Click **Merge pull request** on the page you're directed to.

10. Open the terminal on your computer and navigate to the location of repository abacus.

If not on branch **master**, switch to it by using the `git checkout master` command.

11. Retrieve the changes for the remote master branch by using the `git pull origin master` command as shown in the following screenshot:

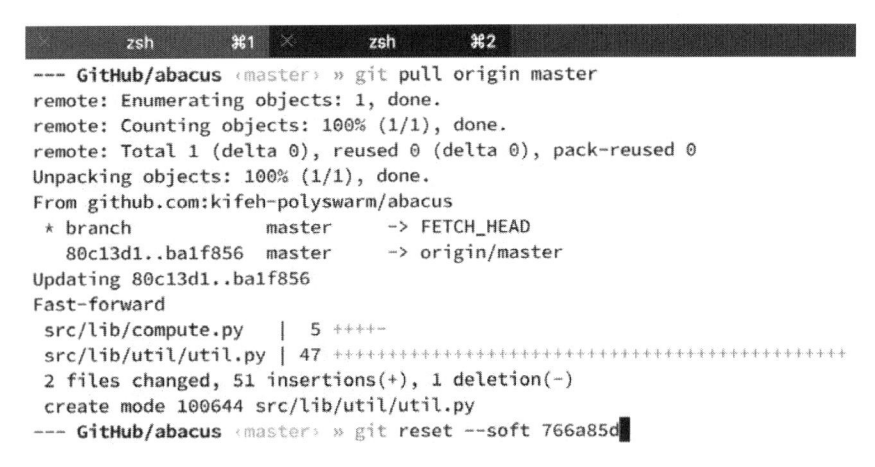

```
--- GitHub/abacus <master> » git pull origin master
remote: Enumerating objects: 1, done.
remote: Counting objects: 100% (1/1), done.
remote: Total 1 (delta 0), reused 0 (delta 0), pack-reused 0
Unpacking objects: 100% (1/1), done.
From github.com:kifeh-polyswarm/abacus
 * branch            master     -> FETCH_HEAD
   80c13d1..ba1f856  master     -> origin/master
Updating 80c13d1..ba1f856
Fast-forward
 src/lib/compute.py  |  5 ++++-
 src/lib/util/util.py | 47 +++++++++++++++++++++++++++++++++++++++++++++++
 2 files changed, 51 insertions(+), 1 deletion(-)
 create mode 100644 src/lib/util/util.py
--- GitHub/abacus <master> » git reset --soft 766a85d
```

Figure 4.63: Retrieving the changes for the master

12. Create a branch called **ft-speed** to implement the speed computation feature using the following command as shown in the following screenshot:

   `git checkout -b ft-compute-speed`

```
--- GitHub/abacus <master> » git checkout -b ft-compute-speed
Switched to a new branch 'ft-compute-speed'
--- GitHub/abacus <ft-compute-speed> »
```

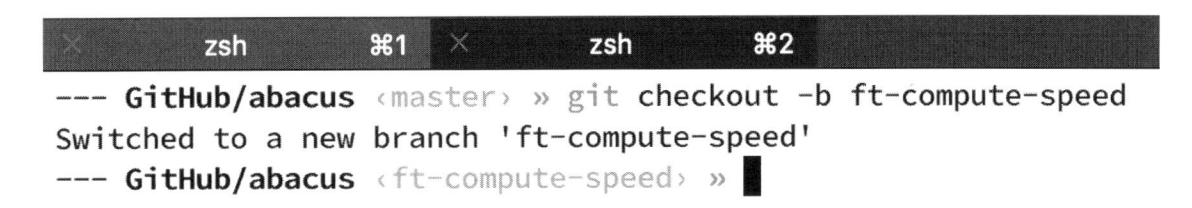

Figure 4.64: Implementing the speed computation

13. Open `src/lib/util/util.py` on your editor and edit the speed method, as follows:

Live Link for file activity_step_13.py: https://bit.ly/2S5SMtu

```python
@classmethod
def speed(cls, unit, *args):
    speed = 0
    speed = reduce(lambda x, y: x*y, args)
    return "%s %s" %(speed, unit)
```

Figure 4.65: Editing the speed method

14. Stage the changes made on `src/lib/util/util.py` / and commit the changes as shown in the following screenshot:

    `git add src/lib/util/util.py`

    `git commit -m "Add speed computation"`

```
--- GitHub/abacus ‹ft-compute-speed* M› » git add src/lib/util/util.py
--- GitHub/abacus ‹ft-compute-speed* M› » git commit -m "Add speed computation"
[ft-compute-speed 55e6a14] Add speed computation
 1 file changed, 4 insertions(+), 2 deletions(-)
--- GitHub/abacus ‹ft-compute-speed› » ▌
```

Figure 4.66: Staging the changes

15. Create a branch called `ft-compute-distance` to compute the distance, given speed, and time:

> **Note**
>
> The history of the branch should start at the point the branch master is currently at.

`git branch ft-compute-distance ba1f856`

```
--- GitHub/abacus ‹ft-compute-speed› » git branch ft-compute-distance ba1f856
--- GitHub/abacus ‹ft-compute-speed› » ▌
```

Figure 4.67: Creating a branch

16. Switch to the ft-compute-distance branch using the following command as shown in the following screenshot: git checkout ft-compute-distance

```
--- GitHub/abacus ‹ft-compute-speed› » git checkout ft-compute-distance
Switched to branch 'ft-compute-distance'
--- GitHub/abacus ‹ft-compute-distance› »
```

Figure 4.68: Switching to the branch

17. Open src/lib/util/util.py on your editor and edit the distance method, as follows:

Live Link for file activity_step_17.py: https://bit.ly/2BmwagP

```python
@classmethod
def distance(unit, *args):
    distance = 0
    distance = reduce(lambda x, y: x*y, args)
    return "%s %s" %(distance, unit)
```

Figure 4.69: Editing the distance method

18. Run the git checkout command to switch to the ft-compute-speed branch by using the git checkout ft-compute-speed command as shown in the following screenshot:

```
--- GitHub/abacus ‹ft-compute-distance* M› » git checkout ft-compute-speed
error: Your local changes to the following files would be overwritten by checkout:
        src/lib/util/util.py
Please commit your changes or stash them before you switch branches.
Aborting
--- GitHub/abacus ‹ft-compute-distance* M› »
```

Figure 4.70: Running the git checkout command

> **Note**
>
> Since the changes in src/lib/util/util.py are yet to be staged and committed, we receive an error warning about an impending overwrite.

302 | Appendix

19. Store away the changes so that you can switch to the `ft-compute-speed` branch by using the `git stash push --message "Adds distance function"` command as shown in the following screenshot:

```
--- GitHub/abacus ‹ft-compute-distance* M› » git stash push --message "Adds distance function"
Saved working directory and index state On ft-compute-distance: Adds distance function
--- GitHub/abacus ‹ft-compute-distance› »
```

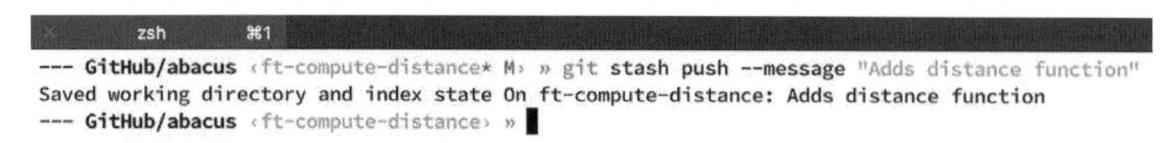

Figure 4.71: Storing away the changes

20. Check the stash list to observe the temporary store that you've created for the yet to be committed `distance` function by using the `git stash list` command as shown in the following screenshot:

```
stash@{0}: On ft-compute-distance: Adds distance function
(END)
```

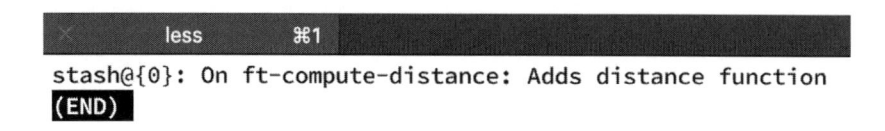

Figure 4.72: Observing the temporary store

21. Switch to the `ft-compute-speed` branch and ascertain that you ordered `speed` to precede `unit` in the returned result by using the `git checkout ft-compute-speed` command as shown in the following screenshot.

> **Note**
>
> The `src/lib/util/util.py` file should have the speed method defined and the arguments ordered, as shown in the following screenshot:

```python
@classmethod
def speed(cls, unit, *args):
    speed = 0
    speed = reduce(lambda x, y: x*y, args)
    return "%s %s" %(speed, unit)
```

Figure 4.73: Switching to the branch

22. Switch back to `ft-compute-speed` by using the `git checkout ft-compute-distance` command.

23. Retrieve the available stash list entries and apply the changes of the relevant stash to the working directory using the following code as shown in the screenshots below:

```
git stash list

git stash show stash@{0}

git stash apply stash@{0}
```

Figure 4.74: Retrieving the available stash list entries

Figure 4.75: Applying the changes of the relevant stash

> **Note**
>
> Examining the `src/lib/util/util.py` file, the source code for the method we defined should be available:

```python
@classmethod
def distance(unit, *args):
    distance = 0
    distance = reduce(lambda x, y: x*y, args)
    return "%s %s" %(distance, unit)
```

Figure 4.76: Examining the file

24. Delete the stash from the stash entry by using the `git stash drop stash@{0}` command as shown in the following screenshot:

```
--- GitHub/abacus <ft-compute-distance* M> » git stash drop stash@{0}
Dropped stash@{0} (54f99bdc8d2bea7fd3a435af0cb0c70b529b1627)
--- GitHub/abacus <ft-compute-distance* M> »
```

Figure 4.77: Deleting the stash from the stash entry

25. Stage the changes and commit them using the code below as shown in the following screenshot:

git add src/lib/util/util.py

git commit -m "Add support for distance"

```
--- GitHub/abacus <ft-compute-distance* M> » git add src/lib/util/util.py
--- GitHub/abacus <ft-compute-distance* M> » git commit -m "Add support for distance"
[ft-compute-distance 9d4924f] Add support for distance"
 1 file changed, 4 insertions(+), 2 deletions(-)
--- GitHub/abacus <ft-compute-distance> »
```

Figure 4.78: Staging the changes

26. As you may have noticed, the methods you've defined have flaws and as such will result in errors when used. Let's solve this. List the branches to obtain the names by using the `git branch` command as shown in the following screenshot:

```
  conflict-branch-4
  ft-add-encapsulating-class
* ft-compute-distance
  ft-compute-speed
  ft-support-addition-tasks
```

Figure 4.79: Listing the branches

27. Switch to the `ft-compute-speed` branch, create a branch called `bg-speed-calc` to resolve the bug, and switch to this branch using the following code:

git checkout ft-compute-speed

git checkout -b bg-speed-calc

28. Edit the **speed** method, as follows:

Live Link for file activity_step_28.py: https://bit.ly/2qvvQJE

```python
@classmethod
def speed(cls, unit, *args):
    speed = 0
    speed = reduce(lambda x, y: x/y, args)
    return "%s %s" %(speed, unit)
```

Figure 4.80: Editing the speed method

> **Note**
>
> Stage and commit the change:
>
> git add src/lib/util/util.py
>
> git commit -m "Rectify calculation"

29. Switch to the **ft-compute-distance** branch, create a branch called **ft-distance-arguments** to resolve the bug, and switch to this branch by using the following code:

    git checkout ft-compute-speed

    git checkout -b fx-distance-arguments

30. Edit the distance method, as follows:

Live Link for file activity_step_30.py: https://bit.ly/2DPmgcb

```python
@classmethod
def distance(cls, unit, *args):
    distance = 0
    distance = reduce(lambda x, y: x*y, args)
    return "%s %s" %(distance, unit)
```

Figure 4.81: Editing the distance method

> **Note**
>
> Stage and commit the change:
>
> git add src/lib/util/util.py
>
> git commit -m "Rectify parameter passing"

31. Rename bg-speed-calc and fx-distance-arguments using the following code as shown in the following screenshots:

    git branch -m bg-speed-calc ft-speed-calc

    git branch -m fx-distance-arguments ft-distance-calc

```
--- GitHub/abacus ‹fx-distance-arguments› » git branch -m bg-speed-calc ft-speed-calc
--- GitHub/abacus ‹fx-distance-arguments› »
```

Figure 4.82: Renaming bg-speed-calc

```
--- GitHub/abacus ‹fx-distance-arguments› » git branch -m fx-distance-arguments ft-distance-calc
--- GitHub/abacus ‹ft-distance-calc› »
```

Figure 4.83: Renaming fx-distance-arguments

32. Delete the ft-compute-distance and ft-compute-speed branches using the following command: git branch -D ft-compute-distance ft-compute-speed

33. Explore the difference in the `distance` method and checkout to the revision prior to the point at which you introduced the fix in the method by using the `git checkout b9aea3e` command as follows:

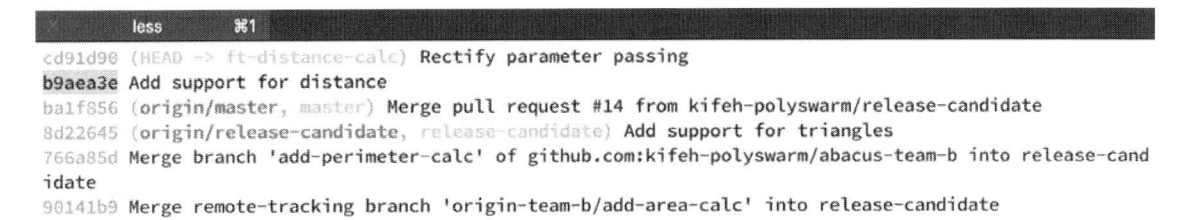

```
cd91d90 (HEAD -> ft-distance-calc) Rectify parameter passing
b9aea3e Add support for distance
ba1f856 (origin/master, master) Merge pull request #14 from kifeh-polyswarm/release-candidate
8d22645 (origin/release-candidate, release-candidate) Add support for triangles
766a85d Merge branch 'add-perimeter-calc' of github.com:kifeh-polyswarm/abacus-team-b into release-candidate
90141b9 Merge remote-tracking branch 'origin-team-b/add-area-calc' into release-candidate
```

Figure 4.84: Exploring the difference in the method

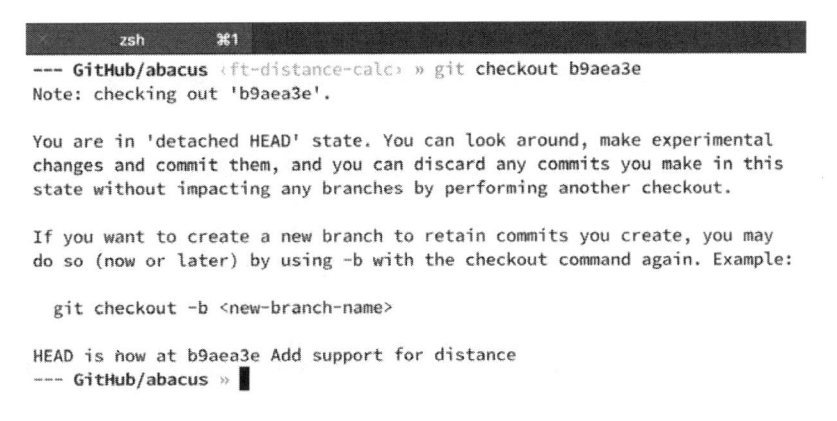

```
--- GitHub/abacus <ft-distance-calc> » git checkout b9aea3e
Note: checking out 'b9aea3e'.

You are in 'detached HEAD' state. You can look around, make experimental
changes and commit them, and you can discard any commits you make in this
state without impacting any branches by performing another checkout.

If you want to create a new branch to retain commits you create, you may
do so (now or later) by using -b with the checkout command again. Example:

  git checkout -b <new-branch-name>

HEAD is now at b9aea3e Add support for distance
--- GitHub/abacus »
```

Figure 4.85: Creating a new branch

> **Note**
>
> Examining `src/lib/util/util.py` shows the difference in the arguments we pass to the distance method. The argument, `cls`, is missing, as shown in the following screenshot:

```
        @classmethod
        def distance(unit, *args):
```

Figure 4.86: Checking the difference in the arguments

34. Switch back to the `ft-compute-calc` branch and create a branch named `util-milestone` using the following code:

    `git checkout ft-distance-calc`

    `git checkout -b util-milestone`

308 | Appendix

35. In `src/lib/util/util.py`, edit the file read as follows:

Live Link for file activity_step_35.py: https://bit.ly/2DnPJ6z

```python
@classmethod
def speed(cls, arg1, arg2):
    speed = 0
    speed = arg1/arg2
    return speed
```

Figure 4.87: Editing the util.py file

> **Note**
>
> Stage the changes and commit them:
>
> git add src/lib/util/util.py
>
> git commit -m "Compute speed"

36. Integrate the functionality to compute speed by using the `git merge ft-speed-calc` command as follows:

```
--- GitHub/abacus <util-milestone> » git merge ft-speed-calc
Auto-merging src/lib/util/util.py
CONFLICT (content): Merge conflict in src/lib/util/util.py
Automatic merge failed; fix conflicts and then commit the result.
--- GitHub/abacus <util-milestone* UU> »
```

Figure 4.88: Integrating the functionality to compute speed

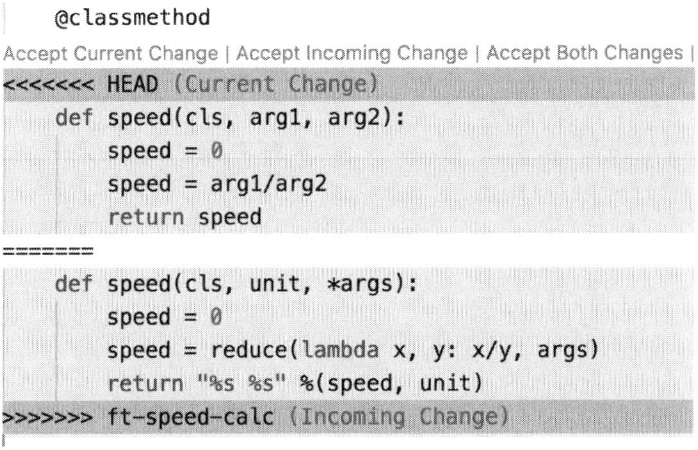

```
        @classmethod
Accept Current Change | Accept Incoming Change | Accept Both Changes |
<<<<<<< HEAD (Current Change)
    def speed(cls, arg1, arg2):
        speed = 0
        speed = arg1/arg2
        return speed
=======
    def speed(cls, unit, *args):
        speed = 0
        speed = reduce(lambda x, y: x/y, args)
        return "%s %s" %(speed, unit)
>>>>>>> ft-speed-calc (Incoming Change)
```

Figure 4.89: Viewing the arguments

37. Resolve the merge conflict by editing src/lib/util/util.py to adopt the incoming change.

> **Note**
>
> The incoming change is the text surrounded by ======= and =>>>>>>> ft-speed-calc:

```
=======
    def speed(cls, unit, *args):
        speed = 0
        speed = reduce(lambda x, y: x/y, args)
        return "%s %s" %(speed, unit)
>>>>>>> ft-speed-calc
```

38. Merge the changes using the following code:

```
git add src/lib/util/util.py
git commit
```

```
--- GitHub/abacus ‹util-milestone* UU› » git add src/lib/util/util.py
--- GitHub/abacus ‹util-milestone* M› » git commit
[util-milestone 058045f] Merge branch 'ft-speed-calc' into util-milestone
--- GitHub/abacus ‹util-milestone› » 
```

Figure 4.90: Merging the changes

310 | Appendix

39. To conclude our work, we need to include a function to calculate time. Create a branch called `ft-time-calc` to compute the time by using the `git checkout -b ft-time-calc` command.

40. In `src/lib/util/util.py`, edit the file to read as follows:

Live Link for file activity_step_40.py: https://bit.ly/2r009nL

```python
@classmethod
def time(cls, unit, *args):
    time = 0
    time = reduce(lambda x, y: x/y, args)
    return time
```

Figure 4.91: Editing the util.py file

> **Note**
>
> Stage the changes and commit them:
>
> g git add src/lib/util/util.py
>
> git commit -m "Compute time"
>
> Obtain the commit hash for use in the next step:
>
> git log --oneline -n .

41. Stage the changes and commit them using the following code:

    ```
    git add src/lib/util/util.py
    git commit -m "Compute time"
    ```

42. Obtain the commit hash for use in the next step by using the `git log --oneline -n` command.

43. Switch to the util-milestone branch by using the `git checkout util-milestone` command.

44. Add the time function to the current branch by using the `git cherry-pick ef9426b` command.

> **Note**
>
> The following are the logs of the branch before and after the cherry-pick:

```
058045f (HEAD -> util-milestone) Merge branch 'ft-speed-calc' into util-milestone
3bb0c9f Compute speed
cd91d90 (ft-distance-calc) Rectify parameter passing
(END)
```

Figure 4.92: Before cherry-pick

```
58bbd4c (HEAD -> util-milestone) Compute time
058045f Merge branch 'ft-speed-calc' into util-milestone
3bb0c9f Compute speed
(END)
```

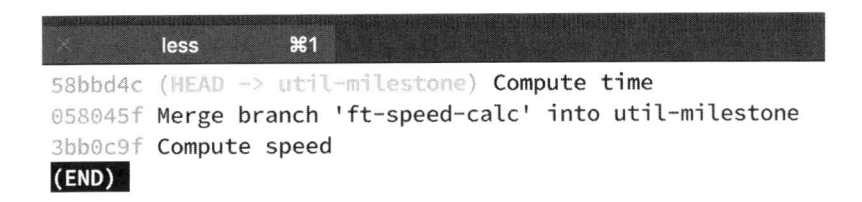

Figure 4.93: After cherry-pick

45. Push the change to the remote repository using the following command:

    ```
    git push origin util-milestone
    ```

    ```
    --- GitHub/abacus (util-milestone) » git push origin util-milestone
    Counting objects: 42, done.
    Delta compression using up to 4 threads.
    Compressing objects: 100% (28/28), done.
    Writing objects: 100% (42/42), 3.04 KiB | 1.01 MiB/s, done.
    Total 42 (delta 15), reused 0 (delta 0)
    remote: Resolving deltas: 100% (15/15), completed with 2 local objects.
    remote:
    remote: Create a pull request for 'util-milestone' on GitHub by visiting:
    remote:      https://github.com/kifeh-polyswarm/abacus/pull/new/util-milestone
    remote:
    To github.com:kifeh-polyswarm/abacus.git
     * [new branch]      util-milestone -> util-milestone
    --- GitHub/abacus (util-milestone) »
    ```

    Figure 4.94: Pushing the change to the repository

46. Visit https://github.com/ [username]/abacus/compare/util-milestone?expand=1 to raise a pull request.

Outcome

The activity in the culmination of this topic should enable you to navigate branches as well as the snapshots represented by their respective commits.

Chapter 5: Collaborative Git

Activity 5: Rebasing

You have been tasked with squashing and dropping select commits.

This aim of this activity is to demonstrate forking a workflow and rebasing.

Ensure that you have a GitHub account:

1. Fork https://github.com/mrmuli/track-it.
2. Checkout to a new branch called `ch-implement-feedback`.
3. Rebase and squash the following commits:

    a. `parse input`

    b. `add extra functions`

    Rebase and drop the commits with the message `remove unused methods`.

4. Fork the repository from https://github.com/mrmuli/track-it.
5. Checkout to `ch-implement-feedback`, as shown in the following screenshot:

```
josephmuli at Friday in ~/Repositories/writing/track-it on master [$]
$ git checkout -b ch-implement-feedback
Switched to a new branch 'ch-implement-feedback'
```

Figure 5.85: Switching to the new branch

6. Rebase and squash the `parse input` and `add extra functions` commits as shown in the following screenshots:

    Run `git log` to list the commits:

```
josephmuli at Friday in ~/Repositories/writing/track-it on ch-implement-feedback [$]
$ git log --oneline
a436365 (HEAD -> ch-implement-feedback, origin/master, origin/HEAD, master) Merge pull request #4 from mrmuli/fx-remove-unused-methods
3df0365 (origin/fx-remove-unused-methods, fx-remove-unused-methods) remove unused methods
17368c9 add gitignore
70a4d83 Merge pull request #3 from mrmuli/ft-parse-input
970517d (origin/ft-parse-input, ft-parse-input) add extra functions
3801712 parse input
488a3d5 Merge pull request #2 from mrmuli/ft-read-data
5450a26 (origin/ft-read-data, ft-read-data) added read_data method
a171ae0 Merge pull request #1 from mrmuli/ch-base-setup
86e9310 (origin/ch-base-setup, ch-base-setup) add application frame
5b42c76 Update README.md
27461a7 Initial commit
```

Figure 5.86: Running the git log command

Rebase HEAD:

```
josephmuli at Friday in ~/Repositories/writing/track-it on ch-implement-feedback [$]
$ git rebase -i HEAD~5
```

Figure 5.87: Running the git rebase command

Update `parse input` on the interactive prompt:

```
git-rebase-todo
1 pick 5b42c76 Update README.md
2 pick 86e9310 add application frame
3 pick 5450a26 added read_data method
4 squash 3801712 parse input
5 pick 970517d add extra functions
6 pick 17368c9 add gitignore
7 pick 3df0365 remove unused methods
8
```

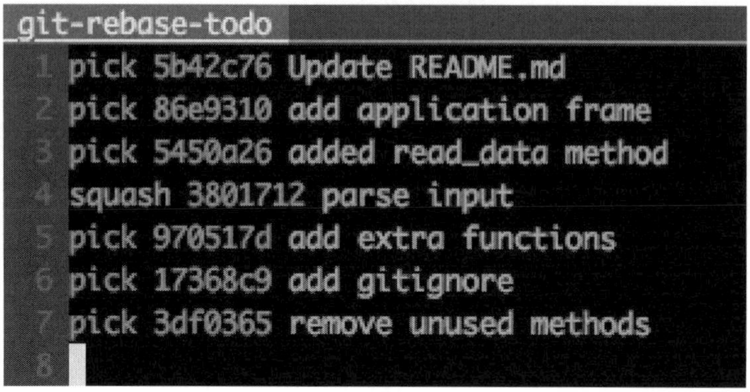

Figure 5.88: Updating the parse input

7. Rebase and drop `remove unused methods`:

    Rebase HEAD:

```
josephmuli at Friday in ~/Repositories/writing/track-it on ch-implement-feedback [$]
$ git rebase -i HEAD~2
```

Figure 5.89: Rebasing and dropping unused methods

Drop the commit on the interactive prompt:

```
git-rebase-todo
1 pick 0d66b22 add gitignore
2 drop 6834a55 remove unused methods
```

Figure 5.90: Dropping the commit

Outcome

You have successfully forked the workflow and removed the used commits and methods.

Activity 6: Utilizing Pre-Commit Hooks for Housekeeping

To have a clean, effective, and resource friendly repository, you have been tasked with getting rid of merged local and remote branches on `track-it`.

The aim of this activity is to demonstrate using pre-commit hooks to remove the merged remote branches on `track-it`.

Ensure that you have a cloned track-it repository from the previous activity:

1. From the hooks directory and on your preferred editor, update the `prepare-commit-msg.sample` script, as shown in the following screenshot. Note that we're only adding the last line:

```
COMMIT_MSG_FILE=$1
COMMIT_SOURCE=$2
SHA1=$3

/usr/bin/perl -i.bak -ne 'print unless(m/^. Please enter the commit message/..m/^#$/)' "$COMMIT_MSG_FILE"

echo " Beware! Commit messages should be descriptive and relate the feature, bug or chore" > $1
```

Figure 5.91: Updating the script

2. Run the following command to update the name of the commit as shown in the following screenshot:

```
josephmuli at Friday in ~/Repositories/writing/track-it/.git/hooks on master
$ mv prepare-commit-msg.sample prepare-commit-msg
```

Figure 5.92: Updating the name

3. Finally, make the script executable by using the following command as shown in the following screenshot:

```
josephmuli at Friday in ~/Repositories/writing/track-it/.git/hooks on master
$ chmod +x prepare-commit-msg
```

Figure 5.93: Making the script executable

4. Back on the root directory, stage a new file, as follows:

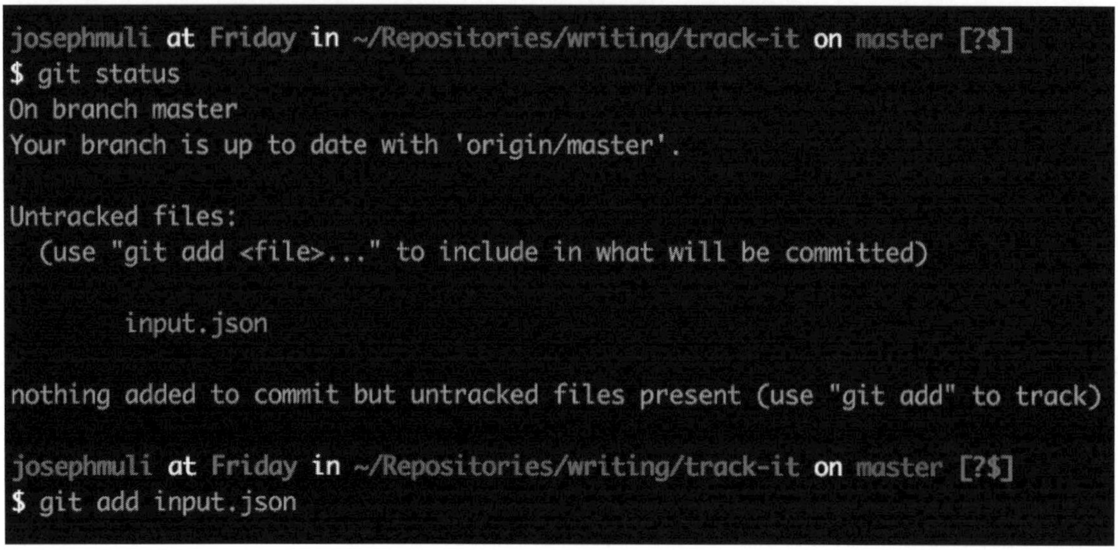

```
josephmuli at Friday in ~/Repositories/writing/track-it on master [?$]
$ git status
On branch master
Your branch is up to date with 'origin/master'.

Untracked files:
  (use "git add <file>..." to include in what will be committed)

        input.json

nothing added to commit but untracked files present (use "git add" to track)

josephmuli at Friday in ~/Repositories/writing/track-it on master [?$]
$ git add input.json
```

Figure 5.94: Staging a new file

5. Commit the file through the `git commit` command to observe the changes:

```
COMMIT_EDITMSG
1 Beware! Commit messages should be descriptive and relate the feature, bug or chore
```

Figure 5.95: Committing the file

6. Run `git branch --merged` to identify all merged branches.

7. For each branch, delete them by using the `git push --delete origin <branchname>` command.

Outcome

You have successfully utilized pre-commit hooks to remove the merged remote branches on `track-it`.

Chapter 6: Automated Testing and Release Management

Activity 7: Integrating a Build Pipeline on CircleCi

You have been instructed to set up a repository and build a pipeline for a new Python API that will serve as a gateway for your current infrastructure. To this, the first requirement is setting up the project's base, involving its repository and pipeline.

The aim of this activity is to create build pipelines and integrate them with GitHub applications.

To get started, you need to have the Git command-line tool installed on your computer. You need to have an account on https://github.com/ and should be logged into it. Follow these steps to complete this activity:

1. Create the repository on GitHub and name it **backend-api.**
2. Clone the repository locally.
3. Ensure that you have the **master** and **develop** branches.
4. From the **develop** branch, ensure that you have a descriptive README file.
5. Checkout from the develop branch into a feature branch with the name **ch-integrate-circleci**.
6. Create a **.circleci** folder, as follows:

```
josephmuli at Friday in ~/Desktop/backend-api on ch-integrate-circleci
$ mkdir .circleci
```

Figure 6.46: Making the directory

7. Push your changes to GitHub.
8. Login to CircleCi and from the dashboard, add the backend-API project and run the first build.

9. In the CircleCi directory, add a **config.yml** file and include the following configuration:

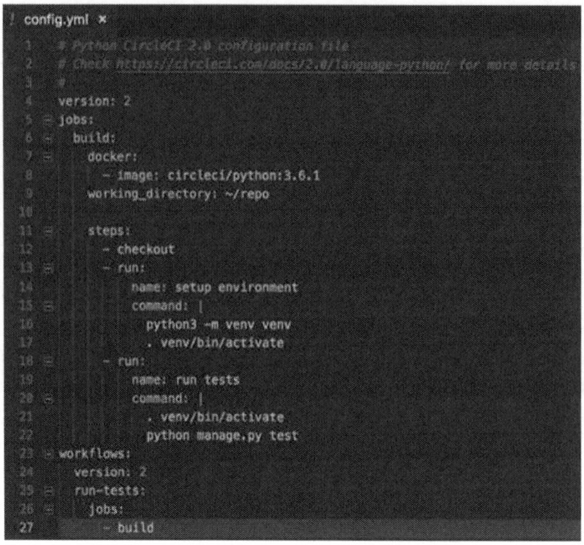

Figure 6.47: Adding the config.yml file

Outcome

You have successfully set up build pipelines and integrated them with GitHub applications.

Activity 8: Tagging and Releasing with Git

You have been instructed to update the abacus documentation, tag the feature, and document the release changes. Tag at least one stage of abacus branching off of the develop branch and document the tags in a Changelog.

The aim of this activity is to tag and release software with Git.

To get started, you need to have the Git command-line tool installed on your computer. You need to have an account on https://github.com/ and should be logged into it. Follow these steps to complete this activity:

1. Make sure that you do not have any pending changes on the branch you are on and checkout to develop.

2. From the develop branch, checkout to a feature branch called **ch-update-readme**.

3. Add the changes shown in the following screenshot to the **README.md file:**

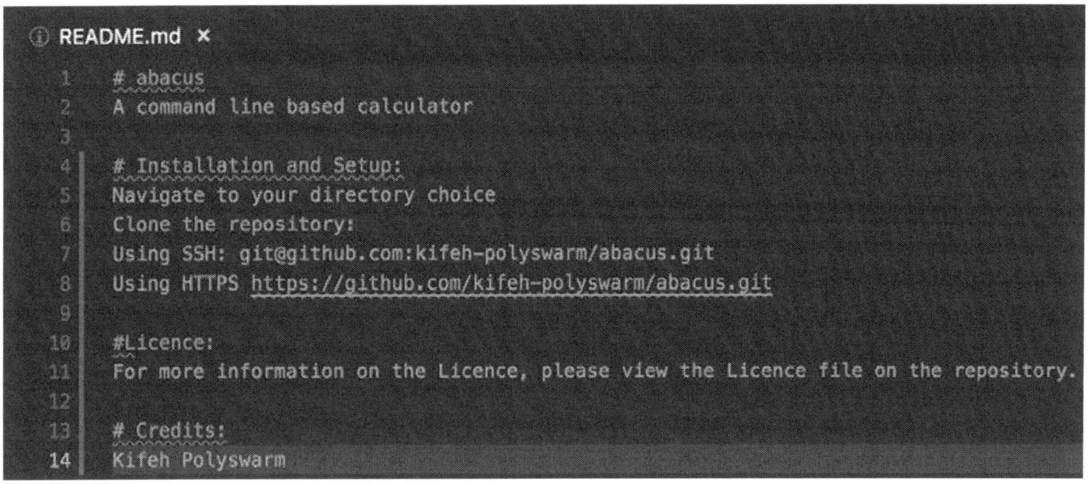

Figure 6.48: Adding the changes

> **Note**
>
> Be sure to use your repository details and your name on the credits.

4. Stage, commit, and push your changes to GitHub.
5. Create a pull request to develop and if everything checks out, including, as a bonus, a request to your peer for a review, merge the branch to develop and delete the feature branch.
6. Create a release branch off of develop and update the Changelog with the new changes to Abacus's documentation.

> **Note**
>
> Your branch should follow the Semver versioning conventions. In our case, it would be release-v1.0.1. This is because we are not making a major or minor release, but a minor patch.

7. Stage and commit the changes.

8. Tag the commit, as shown in the following screenshot, by following the convention described earlier:

```
josephmuli at Friday in ~/Desktop/abacus on ch-update-readme
$ git tag -a v1.0.1 -m"Abacus documentation update"
```

Figure 6.49: Tag the commit file

9. Push the changes to the origin.
10. Create a pull request to the master and when all checks go through, merge the release branch.
11. Finally, merge the release branch to Develop and delete the release branch.
12. Update the release notes on GitHub to reflect the new release changes.

Outcome

You have successfully tagged and released software with Git.

Index

About

All major keywords used in this book are captured alphabetically in this section. Each one is accompanied by the page number of where they appear.

A

abacus: 31, 33, 38, 41, 49-50, 59, 61, 63, 66, 71, 73, 78, 80, 82, 97, 99, 101, 104, 115, 126, 135, 143, 149, 151, 162, 165, 169, 173, 177, 183-184, 187-188, 219-222, 225, 243, 249, 254, 265, 267-268
--after: 92
--amend: 96-97, 103
android: 12
annotated: 2, 43-44, 257-258, 262, 265
annotation: 2
anomaly: 227
apache: 6, 141
architects: 4
automation: 242, 246
autosquash: 210-211, 213
auxiliary: 153

B

badges: 252
barcode: 13
benchmarks: 110
binaries: 266
binary: 132, 227-228
bisect: 224, 227-231
bmtcqa: 127
branches: 5-6, 41, 49, 57-58, 60, 65, 70-71, 106, 109-111, 114-123, 135-137, 139-140, 142, 153, 155, 159, 161-162, 172, 186-188, 204, 210, 231, 236-239, 242, 250, 254, 256, 258
branchname: 158

browser: 13, 115, 184, 187, 192

C

calculator: 262
callback: 14
callbacks: 242
candidate: 30, 58
canons: 165
category: 24
cat-file: 131-133
changelog: 261, 263-264, 268
changelogs: 269
checklist: 43, 166, 175
cherry: 160
circleci: 241, 246-253, 255-258, 269
cloned: 54, 111, 141, 195, 223, 239
clone-demo: 37
clones: 223
cloning: 37
clutter: 237
codacy: 20-23
commission: 141
commit: 4-5, 33-34, 41, 44-45, 47-48, 50, 53, 58, 62, 64-66, 69-70, 73, 77-79, 81-83, 89-90, 92-98, 100-105, 110, 113, 119-120, 125-131, 133-135, 140-142, 150, 153-161, 166, 170, 174-175, 177-180, 182, 185, 187-188, 196, 200, 203-205, 207-208, 210-216, 218, 222, 225, 227-232, 239, 251, 253, 258, 261, 268-269
--commit: 124-125

commits: 3, 41, 54, 57-58, 62-63, 65, 71, 78, 87-88, 91-94, 96, 98-99, 101, 105-106, 110, 117, 119, 122-126, 130, 153, 155-156, 159-161, 182, 188, 205, 207, 209-211, 214, 216, 223-228, 231-232, 238, 242, 262
committed: 6, 141, 211, 226, 236, 259
committer: 131, 153
compressed: 268
concurrent: 3-4
conflict: 139, 159, 172-173, 177, 180, 188
conflicts: 141, 171-173, 177, 210
consensus: 135, 162
convert: 16

D

dependency: 20, 195, 219, 261
deployment: 52, 218-219, 242, 246, 263
devops: 218, 220, 242
downstream: 110
--dry-run: 72, 79-80, 123

E

embedding: 195
executable: 239

F

facets: 2
filters: 250
fork-demo: 192
forked: 41, 110, 141,

195-196, 210, 220, 224, 239
forking: 6, 110, 141, 191-192, 194-195, 199, 223-224, 242
ft-speed: 187
function: 104, 135, 149, 188
functions: 1, 57-59, 62, 106, 224

G

gitconfig: 24
gitflow: 6, 140
github: 1, 3-4, 6-8, 11, 15-16, 18, 20, 24, 26, 28, 30-31, 33-35, 37-38, 41-43, 49, 53-54, 58, 63, 71, 78, 104, 110, 112-115, 121, 135, 141, 143, 151, 162-165, 169, 184, 187-189, 191-196, 199, 201, 206, 211, 216, 223, 237, 239, 241-246, 250-251, 254-257, 262, 264-269
gitignore: 53, 58, 60, 62-63, 71, 78, 230, 233
gitmodules: 191, 218-219, 221, 223

H

hashes: 65, 85, 153, 232
hotfix: 140

I

inception: 2
increments: 54
indexes: 57-58, 106, 110
integral: 4

J

jenkins: 242, 244

K

kanban: 144
keep-index: 157

M

magana: 93-94
metadata: 2

N

nesting: 16
newline: 95
--no-edit: 79, 82, 125-126, 159
--no-ff: 125, 159
no-renames: 125

O

octopus: 125

P

parent: 94, 131, 153, 157, 160-161, 219
pbcopy: 29
polyswarm: 79
--prune: 119
purges: 233
python: 169, 249, 256

Q

qamine: 23
qghnra: 149

R

real-world: 258, 263
refactor: 161
reflog: 224, 231-232, 236
reflogs: 231
refspec: 119, 124
repetition: 226
rescind: 137, 140
rewind: 209

S

saturated: 231
semver: 260, 269
snippets: 131
ssh-add: 28
ssh-agent: 27-28
ssh-keygen: 26
stacks: 242

T

tree-ish: 133-134
trello: 142
two-factor: 11-12, 14-16
type-task: 142

U

upstream: 110-111, 118-119, 122, 124, 154, 194-199, 202-204, 206-207
username: 18, 24-26, 39, 151, 169, 188, 223

V

velocity: 38

W

webhook: 242-245
webhooks: 241-244
workflow: 6, 110,
    139-141, 143, 188, 192,
    199, 202, 223-224,
    238-239, 258, 269
workflows: 1, 6, 54,
    58, 139-140, 186,
    192, 242, 248, 258

Z

zipped: 267